BARBECUE SECRETS

THE VERY BEST RECIPES, TIPS & TRICKS FROM A BARBECUE CHAMPION

DELUXE!

ROCKIN' RONNIE SHEWCHUK

whitecap

Editing by Kate Zimmerman
Proofreading by Paula Ayer
Interior design and illustrations by Setareh Ashrafologhalai
Food photography by John Sinal and food styling by Joanne
    Facchin unless otherwise noted below
Food photography by Greg Athans and food styling by Nathan Fong
    on pages 49, 87, 88, 92, 105, 135, 155, 189, 190, 202,
    251, 274, 296, 303, 318, and 368
Photo on page 37 by Greg Athans
Food photography by Reed Davis on page 177
Photography by Michelle Mayne on pages 20, 27, 28, 46, 90, 98,
    100, 115, 139, 146, 183, 184, 206, 210, 240, 304, 328,
    333, 362, and 382
Other photos kindly supplied by family and friends of the author

Printed in China

Library and Archives Canada Cataloguing in Publication

Shewchuk, Ron
    Barbecue secrets deluxe : the very best recipes, tips & tricks from a barbecue champion / Ron Shewchuk.

Includes index.
ISBN 978-1-55285-949-0

    1. Barbecue cookery. 2. Plank cookery. I. Title.

TX840.B3S553 2009   641.5'784   C2008-905582-9

The publisher acknowledges the financial support of the Government of Canada through the Book Publishing Industry Development Program (BPIDP) and the Province of British Columbia through the Book Publishing Tax Credit.

09 10 11 12 13 5 4 3 2 1

Contents

To Kate, and to the Butt Shredders

PREFACE

What a long, smoky trip it's been. When I sat down to put together the first edition of *Barbecue Secrets* in the summer of 2003, I didn't realize I was literally writing the next chapter of my career. The book was a major milestone along my path to barbecue enlightenment, which began in the '60s when I was a young boy watching my dad grill steak on an open brazier at my family's summer cottage. I've been addicted to the smell of meat searing over charcoal ever since.

Becoming a cookbook author took my passion for outdoor cooking to a new level, turning what was a mere passion into a full-fledged obsession. The first book was just the excuse I needed to abandon my day job and pursue my dream of living the barbecue lifestyle full time. For the next three years I did almost nothing but wield a pair of tongs as I worked to promote the first book and write the second, *Planking Secrets*. As you'll find out in more detail inside, I eventually suffered from barbecue burnout and took a year off to pursue something I'd kind of ignored for a while—a real career and earning a steady paycheck to support my family.

These days, it seems I've finally found the right work-family-barbecue balance, holding down my job as a PR consultant and finding time for family and barbecue on evenings and weekends.

But I have no regrets about my multiyear sidetrack into full-time barbecue excess. I got to visit the barbecue mountaintop, the Jack Daniel's World Championship Invitational Barbecue, competing with my team, the Butt Shredders, three years in a row. I had the privilege of being the first guest cook at the beautiful Mission Hill Family Estate Winery, delivering grilling and barbecue workshops with my friend, winery chef Michael Allemeier. And, best of all, I got to meet hundreds of like-minded outdoor cooks from all over the world to trade stories, share recipe ideas, and celebrate the many pleasures of grilling and barbecue.

This special edition of *Barbecue Secrets* is my attempt to gather everything I've learned and written so far in one comprehensive volume. In *Barbecue Secrets DELUXE!* you'll find many of the recipes from my first and second books. I've taken the opportunity to fine-tune some of them, and I've junked a bunch that just didn't hold up over time. In a few cases, I've taken recipes that were designed initially for the plank, and converted them to straight grilling or barbecue techniques because they just work better that way. And, for good measure, I've added about 50 new recipes to supply some fresh fodder for the grill.

To make this edition even more deluxe, I've included some more reading. In the last few years I've written articles for various publications on my favorite food-related topics, and I'm reprinting some of them here, along with a new barbecue mini-memoir that captures some of the most memorable stories from the years since the first book was published.

As a special treat I've convinced my darling wife, the writer and self-proclaimed barbecue widow Kate Zimmerman, to share a couple of her best humor columns that feature her thinly veiled parody of me as both a typical male cook and a barbecue doofus.

To round things out I'm including a couple of other features that are important to the barbecue lifestyle—an updated and expanded selection of music suggestions to enhance your backyard cooking experience, and a fine collection of drink recipes to help maintain the right barbecue buzz.

I hope you enjoy using this book as much as I enjoyed living through the experiences that formed and inspired it. Most of all, I hope it helps you launch a new chapter in your own barbecue career.

Yours forever in smoke,

Find me at www.ronshewchuk.com

A Smoky History Lesson

THE ORIGINS OF BARBECUE

"The story of barbecue is the story of America: Settlers arrive on great unspoiled continent, discover wondrous riches, set them on fire and eat them."

—Vince Staten

Who the heck can say when the first primitive human being put the first chunk of meat near a fire? It was thousands of years before humans were able to drink beer and use a basting brush, but that's all we know for sure.

What we do have is the first record of American barbecue, as documented by Spanish conquistadors in the early 16th century. Between plundering episodes, the Spaniards noted that the Arawak Aboriginal people of the Caribbean used a raised platform called a *barbaca*, made of green wood, to cook meat over a smoldering fire. Some historians report that the Arawak also used the grill to roast their enemies. The word *barbaca* evolved into the Spanish *barbacòa*, a term still in use today in that language. Over time, *barbacòa* became Americanized, morphing into the term we all know and love.

That's not the only theory about the birth of the term "barbecue," however. There's one possible root of the word that is consistently discounted or thrown out altogether by American barbecue pundits, though I think it is perfectly feasible. Apparently in France, when a butcher or a chef skewers a whole animal for cooking over a fire, he does it from beard to tail, or *de barbe à queue* . . . hence, barbecue. This French derivation could easily have migrated into Southern Creole dialects and then into American English. But in a continuation of the long-standing cultural and political feud between the United States and France, Americans scoff at this theory. Famed barbecue scholar and historian C. Clark "Smoky" Hale discounts the French origin in classic barbecue style: "The French claim . . . is flagrantly fatuous franco-poop," writes Hale, a Texan, in an essay on the origins of barbecue. "If Catherine de Medici had not sent for her [Italian] chefs when she became queen of France, the French would probably still be groveling for gruel." Go, Smoky, go!

Cut to the US southeast coast, where the Aboriginal practice of cooking meat on a barbacòa-style contraption was observed by Spanish explorer Hernando de Soto's crewmen in the 1500s. One account describes a group of natives roasting venison and turkeys on a barbacòa near the Ocmulgee River, which is in present-day Georgia. This was a profoundly historic moment (at least for us barbecue nuts): the first recorded tailgate party in North America.

Meanwhile, on the West Coast, people had been catching salmon and cooking it over smoky fires for about 8,000 years. Their technique was to skewer a big slab of freshly caught salmon on a stick and jab it into the ground close to a hot alder fire, which infused it with a lovely aroma and helped preserve the meat. They didn't call it barbecue, but that's certainly what it was.

But back to the East Coast. It wasn't long before the American settlers, having observed the natives' *barbacòa* cooking technique, started applying it to the descendants of the pigs who had come over with the first European settlers. As the eastern states became populated with European settlers and the rich bounty of North America began to reward those who took the risk of settling there, the pig became an integral part of the early American lifestyle. Hogs were plentiful and easy to raise, but refrigeration did not exist, and salt was at a premium. If you don't have salt or a fridge, the next-best preservatives are sugar and vinegar. And in a fruit-deprived, scurvy-prone society, a big source of vitamin C was the chili pepper.

And so it came to pass that whole hogs were smoked over hardwood fires and mopped with a mixture of vinegar, sugar, and chilies. Pork was the perfect staple food for the pioneers, and this style of cooking is how barbecue is still practiced in that part of the United States to this day.

This take on the history of barbecue happens to be consistent with another tale relating to the origin of the word "barbecue." A wealthy South Carolina rancher named Bernard Quayle was in the habit of throwing huge outdoor feasts for hundreds of guests, which featured pit-roasted sheep, hogs, and steers. The story goes that the name of his ranch (also his cattle brand) was BQ, or Bar-B-Q. The name, over time, became associated

➤GRILLING VS. BARBECUE➤

Before we get on with anything else, I want to make an important distinction between grilling and barbecue. When most North Americans, particularly those north of the Mason-Dixon line, think about "barbecuing" or "having a barbecue," they mean grilling—that is, searing a seasoned steak or some marinated chicken for a few minutes on a propane, natural gas, or charcoal grill. The grill makes nice marks on the meat, the drippings and ensuing flare-ups create a distinctive charred taste, and the high heat makes for convenient, quick, and tasty cooking.

But it ain't barbecue. For die-hard barbecue fanatics, grilling is the culinary equivalent of bait-fishing—as viewed by those who think flycasting is the only true and pure form of angling. (They're the ones who derisively refer to bait fishermen as "worm drowners.")

For the purist, barbecue is not a convenient way of cooking—a 15-minute predinner activity. Rather, it's something you eat at a roadside barbecue joint, or you cook yourself, for a long time, in a special piece of equipment called a smoker or barbecue pit. Traditional, Southern-style barbecue—or "Q," as it's sometimes called—consists of big, tough, fatty cuts of meat, like pork shoulder and beef brisket, that are cooked for many hours in a closed chamber, immersed in the vapors produced by a smoldering charcoal or hardwood fire. It's this style of cooking that is the basis of the growing number of barbecue competitions across the continent. There are even several governing bodies of

(continued)

barbecue, including the Kansas City Barbecue Society (KCBS), which lay down strict rules and judging criteria for barbecue competitions. And, as in professional boxing, there are a number of huge contests that claim to be the world championship of barbecue. But we'll get to that later.

In this book I will be making the distinction between grilling and traditional barbecue, but I will give equal treatment to each. When I say grilling, it means what you do on your propane or charcoal grill. When I refer to barbecue, or barbecuing, it means the traditional, "low and slow" style of cooking that is one of the few truly indigenous American culinary techniques. And then, of course, there's planking, or plank-cooking, which is a kind of hybrid of grilling and barbecue. For me, all of these techniques are great ways to achieve a fulfilling meat-eating experience. In fact, many of the tricks and recipes used in competitive barbecue can be easily adapted for use by the home cook.

So, throughout this book you will see phrasing that might seem awkward at first, like, "The single most important factor in cooking great barbecue is the rub," or "I love barbecue." Get used to it. After you've read and digested this book I expect you to become a barbecue ambassador in your community. If you truly love barbecue, you have to speak it, too!

with his style of entertaining and the term barbecue was born. Although this is an unlikely theory for the origin of the word barbecue, I like to think that old Mr. Quayle had a sense of humor. Seeing the similarity between his initials and what he liked to serve his guests, he turned his cattle brand into a visual pun. Although he may not have come up with the word itself, the spirit of fun that we associate with barbecue may have had its beginnings with this Q-loving rancher.

If we see the East Coast of the United States as the point of entry for barbecue, it's not too hard to document its migration west. From the Carolinas and Georgia to Tennessee, to Missouri, and on to the great state of Texas, barbecue spread across America, with each region adding its own distinctive style. Memphis pretty much followed the whole hog tradition of the East Coast. Kansas City perfected pork ribs and added the thick, sweet, tangy, tomato-y sauce that most people today associate with barbecue. And Texas—well, as we all know, it's a whole other country. More specifically, Texas is beef country, where big briskets are cooked "low and slow" and barbecue's roots go real deep.

To get at how we arrived at the classic American barbecue of today, we need to follow the trail that led from the East Coast of the US down to Texas in the 1800s. Settlers there used open pits to cook game such as squirrel and venison. Then, a major turning point in barbecue history: a wave of European immigrants came to America in the last half of the 1800s, including German and Czech butchers who had their own traditional methods for smoking food. How do you run a butcher shop and sell meat in hot old Texas with no refrigeration? The answer is simple: sell as much fresh meat as you can, and then smoke the leftovers (including sausages and tougher cuts of meat) in a big, brick, wood-fired oven, the precursor of the modern barbecue pit.

There was a growing market for this delicious leftover meat. Cotton farmers from all over the South flooded into Texas in the 1850s to buy cheap land, and with them came thousands of African-American slaves, who were freed in 1865. These folks may have been free in legal terms, but at the time there were few restaurants in that part of the world that would serve them after a long day of picking cotton. But the meat markets would. They sold hunks of smoked meat on sheets of butcher paper to the hungry farm workers, who would enjoy their meals while sitting on a nearby curb. To this day, there are some barbecue joints—and butcher shops—in Texas that serve barbecue exactly the same way.

The rise of German-style meat markets and barbecue restaurants represents an important branch of the history of barbecue. Another key ingredient in the historical mix is the tradition of giant parties hosted by politicians to attract a crowd leading up to election time—and to reward the faithful once they got into power. American president Lyndon Baines Johnson hosted many a barbecue on his sprawling Texas ranch, and First Lady "Lady Bird" would hand out recipe cards for her buttery barbecue sauce to constituents who wrote her at the White House.

THE GOLDEN AGE OF OUTDOOR COOKING

Today everyone in the American South has a personal opinion on what is the best barbecue, generally based on their experiences at their favorite roadside barbecue joint, with its Formica-top tables, dingy lighting, and charmingly grumpy servers. But what of barbecue and the home cook? How did we get to the point where we are today, with most households in North America owning some kind of backyard cooking device, and the proliferation of barbecue contests across the continent?

The history of suburban barbecuing and grilling goes back to the World War II–era aviation fuel drum. My friend Rocky Danner, one of barbecue's greatest storytellers, says the roots of modern backyard cooking can be traced to US Air Force veterans who were posted at American military bases in the Caribbean.

During the war many temporary landing strips had to be built in the West Indies, and the only way to do that on the sandy terrain was to lay down rolls of diamond-patterned steel grating, which allowed planes to land safely. The local natives used leftover grating from the airstrips as a modern replacement for the traditional wooden cooking grates of the barbacòa. To complete the concept, a used fuel drum was cut in half lengthwise, hinged, and placed on metal legs, lifting the traditional barbacòa fire off the ground to create the

☞ THE FIRST ☜ BARBECUE JOINT?

By the 1850s, a flood of German immigrants had created Texas's "German belt" of farm communities stretching into the hills outside of Houston, and people of German descent made up about five percent of the state's total population. Kreuz Market was founded at the turn of the century in Lockhart, Texas, and featured a large brick oven at the back of the store with a firebox on one side and a chimney on the other. Sausages and leftover cuts of beef and pork were smoked there according to European tradition, left unsauced, and seasoned simply with salt and pepper. The meat was sold over the counter on sheets of butcher paper, with no forks, knives, or condiments other than the pickles and crackers sold in the shop. Kreuz Market is one of Texas's best-known purveyors of barbecue to this day, and although it moved to a bigger location in 1999, it is still a butcher shop selling barbecue on sheets of butcher paper, the same way as always, with pickles and crackers.

prototypical modern barbecue pit, which remains in active use throughout the Caribbean today.

The way Rocky tells it, many American servicemen came back from the war having learned to cook on these makeshift devices, and before long there was one on every block of an ever-expanding 1950s suburbia.

At that time we saw a split between grilling and barbecue, the two classic styles of backyard cooking. An open half-drum, with charcoal or hardwood coals directly underneath a grate, is essentially a brazier or grill, designed to sear meat and cook food relatively quickly. But cover that device with the other half of the barrel and you have a closed chamber. Push the fire to one side, keep the heat low, put a pan of water underneath the meat, and you have a mini-smoker. Finally, weld a firebox on one side, and a chimney on the other, and you have the design of today's modern barbecue pit. (It is interesting to note that although very little barbecue is cooked in a hole in the ground these days, the term "pit" has survived and can be used to describe any enclosed wood- or charcoal-fired smoke cooker.) Load that homemade pit in the back of a pickup, head for the stadium, and you were—and still are—the king of the tailgate party.

LET THE CONTESTS BEGIN!

Which brings us into the age of competitive barbecue, which in turn brings us back to Texas. In the post–Second World War oil boom, Texas was the center of the American oil industry and a huge infrastructure was built around the thousands of oil wells spurting black gold out of the ground. Oil rigs, pipelines, and refineries were springing up everywhere, and many of the oil workers in Texas were also barbecue lovers. It wasn't long before some enterprising welders and pipe fitters took advantage of periodic downtime in the equipment storage yard and perfected the design of the big honkin' barbecue pits you see today. Soon, these custom-built behemoths were equipped with dual wheels and towed behind the giant pickup trucks and motor homes of barbecue fanatics and caterers who specialized in feeding Q to big crowds.

At the same time, the tradition of the tailgate party was taking root in American culture. These pregame bashes, which

THE HISTORY OF THE ❧ BACKYARD GRILL ❧

Before the rise of covered grilling in the 1950s, the classic store-bought home barbecue was more like a brazier. It was usually a square or round sheet-metal contraption, in which you placed charcoal. There was a removable grate on top, on which you put your meat. (It might also have had a cowling to hold a rotisserie and a compartment for keeping side dishes warm.) The one we had at our family cottage had a grill that was fixed on a giant screw. To raise or lower the grill, you had to screw or unscrew it from its base. I still remember the squeaky sound the screw made, and the way Dad rolled around in the grass screaming that time he tried to light the coals with gasoline and burned himself. Good times.

The era of modern grilling was born in 1951, when a welder from Chicago named George Stephen got so frustrated with using his open grill in the Windy City that he decided to do something about it. George worked at Weber Brothers Metal Works, welding together large round metal buoys for the Coast Guard. Working with the buoys all day inspired George to build a cooker with the same materials—a bowl-shaped device with a lid, an air vent, and three spindly metal legs that would become the prototype of the Weber Kettle, which in some circles is as recognizable an icon as the Coca-Cola bottle.

Perhaps even more familiar in modern times is the omnipresent outdoor gas grill, which was invented by Walter Koziol, founder of Modern

(continued)

today often overshadow the actual football or baseball game they are celebrating, are called tailgate parties because their hosts create a banquet table and bar out of the back of a pickup truck. In Texas, especially in the parking lot outside the Houston Astrodome, the quality of the barbecue at tailgate parties became such a source of pride that in 1969 a bunch of Texans decided to have themselves a contest. Little did they know at the time that their little informal event would become one of the biggest barbecue contests in the world, and would spawn an entire competitive barbecue circuit, with governing bodies, elaborate judging criteria, and scores of championships across the continent.

Today the World's Championship Bar-B-Que is an integral part of the annual Houston Stock Show and Rodeo, with over 350 teams cooking more than 100,000 pounds (45,000 kg) of meat on giant, custom-built barbecue pits and attracting a crowd of more than 200,000 people.

Photo courtesy of The Brinkman Corporation, www.the brinkmancorp.com

BARBECUE IS HERE TO STAY

With hundreds of regional barbecue cooking contests across North America, and new barbecue restaurants springing up everywhere (there are finally a handful of authentic ones in New York City), barbecue has truly arrived, having entered the new millennium with enough steamy smoke to power it into the future for many more generations. With strong regional styles of cooking, barbecue restaurants—both old and new—all over North America, and a renaissance of backyard barbecue that is giving the grill a run for its money, barbecue is here to stay.

The History of the Backyard Grill (continued)
Home Products (MHP), in Antioch, Illinois. In the 1950s, MHP was a pioneer in decorative gas lighting for homeowners. As the market for gas lighting grew in suburban America, Walter began looking for ways to market other gas devices. After much tinkering, MHP introduced the first commercial gas grill, the Perfect Host, in 1960. The first Perfect Hosts were round and uncovered, with a cowling that held a rotisserie. The next big innovation came in 1963 when MHP introduced the first rectangular gas grill with a hinged lid—the same basic design that is now a fixture in most North American backyards. It's fun to observe that the modern covered gas grill doesn't look all that different from something one might construct out of two halves of an old oil drum!

1960—the world's first outdoor gas grill

The familiar modern gas grill

Photos courtesy of Modern Home Products, Corp.
www.modernhomeproducts.com

PLANKS FOR THE MEMORIES:
A BRIEF HISTORY OF PLANK-COOKING

To chart the history of cooking with wood is to document the evolution of humankind. But the exact origins of plank-cooking are a little obscure.

We know, for example, that ancient Aboriginal tribes on both sides of the North American continent would lash chunks of fish and meat to planks or stakes and lean them close to a fire. On the northwest coast, cooking salmon on planks placed beside a roaring beach fire celebrated the bounty of the sea. Much of the catch would be smoked to preserve it for the winter, but freshly caught, freshly cooked salmon must have been as much of a delicacy back then as it is today—enhanced, of course, by fire and smoke.

On the East Coast, the largest member of the herring family, the shad, makes its annual spawning run up coastal rivers like the Hudson and the Nanticoke. The arrival of the shad marked the start of a rich annual fishery. Sadly, the shad population has been severely depleted, although they are still harvested in limited numbers. In colonial times, the local natives taught European settlers how to cook shad fillets by fastening them to hardwood planks. The settlers adapted the technique, using nails to attach the fish to the planks, which are leaned against a rack running parallel to an open oak fire.

The tradition of the "shad planking," a celebratory feast, lives on, and today it marks the start of the political campaign season in New England. In the same spirit as the famed barbecue gatherings hosted by politicos and preachers in the American South, shad plankings have become a symbol of American democracy.

The technique of plank-cooking in restaurants and home kitchens gained popularity in the United States on both coasts in the mid-1800s. Early American cookbook authors Eliza Leslie and Fannie Farmer documented recipes for planked whitefish, shad, and chicken. The technique was incredibly easy: butter an oak plank (which would be reused), put the fish or meat on it, and bake it in a hot oven.

> **PLANKING SECRETS**
>
> "Pacific Northwest natives later shared the plank-cooking method for wild salmon with European explorers and settlers. In the 1890s, the method gained popularity when some of the first hotels in the Northwest treated guests to this dramatic local cooking style."
> —from *Savory Flavors with Wood* by Nature's Cuisine
>
> ❧
>
> "In olden times shad was smoked on standing oak boards . . . This was called shad planking. The shad was cleaned and split open and nailed flat to the oak boards . . . The board was turned several times to get uniform cooking."
> —from the website of the Chicone Ruritan Club, an article on Nanticoke River shad planking
>
> ❧
>
> "The only true planked salmon consists of fillets bound to a cedar plank, placed around an alder wood fire at a 15 degree angle away from the vertical and basted throughout the cooking process. The salmon fillets may be marinated or merely salted and peppered ahead of time."
> —Bob Lyon, Pacific Northwest columnist, *National Barbecue News*

◀ The history of plank-cooking has its roots in ancient Aboriginal techniques, like this West Coast alder-fired salmon roast.

Meanwhile, hotel chefs in the Pacific Northwest began offering oven-planked dishes inspired by native cuisine, and to this day cedar-planked salmon is a popular dish in restaurants of the region.

This is where things get fuzzy. Despite an extensive search both on the Internet and in cooking reference books, I can't for the life of me find exactly how the plank made its way from the oven to the grill. It's an obvious and natural transition, but who did it first, and when?

As noted earlier in this book, the classic American covered charcoal grill wasn't invented until George Stephen welded together the first Weber Kettle in 1951. We also know that the first covered gas grill—which truly revolutionized backyard cooking—was introduced to the market by Modern Home Products in 1963. So plank-cooking on a covered grill began no more than 50 or 60 years ago. But was its inventor someone on the East Coast, adapting shad planking to a covered grill using an oak board? Or was it someone in the West, planking the first salmon on a cedar shake? I have a standing offer to buy a case of delicious British Columbian Okanagan wine for the person who can prove that they, or someone they know, were the first to plank-cook anything in a covered grill.

On a personal note, the first time I cooked on a plank was just a few years ago, after moving to British Columbia. Many Vancouver restaurants offer cedar-planked salmon on their menus, and I got a chance to taste it. At some point I came across the *Sticks & Stones* cookbook, by Canadian chef and grilling celebrity Ted Reader. Ted's planking techniques and innovative recipes got me hooked, and there was no turning back.

I remember the first time my wife, Kate, tasted cedar-planked salmon, fresh out of my propane grill. "My goodness, it's like having a sauna in my mouth!" she exclaimed. In that instant, she was hooked, too.

YOU, TOO, CAN MAKE BARBECUE HISTORY

It's not hard to understand the enduring popularity of cooking over a fire. Just a hint of the smell of sizzling fat and hardwood smoke sends most of us to a happy place that reminds us of why it's good to be human. The history of outdoor cooking is all about man's quest for balance—whether it's the perfectly balanced flavors of a succulent piece of meat fresh off the grill, or the perfectly balanced life, which includes time for friends, family, good cheer, and great food. As you thumb through the pages of this book I hope you find some ways to achieve the balance that's right for you, and at the same time, make a little history yourself.

Championship Tools & Techniques

"What would keep a man in the backyard all day cooking a
five-dollar piece of meat? . . . the obvious answer: a five-
hundred-dollar rig to play with."
—food writer John Thorne, in his book *Serious Pig*

THE SCIENCE OF COOKING MEAT

As cooking techniques, grilling and barbecue are elegantly simple. You season
some meat, you hold it near a fire until it's done, and then you eat it, often
with your bare hands. And yet there are so many differences in how meats
cook. Fowl, pork, beef, lamb, and venison all have different qualities that
require different techniques. And of course, there are huge differences in the
taste and texture of each cut, too, depending on what part of the animal it's
from, and even differences in flavor from animal to animal, depending on how
each one was raised. Barbecue champions carefully guard the sources of their
meat and stay on very good terms with their butchers. (When I want a brisket
for competition, my favorite butcher orders 10, calls me when they arrive, and
lets me pick the two I want.)

How different meats cook depends for the most part on their protein content—the fiber of the meat. Proteins consist of amino acids that are chemically
bonded to form long fibers, which are in turn bundled together with connective tissue to form the muscles of an animal.

As the muscle fibers of a cut of meat are cooked, the first thing that happens is they begin to shrink and become progressively harder. Think of how
soft and pliable a steak or chicken breast is when you put it on the grill, and
how quickly it firms up as you cook it. This process starts at about 130°F
(55°C) and continues on up through to about 175°F (80°C). A perfectly done
beef tenderloin has an internal temperature of about 140°F (60°C). (Note: this
refers to the final temperature after resting.)

At 140°F (60°C), the meat still has a lot of the tenderness that we love in
rare or medium-rare beef. Now, if you were to quickly cook that tenderloin to
an internal temperature of 175°F (80°C), it would seize up like a brick and the
meat would turn gray. Under these conditions the proteins shrink so much,

and so quickly, that they crack and the fibers become crumbly. So, when you grill a piece of tender, lean meat, you never want the internal temperature to go above about 140°F (60°C) for beef, pork, or lamb and 160°F (71°C) for chicken. Ideally you want to take beef, pork, or lamb off the grill at around the 125 to 135°F (52–57°C) range, and chicken at a slightly higher temperature because of risks related to salmonella. As the meat rests, the core temperature will rise, especially in larger cuts.

With grilling, the goal is to get those proteins to tighten up just enough so the interior of the meat has a perfectly succulent texture—not raw, but not tough and grainy, either. Because you don't want to overcook meat on the grill, it's a very quick cooking technique—well suited to contemporary urban life. Many of us are so busy that the speed and convenience of grilling is hard to resist. What could be faster than seasoning a few chicken breasts and tossing them on a hot grill along with some fresh vegetables? In 10 minutes we can have a tasty meal, and there's virtually no cleanup.

The Alchemy of Barbecue

But now, chemically speaking, it's time to bring this discussion to the next level. There's another process that begins to take place when the internal temperature of meat reaches about 150°F (66°C). It's at this point that the connective tissue—called collagen—that is holding all the protein fibers together begins to break down and turn into gelatin. This is the alchemy that makes great barbecue, and in traditional cooking it's called braising.

When meat is heated very slowly in a moist environment, the proteins don't tighten up as much, although the meat does get firm. Then, when the internal temperature slowly climbs above 150°F (66°C) and starts approaching 170°F (77°C), something magical happens. Inside the moist interior of the meat, protected by a darkening exterior crust, the collagen starts to break down and the meat starts loosening up. The fibers relax. Juice that was squeezed out of the tissue earlier in the cooking process gets reabsorbed. Fat between the fibers liquefies and combines with the gelatin to create a rich primordial broth, basting the meat from the inside. The end result is real barbecue—the most tender, juicy, succulent meat you'll ever taste. This technique works best with meats that have a high fat content, especially the cuts that also have lots of connective tissue, like pork shoulders and beef briskets.

THE LESSON OF MOM'S ⤞ TOUGH POT ROAST ⤝

Remember the time Mom's pot roast was so tough you could hardly chew it? It's not that your mother was a bad cook. The roast just didn't cook long enough! Pot roast is tough when it hasn't simmered for an extended period, or has been heated too fast at the beginning of the cooking process, seizing up the meat's fibers and squeezing out all its juices. Either way, the end result is a chewy, tasteless blob of meat that properly belongs on a soccer field rather than on a plate. The same problems afflict undercooked barbecue, especially beef brisket and pork shoulder. These cuts should be cooked at least an hour and a half per pound (500 g) over a low, smoldering fire at about 200 to 225°F (95–105°C). That means a 12 lb (5.5 kg) brisket needs to cook for 18 hours! And that's why championship barbecue is an all-night affair.

Leaner cuts simply cannot hold up to this process. Anyone who has over-cooked a beef tenderloin or top sirloin steak on an overheated grill can attest to this. As the meat has less connective tissue and a low fat content, its juices are squeezed out by overcooking and its proteins crack and crumble, leaving nothing more than some mealy gray cardboard.

An Outdoor Cooking Equipment Primer

It's difficult, but not impossible, to get a full range of cooking conditions using one piece of equipment. But to be able to use all of the techniques described in this book, I recommend that you have at least two cookers in your backyard: a gas or charcoal grill, and a smoker or barbecue pit. You can emulate the conditions necessary to cook real barbecue on your grill, but it's just not the same as having a smoker or pit. Have a look through this chart and you'll see what I mean. These are the five backyard cooking devices I have in my arsenal and the functions they perform.

TYPE OF COOKER	WHAT IT DOES BEST	DRAWBACKS
Gas Grill	This is your all-purpose suburban backyard cooking device, ideal for quick grilling jobs and adaptable to bigger, more complex cooking projects like pork shoulder roasts and turkeys. The covered gas grill is also ideal for planking because of its high heat and quick adjustability. Everyone should have one of these, but that doesn't mean you should use it to cook the same thing every time.	Its convenience invites laziness. With a gas grill you can have dinner in 10 minutes, and forget what you ate 10 minutes later. And natural gas and propane are odorless and taste-less. This might be an advantage if you were heating a house with them, but it's a huge liability in the flavor enhancement department. In gas-powered grills the extra flavor comes from caramelization, where your food comes into contact with the super-heated grill, and the vaporized drip-pings, which create an interesting taste. Some extra smoky flavor can be added in the form of wood chips (see pages 23–25).
Charcoal Grill	A covered charcoal grill is superb for high-temperature grilling as well as slower indirect cooking. It has the distinct advantage of using a fuel, charcoal, that adds considerable flavor. And simply throwing some hardwood chips or chunks onto the hot briquettes can give you barbecue flavor. In a shorter time than a full-blown smoker or barbecue pit. It's also great for plank-cooking. One of its big advantages is that there's less chance of flare-ups.	The biggest drawbacks with charcoal cooking are smoke and time. Starting up a charcoal cooker can be a smoky process and if you have sensitive neighbors this can cause problems. And, of course, coals take time to start. You can't just turn on the bri-quettes; it takes at least 20 minutes, and more like half an hour, to start your coals and get your grill up to temperature. For weekday family cooking this can be a nonstarter unless you get into the habit of start-ing your coals even before you loosen your necktie!

TYPE OF COOKER	WHAT IT DOES BEST	DRAWBACKS
Water Smoker or Home Barbecue Pit (a "Bullet")	This is what you need to cook real barbecue at home. It produces a low heat and uses charcoal and/or hardwood to create the moist, smoky environment inside the cooking chamber that's needed to produce true Q.	Requires a fanatical devotion to barbecue. You've got to use this gear more than once a season to get good at it. The fire needs to be tended, and it takes up to 18 hours to cook some large cuts of meat. The cooker takes up space in your backyard. It generates quite a bit of smoke. It is a bit of a pain to clean up, especially after a long cooking session. It makes your wife feel like a barbecue widow. But it's worth it for the kind of fabulous food you can make!
Fancy Electric Smoker	Great for barbecue hobbyists who want some extra convenience. Some of these use an auger turned by an electric motor to feed hardwood pellets, or "bisquettes," into a chamber for a consistent, easily adjustable fire. They work like a charm!	Yet another piece of gear to irritate your spouse. And, for some, it's not "old school" enough to qualify as a real barbecue pit.
Portable Charcoal Grill	Indispensable for picnics and vacations. Allows you to bring your backyard expertise anywhere, anytime.	Doesn't hold a huge amount of food. Hot coals can be a challenge to dispose of safely.

If you don't want to invest in multiple pieces of equipment, your best choice for versatility and flavor is a kettle-style covered charcoal grill. For convenience and speed, a gas grill can't be beat. But if you want to cook with the big boys, the minimum requirement is a bullet-style water smoker, and the ideal is a true barbecue pit, preferably one with dual wheels and your team name painted on the side!

Gas grills are designed for cooking under fairly hot temperatures. They are perfect for the kind of quick cooking that we've all grown to love. It's hard, however, to get their chamber temperature below 300°F (150°C), so they're not ideal for cooking real barbecue—although they can be put into service to produce passable pork butt and brisket.

GRILLING 101

Back in the old days of the barbacòa, meat was held above the fire on a grate made from green wood so it wouldn't burn. The end result was probably a dry, chewy product that stored and traveled well, but wouldn't make it past the first judge in a modern barbecue competition.

Most backyard grilling today takes place on a covered grill fueled by natural gas, propane, or charcoal. Almost all grills nowadays have a lid, and the manufacturers all recommend that you cook with the lid down. This creates a cooking chamber, similar to the inside of a barbecue pit, which does several things:

- It cuts off oxygen, which reduces flare-ups. Grease needs oxygen to burn. Anyone who has had a chicken fire on an open charcoal grill or in a drafty gas grill can attest to this.
- It speeds up cooking time by making your grill behave like a convection oven.
- It allows you to cook in the rain, or in a snowstorm, for that matter. In the Deep South or the Caribbean, cooking on an open grill is a lot easier because the ambient temperature is so much higher and the weather is more consistently fair. It's not surprising that modern covered grilling was invented by Midwesterners!
- It allows the food you're cooking to become infused with the aroma of the vapors inside the chamber. This is why charcoal grilling is usually more flavorful than gas grilling. The charcoal gives off vapors that impart flavor to the food, which is further intensified by the addition of the wood chips or chunks you place on top of the coals (see pages 23–25).

The Principles of Grilling

There are basically two kinds of grilling: direct heat and indirect heat. Direct heat means cooking with the meat directly above the coals or burner. This technique allows you to cook quickly and get a nice crust on your meat. Indirect heat means cooking with the meat to the side of the coals or burner, which allows for slower cooking and avoids charring. Within each of these broad categories, it's convenient to define three levels of heat: low, medium, and high. The following chart goes into more detail.

➤ LET IT REST! ≈

Always remember: take your meat off the grill before it gets to the temperature you want. It will continue to cook after you've removed it from the grill or smoker, just from the residual heat left in the meat itself. The core temperature of a prime rib roast, for example, will gain up to 15°F (9°C) within a half hour of taking it out of the oven. Smaller cuts, like steaks or chicken breasts, only need to rest for 3 or 4 minutes and can be kept from cooling too quickly by loosely tenting them in foil.

Resting your meat has another big advantage. While it's still on the grill, the juices inside are expanding with the heat, creating a good deal of pressure. By letting your meat stand for even a few minutes after taking it off the heat, you allow the pressure to subside and the interior of the meat to stabilize. The juices go back into the fibers and the meat itself firms up, sort of like a custard, resulting in a slightly denser, more silken texture. Meat that has not been rested will often spurt juice when it is cut open, thereby releasing the most flavorful part of the steak all over your plate. Don't let this happen to you.

Resting meat is so important to the quality of the finished product that, in competition, we often wrap our brisket in foil, then in a blanket, and then place it in an insulated cooler for as many as 3 hours before we carve it for the judges!

Grilling Techniques at a Glance

NOTE: In this book it is always assumed that cooking is taking place with the cover of the grill or smoker on. Your results will vary greatly if you grill with the lid open. The only time I would recommend grilling with the top off is for steaks, chops, chicken wings, or calamari on a hot, calm summer day.

DIRECT HIGH HEAT	HEAT INTENSITY	HOW IT WORKS	WHAT TO COOK
Gas or Propane All burners on high.	Chamber temperature 500–700°F/ 260–370°C for gas grills, 350– 450°F/180–230°C for covered charcoal grills. (Covered gas grills can achieve much hotter chamber temperatures than charcoal grills.) *Test* You can't hold your hand directly above the grill for more than 1 or 2 seconds.	*Gas Grill* Food is cooked directly above the heat source with the grill at its highest setting.	Excellent for grilling steaks, chops, and chicken parts, quickly searing tender vegetables like zucchini and asparagus, or charring slices of pineapple. Also a useful final step for crisping the skin of whatever you're cooking. Be sure to turn whatever you're grilling at least once or twice during cooking time. Only use this technique for anything that takes 10 minutes or less to cook.
Charcoal A medium-sized bed of hot coals.		*Charcoal Grill* Same food placement as above, but with a full, fresh, hot layer of coals (about 50 briquettes, depending on the size of the cooker) under the grill and with the vents fully open.	

DIRECT MEDIUM HEAT	HEAT INTENSITY	HOW IT WORKS	WHAT TO COOK
Gas or Propane All burners on medium.	Chamber temperature 300–500°F (150–260°C). *Test* You can hold your hand directly above the grill for 3 or 4 seconds.	*Gas Grill* Food is cooked directly above the heat source, but the gas is adjusted to a lower setting.	This is the best all-purpose setting, suitable for almost anything. This is a gentler way to grill that just takes a little more cooking time, but it's worth it because the proteins in the meat don't seize up as much as with direct high heat. Also excellent for plank-cooking and roasting more robust vegetables like potatoes, squash, or onions, which require a longer cooking time.
Charcoal A medium-sized bed of hot coals.		*Charcoal Grill* Same food placement as above, with 30 or fewer briquettes, and the air vents adjusted as necessary.	

DIRECT LOW	HEAT INTENSITY	HOW IT WORKS	WHAT TO COOK
Gas or Propane All burners on the lowest setting.	Chamber temperature 200–300°F (95–150°C). *Test* You can hold your hand above the grill for at least 5 seconds.	*Gas Grill* Food is cooked directly above the heat source, but the gas is adjusted to the lowest possible setting.	This is good for cooking more fragile foods, like tender fish fillets, or slow-roasting bigger cuts of meat. It isn't much different from indirect medium cooking—except there's a slight risk of flare-ups and a better crust.
Charcoal A small bed of hot coals.		*Charcoal Grill* Same food placement as above, but the briquettes are half spent, or use a smaller number, like 15 to 20. This style of cooking takes longer, so be prepared to add a few coals every hour or so.	

INDIRECT HIGH	HEAT INTENSITY	HOW IT WORKS	WHAT TO COOK
Gas or Propane Side burners on high, the middle one turned off, with a drip pan under the middle grate.	Chamber temperature 500–700°F (260–370°C) for gas grills, 350–450°F (180–230°C) for covered charcoal grills.	*Gas Grill* Preheat the grill on high, then turn one burner off and place your meat above it. With fattier cuts you need to put a foil drip pan underneath the cooking grate to catch the drippings.	This technique is great for achieving a high cooking temperature without the risk of excessive charring or flare-ups. It's great for chicken thighs and breasts, fish, steaks, racks of lamb—anything that would do well in a hot convection oven. The high heat lets you achieve a nice crust, after which you can adjust the grill to medium heat for the rest of the cooking time.
Charcoal A pile of hot coals on each side of the drip pan.		*Charcoal Grill* Put the coals to one side of the grill and place your meat on the other side over an aluminum pan to catch the drippings. Modern charcoal grills have special coal baskets that hold the coals on either side of the grill.	

INDIRECT MEDIUM	HEAT INTENSITY	HOW IT WORKS	WHAT TO COOK
Gas or Propane Side burners on medium, the middle one turned off. *Charcoal* Medium piles of charcoal on each side of the drip pan.	Chamber temperature 250–350°F (120–180°C).	*Gas Grill* Preheat the grill on high, turn one burner off, and place your meat above it with a drip pan below if you need it. Turn down the gas on the other burner(s) to medium. *Charcoal Grill* The same food placement as indirect high, but with fewer coals and the air intake vents partially closed if necessary.	This is perfect for whole chickens and turkeys and roasts—meats that require a longer cooking time.

INDIRECT LOW	HEAT INTENSITY	HOW IT WORKS	WHAT TO COOK
Gas or Propane Side burners on low, the middle one turned off. *Charcoal* Small piles of charcoal on each side of the drip pan.	Internal temperature 180–250°F (82–120°C).	*Gas Grill* Preheat the grill on high, turn one burner off, and place your meat above it with a drip pan below if you need it. Turn down the gas on the other burner(s) to as low as they will go. *Charcoal Grill* The same food placement as indirect high, but moderating the air intake and using a modest amount of coals.	This is where grilling and barbecue overlap, especially with the addition of some wood chips. What you have here is essentially a makeshift barbecue pit, suitable for cooking large cuts like briskets, pork shoulders, and turkeys, or slow-cooking chicken, duck, or other smokable foods. The big disadvantage with charcoal is you need to add more coals every hour or so.

Grilling Tips

Here are some grilling techniques that will give your backyard cooking a championship edge.

1. *Don't walk away from your grill.* I once ruined a whole grill full of kebabs because I was more interested in yakking with my friends than in tending the grill. Just 2 or 3 minutes can make the difference between succulent fare and grainy, overdone meat.

2. *Don't cook everything on direct high heat.* In fact, there's almost nothing that can be cooked with direct high heat that won't improve if cooked instead for a little longer over medium heat. Superhigh heat is fine if you want to get nice dark char marks on your steak or zucchini, but it is a violent approach to grilling that can make the most tender cuts of meat seize up, squeezing out their flavor-giving juices. And that results in mediocre food only worth eating by ravenous, boorish guests that you wouldn't want back anyway. Turn the heat down. Have some patience, and get a better product! If you normally cook steaks for 4 minutes per side on a really hot grill, turn the heat to medium and try 6 minutes per side. Instead of getting steaks that are charred to death on the outside and still cold on the inside, you'll get mouthwatering, perfectly rare or medium-rare, juicy steaks that will blow your guests away.

3. *Cook on a clean, oiled, preheated grill.* I don't mean perfectly clean, like putting it through your dishwasher. Your grill should be free of gunk from the last time you cooked, and it should have some oil on it to avoid the dreaded sticking that tears the skin off chicken parts and makes fish impossible to remove. Remember these techniques for smooth, nonstick grilling:

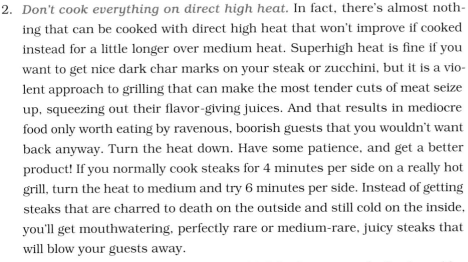

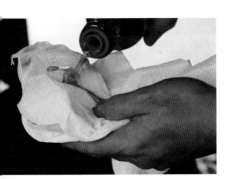

- Always preheat your grill on a high heat for at least 5 minutes before you start cooking, then turn it down if you require a lower chamber temperature. A few minutes before you put on your food, give the grill a good scrape with a wire brush.
- Oil the hot grill just before cooking with a paper towel or clean rag drizzled with cooking oil. Alternatively, you can spray whatever you're putting on the grill with cooking spray (like Pam or whatever else you like) on the side that will hit the grill first. Oiling the grill or the food to be grilled are surefire ways to prevent sticking and they don't add much extra flavor or many calories to your food. (You don't have to spray the food if oil is a major ingredient in your marinade.)
- Don't turn too early. When you first put a burger or a piece of fish on the grill, it automatically sticks to the cooking grate for the first few minutes of cooking. Then a magical thing occurs. Whatever you're cooking carbonizes at the contact points where it's touching the hot grate, which makes it shrink and release itself. You can test for this by nudging the meat with your tongs or spatula. When the edge comes away from the grill easily, it's time to turn!

4. *Turn the meat 3 times for cool grill marks.* This is a fun technique that gets lots of oohs and aahs from your guests. Making sure you've got a hot grill, put on your steak or chop or anything else with a relatively flat surface, and turn it 3 times during cooking, rotating it 90 degrees each time you turn. You'll end up with crosshatched grill marks like the pros.

5. *Don't turn fish at all.* Fish is such a fragile food that it can easily fall apart from excessive handling. Because a covered grill is like a convection oven, you often don't need to turn food at all for it to cook completely, especially if you use indirect heat. But this is coming from a guy with an old grill with cooking grates that have seen better days. New grills, with nice smooth porcelain-coated or stainless steel cooking grates, allow you to turn fish without as much risk of sticking.

6. *Use wood chips for added flavor.* A big disadvantage of gas grills is that they don't add the classic smoky flavor to whatever you're cooking. The more expensive gas grills often have a special little chamber for wood chips to emulate the smoky environment inside a barbecue pit, but you can adapt any covered gas grill in this way:

Step 1 Presoak a handful of hardwood chips (see chart, pages 24–25, for the kinds of flavors they impart) in water, wine, or apple juice for half an hour or so and then wrap them in foil to make a kind of packet.

Step 2 Poke some holes in the packet with a fork and toss the bag onto the lava rocks or spatter guards underneath your cooking grate. They will soon begin to smolder and give off smoke.

Step 3 When the packet is throwing off a good amount of smoke, put your food on the grill and it will take on a bit of smoky flavor. It ain't real barbecue, but it's better than nothin'—and if you get good at it, you can actually create a modest smoke ring (see page 29) using a gas grill!

How to Tell When Your Meat Is Done

Is it done yet? This question haunts anyone who has ruined an expensive piece of meat by overcooking. Every grill, and every plank, and every piece of

➤ BARBECUE SECRETS ➤

Let the food cook a bit before you try to turn it. An uncooked burger patty has a much higher chance of sticking to the grill than one that has started to firm up.

➤ ➤

Flip your meat onto an unused part of the grill for maximum searing power and the best grill marks. The metal that your meat is touching will be cooled by the liquid in the meat. A dry, hot cooking grate makes the darkest char marks! Also, if you want nice dark grill marks, use a rub that has at least a little sugar in it.

➤ ➤

Always cook fish skin side down. When it's done, you can use a spatula to lift the fish right off its skin, which will stick to the grill. For a bonus snack, grill the skin for a few minutes, then pry it off with a spatula and sprinkle it with salt. It's crispy and chewy good—the bacon of the sea!

➤ ➤

Get to know your grill. Every grill has hot spots and cooler areas. Know where they are and use them to your advantage. For example, if you're planking or grilling cuts of meat that are different sizes, put the larger ones on the hotter part of the grill so they all cook at the same rate. Or, if you know someone likes his or her meat extra-rare, place it on the cooler part of the grill.

meat, is different—and so is every day when it comes to weather conditions. With so many variables, adhering strictly to the time specified in a recipe isn't the best approach. Use the times in this book as guidelines only, and test your meat for doneness using either the feel of the meat or the internal temperature as measured by an instant-read or probe thermometer.

Here's how to test by feel: prod the meat with your finger to check the springiness of the flesh. If it gives easily to the touch, it's quite underdone. If it springs back from your touch, it's time to take it off the heat. (With practice you'll learn how to equate the degree of springiness with the doneness of the meat.) And if the meat is hard to the touch, it's been turned into pet food.

⋟ **DUELING DEFINITIONS** ⋞

"barbecue/(bär be kyoo) n. [Sp. *Barbacoa* < framework of sticks] 1. orig., a raised framework for smoking, drying or broiling meat 2. a hog, steer, etc. broiled or roasted whole over an open fire, sometimes in an open pit 3. any meat broiled on a spit over an open fire 4. a party or picnic at which such meat is served 5. a restaurant that specializes in barbecuing 6. a portable outdoor grill —vt. -cued, -cuing 1. to prepare (meat) outdoors by roasting on a spit or broiling on a grill, usually over a charcoal fire 2. to broil or cook (meat) with a highly seasoned sauce (barbecue sauce) containing vinegar, tomatoes, spices, etc."

—*Webster's New World Dictionary, Second College Edition*

⋟ ⋞

"barbecue/(bawr buh kyoo) n. [Amer. Barbecue < greatest food on earth] 1. a big, fat, tough piece of meat cooked for a long time over low heat using a charcoal or hardwood fire until it is tender and succulent 2. the inspiration for a subculture of barbecue enthusiasts who go from city to city all summer, competing to see who can cook the ultimate piece of meat 3. the basis of a restaurant with Formica tables, bad lighting, and watery draft beer that serves big portions of barbecue to its happy, overweight patrons 4. a way of life, emphasizing the consumption of barbecue, drinking, storytelling, and card playing."

—Rockin' Ronnie's New Dictionary of Barbecue

(continued)

MEAT	IDEAL FINAL INTERNAL TEMPERATURE (AFTER THE MEAT HAS RESTED)
Poultry	160°F (71°C) (or until juices run clear when you pierce the meat)
Beef or lamb	125°F (52°C) for rare 140°F (60°C) for medium rare 160°F (71°C) for overdone
Pork	140°F (60°C) for perfectly done 160°F (71°C) for dry and crumbly
Salmon or other fish	135°F (57°C) for perfectly done 160°F (71°C) for flaky and dry

NOTE: The table above lists the ideal finished temperatures of meat and fish. To achieve them, you need to take the meat or fish off the grill before it comes up to the ideal temperature. For example, if I want my beef roast to be rare when I serve it, I'll take it off the heat when it reaches about 115 to 120°F (46–50°C) because I know the core temperature is going to come up at least 5 or 10 degrees while it's resting. The residual heat on the outside of the roast continues to cook the inside of the roast. For smaller cuts like steaks or chops, chicken parts, or smaller fish steaks, this is less important because there's not as much mass, and therefore not as much residual heat.

BARBECUE 101

Okay. This is it. Now that you've mastered the art of backyard grilling, it's time to graduate to the big time. This is barbecue as a noun ("Rockin' Ronnie cooks great barbecue"), as opposed to barbecue as a verb ("Honey, let's barbecue some pork chops"). It's the kind of barbecue people in the American South travel hours to eat. It's the source of fierce rivalries and friendly arguments. It can convert vegetarians, make women swoon, and inspire men to grunt with delight. And, yes, you can cook it in your own backyard. But pay attention. While this isn't rocket science, it's a lot different from searing a rib steak on your gas grill.

Principles of Barbecue

All you need for cooking barbecue are three things: low heat, hardwood smoke, and time. Almost anything can be prepared in this way, from classic chicken, pork, and beef dishes to fresh tomatoes, onions, and hard-boiled eggs.

You can get as fancy as you want when it comes to spicing and saucing your meat. Many traditionalists don't use barbecue sauce at all, or might use it sparingly at the end of cooking as a finishing glaze.

The classic way to turn meat into barbecue is to slather it with prepared mustard and then sprinkle on a dry rub made from salt, sugar, and spices. You can add your personal signature to barbecued meat through the kind of hardwood you choose and the spice combination in the rub. That said, for many pitmasters, particularly in Texas, land of the brisket, the only way to cook barbecue is to put the meat in the pit with nothing on it and just cook it for a long time. The smoke provides so much flavor, and the texture is so succulent, that salt and sugar and spices seem redundant!

Flavoring with Wood: A Rough-Hewn Guide

Unless you have a giant barbecue pit that is fueled by hardwood logs, the basic technique for creating classic barbecue flavor is to place two or three chunks of wood on top of your hot coals. The heat from the coals makes the wood smolder and burn, creating the precious vapor that flavors your food.

Championship Tools & Techniques

Always use dry, untreated woods for cooking. Green wood generates creosote when it's burned, which isn't good.

Hardwood chunks last longer than chips, but their smoke is less intense. Soak hardwood in water or wine before using it if you want to generate more smoke, but be careful. You can oversmoke things, imparting a bitter, acrid aftertaste to your food. Try to use wood chunks that don't have a lot of thick bark, which can make for bitter smoke. If you're burning logs in a pit, burn off the bark before you put your meat in the smoker.

➤ HARDWOOD'S ➤ MAGICAL VAPORS

There's nothing like the aroma and taste of real barbecue. You can smell a good barbecue restaurant from a mile away. That smell is hardwood smoke, which does some magical things in the chamber of a barbecue pit. At the same time as the fat in the meat is liquefying and the connective tissue is breaking down, the hardwood that is slowly burning to produce the heat is also throwing off beautiful vapors called aromatic hydrocarbons. A hardwood fire is nothing more than the combination of oxygen with the organic compounds of the wood, the main by-products being carbon dioxide and water vapor. But, because of the low heat, the wood is not fully combusted, resulting in the microscopic particles we call smoke, along with the invisible, but crucial, aromatics. Interestingly, a smoker that's working properly does not produce much actual smoke. Rather, the temperature is high enough that the wood burns with a controlled flame, rather than smoldering, which produces more smoke than vapor.

Meats cooked with too smoky a fire blacken quickly and have a bitter, acrid crust. Meats cooked in an ideal, vapor-filled environment develop a mahogany-brown exterior crust over time, and the interior of the meat becomes infused with the hardwood fumes, taking on the essential aroma and flavor of the wood itself. Burn fruitwood like cherry, apple, or peach in your smoker and the meat takes on a wonderful smoky sweetness. Use hickory for the

(continued)

WOOD (& OTHER)	FLAVOR/AROMA	USES
HICKORY	The classic sweet, strong smell and hearty taste of American barbecue, this is the wood used in the original American pig roasts of the 16th century. Hickory smoke is so pervasive a flavor in North America today that sometimes we forget where it comes from. Whenever you see "smoke" on the ingredient list in wieners, bacon, or ham, it's probably hickory.	You can't go wrong with hickory. It goes well with everything from pork to chicken and salmon. The only problem: some say it makes everything taste like ham! It is truly one of the "comfort food" flavors.
MESQUITE	A strong, heavy, pungent, slightly acrid aroma that imparts a classic Southwestern flavor to smoked and wood-grilled foods. Burns hot, so watch how much you use.	Use it for smoking beef, game, duck, lamb, or any of the more strongly flavored meats. Great grilling wood for almost anything. Your favorite Tex-Mex restaurant probably cooks your steak with it.
OAK	Lovely dry, nutty aroma, with a slight but noticeable acidity. Available plain, and as the chopped-up remains of wine and liquor barrels, which add another layer of flavor and complexity.	Excellent for beef brisket, but great with almost anything except maybe fish. Perhaps the most versatile hardwood.
MAPLE	Mild, sweet, reminiscent of the smell of a fireplace at a fishing lodge.	Goes well with poultry, ham, and vegetables. Some brands of bacon are maple-smoked.
ALDER	Fresh, pungent, dry aroma, mild flavor.	The classic way to smoke salmon.
PECAN	Similar to hickory but milder and cooler burning. Popular among competitors as well as professional chefs.	Use instead of hickory, maple, or oak as an all-purpose cooking wood.

WOOD (& OTHER)	FLAVOR/AROMA	USES
BIRCH AND WILLOW	Sharply aromatic, pungent, the closest thing to softwood in a hardwood. Scorned by some but used by others, particularly above the Mason-Dixon line.	Fish and game.
APPLE, CHERRY, PEACH	Sweet, mild, fruity, very smooth.	Great with pork and poultry, but they go with almost anything. Also good to blend with other woods, like hickory or oak.
GRAPEVINE	Rich, fruity, aromatic.	Game, lamb, or fish.
CEDAR	A softwood that imparts a distinctive, sharp, astringent aroma and flavor to meat.	Requires a special technique: planking (see page 33). Excellent with fish but also great with cheese, fruits, and vegetables.
DRIED CORNCOBS	Sweet, mild.	Use them like you would a fruitwood for poultry or pork, or combine with a heartier wood like maple or oak.
SEAWEED	Tangy, salty, smoky.	Shellfish and all kinds of seafood. Wash and dry before use.
HERBS (bay leaves, cinnamon sticks, whole nutmeg) and herb wood (branches of rosemary, sage, thyme)	A whole other level of flavor more often used in Europe than in America. Try it sometime! Rosemary adds a piney aroma to lamb.	Lamb and fish, vegetables, cheeses.

Barbecue Techniques for Backyard Cooks

The first thing you need is a water smoker (unless you can afford to shell out a lot of money for a traditional-style barbecue pit, with a side-mounted firebox and a built-in well for water). Water smokers come in many different styles, but most are basically alike, designed in a classic egg shape, resembling *Star Wars*'s famous droid R2-D2. They cost anywhere from $50 to $300. All of them will do the job. Weber and Brinkman make good ones, the Weber Smokey Mountain Cooker being the standard equipment for competitive barbecuers who can't afford big custom pits.

You don't need many tools in addition to your water smoker. Truth be told, you can make do with a good long pair of tongs, some old oven mitts, and a charcoal chimney for starting your coals. But who wants to go with the minimum requirement? (See pages 43–46 for a gearhead's guide.)

Hardwood's Magical Vapors (continued)
classic taste of barbecue that goes back to the plentiful hickory forests of the East Coast. Or burn mesquite for the dark, sharp, tangy flavor of traditional Texas barbecue.

Barbecue competitors often have their own custom mix of hardwoods to add to the richness and complexity of the meat they're cooking. I like to use a combination of cherry, hickory, and mesquite for the bigger cuts like pork butt and brisket, and pure fruitwoods for ribs and chicken to enhance their natural sweetness but not overpower the meat flavor.

Most big barbecue pits run on pure wood—hickory, pecan, or oak logs are favorites. But home cooks who use smaller cookers usually start with a base of charcoal briquettes and then toss hardwood chunks or chips on top of the briquettes to create the vapors essential to classic barbecue. That's what I do.

Where can you find hardwood to fuel your backyard barbecue passion? Sometimes you can find it in someone's backyard. My cherry wood comes from a friend who chopped down a cherry tree as part of a home landscaping project. But most barbecue supply stores and general hardware/building supply outlets display bags of hardwood chunks and chips alongside grills and grilling utensils. If you want to source hardwood logs or more obscure woods, call around to some high-end restaurants in your city; local chefs who use wood-fired ovens often know where to get the best cooking woods.

Getting Started

At the bottom of the water smoker is a basket for your charcoal and hardwood chunks. Better models have adjustable vents at the bottom and top of the unit to help control air flow and temperature. It's best to get your coals going in a chimney-style starter before you put them in the smoker. Charcoal chimneys are designed so you put charcoal briquettes in the chimney and place one or two crumpled pieces of newspaper in a chamber at the bottom. You light the newspaper, and about 15 minutes later you have nice hot briquettes. Never use lighting fluid or any other chemical starter on your charcoal. It can alter the taste of the meat.

The amount of charcoal you use depends on how long you're going to be cooking. One full chimney of briquettes is not really enough to cook anything other than some chicken pieces or a couple of racks of lamb. The trick is to put a layer of cold briquettes in the basket and then pour your hot ones on top to begin. When I'm barbecuing a brisket or pork butt I start out with 10 to 15 lb (4.5–6.75 kg) of coals. To start things going I create a "seed fire" on top of the pile of cold charcoal. You can do this in a couple of ways:

> **BARBECUE SECRET** <

Don't oversmoke! The biggest mistake novice barbecuers make is to put too much hardwood on the coals. The end result is meat that tastes like smoke and not much more. Take it easy on the wood—barbecue is all about balance.

- Light a handful of coals in your charcoal chimney and, when they're burning well, place them on top of the cold coals (see photos opposite), or
- Place a couple of wax-impregnated felt sticks among the coals at the top of the pile and light them. When the sticks are fully burned and the coals around them are nicely lit, cover the smoker and you're ready to go.

The Water Pan

In your smoker, just above the basket where the coals go, there's a water pan. The water helps keep the meat moist and also maintains the internal temperature of the smoker at an ideal 200 to 225°F (95–105°C). Before you fill up this bowl-shaped receptacle, it's best if you coat it with a double or even triple layer of extra-wide foil for ease of cleanup later. Use hot tap water to fill the water pan. (We like to use apple juice in competition.) If you want to get fancy, throw in a bottle or two of dark beer, some wine, or whatever you've been marinating your meat in.

Some very fatty cuts of meat, such as pork shoulder butt, can be cooked at a slightly higher temperature (250°F/120°C) with a drier heat. In cases like this you may leave the water pan in the smoker without any water in it to catch the drippings. Be sure you monitor your water level. For long smoking jobs you may need to add water to the pan once or twice.

❧ BARBECUE SECRETS ❧

About 45 minutes before the end of the cooking time, brush the meat all over with barbecue sauce and add one or two last chunks of wood to "finish" it with a final blast of smoky vapors. After you take your meat out of the smoker, let it rest for at least 20 minutes before you eat it (see Let It Rest! page 16).

A charcoal or wood fire is regulated not by the amount of wood or coal you're burning, but rather, how much air you let into your smoker or barbecue pit. Most charcoal and wood smokers have air vents that can be adjusted to regulate the intensity of the fire. After some practice you should be able to regulate the air vents on your smoker to the point where you can walk away from it for hours, or, in the case of a large brisket or pork butt, overnight.

Spray your meat for a tastier crust. In a spray bottle, combine apple juice with some maple syrup, a glug of Jack Daniel's Tennessee Whiskey, and a pinch of cayenne. Lightly spray the meat every hour or two to give it a shiny glaze and a little more zing.

Preparing the Meat: Mustard & Rub

Take the meat you're going to smoke out of the fridge and let it sit for an hour or so at room temperature. Coat the meat on both sides with a thin layer of prepared mustard (not fancy Dijon, just plain old ballpark mustard). Sprinkle dry rub (see Dry Rub Recipes, pages 50–53) on the meat, giving it a nice even distribution. (If the meat has been brined or heavily marinated, you can often do without the mustard and rub.)

Let the rubbed meat sit for 15 minutes or until tacky (when the salt in the rub starts to draw the moisture out of the meat). Place the meat fat side up on the cooking grate of your smoker, put some hardwood on the coals, and let it cook at 200 to 225°F (95–105°C).

Monitoring the Temperature Inside the Cooking Chamber

Above the charcoal and the water pan are two circular cooking grates on which you place your meat once you've got your smoker up to temperature. Some cheap water smokers come with a temperature gauge, usually one that says WARM, IDEAL, and HOT. This is not good enough. Buy a good metal probe-style thermometer that goes from 100 to 500°F (38–260°C). If you don't have an air vent at the top of your smoker, use a drill to make a single hole big enough to accommodate the stem of the thermometer. When the temperature reaches 200 to 225°F (95–105°C), it's time to put your meat in.

Tending Your Meat

Once you've put your meat on the grill, put some hardwood chips or chunks on the coals (see page 23–25) and place the cover on your smoker. Some barbecue cooks like to soak their wood chunks or wood chips in water or wine before using them.

The wet wood produces more smoke; for a milder flavor, don't soak it.

Now it's time for a long break. The key to great barbecue is to let the cooker do the work. The more you open the smoker to check the meat, the longer the cooking time. Every time you open that lid, you add about 15 minutes. As famed Memphis in May champion Myron Mixon says, "If you lookin', you ain't cookin'."

Allow 1½ to 2½ hours for hamburgers, 2½ to 3 hours for half chickens, 5 or 6 hours for ribs, and 1½ to 2 hours per pound (500 g) for pork shoulder or beef brisket. (Cooking times vary because of differences in equipment and weather conditions. Especially when you're first starting out, it's best to gauge doneness based on internal temperature rather than time. Add one or two more chunks of hardwood to the coals every hour or two.)

Master Barbecue Chart

This chart is designed as a guide for cooking barbecue in a water smoker or a barbecue pit, assuming the internal temperature of the cooker is about 200 to 220°F (95–100°C).

In all cases, make sure to let the meat rest, tented in foil, for at least 15 minutes for small cuts and an hour or more for bigger ones.

MEAT	SIZE	BEST HARDWOOD FLAVORS	COOKING TIME AND DONENESS TEST
PORK			
Pork butt (bone in)	6–8 lb (2.7–3.5 kg)	Hickory, oak, apple, cherry	1½–2 hours per pound (3–4 hours per kg). Butt is done when the internal temperature reaches 185°F (85°C).
Pork loin roast (boneless)	3–5 lb (1.5–2.2 kg)	See above	3–5 hours, or until the internal temperature reaches 145°F (63°C).
Pork tenderloin	1–1½ lb (500–750 g)	See above	1–1½ hours, or until the internal temperature reaches 145°F (63°C) for medium.

⤝ THE SMOKE RING ⤞

Judges in barbecue competitions look for something called a "smoke ring" when meat is presented to them. This bright pink ring is evidence of the depth of penetration of the aromatics into the meat. The more pronounced the smoke ring, the better. The reddish color is caused by nitrogen compounds in the smoke reacting with myoglobin, the oxygen-carrying protein in muscle tissue. Nitrates not only color the meat, but act as a natural preservative, inhibiting bacterial growth. Ever wonder why ham is pink? It's because nitrates are added to commercial meat products. Rumor has it that some modern barbecue competitors add powdered nitrates to their rubs to artificially enhance their smoke rings—a travesty, as far as most competitors are concerned! Some barbecue restaurants publish warnings to guests who are new to barbecue and might mistake the red color of their ribs or beef for raw or undercooked meat. With barbecue, if it's got a red ring, it's done like dinner!

10 SECRETS OF CHAMPIONSHIP BARBECUE

1. *Keep it slow and low.* The thing that sets real barbecue apart from grilling is the low temperature (about 200–225°F/95–105°C) and the long cooking time (3 or 4 hours for chicken and as long as 18 to 24 hours for a big beef brisket). This technique allows the fibers in the meat to gently break down over time, creating the melt-in-your-mouth texture of real barbecue.

2. *The judges eat with their eyes, and so do your guests.* Care about presentation. Just as your car runs better after you've washed it, great barbecue tastes even greater when it looks so good you want to jump into the plate and wallow in it.

3. *Mustard and rub.* This simple yet time-honored technique gives barbecue its fabulous crust, or "bark," as the Southerners call it. The mustard provides a base for your rub to stick to, and gives the crust a nice tang when you bite into it. And the rub, with its combination of salty, savory, bitter, and sweet flavors, accentuates the flavor of the meat without overpowering it.

4. *Two words: Granulated garlic.* The addition of this seemingly modest flavor component makes a difference to that first taste. The judges don't know why, but there's something about it that tugs the old taste buds in the right direction.

5. *The final temperature of your meat is more important than how long you cook it.* Watch the internal temperature of your meat and you will produce great barbecue, time after time.

6. *Let it rest.* Resting your meat after you take it off the heat allows the juices to redistribute inside, within the protective crust. It also allows the protein to set, or gel, almost like custard. Resting lets the meat come to the perfect texture. *(continued)*

MEAT	SIZE	BEST HARDWOOD FLAVORS	COOKING TIME AND DONENESS TEST
PORK *(continued)*			
Ribs (side ribs or baby backs)	Full slab with membrane removed	See above	4–6 hours or to an internal temperature of 165°F (74°C). Ribs should pull easily away from the bone.
Pork sausage, raw (like bratwurst, chorizo or Italian)	1-inch (2.5 cm) diameter	See above	2–3 hours, until the sausages are firm and no longer pink in the center; internal temperature of 160°F (71°C).
BEEF			
Boneless roasts (sirloin, tri-tip, rib, cross-rib)	4–6 lb (1.8–2.7 kg)	Hickory, mesquite, oak, cherry	About 1 hour per pound (2 hours per kg) or until the internal temperature reads 125°F (52°C) for medium rare, 140°F (60°C) for medium. Not worth eating if it's well done!
Brisket	10–14 lb (4.5–6.4 kg)	Hickory, mesquite, oak, cherry	Cook 1½–2 hours per pound (3–4 hours per kg) or until the internal temperature reads 185°F (85°C). When you lift the roast to turn it, it should have a relaxed, jellylike feeling. It is underdone if it feels very firm and tight.
Short ribs	2–3 inches (5–8 cm) thick, preferably on the bone	See above	4–6 hours, or until the meat pulls easily off the bone.
Prime rib bones	Rack with 6–8 bones	See above	3–4 hours or until the internal temperature at the thickest part of the ribs reaches 140°F (60°C) for medium rare.
Hamburgers (Yes, you can smoke hamburgers. Coat them with barbecue sauce and finish them on a hot grill.)	⅓–½ lb (170–250 g) each	See above	Cook for 1½ to 2½ hours, until the internal temperature reaches 160°F (71°C) or until the burgers become springy when touched.

MEAT	SIZE	BEST HARDWOOD FLAVORS	COOKING TIME AND DONENESS TEST
POULTRY			
Turkey, whole (no stuffing, cavity open to allow smoke to circulate)	10–12 lb (4.5–5.5 kg)	Apple, cherry, grapevine, oak, hickory	45 minutes to 1 hour per pound (1½ to 2 hours per kg), or until the internal temperature at the thigh joint is 160°F (71°C).
Chicken, cut in half lengthwise	3–5 lb (1.5–2.2 kg)	See above	2½–3 hours, or until the internal temperature at the thigh joint is 160°F (71°C), or until the meat near the thighbone is no longer pink (cut to test).
Duck, cut in half lengthwise	4–6 lb (1.8–2.7 kg)	Apple, cherry	4–6 hours, or until the temperature at the thickest part of the breast is 160°F (71°C).
Cornish game hen	1–1½ lb (500–750 g)	See above	2–3 hours, or until the meat next to the thigh bone is no longer pink (cut to test).
LAMB			
Leg, bone in	4–6 lb (1.8–2.7 kg)	Apple, cherry, oak	1 hour per pound (2 hours per kg) or until the internal temperature reaches 125°F (52°C) for medium rare or 140°F (60°C) for medium.
Shoulder, whole, bone in	3–4 lb (1.5–1.8 kg)	See above	5–7 hours, or until the internal temperature reaches 170°F (77°C) and the meat pulls easily off the bone.
Rack, whole	1½–2 lb (750 g–1 kg)	See above, but also try a few rosemary branches	1½–2 hours, or until the internal temperature reaches 125°F (52°C) for medium rare, 140°F (60°F) for medium. Not worth eating if it's well done!

10 Secrets of Championship Barbecue
(continued)

7. *Sauce lightly, or don't sauce at all.* The tang of a barbecue sauce (called a finishing glaze in barbecue circles) helps to complete the perfect barbecue flavor. But it can also overpower the flavor of barbecue, so you don't taste much else but the sauce. Go lightly, and then serve some "dipping sauce" on the side.

8. *Use a combo of woods for complex flavor.* Use hardwood as a flavoring agent, but learn what combination works for you. Just like a blended whiskey provides the taster with different flavor notes—some sharp, some sweet—hardwood can be just as subtle. Use mesquite for astringent sharpness, fruitwood for rich sweetness, and hickory, maple, and oak for classic barbecue flavor.

9. *Barbecue is about balance.* Balance your flavors to create a single, complex but unified taste. Balance your temperature, length of cooking time and resting time to achieve the perfect texture. Balance the appearance of the barbecue on your guest's plate or the judges' tray, so your portion looks plentiful but not vulgar, and moist but not oversauced, richly luxurious, but with some fresh green as a visual counterpoint.

10. *Barbecue is life.* Good food and drink, friendship, humor, healthy competition— that's what both barbecue and life are all about. As an old boss of mine once said, "Ronnie, if you use people good, they'll use you good." Be gentle with your barbecue and with your friends, and you shall lead a wonderful life.

EMULATING REAL ⇒ BARBECUE ON YOUR ⇐ COVERED GAS GRILL

Real barbecue has three essential components: time, low heat, and smoke. This makes it difficult, but not impossible, to approximate real barbecue on a gas grill. Here's how to do it.

1. Use indirect low heat. Put a foil pan underneath the cooking grate on one side of your grill to catch the drippings. Preheat the grill by turning on the burner on the other side on high for 5 minutes, then turning it to its lowest setting. Ideally you want the chamber temperature to be somewhere in the range of 200 to 250°F (95–120°C). Place whatever you're cooking (like a pork butt or brisket) on the grate on the cool side of the grill, above the drip pan. Then cook it as if it were in a smoker or barbecue pit, with the lid closed, turning the meat periodically and spraying it with apple juice.

2. Generate some smoke to help flavor the meat. Take some hardwood chips or chunks and soak them in water for about an hour. Wrap them in a double coating of foil to make a neat packet. Pierce the packet with a fork in a few places and then place the packet on the hot side of your grill, below the cooking grate and on top of your lava rocks or drip guard. The wood will heat up and slowly burn, releasing smoke into the chamber of your grill, giving the meat a bit of smoky flavor and producing a mild red smoke ring.

3. Use smoked salt, smoked paprika, or chipotle chili powder in your rub or chipotles in adobo sauce in your finishing glaze. These naturally smoky ingredients add a subtly smoky flavor to whatever you're grilling, and the chipotles also give it some chili heat.

MEAT	SIZE	BEST HARDWOOD FLAVORS	COOKING TIME AND DONENESS TEST
FISH			
Whole, small	1 lb (500 g)	Alder, grapevine, hickory, oak	¾–1½ hours, or until the flesh is just starting to firm up and almost flakes.
Whole fillet (side), large	3–4 lb (1.5–1.8 kg)	Alder, grapevine, hickory, oak. If you're cooking salmon, use hickory or alder for best results.	2–3 hours, or until the flesh is just starting to firm up and almost flakes.
Fillets or steaks	6–8 oz (175–250 g) per piece	Alder, grapevine, hickory, oak	1–1½ hours, or until the flesh is just starting to firm up and almost flakes.
Shellfish—oysters, scallops, prawns	1–2 oz (30–60 g) per piece	Alder, grapevine, hickory, oak	½–1 hour, until they are just heated through and firm to the touch.
OTHER			
Tomatoes	Medium-sized	Hickory, oak, apple, cherry	½ hour, or until the tomatoes start to take on a golden tinge but are still firm to the touch.
Onion	Peeled and cut into ¼–½-inch (6–10 mm) rounds	See above	About an hour, or until the slices take on a golden color.
Red bell pepper	Medium-sized, nice and meaty	See above	¾–1½ hours, or until the flesh is soft.
Garlic	Whole head, trimmed to expose the cloves	Apple or cherry	2–3 hours, or until the head is golden brown and the garlic is soft and tender.
Salt (kosher, Maldon, or fleur de sel sea salt)	1 cup (250 mL) spread evenly in a cake pan or pie plate	Hickory, oak, apple, or cherry	About 1 hour, stirring once or twice, until the salt is golden brown.
Nuts (whole shelled pecans, almonds, or your favorite nut)	½ lb (250 g) spread evenly in a cake pan or pie plate	See above	1 hour, or until the nuts have taken on a slightly darker hue.
Cheese (mozzarella, Jack, Gouda, cheddar, or any other firm cheese)	½ lb (250 g) wrapped in cheesecloth	See above	1–2 hours.

PLANKING 101

For many years, plank-cooking has been an obscure technique practiced by restaurateurs, anglers, and nerdish foodies. But, thanks to the growing availability of quality cooking planks and exposure on network television, hundreds of thousands of people across North America have discovered this easy, delicious grilling technique. For a generation that has grown up on propane and gas grills, plank-cooking is a simple way to add the classic taste and aroma of wood smoke to meat.

And, as you'll find out in the pages that follow, it also happens to be a great way to prepare vegetables, fresh fruit, nuts, and even cheese.

The basic technique couldn't be simpler: soak a cedar or hardwood plank in water. Place it in a hot covered grill. When the plank starts to crackle and smoke, put whatever you want to cook on the plank, then cover the grill and turn the heat down to medium. Soon you'll have juicy, perfectly cooked food, infused with wonderful flavor.

I'll admit there's skepticism in some circles about planking. My friend and longtime mentor Bob Lyon is a correspondent for the *National Barbecue News* and a true barbecue purist. He says the popularity of cooking with planks—particularly in America's Pacific Northwest, where cedar-planked salmon is a restaurant staple—is fueled by "misinformation for tourists and local gullibles." And another old pal, food writer and barbecue queen Kathy Richardier, says, "It's a waste of perfectly good wood. The only wood I advocate for food cooking is long sticks stuck with hot dogs or marshmallows over a campfire."

Unlike my curmudgeonly chums, many backyard cooks are attracted to the idea of plank-cooking but are reluctant to use planks on their grills, perhaps fearing the unknown or worrying about potential flare-ups and fires. The concept can be a bit daunting.

Well, I'm here to challenge the skeptics and calm the concerns of cautious grillers. When done right, plank-cooking is safe, easy, and fun for all backyard grillers. As you try out the planking techniques and recipes in this book, I'm convinced you'll quickly understand just how versatile planking can be, and how it can produce some of the most succulent dishes you've ever tasted. From classic planked salmon with whiskey-maple glaze to planked pears in a pool of rhubarb compote, there's something in here for every taste and skill level.

❧ PLANKING SECRET ❧

To reuse, or not to reuse? That's a good question, and the easy answer is the one my mentor Ted Reader gives: "Planks have two uses, one on your grill, the other in your fireplace." The more complicated answer is that planks can be used maybe two or three times as long as you wash them thoroughly between uses and then store them in a place with good air circulation so they won't get moldy. Hardwood planks like oak or maple stand up best to multiple uses because they're very dense. Cedar, because it's lighter and more porous, tends to get quite charred and crumbly on the first use and therefore doesn't reuse well.

The Basics: Plank-Cooking Made Easy

Why plank in the first place? If you want smoky flavor, you can use a charcoal grill, or toss some soaked wood chips into your gas grill. If you want to slow-roast something, you can put it in a smoker, or use indirect heat on your grill by turning off the burner under your roast or moving the briquettes to either side. Well, it turns out there are distinct advantages to grilling with planks:

- Planking adds great flavor without the mess. Ever try to clean a grill that's got salmon skin stuck to it? With planking, food never touches the cooking grate. If you're adding flavor with wood chips, you're going to get ashes, which have to be cleaned up eventually. Planks stay intact throughout the cooking process. When you're finished, you take the plank off and you're done.
- The plank helps cook food gently. A soaked plank is going to throw off smoke, but it also produces steam, which moderates the heat and helps the food retain its moisture. The plank also insulates whatever you're cooking from the direct heat of the grill, cooking food more gently and evenly.
- Plank-cooking is spectacular. There's a theatrical aspect to planking that plays into the need for backyard cooks (especially men) to show off to their spouses and guests. You've got smoke. You've got campfire-like crackling. Sometimes you've got fire around the edges of the plank, which has to be expertly sprayed to put it out. And, with planked salmon in particular, you've got a magnificent way of presenting and serving the fish, right on the beautifully charred plank.
- Planking is low fat. I'm actually not so sure that's an advantage, but for some people I suppose it's nice to know that you don't need to add oil or fat to the food to enhance the flavor or prevent sticking.

Planking Gear

Like all great pastimes, plank-cooking requires a certain amount of gear, most of which is already in your grilling arsenal. Here are the essentials.

Planks There are all kinds and sizes of grilling planks on the market today, and you can get them at gourmet food and kitchen stores, supermarkets, and home improvement centers. The best kind of wood for beginners is cedar because it soaks up more water than other woods, which makes flare-ups less likely. The ideal size for a grilling plank is about 7 inches wide by 16 inches long (18 × 40 cm), and between ¼ and ⅝ inch thick (0.6–1.5 cm). You want a plank that's not too long to fit in your covered grill but big enough to hold what you want to cook, with a little space on all sides (this protects the food from charring in case you get flare-ups along the edges). Old-timers, purists, and cheapskates will tell you the best way to get planks is to go to your local lumberyard or home improvement center and buy cedar shakes or fencing planks (make sure they're untreated, of course), which you can then saw to whatever length you want. Whatever you do, don't use softwoods like pine, spruce, or fir for planking. They're too resiny and their smoke imparts a bad taste.

Covered charcoal or gas grill Just about any kind of covered grill will do, and even the small portables work fine. As with other styles of grilling and barbecue, you're going to get more flavor using a charcoal-fired cooker. But most households in North America have propane or natural gas grills, and they work just fine with a plank.

Space Grilling with planks produces quite a bit of smoke, which is going to cause you trouble if your grill is in a tight, semi-enclosed space like a covered deck or an apartment balcony. You also need to be far enough away from your neighbors, or at least downwind from them, so you don't smoke them out of their houses.

Fire extinguisher Every cook should have one in the kitchen, and two if the kitchen is far away from where you keep your grill. You may never have to use it, but you'll regret it if you have to put out a fire without one.

Spray bottle I'm talking about your basic garden-variety spray bottle, the kind people use for spraying houseplants or moistening clothes before ironing. You need to keep one on hand (full of water) to put out the little flare-ups that are inevitable with this style of cooking, especially if you didn't soak your plank for very long before putting it on the grill.

Sturdy tongs The longer, the better. You'll use these for placing food on the plank, but you can also remove the plank with the food on it by grabbing it with a good set of tongs (this only works for lighter fare, and on planks that aren't too burnt).

⤳ IS UNTREATED ⤳ REALLY UNTREATED?

When I go into a lumberyard and buy untreated planks to use for cooking, I've always assumed they won't have any unwanted chemicals on them. Even so, I make sure to rinse the planks thoroughly before using them. But I have since talked with cooking plank manufacturers, and they tell me a couple of things that might give pause to those who want to cut their own planks. First, there are some lumber mills that, as a matter of course, spray all the wood coming out of the mill with an agent that helps resist mold and mildew. Who knows whether that's good for your health? On top of that, when you buy an untreated plank, do you know how and where it's been stored? If it's been on a rack, exposed to the rain, with poisonous treated wood above it, have the chemicals leached out of the preserved wood to contaminate the untreated planks below? If this makes you worry, then always look for planks meant for cooking that say they are untreated and have "food grade" on the label.

Metal spatulas The easiest, safest way to take a plank off the grill is with two spatulas. Buy ones that are both long and wide; they give you the most control and allow you to pick up planks that have been weakened by charring.

Large baking pans You can transfer a hot, smoldering plank to a baking pan or baking sheet to let it cool down before serving.

Large stainless steel serving dish Sometimes the most attractive and simplest way to serve planked food is to present it and carve it right on the plank. But you need to put the plank on something that won't melt or burn.

Meat thermometers I recommend you have two kinds—an instant-read thermometer and a probe-style digital thermometer. You can poke the instant-read device into whatever you're cooking to find out the internal temperature within a few seconds. For larger cuts, a probe-style thermometer will give you an ongoing, live reading of the core temperature of your meat without having to open the cover of your grill. Some of the higher-end models come with radio transmitters and remote devices that allow you to monitor the internal temperature of your meat from as far as 50 feet (15 m) away. The good ones have alarm settings so your remote will beep when your meat is ready to take off the grill. Maverick brand remote thermometers are the best I've tried. They're easy to use and reliable, unlike many others on the market today.

Chamber thermometer Most grills nowadays have a built-in chamber thermometer that gives you a pretty good idea of the temperature inside the cooker. If yours doesn't have one, a standard oven thermometer can be used. Just sit it on the plank right next to the food for an accurate reading.

Silicone basting brush If you don't have a silicone basting brush, I recommend that you add one to your gear collection immediately. This is a huge upgrade from your basic pig-bristle paintbrush-style baster. It holds more sauce, spreads it more evenly, stands up to very high temperatures, and cleans up in the dishwasher.

Drip pans When you're planking (or grilling) large, fatty cuts of meat, it pays to put a drip pan beneath the cooking grate to avoid flare-ups and keep your grill clean. I find the large rectangular disposable aluminum trays work best.

Common Types of Planks

WOOD	FLAVORS	USES
Cedar (use only western red cedar)	Spicy, exotic, mildly astringent. Like having a sauna in your mouth.	Goes best with sweeter meats and fish like salmon, pork, and lamb, and tree fruits like peaches and pears, but try it with other foods, including veggies, nuts, and cheese.
Apple, apricot, peach, and other fruitwoods	Mild, sweet, fruity.	Great for pork, poultry, game, and seafood.
Alder	A West Coast classic. Mild, delicate, dry, with hints of vanilla; a bit like oak but much lighter.	Perfect with salmon and other seafood but also good with almost anything else.
Cherry	More flavorful than other fruitwoods, cherry imparts a distinct, sweet, smoky taste.	Ideal for poultry, lamb, and game.
Hickory	The most recognizable flavor in all of barbecue, hickory is the most versatile cooking wood.	Excellent with pork, salmon, red meat, cheese, and nuts. The intense flavor conjures up traditional Southern-style cooking. Anything cooked with hickory becomes a comfort food. Not as good for more delicate meats, fish, or vegetables.
Maple	We all know the smooth, sweet smell of maple because a lot of bacon is flavored with maple smoke.	A classic flavor that works with almost anything you want to cook, but is best suited to pork and poultry.
Mesquite	The strongest flavor of all the hardwoods, it's the classic taste of the American Southwest.	Perfect with pork and beef, it might be too strong for milder and more delicate foods.
Oak	The taste of Texas barbecue (especially red oak). Oak adds a strong, dry, slightly astringent flavor.	Best with beef, but works with almost anything.
Other woods	You can use any hardwood to plank-cook food, but the more exotic you get, the more expensive the wood can be (try buying a walnut plank and you'll see what I mean). Apparently Hawaiian guava wood is superb (but expensive).	

ALDER   CEDAR   CHERRY   HICKORY   MAPLE   WHITE OAK

10 Steps to Planking Perfection

Planking is almost as easy as one, two, three: Soak the plank, preheat it on the grill, put your food on. There's just a little more to it than that. Follow these 10 simple steps to perfect planking every time.

(continued)

1. *Soak the plank.* This step is a must unless you want to convert your grill into an inferno. Ideally, soak your plank overnight, but I recommend you soak planks for at least 1 hour before use. (In a pinch you can get away with only an hour of soaking time, but you've got to be extra vigilant to catch and put out flare-ups during cooking.)

   Longer soaking is especially important with hardwoods like alder, maple, and oak, which are much denser than cedar. Planks float, so to soak them you need to weigh them down. I use a rock from my garden, but you can use a container of water, a heavy jar or jug, or a brick. Don't use cans, because they rust.

2. *Get your food ready to go.* Have all your prep work done before you start the grill. You don't want a plank that's ready for the food but food that's not ready for the plank. By the time you've caught up, the plank will literally have gone up in smoke.

3. *Preheat your grill.* Prepare the grill for direct medium-high cooking. For a gas grill, this means all burners are on high for about 5 or 10 minutes. For a charcoal grill, you want a fairly full, fresh, hot layer of charcoal—maybe 30 briquettes. This will take 15 to 20 minutes.

4. *Take the plank out of the soaking water, rinse it well under a tap, and place it on the cooking grate.* Once you've got the plank on the grill, close the cover immediately. If the plank has a smooth and a rough side, put the rough side facing down.

5. *Let the plank heat up inside the grill.* In about 4 or 5 minutes you'll hear the plank start to gently pop and crackle, and you'll see some smoke coming out of the grill. Don't wait too long or your plank will go up in flames, especially on a gas grill. But remember that if you don't wait for the crackle and smoke you won't get much flavor.

6. *Put your food on the plank.* Leave at least a 1- to 2-inch (2.5 to 5 cm) margin of wood around the edge, and leave a little space between individual pieces of meat.

7. *Immediately turn the heat down.* This applies mainly to gas grills. You should turn it down to medium or medium-low as soon as the plank is ready. This allows the food to cook more gently and reduces flare-ups. You're looking for an internal chamber temperature of 350 to 500°F (180–260°C). I know that's a big range, but some gas grills just don't get much below 500°F (260°C). For most applications, the more moderate the heat, the better the result.

8. *Closely monitor the grill.* Take care to spray water on flare-ups if they occur. (Don't open the lid too often as that will increase the oxygen and encourage the plank to burn.)

9. *Take the planked food, and the plank, off the grill.* You can do this in two ways: Take the food off the plank and then take the plank off the grill, or take the plank off with the food on it (a great way to present salmon).

10. *Put out the plank.* Make sure the plank you're using is safely out of the grill. Dunk it in water or spray it with a hose to make sure it's completely out.

Planking Secrets (continued)

an hour or two. That means the waterlogged plank will need more time to heat up before you put whatever you're cooking on it. Listen for the telltale crackle and pop of a plank that's ready to go, or watch for a haze of bluish smoke coming out of your grill. If you don't wait long enough, you won't get nearly as much flavor out of your plank. (Of course, if you wait too long you'll have a bonfire in your grill, so just watch and listen, and learn as you go!)

If you want to reuse a plank, wash it with mild soap and warm water immediately after use, and rinse it well. When the plank is dry, sand the surface to open the grain and release more flavor the next time you cook with it. As mentioned on page 33, hardwood planks, because they have a tighter grain, are easier to reuse. Wash as soon as it has cooled, and be sure there is good air circulation while the plank is drying.

Keep an eye on food while it's being planked. Never stray too far from your grill while you're plank-cooking. If it's billowing giant clouds of smoke, your plank is on fire and you need to be there with your spray bottle. (This circumstance is rare, and it's usually caused by an undersoaked plank in a too-hot grill with very fatty meat on the wood.) If you get distracted and your plank is completely in flames, a spray bottle might not do. You might need to pour a cup of water along the burning edges of the plank to subdue the fire.

Always turn off the grill after you've taken the food off the plank. I learned this lesson the hard way. One time I was planking some salmon and had two planks in the grill. I took the salmon off, but absentmindedly left the grill on, with the planks still inside. The heat from the grill, combined with a strong, dry crosswind, turned the grill into a furnace and melted the cooking grates. Molten metal actually dripped out of the grill onto the stand below. Since then I always turn the heat off and take the planks off the grill!

PANTRY & TOOLBOX: STUFF YOU REALLY NEED

A Backyard Cook's Pantry

The longer you soak a plank, the more likely it is to warp when you preheat it on the grill. For many applications this doesn't matter much, and sometimes a slight curve to the plank enhances the final presentation. But in other cases, you want a flat plank so things like mushrooms, baked apples, or tomatoes won't roll off. Two tricks here: First, avoid excessive warping by soaking your plank for only an hour, or even less if you're careful to manage flare-ups with a spray bottle. Second, simply turn the plank over when you see it starting to warp, and before it starts to char. Applying direct heat to the other side will make it flat again.

When you take a plank off the grill, after you've removed the cooked food, always douse it with water or spray it with a hose until it stops smoking (unless you're going to serve the food on the plank, in which case you should wait till it stops smoking before bringing it into the house). Never lay a smoldering plank down on something flammable or meltable, like a plastic tablecloth.

If you need to use 2 or even 3 planks at a time, make sure that you leave at least an inch (2.5 cm) of open space between them to allow for good smoke circulation.

(continued)

This is not a comprehensive list of everything you need in your grilling and barbecue arsenal. But these are a few of my favorite ingredients—some more obscure than others—all of which I consider essential to great backyard cooking.

Asian sauces   Light and dark soy, toasted sesame oil, oyster sauce, black bean sauce, hoisin sauce, and chili garlic sauce should be in your pantry. Use them in marinades, combine them to make an Asian finishing glaze, doctor mayo with them for a flavorful dip, or just paint them on meat as you grill it.

Black peppercorns   If you haven't already done so, please throw out any prepackaged ground pepper in your pantry. Pepper loses its aromatic oils shortly after being ground, so always use whole peppercorns and grind them in a pepper mill. If you need a large amount, use a spice mill or coffee grinder. Use finely ground pepper in rubs and a coarser grind for coating steaks and roasts.

Chilies, ground   Dried chilies are some of the essential flavor components of great barbecue. Use them in everything—sauces, marinades, rubs, dips, and dressings. Blend them half and half with kosher salt and sprinkle the mixture on hot buttered corn on the cob. Add them to guacamole and salsa for extra flavor and heat. Be sure to use the real stuff, which is available in Latin food stores and some ethnic supermarkets—don't waste your money on store-bought blended chili powder. These days I do notice that spice giant McCormick is selling small bottles of ground ancho chilies, but they're very expensive. Best to look to ethnic retailers for good-quality, lower-priced products.

Chipotles in adobo sauce   This is common in Latin American pantries and widely available in the Mexican food section of most supermarkets. Dried chipotles are reconstituted, stewed in a tomato-based sauce, and packaged in little tins. One or two chopped chipotles add a wonderful hot, smoky flavor to sauces and marinades.

Cooking spray   For spraying grills and food about to go on the grill.

Cumin seeds   Raw cumin seeds are available just about everywhere these days, and you can buy big bags of them in the Indian spices section of your supermarket. This is one of my favorite spices, with its dark, earthy, slightly smoky taste and pungent aroma. Use the seeds whole to add an interesting texture to dishes and give a little burst of flavor when you bite into them. For most uses I recommend toasting cumin seeds before adding them to whatever you're cooking (see toasting, page 95). There's nothing like the aroma of freshly toasted cumin seeds ground in a spice mill or coffee grinder!

Extra virgin olive oil   There isn't much room for olive oil in traditional barbecue, but for grilled foods there's nothing like a last-minute drizzle of fruity extra virgin olive oil and a squeeze of lemon to brighten the flavors and enhance the richness of your cooking.

Flavored oils   French-style toasted walnut oil, truffle oil, citrus-infused olive oil, and chili-flavored oil add so much to salads and marinades, making it easy to add a distinctive and unusual flavor to everyday fare. A couple of spoonfuls of flavored oil, a squeeze of fresh lemon or lime juice, a little dollop of Dijon, some finely minced shallot, and a pinch of salt and pepper makes a quick dressing that will amaze your guests.

Granulated garlic and onion   Lots of cooks frown on powdered seasonings and I don't blame them. They can often taste rancid and bitter, especially when they're not fresh. But granulated garlic and onion are different. They have a wonderful grainy texture and a rich, roasted taste that add an intense flavor to grilled and barbecued food. Lately, I find myself adding a bit of granulated onion to almost everything I cook, for an extra dimension of flavor. Note: I notice that these days most stuff that's labeled onion powder and garlic powder is actually the granulated product. It should have the same consistency as fine beach sand.

Herbs, dried   The modern kitchen tends to shy away from dried herbs in favor of their aromatic and delicate fresh counterparts, but good dried herbs (that is, ones that haven't spent the last seven years in the back of your spice cupboard) add a richness and complexity to food that fresh herbs can't. I often like to combine fresh herbs with their dried counterparts

More Planking Secrets *(continued)*

A few years back a reader sent me an email with a great tip: next time you're doing some planking, soak a few extra planks. When they're fully saturated, wrap them in cling wrap or foil and stick them in your freezer. Next time you want to plank you've got a presoaked plank at the ready!

Don't plank everything. Part of the joy of planking is the novelty. As my son said, upon being presented with a particularly smoky planked peach, "Dad, you know, everything doesn't have to taste like barbecue. There are other styles of cooking. Sometimes it's nice just to taste a plain peach." Nuff said.

to create a big, balanced flavor with an earthy, bitter bottom and a crisp aromatic brightness.

Ketchup This gives Kansas City–style sauces their classic sweetness and glossy, thick texture.

☞ A GROUND CHILI PRIMER ☜

Store-bought chili powder tastes okay if you don't know what tastes better. But once you have used real ground chilies in your cooking, you'll never go back to the store-bought stuff, which does contain ground dried chilies, but usually also contains table salt and other spices, like oregano and cumin. It's well worth the trouble to find a Latin specialty grocer that carries a selection of real powdered chilies. I like to use a combination of different powdered chilies in my rubs. Here are my favorites:

Ancho, the mildest and sweetest of the dried chilies, has a rich, dark, red-brown color and a mild, fruity flavor with overtones of coffee, raisin, and tobacco.

Cayenne, the ubiquitous source of heat in so many styles of cooking, has a pungent, tart heat that adds a little undercurrent of excitement to almost any food.

Chipotle, a very flavorful chili made from dried smoked jalapeños, has tobacco and chocolate overtones and a strong, even heat. *New Mexico chipotle* has a classic mild, earthy flavor and a nice, crisp heat.

Guajillo is a sharp, tannic chili with lots of heat.

Paprika is made from sweet red chilies and has a lovely mild flavor and beautiful red color. *Smoked paprika*, the European cousin to chipotle powder, is one of the signature flavors in the classic Spanish rice dish paella, but also makes a great component of a barbecue rub.

Pasilla has a dark, herbal flavor.

Kosher salt Please, please, please throw out all your cheap iodized salt, which is too powdery and has a chemical aftertaste from the iodine that is added to prevent goiter. Trust me. You're not going to get goiter (a swelling caused by iodine deficiency). I'm sure we all get enough iodine from the salt in the processed food we eat! You can get kosher salt at almost any specialty food shop, and in many supermarkets these days. Be sure you get a brand like Diamond Crystal—some kosher salts are very coarse and are used mainly for pickling. The kind of kosher salt I'm talking about has a slightly coarser, more granular quality than regular table salt, which gives it a subtle crunchy texture when sprinkled on food just before you serve it. Kosher salt also has a less salty, more well-rounded flavor. If you want to get even fancier, use lovely white crystalline Maldon salt from England, or minerally fleur de sel from France, for putting that finishing sprinkle on food just before you serve it.

Lemons and limes Don't bother with bottled lime or lemon juice. The real thing is so much better! Always keep a few of each of these on hand to add tang to a sauce or salad, to squeeze over meat or vegetables fresh off the grill, or to chew on between shots of tequila!

Mustard Good old ballpark-style prepared mustard is an essential component of barbecued meat, but you should also have some Dijon in your fridge. Flavored mustards like wasabi-lime or honey-mustard add a nice twist to marinades, mayos, and dressings. Grainy mustard gives sauces and glazes an extra bit of texture.

Nuts I like to keep bags of pecan halves, pine nuts, pumpkin seeds, and slivered almonds in the freezer. Quickly toast them in a sauté pan or put them on a baking sheet for a few minutes under your broiler and sprinkle them on a salad or piece of grilled fish to add some crunch and flavor.

Seasoned salts Garlic salt, onion salt, celery salt, and steakhouse seasoning salt are important components of barbecue rubs.

Sours White vinegar, cider vinegar, red and white wine vinegars, and balsamic vinegar are good to have around. Good cooking is all about the balance of salt, sour, bitter, sweet, and savory. Great barbecue would not be complete without an acidic tang.

Sweets Honey, maple syrup, white sugar, brown sugar, and molasses add an important dimension to sauces, marinades, and dressings.

Backyard Gear

If you're serious about backyard cooking, here is the must-have gear list:

Basting brushes Natural bristle paintbrushes work better than the basting brushes normally available in grocery stores. In recent years silicone brushes have come down in price and they're what I like to use for most basting tasks. They're great because they hold a lot of sauce and they go in the dishwasher. You need a range of sizes.

Carving knife Get a long-bladed chef's knife with a good grip. Many competitors use a superlong ham knife to carve their meat for judging.

Charcoal chimney This is an essential component of any charcoal-based system. (Don't get the kind that automatically releases your charcoal when you lift it up. It's too easy to forget about this feature and light your coals in the wrong place; when you try to move them, they're released and you have to scramble to move them with a pair of tongs.)

Cutting boards You need at least two at home—a big one for carving and a smaller one, with a handle, for those little chopping jobs. In competition it's good to have four or five in a variety of sizes.

Filleting knife The short, flexible blade makes it easy to remove chicken breasts from the bone and trim fat off briskets and pork butts.

Fire starter Although some of my teammates have no problem with stinky liquid fire starter, I prefer the chemical-free ones like wax-impregnated felt sticks. I use these instead of newspaper at the bottom of my charcoal chimney because they generate less smoke.

➤ BARBECUE-MAMI! ≺

There's a lot of talk these days of a fifth taste (different from sour, salt, bitter, and sweet) that is related to glutamate, an amino acid found in meat, fish, and legumes. Some call it savory, and the Japanese have named it *umami*. An artificial version of this taste, in the form of monosodium glutamate, is used in many manufactured foods and almost every salty snack you can buy. According to experts, glutamates increase salivation and enhance the salty and sweet flavors of foods. Soy sauce, reduced chicken stock, peas, and seaweed are all rich in umami flavor.

And then, of course, there's the heat in chilies, called capsaicin, an odorless, tasteless chemical that stimulates our taste buds and intensifies all the other tastes.

I like to think of barbecue as the ultimate combination of all the five tastes, enhanced by chili heat, with the most glorious texture of perfectly cooked meat. Call it barbecue-mami.

Grill scraper Essential for quickly and easily getting the crud off the grill from your last cooking session. I prefer the metal-bristle brushes but the scouring-pad-style ones also work fine.

Matches Nothing worse than running out of matches. Keep a box of wooden matches handy and hide a backup somewhere else.

Oven mitts At least two pairs—one ratty old pair for handling greasy grills and lifting and turning extra-large cuts, and a nicer pair for pulling side dishes and appetizers out of the oven.

Poultry shears Good to have around for cutting up chickens and ducks.

Resealable plastic bags Use them for marinating, storing, transporting. Always get the extra-thick freezer bags. Have medium, large, and extra large on hand at all times.

Rib racks These wire frames are extremely handy if you want to cook more than three or four racks of ribs.

Spatula This is a must for flipping burgers and lifting anything fragile, like fish fillets, off the grill. The bigger, the better, and you should probably have at least two so you can remove planks and get bigger pieces of fish off the grill in one piece.

Spice mill Freshly ground spices, especially black pepper and cumin, are so much better than the ones you buy in a jar. A coffee grinder is the perfect device for this.

Thermometers You need two kinds:

- A barbecue thermometer gauges the chamber temperature inside your covered grill, water smoker, or barbecue pit. These usually go from 140 to 600°F (60–315°C). This is an essential tool and can range from a simple backyard model to industrial-style gauges used by pitmasters and barbecue competitors. The bigger and more expensive your thermometer, the more reliable—and the better to intimidate your opponents.
- An instant-read meat thermometer, preferably a digital one, is an extremely important tool for judging the doneness of your meat. Digital ones are more reliable than the fairly fragile analog versions.

Tongs You need a good pair for cooking—the kind with soft rubber grips and a smooth spring action—and a crappy pair (any kind will do as long as they're long) for handling coals and moving around grills.

Enhanced Gear List

A list for barbecue gearheads and die-hard contest entrants:

Alka-Seltzer   Say no more.

Bear paws   A specialized tool for shredding pork, available from barbecue specialty stores and online through sites like www.bulkbbq.com, www.barbecue-store.com, and www.hawgeyesbbq.com.

Brine pump or syringe   Many barbecue champions, particularly in the pork category, inject a mixture of fruit juice, salt, and seasonings into the meat to enhance its succulence. You can do this on smaller roasts with a cooking syringe, or, if you want to literally go whole hog, you need a brine pump, which looks like a horse needle attached to a bicycle pump. My team doesn't do this, but if you're game, get a syringe and experiment!

Card table   See *Cribbage board and cards.*

Coolers   Everyone's got one of these at home, but for competition you need at least four: one for storing raw meat, one for keeping wine and beer, one for lettuce, parsley, butter, and other groceries, and one for keeping your briskets and pork butts warm while they rest before being carved and turned in to the judges.

Cribbage board and cards   This duo, especially when accompanied by Jack Daniel's and Coke, is the competitive barbecuer's best friend. It's an excellent tool for passing the hours between spraying your meat and checking your coals.

Duct tape, shock cord, pliers, scissors, wire, bungee cords, safety pins   You never know.

Extra batteries   Have these on hand in case your digital thermometer runs out of steam just before turn-in time, or your flashlight goes dead.

Flashlight   A late-night tool for checking coals, adding water to the water pan, and finding the corkscrew. If you want the full barbecue-nerd look, go for a caving-style flashlight that straps to your head.

Gazebo-style tent   Protects you from the sun and the rain. It rains at barbecue competitions almost as often as the peanut butter side of your bread hits the ground first.

GRILLING, PLANKING, & BARBECUING INDOORS

So you live in an apartment that doesn't allow gas or charcoal grilling on your balcony. Or you don't have a balcony. Well, you can still grill, plank, and barbecue in your kitchen. For about $100 you can buy an electric grill, or you can use a stovetop grilling pan. For indoor planking, soak your plank as usual, preheat your oven, and place the plank on a cookie sheet. You won't get as much smoke, which is a good thing indoors, but you'll still get a nice, planky flavor. Just pay attention and don't forget to have your spray bottle on hand. You can even add a real barbecue flavor to a smaller piece of meat by putting some hardwood chips in the bottom of a wok and putting the meat on a metal steaming grate above the chips. Close the wok, heat it up till a bit of smoke comes out, and voilà. (Be sure you do this in a well-ventilated kitchen with a fan above the stove and a fire extinguisher nearby.) The point is, with a little experimentation and a lot of safety awareness, you can bring your passion for outdoor cooking indoors.

Heat-resistant silicone oven mitts If you've got the dough, these high-tech mitts withstand heat up to 600°F (315°C). They look cool, too.

Knife-sharpening gear Next to Alka-Seltzer, a sharp knife is a cook's best friend. I carry a knife-sharpening system with five different grains of oilstones. You should also have a steel-honing device for putting a razor edge on your knives just before using them.

Old blanket For wrapping pork butts and briskets, which have long resting times.

Portable lawn chairs For playing cards and napping.

Portable paper towel dispenser Along with vinyl gloves, a critical tool to enhance speed and hygiene.

Prep tables My team likes to use the classic 6-foot (1.8 m) folding tables that you can buy at most big home improvement/hardware stores and raise them to countertop height (see Barbecue Secret this page).

Remote digital meat probe Barbecue competitors are always trying to get a competitive edge, and we are always looking for ways to spend money on high-tech gadgets. One of the most stylish and useful is a digital thermometer that has a central unit that connects to one or two probes. The probes are inserted into the thickest portion of the meat and give you a live digital readout of what's going on inside. This is a godsend because when you poke an instant-read thermometer into meat and remove it, you create a hole that allows precious juices to run out. The probe-style devices avoid this because the thermometer stays in the meat for the entire cooking time.

Tennessee whiskey See *Cribbage board and cards.*

Trouble light Handy for illuminating barbecue equipment and card games in the middle of the night.

Vinyl gloves Keep a box of these disposable gloves on hand at all times. This is a huge convenience in competition, and it also enhances hygiene when you're dealing with raw meat.

⇀ NERD ALERT! ≈

If you're going to compete in barbecue contests, keep a logbook! There's nothing worse than turning in championship barbecue and then not being able to duplicate it later. Use your logbook for two things: planning and recording. Have a written plan for each food category, including a detailed schedule to guide you, covering such things as when to put the meat in the marinade, when to start the coals, when to put the meat in the cooker, when to turn and spray it, and when to take it off. Then keep a record of how you prepared your meat and whether it was any good. At most competitions a detailed record of every judge's score in every category is distributed to contestants after the contest is over. Study this and learn from it!

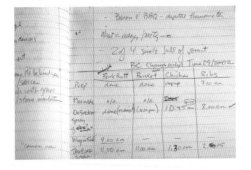

⇀ BARBECUE SECRET ≈

An easy way to raise your prep table to comfortable countertop height is to buy a 6-foot (1.8 m) section of 2-inch (5 cm) PVC pipe and cut it into four equal lengths. The legs of most tables fit perfectly into the pipe sections, giving you a raised, stable surface that will ease your work and save your back.

Bombastic Blasts of Flavor: Rubs, Marinades, Sauces, Salsas, & Spreads

There are some purists who believe great barbecue should be completely unencumbered by any flavor but the smoke of the wood it was cooked over. Although it's easy to overpower the taste of barbecued or grilled meat, it's also possible to take whatever you're cooking to a whole 'nuther level with the right application of rubs, sauces, and other magical preparations.

Please think of the following section of this book as an edible tool kit for the outdoor cook, and a starting point for your own creative concoctions. From the foundational flavor of a great rub or marinade to the finishing touch of a cool salsa or zesty mayo, there is much you can do to enhance your eating experience. And with a little advance work—a few different rubs in your pantry, some flavored butters in the freezer, a bottle or two of sauce in the back of your fridge—you can be ready to whip up a great home-grilled meal or barbecue feast at the drop of a sauce-stained baseball cap.

CHAMPIONSHIP BARBECUE RUB
(A.K.A. BOB'S RUB)

MAKES ABOUT 3 CUPS (750 ML)

RECIPES THAT CALL
⭢ FOR THIS RUB ⭠

Beef Burger with Herbed Butter Core & Caramelized Onions (page 159) / Cheater Ribs (page 181) / Real Barbecued Ribs (page 183) / The King of Barbecue: Beef Brisket (page 259) / Smoked Oysters (page 339)

⭢ BARBECUE SECRETS ⭠

The high sugar content of a barbecue rub works well at the low temperatures needed to cook classic barbecue, creating a rich, dark mahogany color. But for grilling, a sugary rub tends to make your meat char too quickly. When you're cooking over direct high heat, use a rub that has little or no sugar.

⭢ ⭠

If there's one single factor that most influences the taste of barbecue, it's the rub. Every barbecue competitor has his or her secret recipe, but pretty much every barbecue rub has three essential components—salt, sugar, and spices, usually dominated by onion, garlic, and chili flavors.

⭢ ⭠

The ideal barbecue rub should be balanced, with a rich, blended flavor that sparkles on your tongue like biting into a ripe cherry tomato. And it should have an aftertaste, like a good port or scotch, that lingers in the mouth and resonates like a tuning fork.

The Butt Shredders call this Bob's Rub, and it's what we use in competition. Bob Lyon, the granddaddy of barbecue in the Pacific Northwest, shared this at the barbecue workshop that first introduced me to the joys of real barbecue and prompted me to become a barbecue competitor. It follows a rule of thumb that's worth remembering: "a third, a third, a third." Translation: one-third sugar, one-third seasoned salts, and one-third dry herbs and spices.

1 cup [250 mL] sugar	⅓ cup [75 mL] ground black pepper
⅓ cup [75 mL] chili powder (use a commercial blend, or if you want an edge, try a combination of real ground chilies like ancho, poblano, New Mexico or guajillo)	⅓ cup [75 mL] paprika
	¼ cup [50 mL] celery salt
	¼ cup [50 mL] garlic salt
	¼ cup [50 mL] onion salt
	¼ cup [50 mL] seasoning salt (I like Lawry's)

Combine all the ingredients in a bowl and mix them together well.

Add as much heat as you want to this basic rub by using cayenne, hot paprika, or chipotle chili powder. Then add 2 or 3 signature ground spices to suit whatever you're cooking or your personal taste, like thyme, oregano, cumin, sage, ginger, etc. Add only 1 to 3 tsp (5–15 mL) of each signature seasoning so they don't overpower the rub.

⭢ ⭠   *(continued)*

TEXAS-STYLE RUB

MAKES ABOUT 2 CUPS (500 ML)

Everyone has a friend of a friend of a friend who knows some-one in Texas with a great rub recipe. This one came to me through fellow Butt Shredder and barbecue enthusiast Ian "Big Daddy" Baird. The cayenne gives it a nice burn. Use it as an all-purpose rub, but it really makes brisket sing (see The King of Barbecue: Beef Brisket, page 259).

¾ cup [175 mL] paprika
¼ cup [50 mL] kosher salt
¼ cup [50 mL] sugar
¼ cup [50 mL] ground black pepper

¼ cup [50 mL] chili powder
2 Tbsp [25 mL] garlic powder
2 Tbsp [25 mL] onion powder
1 Tbsp [15 mL] cayenne (or to taste)

Combine all the ingredients in a bowl and mix them together well.

ROCKIN' RONNIE'S GRILLING RUB

MAKES ABOUT 1 CUP (250 ML)

I like to use this combination of seasonings for everyday grilling.

¼ cup [50 mL] kosher salt
2 Tbsp [25 mL] granulated onion
2 Tbsp [25 mL] ground toasted cumin seeds
2 Tbsp [25 mL] ancho chili powder

1 Tbsp [15 mL] ground oregano
1 Tbsp [15 mL] granulated garlic
1 tsp [5 mL] ground black pepper
1 tsp [5 mL] chipotle chili powder or cayenne
1 tsp [5 mL] dried parsley

Combine all the ingredients in a bowl and mix them together well.

Barbecue Secrets (continued)

A good rub should have some heat, with sharpness at the beginning and a long, gentle, satisfying burn that stays on your palate and prompts you to want more.

The longer rubs are stored after you mix them, the richer and more balanced the flavor. Try to make a batch of rub at least a few days before using it. Well-sealed and stored in a cool, dry cupboard, rubs keep for at least six months.

To customize your rub, add powdered ginger and some Chinese five-spice powder for an Asian touch; cumin, dried oregano, and coriander seeds for a Southwestern flavor; powdered sage to enhance pork; or allspice, nutmeg, and cloves for an old-world European taste. It's best not to add more than three extra herbs or spices to a classic barbecue rub; more than that and you've got too much going on, and the flavor will not feel true.

Bombastic Blasts of Flavor: Rubs, Marinades, Sauces, Salsas, & Spreads

MEDITERRANEAN DRIED HERB RUB

MAKES ABOUT ¼ CUP (50 ML), ENOUGH TO COAT SEVERAL RACKS OF
LAMB OR A WHOLE LEG OF LAMB OR PORK ROAST

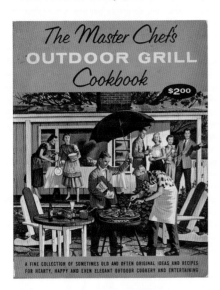
These days, food lovers tend to shy away from dried herbs in favor of the fresh ones that are so readily available. We tend to associate unpleasantly stale, dirty flavors with dried herbs, but that's probably because we use them so rarely that the ones in our pantry are too old. When used within a few months of purchasing them, dried herbs can add a wonderful earthiness and complexity to grilled foods that fresh herbs may not. In fact, the high heat of grilling often destroys the delicate flavors of fresh herbs. In most cases fresh herbs, other than the very strong rosemary and sage, are best used after your meat is off the grill, as a finely chopped sprinkle to add color and aroma. Use this rub for meats like chicken and pork, but it also works well with grilled vegetables. Just toss the veggies with oil and sprinkle them with the rub and some kosher salt.

1 Tbsp [15 mL] dried oregano (not ground)	1 Tbsp [15 mL] dried basil
1 Tbsp [15 mL] dried mint	1 Tbsp [15 mL] dried rosemary
	1 tsp [5 mL] dried parsley

Combine all the ingredients in a bowl and mix them together well.

JAMAICAN-STYLE DRY JERK RUB

MAKES ABOUT ⅔ CUP (160 ML)

Classic jerk is made with a wet marinade and takes time to prep and more time to marinate your meat. This rub gives chicken, pork, or snapper—or whatever else you're grilling—a classic Jamaican flavor without any fuss.

2 Tbsp [25 mL] granulated onion

2 Tbsp [25 mL] dried onion flakes
   (get flakes that aren't too big)

1½ Tbsp [22 mL] dried chives

1 Tbsp [15 mL] ground thyme

1 Tbsp [15 mL] kosher salt

1 Tbsp [15 mL] sugar

2 tsp [10 mL] ground allspice

2 tsp [10 mL] freshly ground black
   pepper

2 tsp [10 mL] cayenne or chipotle
   chili powder

½ tsp [2 mL] freshly grated nutmeg

½ tsp [2 mL] ground cinnamon

Combine all the ingredients in a bowl and mix them together well.

NOTE: Double or quadruple this recipe so you have some on hand. It's supereasy to make a great jerk marinade simply by whizzing ½ cup (125 mL) of this rub in a food processor with a splash of cooking oil, a chopped habanero chili, a chopped onion, and some chopped scallions.

CAJUN RUB

MAKES ABOUT ½ CUP (125 ML)

This great all-around grilling or blackening rub showcases the classic flavors of Cajun cooking.

2 Tbsp [25 mL] sweet paprika

1 Tbsp [15 mL] kosher salt

1 Tbsp [15 mL] granulated garlic

1 Tbsp [15 mL] granulated onion

1 Tbsp [15 mL] cayenne

1 Tbsp [15 mL] freshly ground
   black pepper

1 Tbsp [15 mL] ground white pepper

1½ tsp [7 mL] dried oregano

1½ tsp [7 mL] dried thyme

Combine all the ingredients in a bowl and mix them together well.

MEDITERRANEAN MARINADE

MAKES ABOUT 1 CUP (250 ML), ENOUGH FOR A COUPLE OF RACKS OF LAMB,
4 CHICKEN BREASTS, OR 8 CHICKEN THIGHS

Don't let the anchovy scare you. It adds a wonderful depth of flavor, and the end product doesn't taste fishy at all.

½ cup [125 mL] extra virgin olive oil

1 Tbsp [15 mL] Dijon mustard

1 Tbsp [15 mL] olive paste or 6 kala-mata olives, pitted and chopped

1 anchovy fillet

1 Tbsp [15 mL] coarsely chopped fresh rosemary

1 Tbsp [15 mL] chopped fresh basil

1 Tbsp [15 mL] chopped fresh mint

1 Tbsp [15 mL] Mediterranean Dried Herb Rub (see page 52)

2 Tbsp [25 mL] fresh lemon juice

1 Tbsp [15 mL] balsamic vinegar

Combine all the ingredients in a food processor and whiz them together until they're blended but not totally puréed.

MARINADE FOR PORK

MAKES ABOUT ¾ CUP (175 ML), ENOUGH FOR UP TO 2 LB (1 KG) PORK CHOPS OR
WHOLE TENDERLOINS

Pork tastes great no matter how you prepare it, but this sweet, aromatic marinade nicely offsets its richness and gives it an exotic edge.

¼ cup [50 mL] soy sauce

2 Tbsp [25 mL] dry sherry

2 Tbsp [25 mL] honey

2 Tbsp [25 mL] brown sugar

1 Tbsp [15 mL] grated fresh ginger

1 tsp [5 mL] kosher salt

½ tsp [2 mL] crushed anise seed

½ tsp [2 mL] ground cinnamon

⅛ tsp [0.5 mL] ground cloves

Combine all the ingredients in a saucepan and heat them gently until the sugar is dissolved. Cool the mixture before marinating the meat for at least an hour, or overnight in the fridge if you want a stronger flavor.

HERBED WET RUB

MAKES ABOUT 2 CUPS (500 ML)

This is a cross between a marinade and a paste. It is superb on any meat. Make it a bit thinner with the addition of more olive oil and you can toss vegetables in it to roast them on the grill. It's even great tossed with some fresh cooked pasta!

2 cups [500 mL] chopped
    fresh herbs*
1 Tbsp [15 mL] chopped chives
6 cloves garlic, peeled
1 shallot, peeled and coarsely
    chopped

1 tsp [5 mL] Dijon mustard
1 tsp [5 mL] kosher salt
1 cup [250 mL] oil**

*Use equal parts fresh Italian parsley, mint, basil, cilantro, baby dill, sage, or any combination that goes with what you want to grill.
**Use extra virgin olive oil if you're going with a Mediterranean theme, or a more neutral-flavored oil like canola if you're cooking Asian or Southwestern.

Combine all the ingredients except the oil in a food processor and whiz them together until everything is finely chopped. Keep the processor running and slowly add the oil until the mixture looks like a thin paste (or a very thick marinade). Coat whatever you're grilling with the mixture and let it sit in the fridge for ½ to 1 hour for veggies and seafood and anywhere from 2 hours to overnight for meat.

This rub does not keep well, so make it right when you need it.

⤳ BARBECUE SECRET ⤳

One of the biggest challenges of championship barbecue is finding a way to cook chicken so the skin doesn't turn out rubbery. With grilling, particularly over direct heat, chicken skin crisps up nicely, but in the low, smoky chamber of a smoker or barbecue pit, you run a high risk of getting tough, inedible skin. Here's what some competitors do to get chicken skin that melts in the judges' mouths. The secret is the acid in the marinade, which softens the skin. Marinate chicken overnight in a homemade vinaigrette or good old bottled Italian salad dressing, or in plain or seasoned yogurt. Dry it off with paper towels, coat it with mustard and rub, and you're good to go. As a last bit of insurance to help avoid rubbery skin syndrome, baste the chicken often to keep the skin wet during cooking.

ASIAN POULTRY BRINE

MAKES ABOUT 4 CUPS (1 L), ENOUGH FOR 2 CUT-UP CHICKENS OR A DOZEN THIGHS

> **BARBECUE SECRET** ⌐

There are some who believe that marinades actually tenderize meat, and after over 30 years of grilling I simply do not believe this to be true. In my experience, even an overnight marinade tends to only penetrate maybe ⅛ inch (3 mm) into the meat. That's plenty deep enough to add flavor but not nearly enough to affect the tenderness of the meat. (Brines, which contain a lot of salt, will infuse themselves throughout a piece of meat or fish over a long time, but even they don't seem to affect the texture of the finished product, other than making it a bit firmer and denser.)

The high salt content makes this more of a brine than a marinade, and my barbecue team has used it very successfully in competition. It gives the poultry a nice saltiness and a rich, complex Asian flavor. I marinate duck overnight in this; for milder-tasting chicken, a couple of hours is all you need. Pat the excess moisture from the meat after you've taken it out of the marinade and then use a barbecue rub doctored with Asian flavors, like powdered ginger and Chinese five-spice powder. Barbecue or grill as you like, and finish the meat with your favorite barbecue sauce.

1½ cups [375 mL] water
1 cup [250 mL] soy sauce
½ cup [125 mL] sherry or vermouth
½ cup [125 mL] apple or pineapple juice
¼ cup [50 mL] brown sugar
¼ cup [50 mL] coarse salt
2 Tbsp [25 mL] grated fresh ginger

1 tsp [5 mL] sesame oil
2 cloves garlic, pressed or crushed
1 shallot, minced
1 medium onion, thinly sliced
pinch ground cloves
pinch Chinese five-spice powder

Combine all the ingredients in a bowl, stirring thoroughly to dissolve the salt and sugar.

RON'S RICH, DEEPLY SATISFYING
DIPPING SAUCE

(with acknowledgments to the Baron of Barbecue, Paul Kirk)

MAKES ABOUT 6 CUPS (1.5 L)

Paul Kirk has taught thousands of cooks the essentials of barbecue, and this rich, sweet, tangy sauce is based on his Kansas City classic. If you want a very smooth barbecue sauce, blend it with a hand-held immersion blender or food processor.

2 Tbsp [25 mL] ancho, poblano or
   New Mexico chili powder

1 Tbsp [15 mL] ground black pepper

1 Tbsp [15 mL] dry mustard

1 tsp [5 mL] ground coriander

1 tsp [5 mL] ground allspice

1 tsp [5 mL] cayenne (or to taste)

½ tsp [2 mL] freshly grated nutmeg

¼ tsp [1 mL] ground cloves

¼ cup [50 mL] neutral-flavored oil,
   such as canola

1 onion, finely chopped

6 cloves garlic, finely chopped

1 shallot, minced

1 cup [250 mL] white vinegar

½ cup [125 mL] tightly packed dark
   brown sugar

½ cup [125 mL] clover honey

¼ cup [50 mL] Worcestershire sauce,
   soy sauce, or a combination

1 tsp [5 mL] liquid smoke or hickory
   smoked salt (optional)

4 cups [1 L] ketchup

Mix together the chilies, black pepper, mustard, coriander, allspice, cayenne, nutmeg, and cloves, and set aside.

Heat the oil in a big pot over medium heat and gently sauté the onion, garlic, and shallot until tender, about 5 minutes. Add the spice mixture and combine thoroughly, cooking the mixture for 2 or 3 minutes to bring out the flavors.

Add the remaining ingredients and simmer the mixture for 30 minutes, stirring often (be careful, it spatters). Don't cook it too long or it will start to caramelize and you'll have spicy fudge. This sauce stores indefinitely in the refrigerator.

NOTE: This thick sauce is designed for dipping. If you want to use it as a basting sauce or a glaze, thin it with water, apple juice, or Jack Daniel's.

Bombastic Blasts of Flavor: Rubs, Marinades, Sauces, Salsas, & Spreads

NORTH CAROLINA-STYLE
VINEGAR SAUCE

MAKES A LITTLE MORE THAN 1 CUP (250 ML)

This is old-school barbecue sauce at its finest. Drizzle some of this onto pulled pork just before serving to give it some classic heat and tang, or use it to baste pork butt.

1 cup [250 mL] white vinegar
1 cup [250 mL] cider vinegar
2 Tbsp [25 mL] brown sugar
1 Tbsp [15 mL] crushed dried red
   chili flakes

1 tsp [5 mL] Louisiana-style hot sauce
kosher salt and freshly ground black
   pepper to taste

Combine all the ingredients and stir the mixture until the sugar is dissolved. This sauce stores indefinitely in the refrigerator.

OYSTER SAUCE & BALSAMIC GLAZE

MAKES ABOUT 1½ CUPS (375 ML)

I stumbled across this recipe by Ian Knauer in the May 2008 edition of *Gourmet* magazine. Usually I would try to adapt something like this to my own taste but I honestly can't think of how to improve on the simple combination of bold flavors. Finish any steak or chop with this umami bomb. All I can say is, wow!

1 cup [250 mL] oyster sauce
½ cup [125 mL] balsamic vinegar
4 tsp [20 mL] grainy mustard

2 tsp [10 mL] crushed dried red
   chili flakes

Combine all the ingredients in a bowl. Transfer the glaze to a storage container. This sauce will store indefinitely in the refrigerator.

MUSTARD-BASED BARBECUE SAUCE

MAKES ABOUT 2 CUPS (500 ML)

Who knows why most barbecue sauces are sweet and tomato-based? This tangy, mustardy sauce is very much alive in the Carolinas and Georgia, but almost unheard of in most other places. It's delicious, of course, with pork. It's also great as a dipping sauce for grilled sausages or smokies. Yum!

1 medium onion, finely minced
4 cloves garlic, finely minced
2 Tbsp [25 mL] vegetable oil
1 cup [250 mL] cider vinegar
⅔ cup [160 mL] prepared
    mustard
⅓ cup [75 mL] brown sugar
1 Tbsp [15 mL] ancho chili
    powder

1 Tbsp [15 mL] paprika
1 tsp [5 mL] finely ground
    black pepper
¼ tsp [1 mL] cayenne
2 Tbsp [25 mL] butter or
    margarine
dash soy sauce or Worcester-
    shire sauce

> **BARBECUE SECRET** ≈

Barbecue sauce is often referred to as "dipping sauce," as a way of purposely relegating it to a minor role, as an optional accompaniment to barbecued meat.

Use your favorite barbecue sauce as a glaze or dip for barbecued meats, as a flavoring sauce in fajitas, or, mixed half and half with mayo, as a fabulous dip for french fries.

Gently sauté the onion and garlic in the vegetable oil in a medium saucepan over low to medium heat until they're soft but not browned. Add the vinegar, mustard, brown sugar, chili powder, paprika, pepper, and cayenne. Bring the mixture to a boil and simmer it for 10 minutes.

Stir in the butter or margarine and soy or Worcestershire sauce and remove the sauce from the heat. If you prefer a smoother sauce to one with little chunks of onion and garlic in it, purée it with a hand-held immersion blender before serving. This sauce is good warm, but it stores indefinitely in the refrigerator.

Bombastic Blasts of Flavor: Rubs, Marinades, Sauces, Salsas, & Spreads

COMPLICATED BUT DELICIOUS
TERIYAKI SAUCE

MAKES ABOUT 8 CUPS (2 L)

This homemade teriyaki sauce, which I have adapted slightly from an old recipe by famed Vancouver chef Trevor Hooper, has dimensions of flavor that make the extra work more than worthwhile. It stores for several months in the fridge, and it's great as a marinade for meat or seafood, as a sauce for stir-fries, or just drizzled on steamed rice.

4 cups [1 L] Japanese soy sauce
2 cups [500 mL] brown sugar
1½ cups [375 mL] sake
1½ cups [375 mL] mirin (Japanese sweet rice wine)
½ cup [125 mL] tamari soy sauce
1 small onion, chopped
1 shallot, chopped

4 cloves garlic, chopped
one 2-inch [5 cm] piece fresh ginger, chopped
1 orange, chopped, skin on
1 small pear, chopped
1 small leek, split, washed thoroughly and chopped

Combine all the ingredients in a medium saucepan and bring the mixture to a low boil. Cook it until it's reduced by about 20 percent. Cool the sauce, strain it into a large jar or bottle, and refrigerate it. It stores indefinitely in the refrigerator.

ASIAN BARBECUE SAUCE

The cumin seeds in this sauce give its flavor a twist and an interesting texture. Leave them out if you want a slightly sweeter, smooth sauce. This is great as a marinade and a basting sauce for ribs and steaks, but it's also good with chicken and firm-fleshed fish. Be careful—its strong flavors can overwhelm what you're cooking. Marinate meat for a maximum of four hours and chicken or fish no more than one hour.

one 12 oz [355 mL] bottle hoisin sauce
½ cup [125 mL] light soy sauce
½ cup [125 mL] plum sauce
¼ cup [50 mL] orange juice
2 Tbsp [25 mL] sherry vinegar
2 Tbsp [25 mL] toasted sesame oil
2 Tbsp [25 mL] oyster sauce
2 Tbsp [25 mL] honey

2 Tbsp [25 mL] finely minced fresh ginger
6 cloves garlic, finely minced
1 Tbsp [15 mL] finely chopped chives or
    green onion
1½ tsp [7 mL] Chinese five-spice powder
2 shallots, finely minced
1 tsp [5 mL] toasted cumin seeds

Combine all the ingredients in a nonreactive bowl. Use the sauce soon after making it; it won't keep more than a few days in the refrigerator.

Bombastic Blasts of Flavor: Rubs, Marinades, Sauces, Salsas, & Spreads

QUICK CUCUMBER SALSA

MAKES ABOUT 2 CUPS (500 ML)

Often, the simplest combinations are the best. This one tastes like summer. Try it on grilled fish, spoon it over a cold soup, or split it between two bowls as a starter for a summer lunch.

1 cucumber	1 tsp [5 mL] sugar
2 tsp [10 mL] fresh lime juice	kosher salt
1 tsp [5 mL] chopped fresh dill	

Peel the cucumber, cut it lengthwise into quarters, and remove the seeds. Chop it into a ¼-inch (6 mm) dice. Add the lime juice, dill, sugar, and a pinch of salt, and toss. Use it immediately.

GARDEN SALSA

MAKES ABOUT 1 CUP (250 ML)

I love the crunch of barely cooked asparagus. One day, I thought to myself, why don't we ever eat it raw? This salsa showcases the texture and flavor of fresh raw asparagus, which is a bit like snap peas, in a spectacularly colorful combination. This is excellent with any kind of seafood.

4 spears extremely fresh asparagus, tough ends discarded and spears diced	1 tsp [5 mL] chopped fresh dill or mint
¼ cup [50 mL] diced yellow bell pepper	1 tsp [5 mL] fresh lemon juice
¼ cup [50 mL] diced purple onion	1 tsp [5 mL] sugar
1 medium-sized ripe tomato, diced	pinch cayenne
	kosher salt

Combine all the ingredients in a salad bowl, toss them together, and serve.

PEACH & BLACKBERRY SALSA

MAKES ABOUT 3 CUPS (750 ML)

This salsa, invented by my wife, Kate, is something you should try only when these fruits are at their peak, which on the West Coast of Canada is in August. Paired with grilled or planked chicken, it's a mind-blower.

4 peaches, peeled and diced
1 cup [250 mL] fresh blackberries,
    washed and picked over
¼ cup [50 mL] red onion, diced
½ jalapeño or other hot pepper,
    seeded and minced

4 tsp [20 mL] fresh lime juice
kosher salt and freshly ground
    black pepper

Combine all the ingredients in a bowl. Let the salsa stand, covered, in the fridge for about 1 hour before serving.

TROPICAL SALSA

MAKES ABOUT 3 CUPS (750 ML)

This perfect summer salsa is great on grilled fish or beef. No matter where or when you eat it, you're instantly on a sunny vacation.

2 cups [500 mL] diced tropical fruit
    (any combination of mango, papaya,
    kiwi, pineapple)
2 ripe (but firm) avocados, pitted,
    peeled, and coarsely chopped
3 Tbsp [45 mL] chopped fresh cilantro

3 Tbsp [45 mL] chopped red onion
1 jalapeño, seeded and finely chopped
2 tsp [10 mL] fresh lime juice
pinch sugar
kosher salt and freshly ground
    black pepper

Combine all the ingredients in a bowl. Let the salsa stand, covered, in the fridge for about 1 hour. For a stirring variation of this salsa, leave out the avocados and use 1 cup each of chopped strawberries and mango.

BLACK BEAN & GRILLED CORN SALSA

MAKES ABOUT 5 CUPS (1.25 L)

This salsa is great on grilled fish, but it also stands up on its own as a dip.

3 whole fresh cobs of corn, shucked

one 14 oz [398 mL] can black beans, rinsed and drained

2 medium tomatoes, diced

1 red bell pepper, diced

⅓ cup [75 mL] chopped fresh cilantro

¼ cup [50 mL] red onion, diced

¼ cup [50 mL] fresh lime juice (about 2 limes)

1 tsp [5 mL] minced jalapeño

1 tsp [5 mL] kosher salt

1 avocado, diced

tortilla chips for dipping

Prepare your grill for direct high heat. Grill the cobs of corn until the kernels turn a bright yellow and there's some nice charring. Cool the cobs and remove the kernels with a sharp chef's knife or a mandoline.

Combine all the ingredients, except the avocado and chips, in a bowl. Cover and chill the mixture for at least 2 hours. Dice the avocado and add it just before serving the salsa with the chips.

CHUNKY SMOKED
TOMATO GUACAMOLE

MAKES ABOUT 2 CUPS (500 ML)

The flavor of the freshly smoked ripe tomatoes in this superchunky guaca-mole really jolts your taste buds, but it's also great with regular ripe tomatoes.

2 ripe tomatoes
2 large ripe (but firm) avocados
4 tsp [20 mL] fresh lime juice or
    2 Tbsp [25 mL] fresh lemon juice
1 clove garlic, finely minced
3 canned green chilies, rinsed,
    seeded, and chopped

1 finely minced jalapeño or serrano
    chili (optional)
2 Tbsp [25 mL] chopped fresh cilantro
kosher salt

Prepare your smoker for barbecuing, bringing the temperature up to 200 to 220°F (95–100°C). (Obviously it's easier if you're barbecuing something else and the smoker is already chugging away.) Place the tomatoes in the smoker and cook them for 30 minutes, using a hardwood like hickory or mesquite as a flavoring agent. The idea is to infuse the tomatoes with smoke without overcooking them—when ready, they should be a red-gold color and their skins should be a bit loose, but the flesh should still be firm. Remove them from the smoker and let them cool.

Remove the pits from the avocados and peel them. Coarsely chop the tomatoes and avocados and transfer them to a salad bowl. Add the lime or lemon juice, garlic, green and hot chilies, and cilantro, and gently toss the mixture. Season the guacamole to taste with salt, give it one last toss, and serve.

If you prefer a smoother dip, just use riper avocados and mash them with a fork as you toss the finished dish together. In any case, this is a dish that's best eaten immediately after it's prepared. It's great, of course, with corn chips, but also fabulous on burgers, in fajitas or tacos, or on grilled fish.

CHIMICHURRI

MAKES ABOUT 3 CUPS (750 ML)

⌁ BARBECUE SECRET ⌁

Purée your chimichurri to make a great marinade for flank steak. Thanks for this tip goes to my fellow foodie Angie Quaale.

This is the classic Argentine condiment. It takes various forms; some are finer, like a pesto, and others (like this one) are chunkier, like a salsa. Chimichurri goes well with almost anything grilled, planked, or barbecued, but I like it best on lamb. Make it at least a day before you're going to use it to let the flavors come alive.

½ cup [125 mL] chopped fresh flat-leaf Italian parsley

1 medium red onion, finely chopped

½ red bell pepper, seeded and finely diced (optional)

1 tomato, peeled, seeded and finely chopped (optional)

4 cloves garlic, finely minced

2 Tbsp [25 mL] chopped fresh oregano or 1 Tbsp [15 mL] dried oregano

2 bay leaves

1 Tbsp [15 mL] paprika

1 Tbsp [15 mL] kosher salt

2 tsp [10 mL] crushed dried red chili flakes

1 tsp [5 mL] freshly ground black pepper

½ cup [125 mL] extra virgin olive oil

¼ cup [50 mL] sherry vinegar

¼ cup [50 mL] water

Combine all the ingredients except the oil, vinegar, and water in a large bowl and toss well to make sure the salt is distributed evenly. Let the sauce rest for 30 minutes to allow the salt to dissolve and the flavors to blend.

Add the oil, vinegar, and water, and mix the sauce well. Make sure that the chimichurri looks nice and wet, like a very thick gazpacho. If not, add equal parts of oil, water, and vinegar until the mixture is covered by at least a quarter inch of liquid.

Transfer the sauce to a nonreactive storage container. Cover it and refrigerate it to allow the flavors to blend overnight. It's even better after 2 or 3 days in the refrigerator.

FLAVORED BUTTERS
FOR ALL OCCASIONS

Once you've made any of these savory butters you'll always want to keep some in the freezer. Brought to room temperature, they're incredible on roasted corn on the cob or slathered on cornbread, and a pat of flavored butter on a freshly grilled steak or fish fillet is heavenly.

MEDITERRANEAN BUTTER

¼ cup [50 mL] finely chopped
    fresh flat-leaf Italian parsley
¼ cup [50 mL] finely chopped
    combination of fresh dill, basil,
    or mint (or any combination of
    fresh herbs—try chervil, tar-
    ragon, sage, rosemary, etc.)
1 lb [500 g] unsalted butter, at
    room temperature
kosher salt to taste

RED PEPPER BUTTER

1 red bell pepper, roasted, peeled,
    seeded, and coarsely chopped
½ lb [250 g] unsalted butter, at
    room temperature
1 tsp [5 mL] sweet paprika
kosher salt to taste

GARLIC CHIVE BUTTER

4 cloves garlic, put through a
    garlic press (or 8 cloves
    roasted garlic, squeezed out
    of their skins; see next page)
2 Tbsp [25 mL] finely chopped
    fresh chives
½ lb [250 g] unsalted butter,
    at room temperature
kosher salt to taste

GORGONZOLA BUTTER

¾ cup [175 mL] Gorgonzola
    cheese
¼ lb [125 g] unsalted butter, at
    room temperature
1 tsp [5 mL] fresh lemon juice
kosher salt to taste

Cut the butter into cubes and place them in a food processor. Add the flavoring ingredients and whiz the mixture until it's thoroughly blended, stopping to scrape down the stuff that sticks to the sides of the food processor as needed. If you're serving the butter right away with corn, or on a piece of grilled meat, just place it in a small bowl and serve it.

➤ BARBECUE SECRET ≈

Use flavored butter in your favorite sauté, as a sautéing butter for thinly sliced mushrooms or scrambled eggs, or toss it with some cooked noodles for a quick, easy side.

➤ STORE YOUR ≈
FLAVORED BUTTER

Use a spatula to transfer the butter onto a sheet of waxed paper or plastic wrap, and shape it into a rough cylinder. Fold the wrap around the butter and shape it into an even tube about 1½ inches (4 cm) in diameter. Twist the ends so the tube is sealed and tight, and fasten both ends with twist-ties. Refrigerate or freeze the butter until you need it. To serve, slice off discs of butter. Thaw it a while before dressing steaks or corn, or use it still frozen to stuff inside a burger.

Bombastic Blasts of Flavor: Rubs, Marinades, Sauces, Salsas, & Spreads

DOCTORED MAYONNAISE

Here's a great kitchen staple that works well baked in the oven or planked on the grill. Roasted garlic is as versatile as it is delicious. Use it as a flavor enhancer in mayo, an enricher of mashed potatoes, and a flavor note in soups and sauces—or just spread it on a piece of toasted French bread.

Preheat the oven to 350°F (180°C). With a sharp knife, slice off the top of a garlic bulb, just enough to expose the tops of the cloves. Drizzle it with a little olive oil, season it with salt and pepper, and wrap the bulb tightly in foil. Place it in the oven, cut side up, and roast it for about 1 hour, or until the garlic is soft and lightly browned. Once it's cool enough to handle, you can squeeze the head and the roasted garlic comes out like toothpaste.

To add an extra layer of smoky flavor, roast garlic in your smoker (for 3 hours) or over indirect medium heat in a covered charcoal grill (for 1 hour). Just wrap the bulb fairly loosely in foil to allow the smoke to get in. It's excellent with cherry wood as the flavoring agent. An added benefit: you don't stink up your house.

I love plain old mayo—in sandwiches, as a dip for french fries, and as a simple dressing for hot or cold veggies. But mix in some extra flavor and you've got something that sends your taste buds to new heights. These variations are my favorites, but feel free to create your own.

MARGIE'S CHIPOTLE & ROASTED GARLIC MAYO
MAKES ABOUT 1½ CUPS (375 ML) MAYONNAISE

This invention of Calgary caterer Margie Gibb is particularly good as a dip for pieces of smoked or grilled sausage, but it's also great on just about anything else.

- 1½ cups [375 mL] mayonnaise
- 1 whole head roasted garlic (see sidebar), cloves squeezed out of their skins
- 1 tsp [5 mL] finely ground cumin (preferably made from toasted cumin seeds)
- 1 Tbsp [15 mL] chopped canned chipotle chilies in adobo sauce (add more chipotle if you like it hot)

SESAME MAYO
MAKES ABOUT 1½ CUPS (375 ML) MAYONNAISE

This is the perfect dip for roasted veggies, and it's also great tossed with rice noodles for a cool, creamy side to grilled Asian-flavored meats. Sprinkle it with toasted sesame seeds for extra texture.

- 1 cup [250 mL] mayonnaise
- 1 tsp [5 mL] toasted sesame oil
- ½ tsp [2 mL] soy sauce (or to taste)
- 1 tsp [5 mL] Chinese chili sauce or spicy Szechuan chili oil (or to taste)
- 1 tsp [5 mL] grated or finely chopped lemon, lime, or orange zest
- 1–2 Tbsp [15–25 mL] toasted sesame seeds (or to taste)

CURRY MAYO
MAKES ABOUT 1¼ CUPS (300 ML) MAYONNAISE

This is perfect with veggies or as a sandwich spread.

2 large shallots, peeled and finely
   chopped
4 tsp [20 mL] curry powder

1 Tbsp [15 mL] vegetable oil
1 cup [250 mL] mayonnaise
1 tsp [5 mL] fresh lemon juice

BARBECUE MAYO
MAKES ABOUT 1½ CUPS (375 ML) MAYONNAISE

A great "secret sauce" for your homemade burger, french fries, or grilled chicken wings. Cut it with sour cream for a tasty chip dip.

1 Tbsp [15 mL] barbecue rub of your
   choice (see pages 50–53)
¼ cup [50 mL] barbecue sauce
   of your choice (see pages 57–61)

1 cup [250 mL] mayonnaise
1 tsp [5 mL] fresh lemon or lime juice

WASABI MAYO
MAKES ABOUT 1 CUP (250 ML) MAYONNAISE

Excellent on planked fish, on fried crab cakes, or in a slaw or salad.

1 Tbsp [15 mL] wasabi powder
   or paste

1 cup [250 mL] mayonnaise
1 tsp [5 mL] fresh lime juice

The technique is simple: Combine good-quality store-bought or homemade mayonnaise with the other ingredients in a food processor and whiz them until they're smooth, then refrigerate the result. If possible, store it in the refrigerator for a day, or at least a few hours, before serving to let the flavors marry and intensify.

TO NEWBERG . . . AND GLORY!

⋟How Barbecue Changed My Life⋞

As Vince, Tom, and I barreled south on the I-5 on our way to Oregon, the mood was buoyant. We were loaded for bear . . . and ready to cook barbecue. The van was crammed with coolers full of meat and booze, plus the whole whack of paraphernalia that usually accompanies us to competitions, including our collection of knives, cutting boards, barbecue rubs, sauces, marinades, charcoal, hardwood chips and chunks, electronic thermometers, tables, and patio furniture.

The van smelled of smoke from the four Weber bullets stacked in the back. For amateur competitors like us, bullets—called Smokey Mountain Cookers by their manufacturer, but nicknamed "bullets" for their black, oblong design—are the cooker of choice. On any given day, meat cooked in these cheap, well-designed, and reliable babies can beat whatever the big-time pitmasters can cook in their giant $10,000 dual-wheeled rigs.

We had left Vancouver at 10 a.m. after picking up the pork butts at Penguin Meats near the Canada/US border in White Rock. The butts were perfect nine-pounders, bone in, with creamy white fat caps. We tossed them in the cooler along with the four racks of side ribs, three free-range organic chickens, and two of the best triple A briskets I'd ever seen, each weighing in at about 12 lb (5.5 kg) and costing about 60 bucks apiece.

By 11 o'clock we had reached the Peace Arch border crossing on our way to Newberg, Oregon, the small, rural bedroom community outside of Portland where the big contest was being held. As we pulled away from the border, young Tom yelled what would become the Butt Shredders' rallying cry.

"To Newberg . . . and GLORY!" he shouted, and we couldn't stop laughing. Tom's exclamation had just the right combination of bravado and pomposity for a barbecue team. It also captured the mood of the moment. We felt like an invading army, going deep into alien territory to fight a historic battle on the adversary's home turf. The Oregon State Open was the Pacific Northwest's oldest barbecue championship, and some of the best of the best would be gathering in the storage yard behind Newberg's Ace Hardware, including several state and regional champions. As a Kansas City Barbecue Society (KCBS)–sanctioned event, the Oregon Open would attract everyone in the Pacific Northwest who wanted to take a crack at qualifying for The Royal and The Jack.

We felt like an invading army, going deep into alien territory to fight a historic battle on the adversary's home turf.

⋟ ⋞

Earlier that year I had lost my job as a PR executive. Licking my wounds but armed with a severance package, I began the search for another corporate job, but the pickings were slim. The economy was in the toilet and no one was hiring. Knowing things would not pick up until at least the fall, I applied myself to enjoying the summer with my family. We live in lush, green North Vancouver, British Columbia, one of the most beautiful places on earth, in the middle of the coastal rainforest. It would be a healing summer of picnics on the beach, long walks with the dog, and mountain biking in the woods.

Not to mention barbecue. The hiatus from work also allowed me to focus on my favorite pastime. I had been entering barbecue contests with a group of old friends for seven years, but so far, Rockin' Ronnie's Butt Shredders had not seen an overall victory. Our performance had improved over the years, but in recent contests the Butt Shredders had become barbecue bridesmaids, winning in some categories but consistently placing second overall or, in the overblown barbecue-speak of the competition circuit, finishing as Reserve Grand Champions. With time on my hands and a smoldering passion to win a barbecue contest, I looked forward to the coming season with high hopes.

The plan for 2001 was to take the Canadian Championship in Vancouver by storm in August and keep the momentum going at Barbecue on the Bow in Calgary, Alberta on the Labor Day weekend.

As the summer progressed there was bad news. The founder of the Canadian Barbecue Championship and Canada's best-known promoter of real barbecue, David "The Fire Chef" Valjacic, was dying of cancer, and the big contest was cancelled for that year. Our plans of making a stand

It was time to take a stab at The Big Meat.

at "the Canadians" were off and Labor Day was months away. Around the same time that I found out about the cancellation, the latest edition of *Drippings from the Pit*, the official newsletter of the Pacific Northwest Barbecue Association, arrived in the mail. Among reports on the latest Spring Training barbecue workshops in Washington State and box scores on the results of recent contests, there was a flyer promoting the Oregon State Open Barbecue Championship.

Yes. That's it, I thought. The Butt Shredders had never competed in a US championship before, and the Oregon Open was a qualifier for the American Royal in Kansas City—the World Series of barbecue—and the Jack Daniel's World Championship Invitational, the Holy Grail of competitive barbecue.

It was time to take a stab at The Big Meat.

≈ ≈

After the first couple of hours fighting the Friday afternoon Seattle-area traffic, it was pretty smooth sailing the rest of the way down to Portland, with stops at roadside diners along the way for cheeseburgers and cherry pie, washed down with hot black coffee. Vince, our map man, had downloaded complete travel directions from the Web and we wended our way through the back roads outside of Portland, pulling into Ace Hardware around seven that night.

We were among the last ones to get to the competition grounds. Most of the teams already had their briskets and pork butts on while we hurried to set up. The organizer of the contest, Mark Vergets, treated us like visiting royalty. We were the only Canadians to ever drive that far south in the 14-year history of the contest. Mark had an awning set up for us when we arrived, with a power hook-up all set to go. Sixteen other teams had registered for the contest, including at least four winners of other recent competitions.

After about half an hour of scrambling to unload and do a quick-and-dirty setup, we hooked up our lights and hauled the briskets out of the cooler. With brisket turn-in to the judges only 15 hours away, we had no time to lose. The briskets were big, and should have been in the cooker hours ago.

Working with my filleting knife, I trimmed the fat caps on the two briskets down to the ideal ⅛-inch (3 mm) thickness. Tom, whose father is a surgeon, is our best rub man. He can sprinkle rub on a brisket like a detailer in an auto body shop applies an airbrush to a vintage Chevy.

Working together, we painted the briskets with mustard, applied a light sprinkle of granulated garlic, and hit them with a heavy coating of rub. In the meantime, Vince got the bullets set up, filled the charcoal baskets with briquettes, and started the fires in the two cookers that would hold the briskets and pork butts. It was a race against time.

By nine o'clock the briskets and pork butts were in the smokers and we could relax a bit and start prepping the ribs and chicken. Other competitors whom we knew from previous contests drifted over to say hello, beers were cracked open, and I uncorked a bottle of Oregon Sauvignon Blanc we had picked up at a Fred Meyer megastore on the way into town. We had walked around the huge Fred Meyer in awe, unaccustomed to giant box stores like this. At home, we still buy our wine at the BC Liquor Control Board, and we don't have supermarkets with a produce department and a liquor store that also sell tires and barbecue equipment.

As the evening rolled on we started to get into the rhythm of what barbecue contests are all about. We were happy. We had abandoned our daily lives and become citizens of Barbecueville, a temporary tent city that needs no laws but the rules of judging set out by the Kansas City Barbecue Society. The main industry in Barbecueville is a mild form of debauchery that involves drinking, cooking, eating meat, and staying up all night listening to Waylon Jennings's greatest hits, as hickory smoke wafts across a skyline glittering with chili-shaped patio lights. Throughout the year our chubby nomadic tribe moves from contest to contest, building and then taking down our ramshackle city as if it were a three-ring circus.

We call what we do a championship, but it's the only competition where the event and the tailgate party are exactly the same thing. Even so-called sports like curling and darts don't count cribbage boards as standard equipment. And even though we're all "competing," what we're really doing is what we love—cooking and eating barbecue. Once you have had one aromatic, succulent, deeply satisfying bite of real barbecue, fresh out of the cooker, your life has permanently changed. To taste a perfectly cooked slice of brisket, or to experience the texture of pulled pork, piled high on a fluffy white bun, drizzled with vinegary sauce, and topped with

Throughout the year our chubby nomadic tribe moves from contest to contest, building and then taking down our ramshackle city as if it were a three-ring circus.

crunchy, sweet coleslaw, or to bite into a rib and feel the tender meat come gently off the bone as you taste the tangy, salty, sweet, savory pork, is just one step short of heaven. And when you can claim that you not only cook barbecue, but cook the best barbecue, you are not just a winner but a culinary demigod, bringing a greasy nirvana within reach of those around you.

I had no idea what I was getting into in the summer of 1994, when my old friend Rocco Ciancio invited me over to his ranch on the outskirts of Calgary to show me the new water smoker he had bought on a recent trip to Texas. He and his wife, Denise, had been down to attend a relative's wedding in San Antonio. Rocco was amazed and charmed by the topic of most conversations between Texans—the quality of the brisket they had barbecued over the weekend. Before he left, Rocco visited a Costco and for US$20 got himself a cheap Brinkman water smoker. When he got home he bought a couple of books on home smoking and, from then on, his weekends were spent experimenting with his new toy, smoking sausages, ducks, and chickens, and testing out exotic recipes for things like smoked Peruvian lamb hearts.

He invited me to join in the fun, and before long we were calling his house Rocky's Smokehouse and Commercial Sausage Upgrader. Soon afterward, I got another friend, local restaurant critic Kathy Richardier, interested in smoking food. She and I went halfers on an electric smoker and it just kind of took off from there. But back then we were interested in smoking food and didn't even really know what true barbecue was.

In the spring of 1996 our barbecue journey began in earnest, when Kathy and I and a few other foodie friends joined a group of Calgary cooks for an all-day workshop on championship barbecue. Bob Lyon, the granddaddy of barbecue in the Pacific Northwest and president of the Pacific Northwest Barbecue Association, came up to Calgary from his home base in Washington State to show us Canucks a thing or two about how to cook barbecue for competition.

Bob came to town at the request of Carol and Sandy Dougall, the organizers of Calgary's Barbecue on the Bow. The contest was entering its third year and gaining in popularity, but Carol and Sandy were dismayed that the vast majority of the competitors were US-based teams. They loved hosting the out-of-towners, but they didn't like the fact that the Americans went back with all the shiny hardware every year. By bringing Bob in, they planned to raise the interest and skill level among Calgary barbecue cooks in hopes of increasing the number of Canadian teams—and improving their chances of winning.

Bob, a white-haired, erudite seventysomething, was editor of *Drippings from the Pit*, chief cook of the Beaver Castors (named "Barbecue Road Team of the '90s"), and a seasoned veteran of The Royal and The Jack. He spent the day sharing his knowledge with us and coaching us as we cooked ribs and chicken on our cheap charcoal-fueled covered grills and water smokers. At the end of the day Bob even staged a little contest, showing us how to carve and present our barbecue in competition and giving us a chance to judge each other's cooking according to the KCBS rules.

Shortly after, Rockin' Ronnie's Butt Shredders was formed, and in September we entered our first competition. We won Best New Cooks at Barbecue on the Bow that year, but more importantly, we were on our way to becoming indoctrinated in the culture, values, and mores of Barbecueville.

I had a great team, which spread over two cities after my job took me to Vancouver. In Calgary, my hometown, the core team was made up of Kathy, Rocco, and Ann-Marie ("Amo") Jackson, a great cook who had learned to love barbecue while living in Texas in the 1980s. And in Vancouver, I had convinced my longtime friends Stephen Robertson, Vince Gogolek, and Tom Masterson—the 15-year-old son of my cousin Paula—to be the West Coast contingent of the Butt Shredders.

The two Canadian competitions we entered every year—Barbecue on the Bow in Calgary and the Canadian Championship in Vancouver, British Columbia, were always stacked with ringers. Successful American teams like Sum Say, Mad Momma & the Kids, the Beaver Castors, Smokestack Lightnin', and the Doughboys would come up to Canada because the events were smaller and the few Canadian teams that entered were inexperienced. Winning the Canadian events, which were sanctioned by the Kansas City Barbecue Society, earned the victors an invitation to the big season-ending contests. So, for many teams in the Pacific Northwest, Canada was more than an exotic location. It was a better chance than any to earn a spot at The Royal and The Jack.

There was a lot to learn from the American teams. Each year, as we drifted around the competition grounds, jawing with our fellow competitors, we would pick up a few tips and meet a few more characters. People like the Dakota Kid, known outside of Barbecueville as Harold Froescher, a veteran barbecue competitor whose claim to fame was a perfect 180 score on his ribs at the American Royal in 1994.

The first time I saw Dakota was at Barbecue on the Bow in '97. It was 10 o'clock in the evening, and we had the usual cool Canadian autumn weather. You could see your breath that night. He had a makeshift rig—a homemade Rube Goldberg contraption that combined a sleeping compartment with a rolling barbecue pit, including a fold-out awning and built-in cupboards for all his tools. I came up to him from behind as he hunched over a scrawny pork butt with a fillet knife, muttering to himself. Despite the cold, he was sweating. With his ratty sleeveless undershirt and head-mounted flashlight, he looked like a deranged surgeon—a squat, scowling bowling ball of a man who clearly had some regrets about making the trip to Calgary. After introducing myself I asked him if there was something wrong.

"You can't get a decent pork butt in this town," Dakota grumbled. "The meat up here in Canada is way too lean. Look at this butt. All the fat's been trimmed out of it. How the hell am I supposed to cook this thing?"

I laughed and gave him a friendly, man-style shoulder hug. His big, clammy arms were cold with sweat.

He started to warm up, at least conversation-wise. "'Course nowadays you don't know what the judges want anyway. They don't like seein' any fat at all on your meat." He frowned. "That's stupid. Brisket's gotta have some fat on it to cook right." To get around this, Dakota showed me how he trimmed all the fat off his briskets and then laid strips of it on the meat, moving them to the top every time he turned the brisket over.

A couple of years later I ran into Dakota at the Canadian championships in New Westminster, BC. He was as sad and grumpy as ever, so big that he shambled along like a grizzly bear and wore leather moccasins for comfort. A proud barbecue champion, he spoke with a tinge of anger and resentment about being shut out of the prize money for several contests in a row. He was thinking of giving it up, throwing in the tongs after this year. I asked him what he thought his chances were in tomorrow's judging.

"I dunno. I just don't know any more," he said, hanging his head. "I'm usin' some hickory, some apple, some mesquite. I got the garlic granules. But I just don't know." I first learned about garlic granules from Dakota; it's a secret trick that makes the judges' taste buds stand at attention as soon as they bite into your barbecue.

He was thinking of giving it up, throwing in the tongs after this year.

The Dakota Kid would take it all the next day, winning the Grand Champion title and buying himself yet another ticket to the American Royal. He was beaming as he trundled up to get his trophy.

⤚ ⤙

As dawn broke on judging day of the 2001 Oregon Open, all hell broke loose in our makeshift field kitchen in the back of Ace Hardware. I'd grabbed a couple hours of sleep in our nearby motel room. Hungover from living the barbecue lifestyle the night before, I took a shower, left Vince to sleep for a while longer and headed back down to our tent. It was 7 a.m. The sky was gray and the parking lot was damp from rain that had fallen during the night. Tom, who had taken the graveyard shift to tend the cookers, was fast asleep in a folding chair. When I arrived I took a quick glance around and saw that the chamber temperature on the brisket was down to 140. We had ourselves a situation.

"Tom! Wake up! The briskets have lost temperature!" I bellowed.

Tom rubbed his eyes. "What's the internal?"

"It's down to 140. And the meat's only at 135!"

"I don't know what happened, Rockin' . . . when I closed my eyes an hour ago it was holding steady at test!"

This was bad. Even in ideal conditions at 212 degrees, it was touch-and-go whether we'd have enough time to get the briskets done before turn-in at 11. The probe inside the brisket gave us a reading that showed we were at 130—a full 40 degrees short of a finished product. Thankfully, the pork butts were holding steady, but the cold, rainy night had taken its toll on the briskets. The pitmasters with the big rolling barbecue rigs never had this problem with their huge fireboxes and giant heat-retaining mass.

We opened the vents on the distressed smoker and quickly worked to get a couple of chimneys of hot coals going. There is nothing worse than rubbery, undercooked brisket. We had to get the internal temperature up to at least 170 as soon as possible so the proteins and connective tissue in the brisket would break down, creating the succulent texture of classic barbecue.

In the meantime, the pork butt was doing fine, with the temperature coming up nicely. It was already at 150 and we would take the butts out of the cooker when they reached 165 degrees. With three hours to go before turn-in, there was still plenty of time. Tom worked to replenish the coals under the briskets and butts.

Vince soon arrived and quickly got to work doing his final prep on the ribs, removing the membrane and coating them with mustard and rub. I butchered the chickens, taking care to keep their precious fat-giving skin intact, and got them into the marinade.

By 10 o'clock the internal temperature of the brisket had gone up to 160 or so—still not high enough to cook properly. With only two hours to go before turn-in time, we decided to take drastic measures. We took the water pan out from under the briskets, then wrapped each piece of meat in a thick coating of heavy foil and placed them back in the smoker. Now we needed a quick source of heat, and briquettes would take a good 20 minutes to start up.

I decided to use most of our remaining dry cherry wood chunks to make some natural charcoal, which would burn hotter and faster than briquettes. The goal was to build a healthy fire under the briskets, pushing the chamber temperature to nearly 400 degrees. Our only hope was that the high heat would somehow pressure-cook the foil-wrapped briskets and get them tender enough in time for turn-in.

Paying all that attention to the brisket made us take our eyes off the ribs, which were losing temperature in the cool of the morning. They weren't in as much danger as the briskets, but they definitely needed tending. Suddenly it looked like we might screw up both the ribs and the briskets. At the same time, the coals for the chicken were almost ready.

Again, we had to act quickly. After some frantic discussion we agreed on a course of action. One of the advantages of the Weber bullets is their interchangeability. The modular design allows for the body of the smoker to be removed without disturbing the charcoal basket underneath. We would take the chamber containing the ribs and switch it with the one that the chicken was about to go in, which was full of fresh hot coals. We needed heat on the ribs immediately, and the chicken, which is easy to overcook, would be fine in a cooler chamber with half-spent coals.

All three of us went into action. From a distance it must have looked like a strange, frantic dance, with three men staggering around in oven mitts, switching smoking chambers and yelling instructions at one another.

It was chaos on one level. But, on another, we were playing at the peak of our game. Like a pro golfer who gets caught in the rough, we were drawing on everything we knew to get out of a bad situation. With a foundation of seven years of competitions under our belts, we were at a skill level where we could improvise in response to a crisis. Although what we were attempting looked crazy, we were actually working very hard to keep things under control.

Or so we thought. A few minutes after our little dance I took a quick peek under the lid of one of the smokers, which I thought contained the ribs. But it was the briskets! That meant the ribs were in a 400-degree smoker. Way too hot. And our briskets were languishing in the smoker right next to it.

I felt like an idiot. Like out-of-town rubes drawn into a bizarre shell game, we had lost track of which meat was in which cooker!

> **From a distance it must have looked like a strange, frantic dance, with three men staggering around in oven mitts, switching smoking chambers and yelling instructions at one another.**

More shouting. More stumbling about. More shuffling of equipment. Finally, everything was where it was supposed to be, with only an hour before the first turn-in. Exhausted but full of adrenalin, we put the chicken on and gave the pork butt its final glaze before wrapping it in foil to rest before we carved it for the judges. The ribs were doing fine and the briskets, still wrapped in foil, were steaming away in the chamber above the hot cherry wood coals.

Somewhere in the middle of that chaos, I was tending one of the bullets when I heard a familiar voice.

"How ya doin', boys?" It was Harold Froescher.

"The Dakota Kid!" I gasped, jumping up to shake his hand. "We didn't see you last night. Are you competing?" He laughed as he shambled into our enclosure.

"Nope. I'm semiretired. Got the diabetes, and it's slowin' me down. I got some friends who have a team here. I'm just hangin' around and givin' 'em advice, whether they want it or not!"

"Got any advice for us, Dakota? How do you think we're going to do?"

He looked at me, smiled, laid his big, meaty hand on my shoulder, and said, "Son, there's a lot of good cooks here today. But I wish you the best of luck."

With that, he turned and trundled on back to his buddies.

❧ ❧

The Kansas City Barbecue Society sets out strict rules for the presentation and judging of barbecue. There are four, and only four, official categories in a KCBS-sanctioned event: brisket, pork shoulder (whole or Boston butt), ribs, and chicken. Only green leaf lettuce can be used as a bed for the meat, and only parsley or cilantro can be used as garnish.

Every contestant gets four white, hinged Styrofoam takeout trays, each with a standard door prize–style double ticket taped to the bottom. You tear off one of the tickets when you get your containers and leave the duplicate tickets taped to the container. That way no one knows which team cooked what—until they announce the numbers of the winning contestants for each category. Entries must be turned in within five minutes of the official turn-in times, which are usually an hour apart, starting at 11 a.m. with brisket, then pork shoulder, then chicken, then ribs. Each entry is scored by six judges, on a scale of one to nine, on three criteria: appearance, texture, and taste. The taste score is doubled and the lowest score on each criterion is thrown out.

The taste score is doubled in recognition of the fact that taste is the most important component of great barbecue. But barbecue competitors know that the judges eat first with their eyes. If your presentation looks mouth-wateringly good, it will simply taste better.

In addition to my role as team captain, I'm the knife man, taking the lead in putting together the presentation of each entry. The trick is to find ways to present six or more pieces of meat on a bed of leaf lettuce that makes the judges want to jump right into the container.

❧ ❧

We were *on* that morning in Newberg. When I took the briskets out of the foil they were a bit charred on the bottoms from being directly above the fire with a dry water pan, but otherwise they were perfectly juicy and tender. The six slices of brisket we presented, with their thin layer of tasty fat and bright red smoke ring, looked positively succulent. The pork butts were smoked to a glistening mahogany perfection and we arranged them on the lettuce in our usual style: six half-inch medallions taken from the richest part of the butt and laid neatly across the container diagonally, with a heaping pile of lightly sauced and shredded meat on either side.

The chicken pieces, which had been brined, basted, and sauced meticulously by Vince and Tom, were gloriously shiny and dotted with little bits of parsley as they came out of the cooker. The six beautiful white slices of breast meat seemed

to fall into place in the presentation tray, nestled between a plump leg-thigh combo and a golden brown wing. A small sprig of parsley was all it took to finish it off. It looked like something out of a magazine.

With each successive turn-in we were more confident—except for the ribs, our Achilles heel. In all our years of competition we had never placed better than sixth in ribs. The tiny, lean racks available in fat-conscious Canada didn't help. Our ribs always seemed to come out dry and overcooked, or tough and undercooked. They didn't have a distinctive flavor, and because we knew they were a problem, we always overfussed them, often coating them with too much sauce and drowning out the

flavor of the pork. Our turn-in looked only okay. But what the hell, we thought. No one's perfect.

One of the most important parts of barbecue competitions is the postmortem—the team discussion of what went wrong and what went right as we go over our scores and second-guess the judges. This dialogue begins during the hour and a half after the last turn-in, while the judges' marks are being compiled. As we started breaking down our little camp, dumping our coals and drippings, scouring the grills and putting away our tools, we talked about how it had gone, and it had clearly gone pretty well. But as the ritual of announcing the winners began and the head judge called the numbers, in ascending order from tenth to first place, we were stunned.

On that day in Newberg, the Butt Shredders became the first Canadian team ever to win the Oregon Open, and, in fact, the first Canadians to win any US barbecue competition, ever.

We won brisket. Then pork shoulder. And then chicken. By the time ribs were being announced (we didn't even crack the top 10), it didn't matter because it wasn't a contest anymore. On that day in Newberg, the Butt Shredders became the first Canadian team ever to win the Oregon Open, and, in fact, the first Canadians to win any US barbecue competition, ever.

Adding to the prestige and glamour of the occasion, our big shiny plastic trophies were handed to us by the beautiful Queen of Newberg's Old Fashioned Days and her two smiling courtiers. They were pretty country girls dressed in strapless pink taffeta gowns, complete with classic white beauty queen sashes.

We had made it. We had finally achieved barbecue glory. And in the process we had learned some barbecue secrets—about how to cook and present our meat, and, even more importantly, about how high each of us could reach, and how much our team could achieve. It was a great, great feeling.

Minutes after we walked away from the judging area, I called my wife, Kate, on my cell phone. "Mama, git yerself a new pair of shoes! We're goin' to Kansas City! Woo hoo!"

The seven-hour trip back to Vancouver seemed to go by in about two blinks. Its highlight was going through the border crossing. The unsuspecting guard asked the usual questions.

"Do you have anything to declare?" she asked, looking at our passports.

"Yes," said Vince. "I declare we're the winners of the Oregon State Open Barbecue Championship!"

Or, at least, that's how I remember it. Vince and Tom say it was more like, "Why were you visiting the US?"

"We competed in a barbecue contest."

"Did you win?"

"Yes, we did!"

But part of barbecue culture is embellishing stories and I like my version better.

All the way back to Vancouver we replayed the entire contest, going over the moves we'd made, celebrating every moment, and laughing at the crazy path we had taken to victory that morning. Our little voodoo dance with the bullets had worked.

On Sunday morning, I put out a press release to local Vancouver media, and on Monday, there was a color photo of our team at the top of page three of the *Vancouver Sun* with the headline SIZZLING BUTT SHREDDERS WIN U.S. BARBECUE OPEN and a quote from me saying the event was "a pure meat experience."

That afternoon, I was interviewed by the Canadian Broadcasting Corporation for a show that aired across BC. The owners of the local NHL team, the Vancouver Canucks, sent us a congratulatory note and some free hockey tickets for the team.

But more glorious than anything else was the berth we had earned at the American Royal Invitational that October in Kansas City. Six of us would travel down to the US that fall to compete in The Royal. But that's a whole other story.

EPILOGUE

So, how did barbecue change my life? Some hard work, some laughs, a hangover, a few gaudy plastic trophies, a picture in the paper, and some free hockey tickets do not constitute a profound change in anyone's existence.

But when the Dakota Kid put his hand on my shoulder, I had a barbecue epiphany. I realized that barbecue competitions, and barbecue culture, are not just a goofy sport, and that they are much more than a lifestyle. Barbecue, I realized, is a metaphor for life itself. It's a fat, juicy prism through which we can look at the human condition.

I don't know about you, but I find it hard to get a whole lot of personal fulfillment working in the corporate world. Hamstrung by bureaucracy, stifled by bad internal politics, frustrated by the Kafkaesque absurdity of life in the modern workplace, I am drawn to barbecue for its purity, its simple meaning, and a true feeling of joy that brings me to a happier place. The smoky cocoon of the barbecue contest creates a relaxed, friendly community unlike anything in urban life today.

Being on a barbecue team gives its members a sense of purpose and camaraderie that's hard to find anywhere else. And being the chief cook of a barbecue team has given me a chance to be a leader, making decisions, solving problems, coaching and collaborating with teammates, delegating responsibility, bickering when things go wrong, and sharing in the glory when we win.

Barbecue, I realized, is a metaphor for life itself. It's a fat, juicy prism through which we can look at the human condition.

Finally, I think it's fair to say that our victory on that fateful day in Oregon has led to this book. Being a barbecue champion has given me a unique little niche in an increasingly generic world. It has opened doors that I never knew existed, strengthened my old friendships, and given me new ones. And it has given me a chance to cook, and eat, the most delicious food on earth.

Barbecue has made me whole. God bless barbecue.

Bite This!
Starters &
Finger Foods

When you're having people over to enjoy some of your backyard cookery, you need to give them something to eat before dinner because otherwise they'll get drunk, start to argue, and someone will pass out on your carpet. At the same time, you don't want to stuff them with appetizers because they'll want to have big helpings of whatever succulent fare you've got going on your grill or in your smoker. Whatever you make, keep the portions small and make them easy to grab and eat while holding a drink.

GRILLED VEGETABLE PLATTER

MAKES 10–20 SERVINGS, DEPENDING WHAT ELSE YOU'VE GOT ON THE GRILL

This recipe is pretty elaborate and is designed for when you're entertaining. For everyday cooking, just grill one or two kinds of veggies—they're ready in minutes.

20 nugget potatoes, skins on

20 cauliflower florets (about 1 head of cauliflower)

4 sweet potatoes, peeled and cut into rounds ½ inch [1 cm] thick

2 red bell peppers, cut lengthwise into 2-inch [5 cm] strips

2 yellow bell peppers, cut lengthwise into 2-inch [5 cm] strips

2 green bell peppers, cut lengthwise into 2-inch [5 cm] strips

2 bunches fresh asparagus spears, tough ends snapped off

4 zucchini, cut lengthwise into ½-inch [1 cm] slabs

20 whole ripe cherry tomatoes

1 cup [250 mL] extra virgin olive oil

kosher salt and freshly ground black pepper to taste

3 lemons, cut into wedges

> **BARBECUE SECRETS** ≂

You can grill almost any vegetable, in any quantity, simply by tossing the veggies in olive oil, sprinkling them with salt, and putting them on a hot grill. The more robust the vegetable, the longer the cooking time. The more you grill, the better you'll get!

➤ ≂

Grilled veggies are delicious on their own, but go even better with a nice dip, like a flavored mayo (see pages 68–69). They're also great tossed into a green salad or served as a side with grilled meat or fish. To add more flavor, before grilling, toss them with some dried or fresh chopped herbs, like rosemary, oregano, or basil.

Bring the potatoes to a boil in a large pot of cold water over high heat. Turn down the heat and simmer them for 10 minutes, adding the cauliflower florets when you have 5 minutes to go. Remove the vegetables from the pot, and cool the potatoes and cauliflower in a bowl of cold water. Drain them again and set them aside.

Prepare your grill for direct medium heat.

Put all the vegetables in a large bowl, in batches if necessary, and toss them with the olive oil, salt, pepper, and herbs, if desired. Grill the vegetables over high direct heat, starting with the sweet potatoes, potatoes, and cauliflower, turning them often. Grill the most tender vegetables last, taking care not to overcook the asparagus, zucchini, and cherry tomatoes (which really only need to be heated through).

Arrange all the grilled vegetables on a big platter, drizzle them with a little more oil, garnish the platter with lemon wedges, and serve the vegetables immediately. You can also make this an hour or two ahead of time and serve the vegetables at room temperature.

Bite This! Starters & Finger Foods

GRILLED STUFFED MUSHROOMS

MAKES 2 DOZEN MUSHROOMS

This classic stuffed mushroom recipe is adapted from an old *Gourmet* magazine. The mushrooms are great grilled but this recipe also works well on a plank.

24 large button mushrooms (about 2½ lb/1.2 kg)	pinch crumbled dried thyme
12 oz [375 g] sun-dried tomatoes packed in oil	kosher salt and freshly ground black pepper
⅓ cup [75 mL] finely chopped shallots	3 Tbsp [45 mL] whipping cream
1 tsp [5 mL] finely chopped garlic	¼ cup [50 mL] freshly grated Parmesan cheese

Remove the stems from the mushrooms and finely chop the stems until you have 1 cup (250 mL) chopped stems. Discard the rest of the stems.

Drain the sun-dried tomatoes, reserving ¼ cup (50 mL) of the oil. Mince the tomatoes.

Brush the mushroom caps with some of the reserved tomato oil and arrange them on a baking sheet, stemmed side up.

In a large skillet over medium-low heat, cook the shallots and garlic in the remaining tomato oil, stirring occasionally, until they're softened. Stir in the reserved mushroom stems, minced tomatoes, thyme, salt, and pepper. Cook the mixture, stirring occasionally, for 5 to 10 minutes, or until the liquid has evaporated and the mixture is thick. Stir in the cream, divide the mixture among the mushroom caps, and sprinkle them with the Parmesan.

Preheat your grill for medium direct heat. Quickly and carefully place the mushrooms on the cooking grate. Cook them for 8 to 12 minutes, or until the filling has heated through.

THE BARON'S PLANKED
SWEET HICKORY BACON BITES

MAKES 20 SERVINGS

This recipe comes from one of my mentors and one of the world's best-known barbecue cooks, Chef Paul Kirk. "I don't think that people realize cooking on planks can give food a new and wonderful change from everyday barbecue," says Paul.

1 hickory plank (or plank of your
    choice), soaked in water or apple
    juice for at least 1 hour
20 water-soaked toothpicks

20 roasted unsalted pecan halves or
    whole almonds
20 pitted prunes, dates, or figs
10 slices bacon, cut in half

Stuff 1 pecan half or whole almond in each prune, date, or fig. Wrap a piece of bacon around the fruit and secure it with a toothpick. (When you get to the nutmeat, twist or screw the toothpick; this will keep the nuts from breaking.) Place the bites on a prepared plank. Cook them at 350 to 425°F (180–220°C) for 18 to 25 minutes. Add soaked hickory chips to your hot coals or over your grill burner for more hickory flavor, if you want.

PLANKED
ASPARAGUS & PROSCIUTTO
BUNDLES

MAKES 6 SERVINGS

These are a favorite of my brother Allan, who, like me, is a Ukrainian-Canadian boy somehow transformed into a lover of all things Italian. This classic combination of flavors takes well to the plank. If you can't find real imported fontina, use Parmigiano Reggiano shaved into slivers.

1 plank, soaked overnight or at least
   1 hour
18 choice, thick asparagus spears
½ lb [250 g] Italian fontina cheese,
   cut into thin slices

6 large slices prosciutto
1 Tbsp [15 mL] butter
balsamic reduction (optional, see
   sidebar page 242)
crusty bread as an accompaniment

Trim the asparagus and blanch it in salted water for just a minute or two, until it's deep green and still firm. Stop the cooking by immersing the spears in cold water.

Set aside 12 slices of cheese, reserving the rest. Spread open a slice of prosciutto and place 2 spears of asparagus on it. Place 1 slice of the cheese between the spears and place a third spear on top. Wrap the prosciutto around the spears and cheese. Proceed until you have 6 bundles.

Preheat the grill on medium-high for 5 to 10 minutes, or until the chamber temperature rises above 500°F (260°C). Rinse the soaked plank and place it on the cooking grate. Cover the grill and heat the plank for 4 to 5 minutes, or until it starts to throw off a bit of smoke and crackles lightly. Reduce the heat to medium-low and place the bundles on the plank. Working quickly, place the remaining cheese slices over each bundle in a crisscross pattern. Cook the bundles for 10 to 15 minutes, or until the cheese is melted and a little mottled. Remove them from the grill, drizzle them with a little olive oil or brush them with the butter, and let them sit for a few minutes. Plate them individually with a few drops of balsamic reduction around the edges, if desired. Serve the bundles with crusty bread.

NOTE: If you want to do these on your grill without a plank, use indirect medium-high heat and lay down a sheet of aluminum foil on the cooking grate so you won't lose any cheese while the bundles are cooking.

GRILLED
MUSHROOM OR VEGGIE KEBABS
WITH TARRAGON VINAIGRETTE

MAKES 4 TO 6 SKEWERS OR 24 INDIVIDUAL PORTIONS

The first time I cooked this recipe, I just piled some dressed mushrooms on a grill. Later, I used skewered veggies and adapted it for the plank. This is great as a hot starter, or cooled and served as part of an appetizer platter.

6 or 8 bamboo skewers, soaked for at
    least 15 minutes
½ cup [125 mL] extra virgin olive oil
3 Tbsp [45 mL] white wine vinegar or
    tarragon vinegar
1 Tbsp [15 mL] Dijon mustard
1 shallot, finely chopped
1 clove garlic, smashed or finely minced
1 tsp [5 mL] dried crumbled tarragon

1 Tbsp [15 mL] fresh lemon juice
kosher salt and freshly ground black
    pepper
24 large white button mushrooms (or 24
    bite-sized chunks of mixed vegetables,
    including red onion, zucchini, Japa-
    nese eggplant, red, green, or yellow
    bell peppers, cherry tomatoes, etc.)

Prepare your grill for direct medium-high heat, or until the chamber temperature rises above 500°F (260°C). Whisk together the olive oil, vinegar, mustard, shallot, garlic, tarragon, and lemon juice. Season the vinaigrette to taste with salt and pepper.

Toss the mushrooms or veggies in the vinaigrette. If you're making kebabs, place the veggies on the skewers. Place them on the grill and leave the heat on medium-high. Cook the vegetables for 6 to 8 minutes, turning them once or twice, or until they are heated through and starting to brown around the edges.

Remove the vegetables from the heat and transfer them to a serving dish. Squeeze more lemon over the mushrooms or veggies and season them with more salt and pepper and a drizzle of olive oil, if you like.

TO COOK ON A PLANK: Soak 1 cedar plank overnight or at least 1 hour. Rinse the plank and place it on the cooking grate. Cover the grill and heat the plank for 4 to 5 minutes, or until it starts to throw off a bit of smoke and crackles lightly. Place the veggies on the plank and close the lid. Cook them for 8 to 12 minutes, or until the vegetables are heated through and starting to brown around the edges. Serve as described above.

Bite This! Starters & Finger Foods

GRILLED POLENTA DIAMONDS
WITH CHIPOTLE GOAT CHEESE & ROASTED CHERRY TOMATOES

MAKES 1–2 DOZEN CANAPÉS, DEPENDING HOW LARGE YOU CUT THE DIAMONDS

The recipe for these polenta diamonds comes from my friend Jane Mundy. These delicious one-bite appetizers are easy to prepare, even easier to eat, and look great on a platter. They're also great for those who don't eat gluten.

CHERRY TOMATOES

1 lb [500 g] cherry tomatoes, cut in half, preferably red, yellow, and orange
¼ cup [50 mL] extra virgin olive oil
kosher salt

POLENTA DIAMONDS

2 cups [500 mL] instant polenta
extra virgin olive oil for brushing

CHIPOTLE GOAT CHEESE

1½ cups [375 mL] crumbled goat cheese

1 Tbsp [15 mL] whipping cream or plain yogurt
1 Tbsp [15 mL] minced garlic
¼ cup [50 mL] roughly chopped fresh cilantro or parsley
2 Tbsp [25 mL] minced canned chipotle chilies in adobo sauce
1 Tbsp [15 mL] cumin seeds, toasted and finely ground
kosher salt and freshly ground black pepper to taste

Preheat the oven to 200°F (95°C). Put the halved tomatoes on a baking sheet, cut side up. Drizzle them with olive oil and sprinkle them with salt. Put them in the oven and leave them for 1 to 2 hours, until they've shriveled. Remove the tray from the oven and set them aside to cool.

Prepare the polenta according to the package directions. Cover a large baking sheet, or two regular baking sheets, with parchment paper. While it's still hot, pour the cooked polenta onto the parchment. Spread it out onto the sheet in an even layer (about ½-inch/1 cm thick), smooth the surface with the back of a spoon, and allow it to cool. Once it's cool and firm, cut it into bite-sized diamonds or squares.

Prepare the grill for direct high heat. Brush the polenta pieces with olive oil and grill them, turning them once or twice, just long enough to give them some nice char marks. Remove them from the grill and set them aside to cool.

In the bowl of a food processor, combine the ingredients for the goat cheese mixture and process the mixture until it's blended. Put about a teaspoon of the paste onto each polenta square. Top each one with a roasted cherry tomato.

PLANKED BRIE
WITH ROASTED TOMATO-CHERRY RELISH

MAKES 8–12 SERVINGS

I know. Just the name of the recipe sounds luscious. And it is. Roasting the cherries and tomatoes takes a while, but there's no heavy lifting involved, and planking the cheese is a snap. One taste of this molten, smoky, tangy, sweet concoction and you'll be addicted. I want to acknowledge my friend Gail Norton for the relish recipe, and planking god Ted Reader for the cooking technique, which he showcases in his great *Sticks & Stones* cookbook.

1 maple, fruitwood, or cedar plank, soaked overnight or at least 1 hour	1 cup [250 mL] Roasted Tomato-Cherry Relish (recipe follows)
two ¼ lb [125 g] (small) rounds brie	2 Tbsp [30 mL] balsamic reduction
freshly ground black pepper	(see sidebar page 242)

Preheat the grill on medium-high for 5 to 10 minutes, or until the chamber temperature rises above 500°F (260°C). Cut the top of the rind off each of the rounds of brie. Grind a little pepper over the exposed cheese. Spread about ½ cup (125 mL) of the relish over the brie rounds.

Rinse the soaked plank and place it on the cooking grate. Cover the grill and heat the plank for 4 to 5 minutes, or until it starts to throw off a bit of smoke and crackles lightly. Place the cheese on the plank and cook it for 10 to 12 minutes, or until the cheese turns golden and starts to soften (be careful not to overcook it—the cheese can fall apart, and then you've got a tasty mess on your hands). Remove the brie from the grill and drizzle it with the balsamic reduction. Garnish it with a few fresh grape tomatoes and/or cherries and serve it, on the plank, with crusty bread, rye crisps, or your favorite crackers.

(continued)

Planked Brie with Roasted Tomato-Cherry Relish *(continued)*

ROASTED TOMATO-CHERRY RELISH
MAKES ABOUT 2 CUPS (500 ML)

1 lb [500 g] ripe fresh cherries, pits
   removed
1 lb [500 g] grape tomatoes or small
   cherry tomatoes

¼ cup [50 mL] extra virgin olive oil
1 tsp [5 mL] kosher salt
balsamic reduction (see sidebar
   page 242) for drizzling

Preheat the oven to 350°F (180°C). Spread the cherries and tomatoes on a
large baking sheet in 1 layer. Drizzle the oil and sprinkle the salt over the
fruit and toss the cherries and tomatoes to coat them. Place the fruit in the
oven and roast it for 1 hour, mixing it around once or twice. Reduce the heat
to 300°F (150°C) and roast the fruit for another hour, again mixing it once
or twice. The tomatoes and cherries should be nicely caramelized. Drizzle
the relish with a little more oil and a splash of balsamic vinegar, mix them
in thoroughly, and transfer the mixture to a storage container. This relish
keeps in the fridge for 1 or 2 weeks and freezes well.

A GRILLED QUESADILLA LIBRARY

Easy to make and quick to cook, quesadillas are the perfect summer party food. Think of the soft flour tortilla as a palette upon which you can paint beautiful taste-scapes for your guests. Or something like that. Preparing a quesadilla is as easy as one, two, three, four, five.

1. Place a large flour tortilla on a cutting board or baking sheet and cover it with a ¼-inch (6 mm) layer of shredded cheese. (What you want is a gooey but bland cheese like mozzarella or Jack for the right texture, plus, if you want to get fancy, a more robust-tasting cheese like Asiago, Gouda, or blue cheese for extra flavor.)
2. Layer on the toppings (see page 97), taking care to distribute them evenly.
3. Sprinkle the toppings with salt, pepper, and a little hot sauce to taste. (If you've used a salty cheese like blue, go easy.)
4. Coat the toppings with another thin layer of shredded cheese.
5. Top with another flour tortilla.

Preheat your charcoal or gas grill to a medium-high heat. Place the quesadilla directly on the grill and cook it for 2 or 3 minutes, until the cheese starts to melt and the tortilla is toasted and slightly charred. Flip it with a big spatula and cook the other side for another 2 or 3 minutes. Take it off the grill, place it on a cutting board, and let it rest for a minute or two. Cut it into pizzalike slices with a big, sharp knife.

   Accompany the quesadillas with fresh salsa, guacamole, and sour cream for dipping. Quesadillas can also easily be made on a stovetop or on the propane burner on the side of your grill in a large, lightly oiled skillet over medium-high heat. You can prepare the quesadillas in advance and keep them covered and refrigerated for an hour or two before grilling (if you try to keep them overnight, however, the tortillas will get soggy).

(continued)

⤳ A TOAST TO ⤳ SPICES & NUTS!

In India, the first step in almost every home-cooked dish is to toast some spices in a hot pan. The heat refreshes the spices, bringing to life the natural oils that carry their flavor. This technique works especially well with robust whole spices like cumin, coriander, and fennel seeds. All you have to do is preheat a dry sauté pan on a medium setting and toss in a handful of seeds. Shake the pan constantly, watching carefully. After about a minute, when the spices start to brown a little and give off a strong aroma, empty the pan into a cool bowl or plate to stop the toasting before they burn. In a few minutes the seeds will be ready to go into a spice mill, mortar, or coffee grinder. The difference between raw and toasted spices is like night and day.

   This technique also works fabulously to toast pecans or other nuts, sesame seeds, pumpkin seeds, and pine nuts. Toast up a handful of nuts and sprinkle some on a salad for sharp, crunchy bursts of nutty flavor!

Bite This! Starters & Finger Foods

NOTE: This technique takes a little skill and, until you get good at it, it's easy to botch the quesadilla flip and send half-melted cheese all over your grill. To avoid this, make smaller quesadillas by placing all the ingredients on half of 1 tortilla and then folding the other half over the filling. Now you can easily flip the tortilla by grabbing the open end with a pair of tongs and gently turning it over, folded side down, to avoid spillage.

Variations

Simple but Great   Just plain shredded Jack or cheddar cheese with pickled jalapeño slices.

Classic   Equal parts shredded Asiago and Jack cheese, with pickled jalapeño slices, a bit of tomato salsa, and some chopped cilantro, salt, and pepper. Sour cream and guacamole are perfect accompaniments.

Hiker's Dream (from Calgary foodie Dee Hobsbawn-Smith)   Equal parts shredded Jack and smoked Gouda, thinly sliced Granny Smith apple, fresh chopped rosemary, salt, and pepper. Unusual and delicious!

Funky   Shredded Jack cheese, chunks of chèvre (creamy goat cheese), slices of roasted red pepper, lightly toasted pine nuts, salt, and pepper. Serve with jalapeño jelly.

Heavenly   Shredded Jack cheese, chopped cilantro, and a few spoonfuls of leftover chili or chorizo. Dip in sour cream or fresh salsa.

Wolfgangpuckadilla   Shredded Jack cheese with daubs of cream cheese, slices of lox, a few capers, some thinly sliced red onion, salt, and pepper. Serve with sour cream and . . . caviar?

Blue Cheese Dream   Shredded Jack, crumbled strong blue cheese like Roquefort or Gorgonzola, ripe pear slices, and coarsely chopped toasted walnuts. Maybe even a little caramelized onion.

Blue Cheese Dream (II)   Danish blue cheese, shredded Jack, lightly toasted chopped walnuts, and caramelized onions (see recipe page 160).

Calicado   Shredded Jack with chopped, pitted canned black olives, avocado slices, chopped cilantro, chopped fresh red bell pepper, salt, pepper, and a squeeze of fresh lime.

Tropical   Mozzarella and brie, thinly sliced ripe mango or papaya, chopped cilantro, thinly sliced onion, and chopped fresh jalapeño. Serve with sour cream as a dip.

NOTE: Flavored cheeses like jalapeño Jack, peppered goat cheese, or spiced Gouda are excellent in quesadillas.

SEARED CALAMARI
WITH FRESH TOMATO-BASIL SALSA

MAKES 4 SERVINGS

The secret to great grilled squid is to use the freshest and smallest squid you can find, and to cook it over direct high heat for no more than a minute per side. Any longer and it turns rubbery. In this recipe, the tomato salsa provides a cool, tangy, herbal complement to the hot, garlicky calamari. You can also cook this dish on a plank to give it some extra smoky flavor, but you won't get the nice charring that happens when you grill it over direct heat.

1 lb [500 g] cleaned squid, equal parts bodies and tentacles	2 cups [500 mL] small, ripe cherry or grape tomatoes
1 Tbsp [15 mL] kosher salt	1 Tbsp [15 mL] fresh basil
½ cup [125 mL] extra virgin olive oil	1 Tbsp [15 mL] rice vinegar or white wine vinegar
½ tsp [2 mL] crushed dried red chili flakes	kosher salt and freshly ground black pepper
2 cloves garlic, finely chopped	

Coat the squid in the salt, then rinse it thoroughly with cold water. Pat it dry with paper towels. Slit the bodies and score the inside surfaces with diagonal cuts. Cut each squid into large bite-sized pieces. Place them in a bowl with ¼ cup (50 mL) of the olive oil, the chili flakes, and the garlic. Toss the squid to coat and marinate it in the refrigerator for about an hour.

Preheat your grill on high. While the grill is heating, coarsely chop the tomatoes (halves or quarters are fine), slice the basil leaves into fine shreds, and toss them together in a bowl with the vinegar and the remainder of the olive oil. Distribute the salsa among 4 plates.

When the grill is hot, open it up and gently place the calamari on the cooking grate, taking care not to let the pieces slip through the cracks (you may even want to use a grill-topper with small holes designed for this kind of task). Don't walk away! Stand at the grill and tend the squid with a set of good tongs, turning the pieces often so they are cooked quickly and evenly, no more than a minute per side. Remove the squid from the grill, transfer it to the plates, and season it with a pinch of salt and pepper.

Drizzle the calamari with a little more olive oil and serve it immediately with a crisp, fruity white wine.

BACON-WRAPPED OYSTERS

MAKES 4–6 APPETIZER-SIZED PORTIONS

This is a simple, old-fashioned way to grill oysters that makes a great party appetizer.

one 1-pint [500 mL] container of large, fresh, shucked oysters (about a dozen oysters)

¼ lb [125 g] thinly sliced bacon, each slice cut in half

kosher salt and freshly ground black pepper to taste

Louisiana-style hot sauce

Fry the bacon over medium heat in a heavy skillet until it's cooked but not quite crispy. Place the cooked bacon strips on a paper towel and set them aside.

Prepare your grill for direct high heat. Drain the oysters and pat them dry with a paper towel. Wrap half a slice of cooked bacon around each oyster, skewering it with a wooden toothpick. Place the oysters on the cooking grate and grill them for 2 or 3 minutes per side, or until the bacon crisps and the oysters are cooked through and just starting to char. Remove them from the heat, place them on a platter, season them with salt and pepper, and pass them around with a bottle of hot sauce.

OYSTERS GRILLED IN THE SHELL

Beach-grown West Coast oysters usually come pre-shucked in tubs, and they're great smoked or grilled. If you can find them live, in their shells, it's a huge treat. I'm lucky enough to have a friend, Chef Eric Giesbrecht, who is the owner/operator of The Royal We Shellfish Company, based in Calgary. Eric is a wholesaler of oysters and other fresh seafood, and he's also a caterer. I asked him to teach me the secrets of grilling oysters in the shell and I thank him for the following guide. His website is www.meta4foods.com.

1. Use large West Coast beach oysters for the best results. Ask your fishmonger for Royal Miyagis.
2. Prepare your grill for direct medium heat.
3. Rinse the oysters of any extraneous material such as loose barnacles, rocks, sand, or any other hangers-on.
4. Put the oysters "cup side" down on the cooking grate. This will help ensure that you don't lose any of the precious liquor, in which the oysters will slowly poach.
5. Grill the oysters for 5 or 6 minutes. You can tell when they're done when the top shell starts to lift and the nectar begins to spill out.
6. Remove the oysters from the grill and shuck them. If you just try to pull the shells apart, you'll risk getting unappetizing broken bits of shell in the oysters. Eric recommends using an oyster shucking knife or paring knife to separate the top and bottom shells, cut the muscle attaching the oyster to the shell, and lift the flesh out. Some restaurants like to serve them cooked and in the shell with a little sauce spooned in, leaving it to their guests to do the shucking.

⤳ BARBECUE SECRET ⤳

To preserve your grill from the caustic effects of the briny juice that comes out of oysters when you grill them in their shells, place a baking sheet on top of the cooking grate before you preheat the grill. Place the oysters on the baking sheet and it'll catch the juices and preserve the grate.

A FEW OF ERIC'S ⤳ FAVORITE SAUCES ⤳

Verde Use a fistful of fresh herbs pounded to a pulpy paste with a mortar and pestle, adding some nice olive oil, a clove of garlic, a minced shallot, the zest and juice of 1 lime (or lemon), some coarse sea salt, and black peppercorns. Kick this one out of the known galaxy by adding freshly grated Parmesan cheese.

Compound butter Mix ½ lb (250 g) of softened butter with 1 to 2 Tbsp (15–25 mL) of smoked paprika, a pinch of chili flakes, the zest and juice of 1 lemon, 1 Tbsp (15 mL) of liquid honey, 1 clove of crushed garlic, and some chopped parsley for color.

Gratin Eric likes to transfer the grilled oysters onto an oiled baking sheet, plane off slices of Gruyère, Comté, or Appenzeller cheese on top of the oysters, and place the baking sheet back onto the grill. "Close the lid until the cheese is melted and unbearably sexy," he says. "Top with sliced chives or scallions for a contrasting garnish."

Bite This! Starters & Finger Foods

GRILLED OYSTERS
WITH ORANGE-WALNUT VINAIGRETTE

MAKES 4–6 APPETIZER-SIZED PORTIONS

My friend Kosta the fishmonger suggested this flavor combination to me, and when I tried it out I was astonished at how well the light, refreshing vinaigrette complemented the robust flavor of the grilled oysters.

VINAIGRETTE

3 Tbsp [45 mL] French toasted
   walnut oil

1 Tbsp [15 mL] rice vinegar or
   champagne vinegar

1 tsp [5 mL] finely grated orange zest

1 tsp [5 mL] maple syrup

one 1-pint [500 mL] container of large,
   fresh, shucked oysters (about a
   dozen oysters)

kosher salt and freshly ground
   black pepper

neutral-flavored oil like canola or corn oil

1 orange, cut into wedges

Make the vinaigrette by whisking together the walnut oil, vinegar, orange zest, and maple syrup. Set the mixture aside.

Drain the oysters and pat them dry with paper towels. Put them on a baking sheet and set them aside.

Prepare your grill for direct high heat, making sure the cooking grate is thoroughly scraped. Season the oysters with salt and pepper and drizzle them with a light coating of oil. Just before you put the oysters on the hot grill, oil the cooking grate using a paper towel dipped in some oil. Carefully place the oysters on the cooking grate, making sure they don't fall through. Grill them for a couple of minutes per side, or until they're just cooked through and the outside edges are a bit charred. Transfer the oysters to serving plates, top them with a drizzle of the vinaigrette, and garnish with orange wedges.

Bite This! Starters & Finger Foods

PLANK

GAZPACHO
WITH PLANK-SMOKED TOMATOES

MAKES 6–8 SERVINGS WITH LEFTOVERS

⌁ PLANKING SECRET ⌁

Lightly smoked tomatoes are great in guacamole or gazpacho, and smokier and softer tomatoes are wonderful in soups, stews, and sauces.

SMOKE IT WHILE
⌁ YOU'VE GOT IT ⌁

Your smoker or barbecue pit takes a while to get going, and it chugs away after you've finished cooking. It's a shame to waste all those good vapors. Once your smoker is going, take advantage of the situation by smoking other foods to eat another time. Cheap breakfast sausages turn to gold, both literally and figuratively, with a couple of hours in the smoker. Smoked chicken refrigerates and freezes well, and you can fit 4 to 6 whole birds in a small water smoker. You can smoke almost anything. Try some of these ideas.

- Hard-boil some eggs until they are just done, peel them, and put them in your smoker for half an hour to an hour, or until the eggs take on a light golden color. This adds a certain what-the-heck-is-that-delicious-taste to your deviled eggs or egg salad.

- Smoke fresh, ripe tomatoes for about half an hour—just until they are infused with smoke but the flesh is still firm. Use them wherever you'd use fresh tomatoes and give your salsa, guacamole, pasta sauce, or salad a smoky kick.

I introduced smoked tomatoes to backyard cook Lawrence Davis at one of my cooking classes, and he developed this recipe to showcase them in a classic gazpacho, the refreshing cold Spanish summer soup. The recipe serves eight, but Lawrence says it can be doubled or tripled for a large crowd. For extra flavor and variety, add corn, pitted Greek olives, or any seasonal vegetable, coarsely chopped. You can also serve some chopped hard-boiled egg or crumbled bacon on the side for guests to add at the table.

1 maple, hickory, oak, or mesquite plank, soaked overnight or at least 1 hour (you can use cedar, too, which makes for an unusual and delicious flavor, but a hardwood plank will impart classic barbecue taste and aroma)	6 cups [1.5 L] tomato juice
	⅔ cup [160 mL] extra virgin olive oil
	⅓ cup [75 mL] balsamic vinegar
	2 Tbsp [25 mL] fresh lemon juice
	dried or chopped fresh herbs, such as rosemary, thyme, and basil, to taste (if you use dried, don't use too much or you'll add a bitter taste to the soup)
4 large, ripe, firm tomatoes	
1 long English cucumber	
1 green bell pepper	kosher salt and freshly ground black pepper
1 yellow bell pepper	
2 medium onions	Worcestershire sauce
2 stalks celery	Louisiana-style hot sauce

Preheat the grill on medium-high for 5 to 10 minutes, or until the chamber temperature rises above 500°F (260°C). Rinse the soaked plank and place it on the cooking grate. Cover the grill and heat the plank for 4 to 5 minutes, or until it starts to throw off a bit of smoke and crackles lightly. (You may want to put a brick on the plank as it's preheating. This will prevent warping

(continued)

(continued)

- Peel and cut some onions in half, or in ½-inch (1 cm) rounds, and toss them into the smoker for an hour. They make delicious onion soup, and they freeze well. Also try smoking whole heads of garlic for a couple of hours, using the same technique as for roasted garlic (see page 68), except leave the foil slightly open to let the smoke in.

- Put a cup or two of kosher or Maldon salt in a cake pan and put it in the smoker. Smoked salt allows you to give a rich, smoky flavor to anything without having to fire up the cooker.

- Nuts—especially almonds and pecans—take to smoking extremely well. Toss them with a little neutral-flavored oil and some of your barbecue rub, curry powder, Louisiana-style hot sauce, or other seasonings, and place them in a cake pan or on a greased sheet of foil big enough to hold them in 1 layer. Smoke them for about an hour. They're great fresh out of the cooker but you can store them for a few days in a covered container.

- Duck is one of the very best smoked meats and it freezes well. Barbecue half ducks using the usual mustard-and-rub technique. Use Championship Barbecue Rub (page 50) but doctor it with 1 Tbsp (15 mL) each of powdered ginger, mustard powder, and Chinese five-spice powder.

Gazpacho with Plank-Smoked Tomatoes (continued)

so your tomatoes don't roll off the plank.) Reduce the heat to low, place the whole, unpeeled tomatoes on the plank, cover, and cook the tomatoes for 15 to 30 minutes, depending on how smoky and soft you want the tomatoes. The skins will split and take on a yellowish cast from the smoke.

Remove the tomatoes from the plank, peel them, and coarsely chop them. Prepare and coarsely chop the remaining vegetables; combine them with the tomatoes in a large bowl. Pour in the tomato juice, olive oil, vinegar, and lemon juice. Season the soup with herbs, salt, pepper, Worcestershire sauce, and hot sauce to suit your taste.

Refrigerate the soup for several hours or overnight to allow the flavors to meld. (Taste it after several hours and add more seasoning if needed.) Serve the gazpacho cold, in bowls or mugs taken straight from the freezer. Have the Worcestershire and hot sauce on hand for those who want to spice it up!

NOTE: You can smoke tomatoes very easily in a water smoker or barbecue pit, although it's most convenient if you're about to barbecue something else. It's hard to justify getting a smoker going for a half-hour cooking job (see sidebar).

PLANKED CHEESY GARLIC BREAD

MAKES 6 APPETIZER PORTIONS

I guess this is the closest I'll ever get to a wood-fired bread oven. Get the plank going and make these in batches, because they're going to disappear fast. You could also make these in a hot oven if you don't have a plank, but the smoky flavor adds a nice twist to this classic appetizer.

1 fruitwood or alder plank, soaked overnight or at least 1 hour

2 cloves garlic, smashed or pushed through a garlic press

½ cup [125 mL] extra virgin olive oil

1 loaf French bread, sliced at an angle for longer pieces

½ lb [250 g] finely grated Asiago cheese

¼ lb [125 g] finely grated Parmesan cheese

finely chopped green onions or chives, chopped fresh basil, and/or chopped fresh tomatoes with olive oil for garnish

1 part balsamic vinegar to 2 parts extra virgin olive oil for dipping

Combine the garlic and olive oil in a bowl. Prepare the bread slices by brushing them with the garlic oil. Place a layer of grated Asiago on each slice, then sprinkle some Parmesan on top.

Preheat the grill on medium-high for 5 to 10 minutes, or until the chamber temperature rises above 500°F (260°C). Rinse the soaked plank and place it on the cooking grate. Cover the grill and heat the plank for 4 to 5 minutes, or until it starts to throw off a bit of smoke and crackles lightly. Reduce the heat to medium. Put the bread slices, cheese side up of course, on the plank. Cook for 3 to 5 minutes, or until the cheese is melted. Serve the bread with the garnishes, or unembellished just as it comes off the grill.

BBQ

THE DEVILED EGGS
WENT DOWN TO GEORGIA

MAKES 2 DOZEN DEVILED EGGS

You don't see much of this old-school appetizer, but smoking the eggs makes it modern again.

12 eggs
½ cup [125 mL] Margie's Chipotle and
   Roasted Garlic Mayo (see page 68)
1 Tbsp [15 mL] Dijon mustard
2 Tbsp [25 mL] finely chopped
   fresh cilantro

1 lemon
1 tsp [5 mL] paprika
fresh cilantro sprigs for garnish

Choose eggs that are at least a few days old (fresh eggs are harder to peel). Put them in a pot of lukewarm water with a bit of white vinegar. Bring the water to a boil, and at the moment the water starts boiling, remove the pot from the heat. Cover and leave the eggs in the water for 15 minutes. Cool the eggs under cold running water and peel them. Prepare your smoker for barbecuing, bringing the temperature up to 200 to 220°F (95–100°C).

Place the peeled eggs on the cooking grate and smoke them for about half an hour using hickory, maple, or oak as the flavoring agent. Sprinkle them lightly with dry rub if you want a little more flavor. The eggs will turn an amber color. Let them cool.

Slice them in half lengthwise and remove the yolks, setting the whites aside. In a nonreactive bowl, mash the yolks with a fork and add the mayo, mustard, and cilantro, along with the juice of half the lemon. Mix together thoroughly, and spoon or pipe the mixture back into the egg whites.

Sprinkle the deviled eggs with paprika and garnish them with cilantro sprigs and lemon slices.

Get Your Fresh On: Salads

People joke all the time about how I'm such a big meat lover. My brother, for instance, refers to me as "Shrek," after the carnivorous animated ogre. And, indeed, I often say that when I was a young boy I had a balanced diet, eating from the three pork groups—ham, bacon, and sausage—and that the only green thing in my mother's kitchen was the avocado-colored fridge. But it turns out I love salad. I love it because it enhances the meat-eating experience by providing some delightful contrast. The salads in this collection are so good you might not even need any meat yourself . . . just pass it over to me and I'll finish it for you.

PANZANELLA SKEWERS
[SALAD ON A STICK!]

MAKES 6 SERVINGS

My friend Angie Quaale runs Well Seasoned, a gourmet food store in Langley, BC. She's a superb cook and a huge supporter of traditional Southern-style barbecue, hosting a great annual cookoff, the Barbecue on the Bypass. It's a classic local contest, held in the parking lot outside her store. This is one of her favorite grilled appetizers. I love the contrasting flavors and textures.

12 bamboo skewers, soaked for
   15 minutes to half an hour
1 lb [500 g] mozzarella cheese, cut
   into 1½-inch [4 cm] cubes
1 cup [250 mL] fresh whole basil leaves
12 thin slices prosciutto

1 loaf fresh focaccia bread, cut into
   1-inch [2.5 cm] cubes
12 cherry tomatoes
¼ cup [50 mL] garlic-infused olive oil
kosher salt and freshly ground black
   pepper to taste

Cut a pocket into each piece of cheese with a sharp knife and carefully insert 1 basil leaf into each cube. Cut each slice of prosciutto in half and wrap a half-slice around each piece of cheese to enclose it.

To assemble the kebabs, place 1 piece of bread on each skewer, followed by a prosciutto-wrapped cheese chunk and a cherry tomato, and repeat, finishing with a tomato. Brush each skewer liberally with the olive oil and season with salt and pepper.

Prepare the grill for direct medium-high heat. Grill the skewers, turning them once, until the prosciutto is golden brown, the cheese starts to melt, and the bread is golden.

Serve the "salads" on the skewers as an appetizer or as a side.

Get Your Fresh On: Salads

TIDEWATER COLESLAW

MAKES 8–10 SERVINGS

This pungent, high-sugar slaw is best as a condiment, piled high on top of a pulled pork sandwich or burger, or on the side of a few slices of barbecued brisket.

1½ cups [375 mL] mayonnaise
½ cup [125 mL] white vinegar
⅓ cup [75 mL] sugar

1 Tbsp [15 mL] toasted cumin seeds or celery seeds
1 small head cabbage, finely shredded
2 carrots, peeled and finely grated

Whisk the mayonnaise, vinegar, sugar, and cumin together in a bowl. Toss the dressing with the cabbage and carrots, and refrigerate. You can make this slaw a few hours ahead of time. Toss it just before serving to redistribute the dressing.

GOOBER SLAW

MAKES 8–10 SERVINGS

My old pal Ian "Big Daddy" Baird was kind enough to share this crunchy, nutty slaw recipe with me.

1¼ cups [300 mL] good-quality store-bought mayonnaise
⅓ cup [75 mL] apple cider vinegar
⅓ cup [75 mL] sugar
2 Tbsp [25 mL] milk
1 clove garlic, finely minced

½ tsp [2 mL] celery salt
1 small head cabbage, finely grated
2 carrots, peeled and finely grated
¾ cup [175 mL] chopped, salted dry-roasted peanuts

Put the mayonnaise, vinegar, sugar, milk, garlic, and celery salt in a container with a secure lid and shake it until it's well blended. Combine the cabbage and carrots. Pour the dressing over the coleslaw, toss it, and refrigerate it for 1 hour. Just before serving, add the peanuts and toss the slaw again.

JAMAICAN COLESLAW

MAKES 6 SERVINGS

This recipe, adapted slightly from the excellent *Jerk from Jamaica* cookbook by Helen Willinsky (I've added chopped fresh apples), is a superb side. If you want to serve it with something other than jerk, substitute your favorite rub for the jerk seasoning.

4 cups [1 L] shredded cabbage

¾ cup [175 mL] grated carrots

2 apples, peeled, cored, and chopped

½ cup [125 mL] chopped toasted
    nuts (pecans, walnuts, pistachios,
    almonds, or anything else you like)

½ cup [125 mL] mayonnaise

2 Tbsp [25 mL] sugar

1 Tbsp [15 mL] cider vinegar

1 Tbsp [15 mL] Jamaican-Style
    Dry Jerk Rub (see page 53)

Combine all the ingredients in a salad bowl and toss them together. Cover the salad and chill it for at least 1 hour. Toss it again just before serving.

ASIAN SLAW

Asian-flavored meat demands an Asian-inspired slaw, and the peanuts add a nice crunch.

DRESSING

¼ cup [50 mL] creamy peanut butter

2 Tbsp [25 mL] soy sauce

2 Tbsp [25 mL] rice vinegar

1½ tsp [7 mL] finely minced fresh ginger

1 tsp [5 mL] toasted sesame oil

1 tsp [5 mL] Vietnamese chili sauce

1 tsp [5 mL] sugar

1–2 tsp [5–10 mL] water (if needed)

SALAD

2 cups [500 mL] savoy or napa cabbage, grated or shredded into fine slices

1 cup [250 mL] purple cabbage, grated or shredded into fine slices

1 carrot, peeled and grated

1 green onion, chopped

1 small red bell pepper, julienned

¼ cup [50 mL] fresh bean sprouts

¼ cup [50 mL] dry-roasted peanuts, coarsely chopped, for garnish

2 Tbsp [25 mL] chopped fresh cilantro

Combine the dressing ingredients and whisk them together, adding water a little at a time until the mixture is a smooth, fairly thick liquid. Combine all the salad ingredients in a large bowl. Add the dressing and toss to coat. Serve the slaw immediately, garnished with the chopped peanuts.

TOMATOES IN PARADISE

Simple and sensational.

3 Tbsp [45 mL] extra virgin olive oil

1 Tbsp [15 mL] fresh lemon juice

1 tsp [5 mL] Dijon mustard

1 clove finely chopped or pressed garlic

1 Tbsp [15 mL] chopped fresh herbs
   (mint, basil, rosemary, etc.)

kosher salt and freshly ground
   black pepper

4 exceptional tomatoes, cut into quarters

½ cup [125 mL] chopped red onion

1 cup [250 mL] kalamata or other
   Mediterranean olives

Whisk together the olive oil, lemon juice, mustard, garlic, and herbs in a
salad bowl. Season the dressing with salt and pepper. Add the remaining
ingredients and toss them together gently. Let the tomatoes stand for half an
hour at room temperature, then serve.

FIELD GREENS
WITH TOASTED WALNUT OIL & PUMPKIN SEEDS

MAKES 4 SERVINGS

Toasted walnut oil is a dark and delicious French specialty. It's expensive, but a little goes a long way. Its smoky richness perfectly offsets the bitterness of the greens and brings out the nuttiness of the pumpkin seeds in this simple, elegant salad. Serve it as a side salad, garnish a burger with it, or put a pile under a grilled steak or fish fillet.

¼ cup [50 mL] raw pumpkin seeds
3 cups [750 mL] mesclun greens,
    fresh arugula, fresh watercress, or
    a combination
1 bunch fresh basil, stems removed
    and leaves gently torn in half
1 crisp apple, peeled, cored, and cut
    into ½-inch [1 cm] chunks

2 Tbsp [25 mL] French toasted
    walnut oil
½ tsp [2 mL] kosher or Maldon salt
    (or to taste)
freshly ground black pepper
lemon wedges for garnish

Toast the pumpkin seeds in a dry sauté pan over medium heat or under a broiler until they start popping and turning light brown. Set them aside to cool. Place the greens in a salad bowl, and add the toasted pumpkin seeds, apple chunks, walnut oil, salt, and a few grindings of pepper. Toss the salad thoroughly. Garnish it with lemon.

NOTE: Don't substitute the regular untoasted walnut oil that you'll find in health food stores. It doesn't taste of anything. If you can't find toasted walnut oil and you have to substitute, use a flavored extra virgin olive oil. These are lots of different kinds on the market—a lemon- or orange-flavored oil would work great.

PAULINE'S WILD RICE SALAD

MAKES 4–6 SERVINGS

I had this salad at a big family gathering and just had to have the recipe, which Pauline Bahnsen kindly shared with me. She says it's quite versatile, and she has made substitutions and additions over the years (you can substitute dried cranberries for the raisins or use whatever kind of rice you want). It's a great party salad because it keeps well when made the day before. If you're cooking it for a big party, you can easily multiply the ingredients to suit the size of the crowd you're serving.

SALAD

2¼ cups [550 mL] water

¼ tsp [1 mL] kosher salt

¾ cup [175 mL] brown basmati rice or brown rice

½ cup [125 mL] wild rice (or substitute with other kinds of rice to increase the variety of textures and tastes)

one 8 oz [227 mL] can water chestnuts, drained and sliced

1 green bell pepper, diced

1 red bell pepper, diced

2 stalks celery, diced

½ cup [125 mL] raisins

½ cup [125 mL] diced red onion

½ cup [125 mL] chopped toasted almonds

¼ cup [50 mL] chopped fresh parsley

DRESSING

⅓ cup [75 mL] orange or grapefruit juice

2 Tbsp [25 mL] fresh lemon juice

2 Tbsp [25 mL] tamari or soy sauce

1 Tbsp [15 mL] vegetable oil

1 Tbsp [15 mL] finely chopped or grated lemon zest

1 Tbsp [15 mL] dry sherry vinegar or rice vinegar

1 large clove garlic, minced

¼ tsp [1 mL] kosher salt

Bring the water to a boil in a large saucepan. Add the salt and the brown and wild rice; reduce the heat, cover the pot, and simmer the rice until it's tender and no liquid remains (about 45 minutes, depending on the rice mixture used). Transfer the rice to a large bowl. Add the water chestnuts, bell peppers, celery, raisins, onion, almonds, and parsley, tossing the ingredients together to combine.

Whisk the dressing ingredients together in a small bowl. Pour the dressing over the salad and toss it. This salad can be made ahead and refrigerated for up to 24 hours.

POTATO SALAD ADOBO

MAKES 6–8 SERVINGS

➤ BARBECUE SECRET ≈

Roasting red bell peppers on the grill brings out incredible flavor and gives the flesh of the pepper a silky, meaty texture. Buy the biggest, firmest, heaviest peppers you can get. Prepare your grill for direct high cooking. Place the whole peppers on the grill and roast them, turning every few minutes, until the skin is blistered and blackened on all sides. Take the peppers off the grill and place them in a bowl or heavy-duty freezer bag, and cover or seal them. By the time they're cool enough to handle, the skins should be nice and loose—peel the peppers with your hands and discard the skins. Tear the peppers open and remove the stems and seeds, but be sure not to lose any of the precious juices, which contain a lot of flavor. At this point you can tear the flesh into big strips and use them immediately as a burger or sandwich topping or part of a tossed salad, or store them in the fridge or freezer for later use but not before drizzling them with olive oil and adding a few fresh basil leaves. Roasted peppers are also great in soups and sauces.

This Southwestern take on potato salad is a perfect side dish for whatever you're cookin' and makes a great potluck contribution to someone else's barbecue.

2 lb [1 kg] small red potatoes
2 Tbsp [25 mL] olive oil
1 medium onion, finely minced
½ cup [125 mL] cider vinegar
2 Tbsp [25 mL] sugar
2 canned chipotle chilies in adobo sauce, seeded and finely chopped
1 cup [250 mL] mayonnaise
1 tsp [5 mL] toasted sesame oil

2 green onions, chopped
2 Tbsp [25 mL] chopped fresh cilantro
1 roasted red bell pepper (see sidebar), roughly chopped
kosher salt and freshly ground black pepper
½ cup [125 mL] toasted pecans, roughly chopped
fresh cilantro sprigs for garnish

Boil the potatoes in a large pot of lightly salted water until they're just tender. Drain them and set them aside.

Heat the olive oil and cook the onions in a heavy skillet over medium heat until they're soft but not brown, about 6 minutes. Add the vinegar and sugar to the skillet, stir the onions to dissolve the sugar, and remove the skillet from the heat.

Combine the chipotles, mayonnaise, and sesame oil in a food processor and blend the mixture until it's smooth. Cut the still-warm potatoes into halves or quarters and add them to the vinegar/onion mixture, tossing so the potatoes absorb the vinegar. Add the flavored mayonnaise, green onions, cilantro, and roasted bell pepper, tossing to coat everything. Season the salad with salt and pepper, toss it one last time, transfer it to a serving bowl, and top it with the toasted pecans and cilantro sprigs.

ASIAN NOODLE SALAD
WITH SESAME MAYONNAISE

MAKES 4 SERVINGS

This is a great summer salad that goes well with grilled chicken or any Asian-flavored grilled or barbecued meat. I like to use rice spaghetti noodles (as opposed to Asian rice vermicelli, which doesn't have the same chewiness). You can find rice spaghetti noodles in health food stores, but plain old durum wheat spaghetti also works well.

SESAME MAYO DRESSING

1 cup [250 mL] mayonnaise

1 Tbsp [15 mL] lemon, lime, or orange zest

1 tsp [5 mL] toasted sesame oil

1 tsp [5 mL] Chinese chili sauce or spicy Szechuan chili oil (or to taste)

½ tsp [2 mL] soy sauce (or to taste)

SALAD

one 1 lb [500 g] package rice or wheat spaghetti noodles

2 Tbsp [25 mL] chopped fresh cilantro

2 Tbsp [25 mL] toasted sesame seeds

2 limes, cut into wedges

Combine the dressing ingredients in a bowl. Cover the sesame mayonnaise and refrigerate it for at least a few hours or overnight.

Cook the noodles in a large pot of boiling salted water for 8 to 10 minutes, or until they're al dente. Drain the noodles and rinse them with cold water. Drain them again thoroughly. Toss the noodles with the sesame mayo, cilantro, and sesame seeds. Serve the salad garnished with lime wedges.

MIMI'S TABOULEH

This recipe from my friend Michelle Allaire uses instant couscous, which is moistened by all the juices that come out of the vegetables as they sit with the grain in the fridge. It is usually served as a side with lamb but can be an attractive alternative main course for a vegetarian guest. To "beef" it up, add blanched green beans, blanched carrots, and cooked chickpeas.

one 10 oz [300 g] package instant couscous

1 cup [250 mL] good-quality extra virgin olive oil

1 cup [250 mL] fresh tomato, cut into ¼-inch [6 mm] dice

½ red or green bell pepper, cut into ¼-inch [6 mm] dice

1 cup [250 mL] long English cucumber, cut into ¼-inch [6 mm] dice

1 cup [250 mL] chopped fresh parsley

½ cup [125 mL] red onion, cut into ¼-inch [6 mm] dice

¼ cup [50 mL] fresh lemon juice

4 green onions, thinly sliced

1 Tbsp [15 mL] finely chopped fresh mint

1 Tbsp [15 mL] ground cumin

1 tsp [5 mL] kosher salt

½ tsp [2 mL] freshly ground black pepper

Pour the entire package of uncooked couscous into a large bowl. Add the remaining ingredients, mix them together well, and let the tabouleh sit in the fridge for at least 4 hours. Remove it from the fridge at least 1 hour before serving. Mix it again, taste it, and adjust the seasoning and oil to taste.

BEAN & CORN SALAD
WITH MAPLE SYRUP-BALSAMIC
VINAIGRETTE & JALAPEÑO

MAKES 8 SERVINGS

This sweet, fresh, tangy, spicy bean salad has wonderfully bright flavors and contrasting textures. It goes extremely well with barbecue or roast beef. Leave the bacon out if you want a nice vegetarian side.

6 slices maple-flavored bacon

3 cans mixed cooked beans (an assortment of types in 1 can, or cans of 3 different types, like pinto, red kidney, and black), drained and rinsed

6 fresh cobs of corn, shucked

2 red bell peppers

VINAIGRETTE
5 Tbsp [75 mL] balsamic vinegar

1 tsp [5 mL] Dijon mustard

1 shallot, peeled and chopped

3 Tbsp [45 mL] maple syrup

1 jalapeño, seeded and chopped

1 cup [250 mL] extra virgin olive oil

kosher salt and freshly ground black pepper to taste

fresh lime juice to taste (optional)

fresh cilantro, chopped

Over medium heat, fry the bacon strips in a sauté pan until they are crisp. Drain the bacon on paper towels. Coarsely chop it and set it aside.

Rinse and drain the beans and put them in a large bowl.

Prepare the grill for direct high heat. Roast the corn cobs and bell peppers on the hot grill, turning them frequently, until the corn is slightly charred and the peppers are completely blackened and blistered (the peppers will take longer to roast than the corn). Remove the vegetables from the grill when they're ready and let them rest until they're cool enough to handle, placing the red peppers in a covered nonreactive bowl. Slice the kernels off the corn cobs with a large, sharp knife on a cutting board. Peel the charred skin from the peppers, discard the cores and stems, and dice the flesh. Add the corn and diced peppers to the beans.

Make the vinaigrette by mixing the first 5 ingredients together, then slowly whisking in the oil. Season the vinaigrette with salt and pepper. Add lime juice if desired.

Pour the vinaigrette over the beans, corn, and red peppers and let the salad sit, covered, in the refrigerator for a few hours. Adjust the seasonings. Add the bacon and cilantro, toss, heap into a salad bowl, and serve.

Get Your Fresh On: Salads

121

ENOTECA SMOKED DUCK SALAD

MAKES 8 APPETIZER SERVINGS OR 4 MAIN COURSE SERVINGS

My wife, Kate, found this recipe many years ago in a 1990s collection of recipes from American bistros. Seattle's Enoteca does not exist any more, but as long as I barbecue, I will have this recipe in my repertoire. I like to keep a few smoked duck halves in the freezer in case we have dinner guests we want to blow away. The original recipe calls for fresh papaya, which is excellent, but I like slightly tangier mango as the fruit component.

DRESSING

⅔ cup [160 mL] red wine vinegar

½ cup [125 mL] soy sauce

½ cup [125 mL] sugar

¼ cup [50 mL] vegetable oil

¼ cup [50 mL] rice wine vinegar

¼ cup [50 mL] raspberry vinegar

1 Tbsp [15 mL] fresh lime juice

SALAD

1 lb [500 g] smoked duck or smoked chicken (see the section starting on page 22 and the chart on page 31)

2 whole fresh mangoes

2 bags fresh baby spinach, washed and dried well

½ small purple onion, diced

freshly ground black pepper

1 lime

1 cup [250 mL] toasted walnuts or pecans, coarsely chopped

1 lime, quartered, for garnish

To prepare the dressing, bring the vinegar, soy sauce, sugar, and oil to a boil in a medium saucepan over medium heat. Cook the mixture until the sugar is dissolved. Add the remaining ingredients and let the dressing cool. This makes enough dressing for 4 salads, but it keeps for at least a few weeks in the refrigerator.

Cut the smoked duck into bite-sized pieces. (If you are using duck that is frozen, thaw it first, heat it up in a 350°F/180°C oven, then let it rest until it's cool enough to handle.) Peel the mangoes and slice the flesh off the pits; reserve a few slices for garnish. Place the spinach, duck, mango, and onion in a salad bowl. Grind the pepper over the mixture and squeeze the juice of the lime over it. Add the nuts and just enough dressing to coat and toss. (Too much dressing drowns out the other salad fixings.) Garnish the salad with the lime quarters and the reserved mango slices.

GRILLED SCALLOP & CUCUMBER SALAD

MAKES 6 SERVINGS

This recipe is a little fancier than most of the others in this book, but it's so good I have to share it with you. It comes from Jenni Neidhart, a Calgary caterer I've had the pleasure of working with.

4 Lebanese cucumbers (or 1 small long English cucumber), finely diced (leave the skin on)

1 red bell pepper, seeded and finely diced

1 yellow bell pepper, seeded and finely diced

½ red onion, finely diced

juice and zest of 1 orange

juice and zest of 1 lemon

juice and zest of 1 lime

1 jalapeño, seeds removed and finely diced

extra virgin olive oil

champagne vinegar*

kosher salt and freshly ground black pepper

¼ cup [50 mL] finely chopped fresh mint

12 large scallops

sesame sea salt (optional; make it by combining sea salt and toasted sesame seeds in a mortar with a pestle or in a food processor)

*For extra flavor Jenni infuses her champagne vinegar, which is available in gourmet food stores, with leftover vanilla pods.

Combine the cucumber, bell peppers, and onion in a medium-sized bowl. Make a vinaigrette by mixing the juices and zests of all the citrus, the jalapeño, a splash each of olive oil and vinegar, and the salt and pepper. Toss the vinaigrette with the diced vegetables and mix in the mint. Easy as that! Chill it until serving time.

Preheat the grill on medium-high for 5 to 10 minutes, or until the chamber temperature rises above 500°F (260°C). Season the scallops with a little kosher salt, drizzle them with olive oil, and place them on the grill, keeping the heat on medium-high. Cover the grill and cook the scallops for 1 or 2 minutes, then turn them and cook them for another couple of minutes, until they're springy to the touch.

Serve the scallops hot over the chilled cucumber salad and finish the dish with a few drops of olive oil and a light sprinkle of sesame sea salt, if desired.

WATERMELON SALAD

MAKES 4 SERVINGS

This lovely summer salad, created by my friend Michelle Allaire, is as refreshing as it sounds.

½ watermelon, rind removed and flesh cut into 1-inch [2.5 cm] chunks
½ lb [250 g] feta cheese, cut into small chunks

2 Tbsp [25 mL] fresh lemon juice
3 Tbsp [45 mL] extra virgin olive oil
freshly ground black pepper

Place the watermelon chunks in a salad bowl. Add the feta cheese. In a separate bowl, mix together the lemon juice, olive oil, and a grinding of black pepper. Add the dressing to the salad at the last minute, just before serving.

KICKIN' CRAB SALAD

MAKES 4–6 SERVINGS

Just read this recipe, invented by my friend Diane Read, and tell me if your mouth doesn't start watering. This tangy, spicy, colorful salad is just the thing to get your guests' appetites going, or a great main dish for a summer lunch. Serve it with a crisp, dry, fruity white wine.

1 lb [500 g] Dungeness or snow crab meat (make sure there are a few whole claw pieces in the mix to make the salad look pretty)

2 Tbsp [25 mL] finely chopped red bell pepper

2 Tbsp [25 mL] finely chopped long English cucumber

2 Tbsp [25 mL] chopped green onion

½ small lemon

½ cup [125 mL] regular or light mayonnaise

2 tsp [10 mL] wasabi paste (or to taste)

¼ tsp [1 mL] crushed dried red chili flakes

1 head butter lettuce, separated into individual whole leaves

lemon wedges or slices for garnish

Place the crab in a large bowl. Carefully fold in the red pepper, cucumber, and green onion, and squeeze the lemon juice over the mixture. In a separate bowl, combine the mayonnaise, wasabi paste, and chilies, and fold the dressing into the crab mixture.

Wash and dry the butter lettuce and either line a platter with small leaves to serve the salad in appetizer-sized portions, or place large leaves on individual plates. Use an ice cream scoop or a tablespoon to place the crab mixture on the lettuce leaves. Garnish the salad with lemon wedges.

All the Fixin's: Veggies, Potatoes, Beans, Rice, & More

I'm not going to get fancy here. When you are entertaining using your grill or barbecue, the meat is the center of attention, and what you want are things that complement it, like beans, rice, potatoes, grilled vegetables, cornbread, and corn on the cob.

The side dishes may not be the main attraction, but I'm not saying you shouldn't take care to make the best accompaniments possible. As important as the meat is, the delicious forkful of mashed potatoes, or spoonful of tasty rice and beans, or perfectly cooked bite of grilled asparagus, or the salty, buttery bite of grilled corn on the cob are integral components of the perfect meal (Texans, for example, will tend a simple pot of red beans all afternoon just to make sure they have a perfect side dish to accompany the brisket that's been in the pit all night).

The great thing about perfect sides is that they're easy. They require not much more than putting some good-quality ingredients in a pot or throwing them on the grill, and cooking them until they are done.

So save the fancy stuff for indoor meals. Here are some superb variations on the classic accompaniments.

GRILLED ASPARAGUS

MAKES 6–8 APPETIZER SERVINGS OR 4 SIDES

The key here is to grill the asparagus very quickly over high heat, so it chars on the outside but remains almost raw in the center. The flavor and texture of this easy dish can earn you more wows than far more complicated recipes. And it's good for you, too.

Try to choose very fresh asparagus that's relatively thick; pencil-thin spears don't stand up to grilling.

1 bunch (about 20 spears) fresh asparagus	kosher salt
extra virgin olive oil	½ lemon

Wash and trim the asparagus and pat it dry on a paper towel. Transfer it to a large bowl or dish. Preheat your grill on high until the chamber temperature rises above 500°F (260°C). Drizzle the olive oil on the asparagus and sprinkle it with kosher salt. Toss the spears with your hands to coat them evenly with the oil and salt.

Place the asparagus spears on the hot grill, taking care to put them across the cooking grates so they won't fall through. Close the grill and cook for just 1 or 2 minutes. Turn the spears with a set of tongs, close the grill, and cook them for another minute or two. The asparagus will turn an intense green and have nice little char marks.

Transfer the spears back to the bowl and immediately squeeze the lemon over them, tossing to coat them with juice. Serve the asparagus immediately as an appetizer or side dish, or cool it and add it to a vegetable platter. Grilled asparagus goes extremely well with doctored mayos (see pages 68–69).

SUPERCHARGED
GRILLED CORN ON THE COB

Roasted corn is excellent with plain soft butter and a sprinkling of a simple rub consisting of 1 part kosher salt and 1 part ancho chili powder.

➤ ≈

If you feel like fussing a little, you can bend the husk back to one end of each corncob and tie the leaves together with a bit of twine. This will help you turn the corn on the grill and also give your guests a rustic handle to hold on to while they munch.

Almost nothing goes better with grilled or barbecued meat than good old corn on the cob, and it's so easy on the grill. It's also easy to do a little bit more to give it an extra jolt of buttery flavor.

1 unshucked ear of corn per guest	herbed butter or butters (see page 67)
	kosher salt

Soak the whole, unshucked corn in cold water for an hour. Prepare your grill for direct high heat. Remove the corn from the water and place it on the grill. Cook it for about half an hour, turning it regularly. Don't worry if the husks turn brown or black—the corn inside will be protected. Remove the corn from the grill, let it cool enough that you can handle it, remove the husks, and serve the corn with herbed butter and kosher salt. (If you want a more rustic, charred look and flavor, husk the corn cobs before cooking them, then grill them naked for 10 to 15 minutes, watching to make sure they char but don't burn.)

FLORIDA-STYLE GRILLED ZUCCHINI

MAKES 4 SERVINGS

Why Florida? In 1990 there was a feature in *Gourmet* magazine about cooking dinner in Florida. Must have been about low-cal eating for the diet-conscious retiree. That's all I remember, except for this incredibly simple and delicious grilled zucchini. I made it to accompany roast turkey on Thanksgiving that year. My wife had toiled for days on the dinner and had cooked an elaborate and complicated turkey recipe. When the meal was served, it was the zucchini that got the raves. (Not me. Right, honey?)

1 large clove garlic, minced and
    mashed to a paste with ½ tsp
    [2 mL] kosher salt
2 Tbsp [25 mL] fresh lemon juice
1 tsp [5 mL] white wine vinegar

¼ cup [50 mL] vegetable oil
freshly ground black pepper
2 zucchini, each about 1½ inches
    [4 cm] in diameter

Whisk together the garlic paste, lemon juice, vinegar, oil, and pepper. Pour the mixture into a large baking dish. Halve the zucchini lengthwise and toss the pieces in the marinade, making sure they're well coated. Cover and refrigerate the zucchini overnight, turning it several times.

    Prepare your grill for medium heat. Grill the zucchini for 4 to 5 minutes, cut side down. Turn them, brush them with some marinade, and grill the other side for 4 to 5 more minutes, or until they're just tender. Transfer the zucchini to a cutting board, slice them diagonally, and serve. This is a perfect dish to make while a large cut of meat is off the grill and resting.

RATATOUILLE

The rich meatiness of barbecue is nicely offset by this classic European accompaniment. This recipe comes from my Franco-Canadian friend, Michelle Allaire. It's best with lamb or pork.

1 eggplant, peel on, cut into 1-inch [2.5 cm] cubes

1 tsp [5 mL] kosher salt

2 Tbsp [25 mL] extra virgin olive oil, divided

4 cloves garlic, coarsely chopped

1 large onion (white or red), coarsely chopped

1 red or green bell pepper, cut into 1-inch [2.5 cm] dice

2 medium zucchini, cut into 1-inch [2.5 cm] cubes

2 ripe plum tomatoes, coarsely chopped

kosher salt and freshly ground black pepper to taste

1 Tbsp [15 mL] fresh thyme or 1 tsp [5 mL] dried thyme

1 Tbsp [15 mL] fresh rosemary or 1 tsp [5 mL] dried rosemary

Put the eggplant cubes in a colander and sprinkle them with the 1 tsp (5 mL) of salt. Mix them together well and set the colander over a bowl or in the sink for at least 2 hours. (Water will be drawn out of the eggplant, making it easier to cook without soaking up a lot of oil.) Rinse the eggplant in cold water and pat it dry.

Place 1 Tbsp (15 mL) of the olive oil in a large skillet. Add the chopped garlic to the cold oil and turn the heat to medium, warming the pan slowly so the oil absorbs the flavor gradually. Add the onion and bell pepper and sauté them until they're soft and shiny. Add the eggplant and the remaining 1 Tbsp (15 mL) of oil. Sauté the eggplant for a few minutes and then add the zucchini. Cook the vegetables for at least 8 more minutes, until they are all soft. Remove them from the heat and transfer them to a heavy pot. Place the pot over medium heat and add the tomatoes. Season the mixture with salt and pepper and add the herbs. Bring it to a boil, then turn the heat to low. Simmer the ratatouille uncovered for at least 1 hour, stirring it frequently to allow the juices to reduce slightly. Serve it hot or cold.

DILLED SMASHED POTATOES

Fresh dill and nutmeg enhance the sweetness of the butter and potatoes in this classic dish. This is true comfort food that goes well with any kind of grilled meat or fish. If you are a garlic lover, squeeze in a few cloves of roasted garlic or sprinkle in some granulated garlic before mashing.

2 lb [1 kg] red nugget potatoes
½ cup [125 mL] butter, at room
   temperature
1 tsp [5 mL] granulated onion
¼ tsp [1 mL] freshly grated nutmeg

2 Tbsp [25 mL] chopped fresh dill
pinch cayenne
roasted garlic (optional, see page 68)
kosher salt and freshly ground black
   pepper to taste

Trim any blemishes from the potatoes, leaving the skins on, and cut them in halves or quarters so you have 2-inch (5 cm) chunks. Place the potatoes in a large pot of cold water and bring them to a boil over high heat. Reduce the heat to medium and boil the potatoes for 10 to 15 minutes, or until a fork goes easily through a chunk of potato. Drain the potatoes and return them to the pot, reducing the heat to low. Add the butter, granulated onion, nutmeg, dill, cayenne, and roasted garlic, if you like. Mash the potatoes just until they are half-mashed. Season them with salt and pepper and serve them immediately.

PLANK-BAKED STUFFED POTATOES

MAKES 5 SERVINGS

These potatoes are baked in the oven and finished on a plank, which adds an extra dimension of smoky flavor that's brought out further if you use smoked Gouda instead of cheddar. (My kids thought the smoked Gouda version was too smoky, but I loved it.)

1 hardwood plank (alder, maple, or oak works best here), soaked overnight or at least 1 hour

3 baking potatoes

1 Tbsp [15 mL] kosher salt (or even coarser salt like Maldon or fleur de sel)

½ medium onion, chopped

2 cloves garlic, minced

¼ cup [50 mL] butter, divided

¼ cup [50 mL] whipping cream

½ tsp [2 mL] freshly grated nutmeg

1 cup [250 mL] grated cheddar cheese or smoked Gouda

½ cup [125 mL] grated Parmesan cheese

1 Tbsp [15 mL] extra virgin olive oil

paprika

sour cream

chopped chives

Preheat the oven to 400°F (200°C). Wash and scrub the potatoes under cold water and puncture the skin in a few places with a fork. While the potatoes are still damp, coat them generously with the salt, reserving about 1 tsp (5 mL) for seasoning the filling later. Bake the potatoes for about 1 hour.

Gently sauté the onion and garlic in 2 Tbsp (25 mL) of the butter in a saucepan over medium heat until they're tender and translucent, about 5 minutes.

When the potatoes are cool enough to handle, cut them lengthwise. Let them cool a few minutes until you can handle them. Trying not to break the skins, scoop out the pulp, leaving about ¼ inch (6 mm) of potato flesh on the skin. Discard or eat the skin that's in the worst shape. (Only 5 potatoes will fit on the average cooking plank, so the sixth potato half will just add volume to the filling.)

Combine the potato pulp, sautéed vegetables, remaining butter, cream, nutmeg, and reserved 1 tsp (5 mL) of salt in a medium bowl. Mash

(continued)

Plank-Baked Stuffed Potatoes *(continued)*

everything together until it's smooth. Add the cheddar or Gouda and mix the potatoes with a wooden spoon until the cheese is barely combined with the mash. Add extra milk or cream if the mixture seems too dry. Spoon the filling into the potatoes, top them with the grated Parmesan, and gently shape them with your hands if they've drooped a bit. Drizzle each potato with a little olive oil and sprinkle a pinch of paprika on top.

Preheat the grill on medium-high for 5 to 10 minutes, or until the chamber temperature rises above 500°F (260°C). Rinse the soaked plank and place it on the cooking grate. Cover the grill and heat the plank for 4 to 5 minutes, or until it starts to throw off a bit of smoke and crackles lightly. Reduce the heat to medium-low. Arrange the potatoes on the plank and cook them for 10 to 15 minutes, or until the cheese is nicely browned and blistered. Serve the potatoes with the sour cream and chopped chives.

WASABI MASHED POTATOES

MAKES 6–8 SERVINGS

You don't always have to serve rice with Asian dishes. This mashed potato recipe is easy to make and packs an unexpected punch. You can get wasabi paste at Asian specialty stores.

3 lb [1.5 kg] yellow-fleshed potatoes
¾ cup [175 mL] cream or whole milk
1 Tbsp [15 mL] wasabi paste
¼ cup [50 mL] butter, at room
   temperature

kosher salt and freshly ground
   black pepper

Peel the potatoes and cut them into quarters. Place them in a large pot and fill it with cold water to cover them. Bring the water to a boil over high heat and then reduce the heat to medium for 15 to 20 minutes, or until a fork goes easily through a chunk of potato. Drain the potatoes, reserving ½ cup (125 mL) or so of the water, and return them to the pot. Mash them until they're smooth. Combine the cream or milk and wasabi in a small bowl and mix them together until they're smooth. Add the wasabi mixture and butter to the potatoes and mash them thoroughly, adding some reserved potato liquid if necessary, until they're creamy smooth. Season the potatoes with salt and pepper and serve them hot.

MINTY POTATO HOBO PACK

MAKES 4–6 SERVINGS

➤ BARBECUE SECRET ≈

It's easy to burn the bottom of a hobo pack, but it's hard to screw up using this basic technique. Make sure to use heavy-duty foil and double it. Coat the foil with oil or butter, then put whatever ingredient will take the most direct heat, like bacon or onions, first. Then lay on the rest of your ingredients in order of vulnerability and cooking time—potatoes next, then bell pepper, and so on, with any fresh herbs on top. Finish the package with a couple of dabs of butter or a drizzle of oil, seal it tightly, and place it on direct medium heat. If the bottom layer of onions and/or bacon get charred, they'll add to the flavor. To avoid the risk of burning altogether, cook hobo packs using indirect high heat.

Why, oh why, do we ignore the glories of fresh mint in North American home cooking? It's delicious and refreshing, and its aroma is like nothing else. This dish is insanely simple to make, and the combination of mint and potatoes will wow your guests. Because this recipe calls for indirect heat, you can use the hot side of the grill to cook your steaks and grill your veggies.

6 medium Yukon Gold potatoes	extra virgin olive oil for drizzling
2 tsp [10 mL] dried mint	2 Tbsp [25 mL] finely chopped
1 large yellow onion	fresh mint leaves
¼ lb [125 g] butter, at room	kosher salt
temperature	

Take 6 feet (1.8 m) of wide, heavy-duty aluminum foil and fold it in half. Place the foil on a counter and coat it with about one-quarter of the butter, leaving about a 4-inch (10 cm) margin all the way around the rectangle.

Peel the onion and slice it into ¼-inch (6 mm) rounds. Split the rounds into rings, and spread the rings to cover the buttered area of the foil. Cut the potatoes into ½-inch (1 cm) slices, leaving the skins on, and layer them on top of the onions, sprinkling a little dried mint and salt on each layer. Top the potatoes with a few dabs of the butter, reserving half of it for finishing the dish.

Gather up the foil around the edges and close up the hobo pack, making it into a loaflike cylinder. Make sure you have a tight seal all the way around.

Prepare your grill for indirect medium-high heat. Place the hobo pack on the grill (away from direct heat), and cook for 15 to 20 minutes.

Let the hobo pack rest at least 5 minutes. Place it on a heatproof platter, open the foil, and sprinkle with the mint and dab with butter. Gently toss and serve.

MAPLE BUTTERNUT SQUASH PURÉE

MAKES 8–10 SERVINGS

This squash dish, based on a recipe in Diane Rossen Worthington's great cookbook *American Bistro*, goes with just about any meat. It can even be made early in the day if you've got an ambitious dinner on the go, like at Thanksgiving. Reheat it gently in the microwave. I recommend organic carrots because they usually have so much more flavor.

2 butternut squashes, peeled, seeded, and cut into 1-inch [2.5 cm] slices (about 3 lb/1.5 kg of flesh in total)
6 carrots, peeled
1 tsp [5 mL] ground ginger (or to taste)
1 tsp [5 mL] maple syrup

3 Tbsp [45 mL] butter
2 Tbsp [25 mL] olive oil
kosher salt and freshly ground black pepper
1 Tbsp [15 mL] finely chopped fresh parsley for garnish

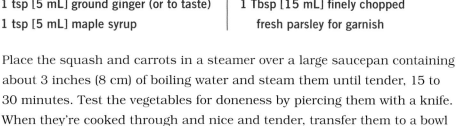

Place the squash and carrots in a steamer over a large saucepan containing about 3 inches (8 cm) of boiling water and steam them until tender, 15 to 30 minutes. Test the vegetables for doneness by piercing them with a knife. When they're cooked through and nice and tender, transfer them to a bowl to cool.

Combine the steamed vegetables with all the ingredients except the parsley in a food processor. Process the mixture using the metal blade until the mixture is smoothly puréed, scraping down the sides of the bowl as required and adding a little hot water, if necessary. Taste the purée for seasoning. Sprinkle it with parsley and serve it hot.

CORN MUFFINS WITH ROASTED PECANS

MAKES 12 MUFFINS

The rich, mild nuttiness of toasted pecans and the chewy texture of the roasted corn kernels make these slightly sweet corn muffins, based on a recipe by Southwestern food guru Mark Miller, the perfect side. Try them with barbecued meat, chili, or scrambled eggs . . . and don't skimp on the butter!

vegetable cooking spray

¾ cup [175 mL] pecans

⅔ cup [160 mL] fresh or thawed
    frozen corn kernels

1½ cups [375 mL] unbleached
    all-purpose flour

1½ cups [375 mL] cornmeal

⅓ cup [75 mL] sugar

1 Tbsp [15 mL] baking powder

¾ tsp [3 mL] kosher salt

3 large eggs, separated

1½ cups [375 mL] milk

⅓ cup [75 mL] honey

¼ cup + 2 Tbsp [75 mL] unsalted
    butter, melted

2 Tbsp [25 mL] chopped fresh
    thyme (optional)

Preheat the oven to 375°F (190°C). Grease a 12-cup muffin pan with the cooking spray. Toast the pecans on a baking sheet until they're golden brown, about 3 or 4 minutes. Transfer them to a plate and let them cool. Cook the corn in a skillet over low heat, stirring it often, until it's browned and slightly dry, 6 to 8 minutes. Transfer it to a plate to cool. (Alternative method: Roast the corn on the cob over direct heat to char the kernels and then cut them off the cob.)

Mix together the flour, cornmeal, sugar, baking powder, and salt in a large bowl. Beat the egg whites in another bowl until they're stiff but not dry. In another bowl, combine the egg yolks, milk, honey, and melted butter and mix them together thoroughly.

Make a well in the middle of the dry ingredients and pour in the milk mixture, along with the pecans and corn; stir the batter just enough to combine. Fold in the beaten egg whites and thyme. Spoon the batter into the prepared pan and bake for 20 to 25 minutes, until a toothpick or knife blade comes out clean. Let the muffins cool for a few minutes in the pan, then turn them onto a cooling rack.

TEXAN RED BEANS

MAKES ABOUT 10 SERVINGS

This is how my Texan friend Amy Walker's mom makes beans. It's a simple recipe but requires some tending, so it's best made on an afternoon when you have other tasks in the kitchen or the backyard. This is definitely worth the effort!

3 cups [750 mL] dried pinto beans	½ lb [250 g] chunk salt pork, cut in 2 pieces

Soak the beans in water in a large, nonreactive bowl overnight, or at least 5 hours. Drain and rinse the beans, discarding the old water. Place the beans in a large pot, add water to cover them, and bring them to a boil. Turn the heat down to low and simmer the beans for about 2 hours, or until they're tender. Stir the beans occasionally to keep them from sticking to the bottom of the pot, and add boiling water as necessary as the beans soak up the water. (Tip: Keep a kettle of warm water on the stove, so when you need to add water, the beans will keep boiling.)

During the second hour, test for tenderness by squashing some of the beans against the side of the pot with your stirring spoon. Keep the squashed ones in the pot to help make good, soupy beans. Also, taste them once in a while to see if they are soft. During the second hour, add the salt pork. (Be sure not to add it too soon, or the beans will be tough.) In the final 15 minutes, squash some more beans against the side of the pot to thicken the juice. Add a little cayenne, if you like.

> ❧ **BARBECUE SECRET** ❧

Smoke your beans! Your favorite bean recipe will take on a whole new dimension if you pop the open pot of beans into the smoker for about an hour over hickory wood (or whatever wood is going). This works especially well when doing ribs. While the ribs are wrapped in foil and finishing on the bottom rack, the beans can be smoking on the top rack.

All the Fixin's: Veggies, Potatoes, Beans, Rice, & More

141

CLASSIC BAKED BEANS FOR A CROWD

MAKES 14 SERVINGS

This classic bean recipe, by friend and caterer Margie Gibb, is a perfect accompaniment to barbecued brisket or ribs, or just about anything else, for that matter!

two 14 oz [398 mL] cans each of red, white, and black beans
1 lb [500 g] double-smoked bacon, cut into large dice
2 large onions, cut into ¼-inch [6 mm] dice
4 cloves garlic, minced
1 Tbsp [15 mL] chili powder
1 tsp [5 mL] freshly ground cumin

2 tsp [10 mL] finely chopped canned chipotle chilies in adobo sauce
1¼ cups [300 mL] packed dark brown sugar
3 Tbsp [45 mL] mild-flavored molasses
one 12 oz [355 mL] bottle dark beer
kosher salt and freshly ground black pepper to taste

Rinse and drain the beans, place them in a large Dutch oven or flameproof pot, and set them aside.

Cook the bacon in a heavy skillet until crisp. Remove the bacon, place it on a paper towel, and set it aside.

Pour off all but 3 Tbsp (45 mL) of the rendered bacon fat. Add the onions and cook them over low to medium heat, stirring, until they are soft but not brown, about 10 minutes. (If you are short of bacon fat, add olive oil as necessary.)

Add the garlic, chili powder, cumin, and chipotles to the onion mixture; cook a further 5 minutes, until the flavors are well blended. Add the onion mixture, sugar, molasses, and beer to the beans and bring them to a boil.

Reduce the heat to medium and cook the beans, covered, stirring occasionally, for about 1 hour. Stir in the bacon and season the beans with salt and pepper. Serve them hot.

This dish improves if prepared 1 day in advance. Refrigerate the beans overnight and then gently reheat them.

JAMAICAN-STYLE RICE & BEANS

MAKES 6–8 SERVINGS

In Jamaica, this dish is a staple. Jamaicans call it rice and peas, but it often features red kidney beans so I've renamed it to avoid confusion. The creamy, sweet richness of the coconut milk helps make this dish a perfect complement to jerk chicken or any spicy grilled meat.

2 thick slices double-smoked bacon, chopped

two 14 oz [398 mL] cans red kidney beans, drained and rinsed

one 14 oz [398 mL] can unsweetened coconut milk

1 green onion, chopped

2 sprigs fresh thyme

1 habanero chili (whole—do not chop!)

2 cups [500 mL] boiling water

2 cups [500 mL] long-grain white rice

kosher salt and freshly ground black pepper

Sauté the chopped bacon in a sauté pan until it's starting to brown, but not yet crispy. Drain off the excess fat.

Combine the beans, coconut milk, bacon, green onion, thyme, and habanero in a large saucepan. Cook the mixture over medium-high heat just until it comes to a simmer. Add the boiling water and stir in the rice. Cover the saucepan tightly, reduce the heat to low, and cook the rice without disturbing it for about 25 minutes, until the liquid has been absorbed and the grains are tender. Fluff the rice before serving and don't forget to remove the habanero so it doesn't surprise anyone!

CONFETTI RICE

This colorful dish is comfort food at its finest. How can you beat the combination of rice and butter? The diced bell pepper and cilantro give it a festive look and wonderful aroma. The use of cilantro stems—which are surprisingly tender and flavorful—make the dish especially delicious.

2 cups [500 mL] short-grain rice (sushi rice works best)
3 cups [750 mL] cold water
½ cup [125 mL] diced red bell pepper
2 Tbsp [25 mL] finely chopped fresh cilantro stems

2 Tbsp [25 mL] butter
coarsely chopped fresh cilantro leaves for garnish
extra butter, at room temperature, for slathering (optional)

Place the rice and water in a saucepan and bring the water to a boil over high heat. Just as the water is starting to boil, add the bell pepper, cilantro stems, and butter, stirring to incorporate them into the rice. When the mixture comes back up to a boil, cover the saucepan and turn the heat down to low. Cook the rice for 15 minutes (no peeking!). Transfer it to a serving bowl, gently fluff it with a pair of forks, and serve it garnished with chopped fresh cilantro leaves. If you're like me, slather on a little more butter.

DILLED LEMONY RICE

This sticky, fragrant rice is a great accompaniment to just about anything.

2 Tbsp [25 mL] butter

1 shallot, finely chopped

4 cups [1 L] homemade or canned
   low-salt chicken stock

2 cups [500 mL] short-grain rice

zest of 2 lemons, finely chopped

¼ cup [50 mL] chopped fresh baby dill

½ tsp [2 mL] kosher salt

¼ tsp [1 mL] black or white pepper

2 Tbsp [25 mL] fresh lemon juice

fresh dill fronds and lemon wedges
   for garnish

Heat half the butter in a sauté pan over medium-low heat. Add the shallot and cook it until it's soft, stirring frequently, about 2 minutes. Set it aside.

Bring the stock to a boil in a saucepan over high heat. Add the rice and return the stock to a boil. Just as the stock begins to boil, reduce the heat to low. Add the sautéed shallot, lemon zest, dill, salt, pepper, and the remaining butter. Gently stir the rice to evenly distribute all the ingredients. Cover the saucepan and cook the rice for 15 minutes. Add the lemon juice, gently fluff the rice with a fork, transfer it to a serving bowl, garnish it with dill and lemon, and serve.

GRILLED RICE CAKES

MAKES 3–5 SERVINGS

These traditional Japanese rice cakes are often found, stuffed with tuna or salmon, in Japanese takeout shops. They take on a wonderful crunchy, chewy texture when grilled, and they go well with any Asian-flavored grilled or barbecued meat. I learned how to make them from Vancouver chef Trevor Hooper's cookbook, *Asian Tapas and Wild Sushi*. You can get sushi rice at just about any supermarket these days. If you can't find it there, look for it at an Asian market or gourmet food store.

3 cups [750 mL] sushi rice
3¾ cups [925 mL] water
neutral-flavored oil, like peanut
    or canola

Complicated but Delicious Teriyaki
    Sauce (see page 60)

Place the rice and water in a medium pot and bring it to a boil over high heat. Boil the rice for 2 minutes, then cover it and reduce the heat to medium. Cook it for another 5 minutes, reduce the heat to low, and cook it for 15 more minutes. Do not remove the lid. Turn off the heat and let the covered pot stand for another 10 minutes.

Empty the rice into a bowl and let it stand for 5 minutes, or until it's cool enough to handle with your bare hands. Have a bowl of cold water handy so you can wet your hands before you form each rice cake.

Wet your hands and grab about ½ cup (125 mL) of the rice. Press it together firmly, cupping your hands to shape the rice into a triangular shape, about the size of a modest wedge of pie. Squeeze it tightly so it will stick together well when it's grilled. Once you have formed all the rice into about 10 neat wedges, the rice cakes can be covered and refrigerated for a day or two before grilling.

To cook the cakes, use a basting brush to paint each one with the oil. Grill them over direct high heat until they are crisp and golden brown, with nice char marks. Drizzle each rice cake with teriyaki sauce. Allow at least 2 per person.

Barbecue Secrets DELUXE!

THE BURGS OF ⋟SUMMER⋞

by Kate Zimmerman

My wife, Kate Zimmerman, writes a popular humor column in a local paper in which she often makes fun of me and my barbecue ways. Here's one of my favorites.

It's that time of the year again—the season when I need to remind myself that I'm sleeping with the best hamburger maker in Canada.

Every hooked-up female on the continent says the same thing, if she knows what's good for her. Men pride themselves on their burgers, whether they deserve to or not, and they like their beloveds to go along with the ruse. So if a gal can't bring herself to rave about her guy's way with a ground beef sandwich, she's certainly obliged to wax euphoric about her dad's.

Being able to slap a round of meat into a palatable patty is a crucial aspect of dudehood. Consequently, when a fellow cannot with a straight face boast that his homemade burger is *numero uno*, he might find it hard to live with himself.

The more spiteful sort of person may even force his family to make do with those premade frozen beef flip-flops beloved of supermarkets. It's like women and Christmas turkeys. Those who can't do order in from KFC.

Suffice it to say that my own champion has walked with a swagger since his triumph at a Whistler burger-grilling contest. Rockin' had always made a wicked Wimpy, but for the contest he decided to gild the lily. His prize-winning meat disc contained a core of herbed butter and featured lashings of roasted red peppers, caramelized onions, and goat cheese. The objective seemed to be that no judge would emerge from the sandwich without a waterfall of fat rushing down his chin. Mission accomplished.

My dad, too, made the claim of burger godhood back when he used to man the barbecue on summertime Saturday nights. As far as I know, his version consisted of ground chuck and garlic powder, but it always enabled him to fish shamelessly for compliments as he brandished his spatula like a scepter.

My uncle probably thought he was the ultimate burger-meister as well, although his creations were the size and diameter of a golf ball and were invariably blackened, completely raw in the middle, and distasteful in the extreme to the hungry children in the crowd.

Sacred cows make the best hamburger.
—Mark Twain

The hamburger phenomenon is odd. It doesn't matter how accomplished one is as a cook, keen carnivores—especially male ones—never tire of the limited challenge posed by sliding a saucer of cooked cow onto a bun.

A round of ground beef is essentially just a blank slate. Yet what red-blooded *hombre* boasts, "I toast a mean scone"? Burgers take little more effort than smearing warm butter on hot bread, but still, their flavors are made surprisingly various through seasonings, options like minced onion, and fillers—from eggs to breadcrumbs to cornflakes. That's why as summer approaches, men start dusting off their barbecues and polishing their tongs. I'd wager that ground-beef sales leap like the NBA's Steve Nash.

Sadly, the meat aspect of the burger—at least, the burger now served to the public—has undergone a drastic transformation for the worse over the past 23 years because of concern about the food-borne bacteria E. coli. In 1982, a particularly nasty strain of E. coli contaminated some McDonald's hamburgers in the US, sickening dozens of people. In 1993, there was another outbreak as a result of undercooked hamburgers at Jack-in-the-Box outlets, in which, according to the *L.A. Times*, more than 700 people became ill, 170 were hospitalized, and four died.

Since then, cooks in North America, both commercial and private, have been leery of serving any ground beef item that hasn't had the living hell cooked out of it.

Burger makers have diverged from their former cow-centrism. Now you'll find patties made of lamb, poultry, salmon, oyster, bison, ostrich, and even veggie blends of oats and nuts—the variations range from delectable to disgusting.

And toppings have also been torqued. This may not be evident at pedestrian fast-food outlets, but more ambitious restaurants and households have bumped them up way more than a notch over the past two decades. From the Kraft single, ketchup, mustard, relish, tomato, iceberg lettuce, onion, and dill pickle that used to constitute hamburger heaven, we've moved on to Gorgonzola, brie, and applewood-smoked cheddar, flavored mayos, designer lettuces, heirloom tomatoes, ciabatta buns, grainy mustards, and homemade ketchups.

I used to enjoy a beef burger at one restaurant that served 'em topped with peanut butter and bacon. The combination may sound like something that killed Elvis, but it was heavenly. Lately, we can even get our burgers capped with foie gras, compliments of high-end chefs continent-wide. Vancouver chef Rob Feenie used to serve one at his restaurant Feenie's; if extreme eating is your mantra, you might have found it worth the 25 dollars. One New York chef got his name in the papers for offering a 50-dollar version that contained short ribs and shaved truffles, and was served on a poppy-seed bun. Take that, Big Mac.

When we eat a burger, we are searching for the Holy Grail of comfort foods.

These embellishments are exciting, but they don't address the fact that when we eat a burger, we are searching for the Holy Grail of comfort foods. It needs to be like our dad's (or mom's, in the unlikely event that she took charge) in some indefinable way—but, if possible, better.

Unfortunately, what often eludes us in these days of low-fat, well-cooked beef is the thing that most appealed to us about the homemade hamburger in the first place—the contrast of crunchy, semiscorched exterior with moist, meaty—ideally, juicy—center.

There is one thing we can count on, however. Whether it's a beaming dad, husband, boyfriend, buddy, brother, or son who hands us our hamburger, he'll ask us with poorly concealed eagerness how we like it.

To that question, the answer must always be, "It's the best I've ever had."

The Burger Connection

The rest of this book is organized under categories relating to specific kinds of meat or seafood, but for backyard cooks, the burger is in a category all its own. Today the hamburger is ubiquitous. There's almost no menu without one, and the range of burgers available in restaurants ranges from the cheap and tasteless cardboard abominations of the fast-food chains to the outrageous $100-plus foie gras, truffle, and short rib–stuffed burgers of New York's trendiest kitchens.

Just as we have traced the origins of barbecue to European immigrants to America, we can follow the roots of the modern hamburger back to, well, Hamburg, Germany, where cheap cuts of beef were chopped, seasoned, and served cooked or raw to the lower classes. The "Hamburg Steak" first appeared on New York menus in the mid-1800s, and by the end of the 19th century it was served in restaurants as far away as Walla Walla in Washington state. It's a lot harder to determine exactly which American state's residents first had the idea to create a sandwich out of that chopped beefsteak to create the burger we know and love today—there are at least five different claims ranging from Wisconsin to Texas. What we do know is that the hamburger made a successful leap from the restaurant kitchen to the backyard grill.

While we may not know exactly who cooked the first burger, everyone knows who makes the best burgers in the world—your dad, of course! Up until now, that is. Armed with this short but powerful collection of burger recipes, I guarantee you will become a legend in your own mind—and maybe even in your entire neighborhood. Whether you cook the simplest Dadburger or the most exotic Oyster Burger, you'll find something here to sink your teeth into.

STEALTH BACON CHEESEBURGER

MAKES 4 LARGE BURGERS

This simple and delicious burger, invented by my friend and barbecue teammate Vince Gogolek, uses back bacon instead of the usual fried strips found on most commercial burgers. The stealth part is that both the bacon and cheese are put in the middle of the burger. The cheese melts into the beef, making it juicy and messy—"a good thing if you're forced by West Coast health freaks to use only extra-lean ground," says Vince.

BURGER PATTIES

2 lb [1 kg] extra-lean ground beef

1 Tbsp [15 mL] onion soup powder

¼ tsp [1 mL] cayenne

1 egg

¼ cup [50 mL] cold water

four ½-inch [1 cm] thick slices
    back bacon

thin slices of medium cheddar

Championship Barbecue Rub (optional,
    see page 50)

FIXIN'S

4 large kaiser buns

mustard

caramelized onions (see page 160)

roasted red peppers (see sidebar page
    118), peeled and torn into quarters

Line a baking sheet with waxed paper.

Combine the beef, soup powder, cayenne, egg, and water in a large bowl, mixing them together gently with your hands, and taking care not to overwork the meat. Wet your hands with cold water and shape the mixture into 8 thinnish patties, each at least 1 inch (2.5 cm) larger in diameter than the slices of back bacon. On 4 of the 8 patties, place some thinly sliced cheese, covering about the same area as the back bacon. Put a slice of back bacon on top of the cheese, and put more thinly sliced cheese on top of the back bacon.

Put another burger patty on top and seal the edges. Coat each patty with mustard and sprinkle it with barbecue rub, if desired.

Prepare the grill for direct medium heat. Grill the burgers for 12 to 15 minutes, flipping them once or twice. If cheese begins to leak through the burger, it's done. Place the burgers on the buns with the garnishes and enjoy.

NOTE: For a different taste, experiment with flavored cheeses, like jalapeño Jack or caraway havarti, instead of the cheddar.

The Burger Connection

151

CLASSIC DADBURGER DELUXE

MAKES 12–16 PATTIES, DEPENDING ON HOW BIG YOU LIKE THEM

This recipe will feed a crowd, or four teenagers. You can easily halve the recipe. If your kids are like mine and don't like bits of onion and garlic in their burgers, substitute 1 tsp (5 mL) each of granulated onion and granulated garlic for the fresh variety.

BURGER PATTIES

6 lb [2.7 kg] ground beef (or equal amounts of ground beef and ground pork)

1 medium onion, finely chopped

1 head roasted garlic (see page 68), cloves squeezed out and mashed with a fork

1 Tbsp [15 mL] toasted sesame oil

2 Tbsp [25 mL] dark soy sauce, Worcestershire sauce, or a combination

½ tsp [2 mL] freshly grated nutmeg

¼ tsp [1 mL] cayenne (or more, if you like more heat)

lots of freshly ground black pepper

2 eggs

½ cup [125 mL] cold water

FIXIN'S

barbecue sauce

12–16 cheese slices (optional)

12–16 hamburger buns

Line a baking sheet with waxed paper.

Gently combine the burger ingredients in a large bowl with your hands, taking care not to overwork the meat. Wet your hands in cold water before you form the mixture into chunks the size of tennis balls. Flatten them into patties, placing them on the baking sheet. Each patty will be about ½ lb (250 g) before cooking. Place the patties in the freezer for 1 hour to firm them up.

Preheat your grill for direct medium heat. Take the burgers out of the freezer and grill them for 6 minutes per side, or until they are springy to the touch, glazing them on both sides with barbecue sauce. Top each patty with a slice of cheese for the last couple of minutes of cooking. Serve the burgers on buns with your favorite condiments.

❧ A LIBRARY OF ❧ BURGER FIXIN'S

We're all so used to iceberg lettuce, ketchup, mayo, ballpark mustard, green relish, and sliced onion and tomato on our burgers that we hardly notice them anymore. Try these unusual burger toppings for a change and experiment with your own combinations.

- Thinly sliced button mushrooms sautéed with a smashed garlic clove in butter and olive oil
- Crunchy-style peanut butter, bacon, raw onion, and lettuce
- An egg fried in butter, over easy, with a leaf of iceberg lettuce and a slather of mayo
- Avocado slices, bacon, and salsa
- Caramelized onion (see page 160), roasted red pepper (see sidebar page 118), and goat cheese
- Tomato slices, thinly sliced red onion, and fresh arugula
- Black olive paste, mayo, and slices of hard-boiled egg
- Brie or Gorgonzola cheese

❧ BARBECUE SECRET ❧

Ground meat is best, and safest, when cooked on the same day it is ground. Get to know your butcher and ask for freshly ground chuck, which has the best flavor for burgers.

The Burger Connection

153

BEEF BURGER WITH CHILI BUTTER CORE
TOPPED WITH CHIPOTLE & ROASTED GARLIC MAYO & GUACAMOLE

MAKES 4 LARGE BURGERS

Disclaimer: This isn't a simple recipe and it involves quite a bit of prep work. The chili butter and mayo need to be made in advance, so a little planning is necessary. Stuffing a frozen disc of flavored butter into the burger patties takes a little practice, but the result will blow your guests away. Be sure not to turn the burgers until they've started to get firm, and keep an eye out for flare-ups.

CHILI BUTTER
½ lb [250 g] butter
1 head roasted garlic (see page 68)
2 canned chipotle chilies in
    adobo sauce
2 Tbsp [25 mL] ancho chili powder
½ tsp [2 mL] kosher salt

BURGER PATTIES
1½–2 lb [750 g–1 kg] lean ground beef
¼ cup [50 mL] cold water
½ tsp [2 mL] garlic salt
½ tsp [2 mL] onion salt

GUACAMOLE
2 large, ripe, but still firm avocados
2 ripe tomatoes
2 Tbsp [25 mL] fresh lime or
    lemon juice

1 clove garlic, finely minced
2 Tbsp [25 mL] chopped fresh cilantro
3 canned green chilies, rinsed, seeded,
    and chopped
1 finely minced jalapeño or
    serrano chili (optional)
kosher salt

FIXIN'S
1 Tbsp [15 mL] prepared mustard
granulated garlic
Championship Barbecue Rub (see
    page 50) or your favorite grilling rub
¼ cup [50 mL] Margie's Chipotle &
    Roasted Garlic Mayo (see page 68)
4 slices Jack cheese (optional)
4 hamburger buns

To make the chili butter, combine all the ingredients in a food processor and blend them together until they're smooth. Transfer the butter onto a sheet of plastic wrap and shape it into a tube 1½ inches (4 cm) in diameter. Twist the ends of the tube to close it, and place it in the freezer for at least

(continued)

Beef Burger with Chili Butter Core Topped with Chipotle & Roasted Garlic Mayo & Guacamole *(continued)*

2 hours, and preferably overnight. (It's a good idea to make the mayo at the same time as you make the chili butter, as both improve when you let the flavors marry.)

The guacamole doesn't keep well and should be made no more than 1 hour before you put the burgers on the grill. To make it, peel the avocados and remove the pits. Coarsely chop the tomatoes and avocados. (You can mash the avocados as much as you like, but I prefer a chunky guacamole.) Blend in the lime or lemon juice, garlic, cilantro, green chilies, and hot chilies, if desired. Season the guacamole to taste with salt. Cover it and set it aside in a cool place.

Combine the burger ingredients in a large nonreactive bowl. Mix the ingredients lightly with your hands, being careful not to overwork the beef. Split it into 4 equal portions and roll it into balls. Take the butter out of the freezer and slice off four ¼-inch (6 mm) discs. Poke your thumb in the middle of each ball to create a hole and insert the disc of chili butter. Encase the butter in the burger as you shape it into a classic burger shape about ¾ inch (2 cm) thick, ensuring that there are no openings where molten butter could run out. Set the rest of the chili butter aside to soften.

Coat the burger patties lightly with the mustard and sprinkle them with a light coating of granulated garlic, then a light coating of the rub.

Preheat the grill on medium-high for 5 to 10 minutes, or until the chamber temperature rises above 500°F (260°C). Place the burgers on the grill, close the cover, and reduce the heat to medium. Cook them for about 5 minutes, keeping an eye out for flare-ups. Turn them carefully and cook them for another 5 to 8 minutes, or until the patties become firm, but not hard, to the touch. If you want to add cheese, place a slice on top of each patty about 2 minutes before you plan to take them off the grill.

Transfer the burgers from the grill to a serving plate. Tent the burgers with foil and let them rest for 2 to 3 minutes. In the meantime, coat the cut side of each half of the buns with some softened chili butter, sprinkle them with a little granulated garlic, and toast them for 30 to 60 seconds on the grill.

Dress the buns with a generous slather of chipotle mayo. Place the burgers on the buns and top each burger with a big dollop of guacamole. Cover the patties with the top half of the buns and serve.

NOTE: Warn your guests that the burgers have a molten filling or they could be in for a shock! In any case, have plenty of napkins at the ready. These are very juicy burgers.

BEEF BURGER
WITH HERBED BUTTER CORE
& CARAMELIZED ONIONS

MAKES 4 BURGERS

This recipe won the burger category at the Canadian National Barbecue Championships in Whistler, British Columbia, in the summer of 2003. More than a burger, it is the Atkins Diet equivalent of a jelly doughnut (if you forgo the bun). It's a life-shaping experience that should probably be accompanied by some kind of parental guidance message. Be careful to whom you serve this—your guests may stalk you until you cook it for them again.

BURGER PATTIES

1½–2 lb [750 g–1 kg] lean
    ground beef
½ tsp [2 mL] freshly grated
    nutmeg
four ½-inch [1 cm] discs of
    frozen Mediterranean Butter
    (see page 67)

FIXIN'S

1 Tbsp [15 mL] Dijon mustard
Championship Barbecue Rub
    (see page 50)

4 hamburger buns
softened Mediterranean Butter
    for the buns
granulated garlic
½ cup [125 mL] chèvre (creamy
    goat cheese), at room
    temperature
2 large roasted red bell peppers
    (see sidebar page 118, torn
    into quarters)
Caramelized Onions (see page
    160)

⮞ BARBECUE SECRET ⮜

For extra-juicy burgers, add some cold water to your raw burger meat before you mix it. You only need about 1 Tbsp (15 mL) per pound (500 g) of meat. For extra-tender burgers, don't overwork the burger mix.

Combine the beef and nutmeg in a large nonreactive bowl. Mix together the spice and the meat lightly with your hands, being careful not to overwork it. Split the meat into 4 equal portions and roll it into balls. Poke your thumb in the middle of each ball to create a hole and insert a frozen disc of herbed butter. Encase the butter in the burger as you shape it into a classic burger shape about ¾ inch (2 cm) thick, ensuring that there are no openings where molten butter could run out. (It may be helpful to dip your hands periodically into cold water to prevent the meat from sticking to them.)

The Burger Connection

(continued)

Beef Burger with Herbed Butter Core & Caramelized Onions *(continued)*

Coat the burger patties lightly with the mustard and sprinkle them with a light coating of the rub. Preheat your grill to medium heat. Either spray the burgers with vegetable oil spray or coat the grill with oil. Place the burgers on the grill and cook them for 4 to 5 minutes per side, or until the patties become firm, but not hard, to the touch.

Remove the burgers from the grill, tent them with foil, and let them rest for 4 to 5 minutes. In the meantime, coat the buns with the softened herbed butter, sprinkle them with a little granulated garlic, and toast them for 30 to 60 seconds on your grill.

Dress the burgers with a slather of chèvre, a piece or two of roasted red pepper, and a dollop of caramelized onion. Inhale.

NOTE: Warn your guests that the burgers have a molten filling or they could be in for a shock! In any case, have plenty of napkins at the ready. These are very juicy burgers.

CARAMELIZED ONIONS
MAKES ABOUT 1 CUP (250 ML)

This makes a great topping for burgers, but also an excellent all-purpose condiment. Try it as an omelet filling or as a topping for grilled pork chops. Mix it with chèvre and spread it on crackers for a tangy, sweet appetizer. It's also a great topping on a planked round of brie.

2 Tbsp [25 mL] butter, olive oil, or a combination	½ tsp [2 mL] kosher salt
	1 tsp [5 mL] sugar
4 medium onions, peeled and sliced into rings	½ tsp [2 mL] ground cinnamon
	pinch cayenne

Heat the butter or olive oil in a large skillet over medium heat. Add the onions and salt and sauté them until they're soft, about 5 minutes. Add the sugar, cinnamon, and cayenne. Continue to sauté the onions, stirring them regularly, until they are shiny and brown (about 15 minutes), being careful not to burn them (add a little water, if necessary, to prevent burning).

THAI-FLAVORED BEEF BURGER
WITH SAUTÉED SHIITAKES

MAKES 4 BURGERS

This recipe, adapted from Weber's *Big Book of Grilling*, features lightly sautéed shiitakes and needs no further condiment to give your taste buds a trip around the world.

BURGER PATTIES

1½ lb [750 g] ground chuck (20% lean)

2 Tbsp [25 mL] finely chopped fresh
　Thai or Italian basil

1 Tbsp [15 mL] fresh lime juice

2 tsp [10 mL] Thai fish sauce

2 cloves garlic, finely minced

1 tsp [5 mL] grated or finely chopped
　lime zest

1 tsp [5 mL] grated fresh ginger

½ tsp [2 mL] freshly ground
　black pepper

MUSHROOMS

3 Tbsp [45 mL] unsalted butter

2 Tbsp [25 mL] canola or peanut oil

1 small shallot, finely chopped

2 tsp [10 mL] grated fresh ginger

8 oz [250 g] fresh shiitake mushrooms,
　stems removed, cut into ¼-inch
　[6 mm] slices

few drops sesame oil

¼ tsp [1 mL] kosher salt

¼ tsp [1 mL] freshly ground black
　pepper

TO FINISH

4 hamburger buns, lightly buttered and
　sprinkled with granulated onion

1 tsp [5 mL] toasted sesame seeds

Line a baking sheet with waxed paper. Gently mix the burger ingredients in a large bowl with your hands, taking care not to overwork the meat. Wet your hands with cold water and shape the mixture into 4 patties about ¾ inch (2 cm) thick. Cover the patties and refrigerate them for at least 30 minutes and up to 4 hours.

Prepare your grill for direct medium heat. While the grill is heating, prepare the mushrooms. Melt the butter with the oil in a sauté pan over medium heat, and add the shallot and ginger. Add the mushrooms and cook the mixture, stirring occasionally, until the mushrooms are tender, 4 to 6 minutes. Add the sesame oil, salt, and pepper and mix them in thoroughly. Set the mushrooms aside and keep them warm.

(continued)

Thai-Flavored Beef Burger with Sautéed Shiitakes *(continued)*

Brush the burger patties with oil and grill them over direct medium heat for 4 to 5 minutes per side, or until the internal temperature reaches 160°F (71°C). Remove them from the heat. Grill the buns for 30 to 60 seconds, butter side down, until they're nicely toasted. Serve the hot burgers on the toasted buns, topped with the mushrooms and a sprinkling of sesame seeds.

LAMB BURGER
WITH MOLTEN GOAT CHEESE CORE

MAKES 4 BURGERS

We North Americans eat so much ground beef that we almost forget what beef tastes like. When you eat a lamb burger you actually taste the lamb and it makes for a deliciously different grilling experience. The goat cheese stuffing adds an orgiastic twist. Don't forget to freeze the goat cheese!

TZATZIKI

1 tsp [5 mL] ground cumin

1 cup [250 mL] plain Greek full-fat
    yogurt

1 Tbsp [15 mL] finely chopped
    fresh mint

⅓ long English cucumber, finely grated

BURGER PATTIES

1½ lb [750 g] ground lamb

2 Tbsp [25 mL] chopped fresh mint

1 tsp [5 mL] dried oregano

½ tsp [2 mL] kosher salt

freshly ground black pepper

3 oz [90 g] chèvre (creamy goat cheese),
    frozen and sliced into four ½-inch
    [1 cm] discs

kosher salt and freshly ground black
    pepper to taste

2 Tbsp [25 mL] softened Mediterranean
    Butter (see page 67)

FIXIN'S

2 large fresh rounds of pita bread

sliced tomatoes

½ red onion, very thinly sliced

1 bunch fresh arugula, washed and dried

To make the tzatziki, toast the ground cumin in a dry nonstick skillet over medium heat for 30 seconds, or until it becomes fragrant and browns just slightly. Transfer the cumin from the hot pan into a bowl. Add the yogurt, mint, and cucumber, mix them together thoroughly, cover the tzatziki, and refrigerate it until it's needed.

Gently mix the lamb with the mint, oregano, salt, and a few grindings of pepper in a nonreactive bowl with your hands. Divide the meat into 4 equal portions and shape them into balls. Make a hole in each patty with your thumb and insert a disc of frozen goat cheese. Carefully seal the hole and shape the ball into a patty ¾ inch (2 cm) thick, making sure to cover the

(continued)

The Burger Connection

163

Lamb Burger with Molten Goat Cheese Core *(continued)*

cheese with the meat. Season the outside of the patties with salt and pepper. Lightly brush them with olive oil and grill them over direct medium heat for 4 to 5 minutes per side, or until the internal temperature is 160°F (71°C).

Take the burgers off the grill and spread a thin layer of the herbed butter on top of each one (if you don't have any herbed butter, drizzle them with a little olive oil—just enough to make them glisten). Let them rest for 3 to 4 minutes. Just before you're ready to serve them, toast the pitas on the grill for 10 to 15 seconds per side. Cut the pitas in half, open them up, and stuff the burgers inside. Dress them with the tomatoes, onion, arugula, and tzatziki.

ASIAN CHICKEN BURGERS

MAKES 4 BURGERS

This chicken burger has a light, fluffy texture and the kind of comfort-food taste we associate with takeout Chinese food. Serve it with ice-cold Asian beer like Tsingtao, Kingfisher, or Kirin.

SAUCE

½ cup [125 mL] mayonnaise

1 tsp [5 mL] hot Asian chili sauce
(like Sriracha)

½ tsp [2 mL] fresh lime juice

½ tsp [2 mL] sesame oil

BURGER PATTIES

1½ lb [750 g] freshly ground chicken

1 cup [250 mL] fresh breadcrumbs

¼ cup [50 mL] minced green onions

¼ cup [50 mL] finely chopped
fresh cilantro

1 large egg, lightly beaten

1 Tbsp [15 mL] oyster sauce

1 Tbsp [15 mL] hoisin sauce

1 Tbsp [15 mL] soy sauce

1 Tbsp [15 mL] liquid honey

2 tsp [10 mL] Dijon mustard

1 tsp [5 mL] toasted sesame oil

½ tsp [2 mL] kosher salt

½ tsp [2 mL] freshly ground
black pepper

FIXIN'S

1 Tbsp [15 mL] neutral-flavored oil
(like canola or corn oil)

4 hamburger buns, lightly buttered and
sprinkled with granulated garlic

Asian Barbecue Sauce (see page 61)

4 lettuce leaves

four ½-inch [1 cm] slices grilled
pineapple (optional)

Combine the sauce ingredients in a medium nonreactive bowl. Cover and refrigerate (you can make this a day in advance).

Line a baking sheet with waxed paper. Gently mix all the burger ingredients together with your hands. Wet your hands with cold water and shape the mixture into 4 patties ¾ inches (2 cm) thick. Place them on the baking sheet, cover, and refrigerate them for at least 1 hour.

Prepare your grill for direct medium heat. Brush the patties with oil and grill them until they're well done (an internal temperature of 160°F/71°C), about 5 to 6 minutes per side. Transfer the burgers to a platter, tent them with foil, and let them rest for 4 to 5 minutes. Lightly toast the buns on the grill. Generously slather the buns with the sauce, add the patties, top them with some lettuce and a slice of grilled pineapple, and serve.

CATHY'S

CATHY'S
KID-FRIENDLY TURKEY BURGERS

MAKES 5–6 BURGERS

Every so often, out of the blue, I'll get an email from someone who is enjoying one of my cookbooks and wants to share a recipe with me. Terry Kelly of Presque Isle, Maine, sent me this easy and delicious burger recipe created by his wife, Cathy.

BURGER PATTIES

1–1½ lb [500–750 g] ground turkey (15% fat)

1 egg

½ tsp [2 mL] freshly ground black pepper

¼ tsp [1 mL] kosher salt

2 Tbsp [25 mL] bottled salad dressing (French or Catalina)

1 small yellow onion, finely chopped

½ tsp [2 mL] granulated garlic

⅔ cup [160 mL] Italian-style dry breadcrumbs

1 Tbsp [15 mL] neutral-flavored oil (like canola or corn oil)

FIXIN'S

cheese slices

4 hamburger buns

burger condiments—Terry likes sliced red onion, ketchup, and Miracle Whip; Doctored Mayo (see page 68) also works nicely

Mix the turkey, egg, pepper, salt, salad dressing, onion, garlic, and breadcrumbs together in a bowl and shape the mixture into 5 to 6 patties.

Prepare your grill for direct medium heat.

Paint the burger patties with a light coating of oil and place them on the grill. Cook them for 3 to 5 minutes, flip them carefully, and cook them another 3 to 5 minutes, or until the burgers are springy to the touch. Put a cheese slice on each patty and cook them another 1 to 2 minutes. Remove them from the grill and serve them immediately with your favorite burger fixings.

THE WAKEFIELD INN OYSTER BURGER

MAKES 4 BURGERS

Years ago the Wakefield Inn, a pub on British Columbia's Sunshine Coast, invented the ultimate burger—and it's not grilled. To get the right texture, you need to pan-fry the oysters. The Wakefield Inn used seasoned flour to coat the oysters, but I prefer the extra crunch of cornmeal. Serve the burger with a dill pickle and a big mug of cold beer. Sadly, the Wakefield Inn has fallen to a condo developer's wrecking ball and all that's left is the great view . . . and this recipe.

1 tsp [5 mL] ground cumin
1 tsp [5 mL] ancho chili powder
1 tsp [5 mL] freshly ground black
    pepper
½ cup [125 mL] cornmeal
1 Tbsp [15 mL] butter
1 Tbsp [15 mL] extra virgin olive oil
12 medium-sized fresh West Coast
    oysters, pre-shucked (you can buy
    them in tubs)

FIXIN'S
¼ cup [50 mL] commercial tartar sauce
    (or Margie's Chipotle & Roasted Garlic
    Mayo, page 68)
4 hamburger buns, toasted and buttered
green leaf lettuce
4 slices crisply cooked bacon
1 thinly sliced ripe tomato
pickle slices and sprigs of fresh parsley,
    for garnish

Combine the cumin, ancho chili powder, pepper, and cornmeal in a small bowl. Mix well and pour onto a dinner plate. Heat the butter and oil in a heavy skillet over medium-high heat until the butter is sizzling. Lightly coat the oysters in the cornmeal mixture and fry them in the oil and butter until they're crisp on the outside and done inside, about 2 to 3 minutes per side.

Spread 1 Tbsp (15 mL) of tartar sauce on each toasted and buttered bun. Add a leaf or two of lettuce, 3 of the fried oysters, 1 crispy slice of bacon (ripped in half), and 1 or 2 slices of tomato. Sprinkle the works with salt and pepper. Top with the other half of the bun, and garnish with a pickle and a parsley sprig.

The Burger Connection

167

SALMON BURGER, WEST COAST STYLE

MAKES 4 BURGERS

White Spot restaurants, known for their excellent old-fashioned hamburgers, are a fixture in British Columbia. In recent years they've gone a bit upscale, adding more gourmet fare to their classic dishes, including a phenomenal salmon burger. Executive chef Chuck Curry likes to play his recipes close to the chest, so I've had to re-create this dish based on my experience of eating it, but this comes pretty close to the real thing. If you don't have the time or the inclination to make the aïoli, substitute with regular commercial mayo doctored with finely chopped fresh basil, a squeeze of lemon juice, and some freshly ground black pepper.

BASIL AÏOLI
2 large egg yolks
2 Tbsp [25 mL] fresh lemon juice
1¼ cups [300 mL] extra virgin olive oil
¼ cup [50 mL] tightly packed fresh
    basil leaves
kosher salt and freshly ground black
    pepper to taste

BURGERS
four 8 oz [250 g] boneless, skinless wild
    BC salmon fillets (farmed salmon will
    do, but it's just not as good)

kosher salt
freshly ground black pepper
extra virgin olive oil

FIXIN'S
4 large sesame hamburger buns
butter
1 large, perfectly ripe beefsteak tomato,
    cut into 4 slices
1 red onion, thinly sliced
green leaf lettuce

Combine the egg yolks and the lemon juice in the bowl of a food processor; process the mixture for 5 seconds. With the machine running, drizzle the olive oil through the feed tube in a slow, steady stream, processing until the mixture is combined. Coarsely chop the basil and add it to the mixture. Whiz the machine again until the basil is incorporated into the aïoli. Season it with salt and pepper and set it aside. It will keep for up to 3 days in the refrigerator.

(continued)

Salmon Burger, West Coast Style *(continued)*

Prepare the grill for direct medium heat. Season the salmon fillets with salt and pepper and drizzle them with a little olive oil. Make sure the cooking grate is scrubbed clean. In this case, you may want to coat the cooking grate with a little oil just before you put the salmon on. Place the salmon on the grill, cover it, and cook the fish for 3 to 4 minutes per side, or until the core temperature of the fillet reaches 130°F (55°C).

Take the salmon off the grill and loosely tent it with foil. While the salmon is resting, butter the buns, place them buttered side down on the cooking grate, cover the grill, and toast the buns for maybe half a minute, taking care not to burn them.

Slather both sides of each toasted bun with the basil aïoli. Place the salmon fillets in the buns and top them with tomato, onion, and lettuce. Serve the burgers with a cold beer or a glass of crisp, fruity white wine.

NANOOK OF THE PORK

❧ Winter Grilling ❧

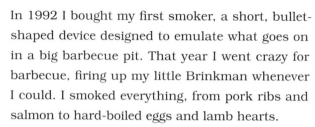

In 1992 I bought my first smoker, a short, bullet-shaped device designed to emulate what goes on in a big barbecue pit. That year I went crazy for barbecue, firing up my little Brinkman whenever I could. I smoked everything, from pork ribs and salmon to hard-boiled eggs and lamb hearts.

Nothing could stop me, to my wife's chagrin. Not even the brutal Calgary winter, where a sunny January afternoon can turn into a raging blizzard in the space of an hour. When it hit –4°C (–20°F) I had trouble keeping the barbecue's temperature up. Undaunted, I dug out an old curling sweater and put it on the smoker. With its woolen arms dangling at its sides, it looked like a cross between John Candy and R2-D2. Worked like a charm. And the zipper made it easy to check the coals.

I still cook outdoors all winter long, and I'm not alone. Every weekend in North America, no matter what the weather, an army of backyard cooks walks precariously across icy patios to toss the Saturday night steaks onto a grill that seems to hiss disapprovingly, as if to say, "Get back in the housssssssssssse, you fool!"

But we forge on. We do it for convenience. We do it for speed. We do it because, damn it, we just love to grill. The smell of fat hitting the fire becomes even more appetizing when one's nostrils are chilled to near frostbite. Besides, you can't get the same flavor in a sauté pan. Plus, the praise you get from your guests—one of man's primary reasons for cooking—diminishes significantly if you're not grilling. ("Gee, Stanley. You really know how to scallop a potato!" Not.)

Weber's annual GrillWatch survey on *al fresco* cooking tells us that three-quarters of all households own outdoor grills or smokers, and more than half of them use their equipment year-round. About a third say they have cooked in a snowstorm.

It wasn't always so. In the early 1950s, backyard grilling was done on open, charcoal-fueled braziers that performed miserably in anything but hot, calm weather. Enter our hero, George Stephen, a welder working in Chicago for the Weber Brothers Metal Works. George was fabricating round metal buoys for the US Coast Guard. Frustrated with cooking outdoors in the Windy City, he performed the hardware equivalent of a sex change, turning a buoy into a grill. The big innovation: George's invention had a lid that kept the weather out and the heat in. Today the Weber kettle is an American icon, as familiar as the Golden Arches.

> **I dug out an old curling sweater and put it on the smoker. With its woolen arms dangling at its sides, it looked like a cross between John Candy and R2-D2. Worked like a charm.**

In the early '60s, another enterprising Illinois inventor, named Walter Koziol, made the next

But it's not the grill that does the cooking. It takes big, steely Northern balls to cook outdoors all winter long.

big breakthrough in all-season grilling. Walter's company, Modern Home Products, made decorative gas lighting for suburban backyards. In search of ways to market other gas-powered devices, Walter invented the world's first gas-fueled, covered outdoor grill, which took George Stephen's concept to the next level. The easy starting and convenience of gas would change backyard cooking forever. In 2007 alone, more than 10 million covered gas grills were sold in North America.

But it's not the grill that does the cooking. It takes big, steely Northern balls to cook outdoors all winter long. Here are a few tips to make it safer and easier:

1. For God's sake, don't grill indoors. The fumes can kill you.

2. Position your grill out of the wind to conserve heat and keep your nose from getting frostbitten. Even with the grill closed, cross-drafts can seriously reduce the efficiency of your cooker.

3. Brush the snow off to speed preheating and avoid melt water, which can create a dangerous skating rink under your grill.

4. Close the cover and don't check the food too often. Remember, if you're lookin', you ain't cookin'.

5. Cook things that only need one or two turns, or make larger roasts that don't require much tending.

6. Choose a grill with higher BTUs (50,000 plus is ideal) to help you get up to grilling temperature faster. Also, look for a grill with a heavy cast iron cooking grate, which retains heat better than porcelain-coated steel.

7. At around –4°C (–20°F), knobs freeze. Yours, and the grill's. Handle them gently to avoid snapping them off.

8. Get a good outdoor-rated patio light so you can see whether your meat is burning. You can also get nifty battery-powered lights that attach to the handles of your grill cover.

9. Get a good meat thermometer and cook to internal temperature rather than time.

10. Heat your serving plate so your meat stays warm when you take it off.

ONE LAST NOTE: You can throw the usual stuff on your grill in the winter, but it's more fun to cook seasonal foods, like turkey, venison, squash, carrots, apples, and pears. Use indirect heat to slow-roast almost anything. All you do is preheat your grill, turn off one burner, and place your meat on the grate directly above it. For big cuts, put a pan underneath to catch the drippings.

This article first appeared in Toro *magazine.*

All Praise the Mighty Pig: Pork

There was a time in the 1990s when pork producers decided that the public wanted to avoid fatty foods, so they fed and bred their hogs to a point where they were competing with skinless chicken breasts for a place on the diet-conscious yuppie's plate. They had forgotten one of the most profound barbecue secrets of all, the formula that says: FOOD + FAT = FLAVOR.

And of all the fats, pork fat is one of the most flavorful. Thank goodness the North American palate has come to its senses and richer foods are once again socially acceptable. Pork producers have responded to this positive trend by offering cuts of pork that are worth eating again. When you choose pork at your local butcher shop or in the supermarket, look for nice lines of creamy fat around the meat and a rich, marbled texture in the muscle itself. Fat is what literally creates the sizzle when you grill, and without it, your barbecued pork would taste like cardboard.

Fat is not only flavorful, it is supremely nutritious. Pig meat fed North American's earliest settlers, and as an inexpensive source of energy-packed protein it has always been a staple of working folks everywhere. And, of course, pork is the lead player on the competitive barbecue stage and the image of the happy pig is synonymous with barbecue culture. All hail the mighty pig, provider to us all!

PORK & APPLE KEBABS

MAKES 8 APPETIZER SERVINGS OR 4–6 MAIN COURSE SERVINGS

This is a great late-summer grilling dish. Use the tangiest, firmest new-crop apples you can find. Serve these kebabs as an appetizer, or with Grilled Asparagus (page 129) and Dilled Smashed Potatoes (page 133) as a main course.

8 long metal skewers, or 12 bamboo
   skewers soaked for 15 minutes to
   half an hour
2 lb [1 kg] boneless pork loin

MARINADE
¼ cup [50 mL] cider vinegar
1 clove garlic, forced through a
   garlic press
1 Tbsp [15 mL] fresh rosemary
1 tsp [5 mL] dried rosemary
1 tsp [5 mL] granulated onion

½ tsp [2 mL] ground allspice
¼ tsp [1 mL] freshly grated nutmeg
pinch cayenne
pinch cloves

KEBABS
6 apples, peeled, cored, and cut into
   bite-sized chunks
kosher salt and freshly ground black
   pepper to taste
extra virgin olive oil

Cut the pork into bite-sized chunks. Combine all the marinade ingredients in a nonreactive bowl and add the pork, mixing to coat it thoroughly. Marinate the pork for about 1 hour at room temperature or 2 to 3 hours in the fridge.

Prepare your grill for direct medium heat. Thread the pork chunks onto the skewers, alternating them with the chunks of apple. Grill the kebabs for 3 to 4 minutes per side, or until the pork is just done. Season the kebabs with salt and pepper and drizzle them with a little olive oil. Serve them hot.

SPICE-CRUSTED PORK BLADE STEAKS

MAKES 6 SERVINGS

I developed this recipe for the folks at *Food & Wine* magazine for their 2005 summer barbecue issue. I love pork blade steaks because they're inexpensive, extremely tasty, and very hard to ruin. The cumin seeds add an earthy tang and interesting texture to these rich, flavorful, chewy steaks. Serve them with your favorite summer sides.

RUB

2 Tbsp [25 mL] ancho chili powder
　or any other chili powder
1 Tbsp [15 mL] granulated garlic
1 Tbsp [15 mL] granulated onion
1 tsp [5 mL] freshly ground black pepper
1 tsp [5 mL] chipotle chili powder
　or cayenne
1 tsp [5 mL] dried oregano
1 tsp [5 mL] dried parsley

STEAKS

1 Tbsp [15 mL] cumin seeds
six 8–10 oz [250–300 g] pork blade
　steaks
kosher salt
2 Tbsp [25 mL] Dijon mustard or
　regular prepared mustard
extra virgin olive oil

Combine all the rub ingredients in a small bowl and set the rub aside.

Toast the cumin seeds in a dry sauté pan over medium heat until they're fragrant and just starting to turn light brown. Remove the cumin from the pan and set it aside.

Generously season the blade steaks with salt. Using the back of a spoon or a basting brush, coat the steaks with a thin layer of mustard. Sprinkle the cumin seeds on both sides of the steaks and pat them in so they stick to the mustard. Sprinkle a generous coating of rub on the steaks and drizzle them with a little olive oil. (You'll have rub left over, which is great for grilling just about anything.)

(continued)

Spice-Crusted Pork Blade Steaks *(continued)*

Prepare your grill for direct high heat. Place the steaks on the cooking grate, close the grill, and immediately reduce the heat to medium.

Cook the steaks for 8 to 10 minutes, turning them once or twice, or until they are springy to the touch. Remove the steaks from the grill, tent them with foil, and let them rest for 5 minutes. Drizzle them with a little olive oil and serve.

WARNING: These steaks have a lot of juice and fat in them, so be on the alert for flare-ups.

PORK CHOPS WITH GRILLED APPLES
& FRESH SAGE LEAVES

MAKES 4 SERVINGS

This classic flavor combination is a perfect late summer dish. Serve it with some Maple Butternut Squash Purée (page 139).

PORK CHOPS

4 pork chops, each about 1½ inches [4 cm] thick

kosher salt and freshly ground black pepper

1 Tbsp [15 mL] Dijon mustard

pinch cayenne

1 tsp [5 mL] granulated onion

1 tsp [5 mL] Mediterranean Dried Herb Rub (see page 52)

extra virgin olive oil

8 large fresh sage leaves

sprigs of fresh sage for garnish

APPLES

4 large, tangy, firm-fleshed apples (Granny Smiths or Rome Beauties would do)

1 lemon

kosher salt and freshly ground black pepper

1 Tbsp [15 mL] chopped fresh rosemary

¼ cup [50 mL] honey

2 Tbsp [25 mL] extra virgin olive oil

1 Tbsp [25 mL] Calvados (French apple brandy), optional

Season the pork chops with salt and pepper. Brush on a light coating of Dijon mustard. Combine the cayenne, granulated onion, and herb rub, and sprinkle the mixture over the chops, coating them lightly and evenly. Drizzle the chops with a little olive oil, patting the oil onto the chops so there's just enough to moisten them and make them shiny. Put the sage leaves in the palm of your hand and clench your fist. This crushes the leaves, releasing their aromatic oils. Paste 1 leaf on both sides of each chop, pressing them onto the surface. They should stick nicely. Let the chops sit at room temperature for 1 hour, or you can refrigerate them for several hours or overnight.

Slice the apples into ½-inch (1 cm) thick rounds. There's no need to peel them. (If you want to get fussy, you can use an apple corer to core the apples before you slice them.) Squeeze half of the lemon over the apples and

(continued)

Pork Chops with Grilled Apples & Fresh Sage Leaves *(continued)*

season them with salt and pepper. Combine the juice from the other half of the lemon with the chopped rosemary, honey, olive oil, and Calvados, if you like, in a bowl, and gently toss the apples in the mixture to coat them. Set the bowl of apple slices aside.

Prepare your grill for direct medium heat. Grill the pork chops for 4 to 6 minutes per side, or until the internal temperature of the thickest part of the chops is about 130°F (55°C). The sage leaves may burn or fall off during cooking, but don't worry; they will have done their work to flavor the chops. Transfer the chops to a serving platter and loosely tent them with foil.

While the chops are resting, turn up the heat to medium-high. Remove the apple slices from the honey mixture, reserving the liquid. Grill the apple slices for 1 or 2 minutes per side, or until they've got some nice grill marks and have softened a bit. When you turn them, you can brush them with a bit of the apple marinade.

To serve, top the chops with the apple slices and drizzle the rest of the honey mixture over the apples and chops. Garnish the dish with the fresh sage leaves and serve.

CHEATER RIBS

MAKES 4 SERVINGS

Die-hard barbecue people don't even like to consider this technique, which goes against all the principles and values of barbecue culture. These ribs may not be smoky, and they may not be quite as flavorful as true barbecued ribs, but they're wonderfully tender, they taste great, and they don't take all day to cook.

2 racks side or back ribs,
    trimmed by your butcher
1 medium onion, peeled and
    halved
1 tsp [5 mL] peppercorns
3 or 4 whole cloves
2 Tbsp [25 mL] prepared
    mustard

½ tsp [2 mL] granulated garlic
¼ cup [50 mL] or so Champion-
    ship Barbecue Rub (see
    page 50)
1 cup [250 mL] barbecue sauce,
    the sweeter and tangier the
    better

➤ **BARBECUE SECRET** ≈

To test ribs for doneness, use the pull test. Grab the outer 2 ribs with your thumbs and forefingers and gently pull them apart. If they are bonded tightly, the ribs are not yet done. If the meat pulls apart easily, the ribs are ready to take out of the cooker.

Remove the membrane from the ribs if your butcher hasn't already done it for you. Fill a large pot with cold water and completely submerge the ribs. Add the onion, peppercorns, and cloves. Bring the water just to a boil. With a spoon or ladle, quickly skim off the soapy scum that forms on the top of the water and reduce the heat to low. Gently simmer the ribs for about 1¼ hours, or until they just pass the pull test (see sidebar). Take the ribs out of the water and cool them on a cooking sheet until they are easy to handle.

Prepare your grill for direct medium heat. Coat the ribs with the mustard, sprinkle them lightly with the granulated garlic, and coat them with the rub. Let them sit until the rub starts to glisten, about 10 minutes. Grill the ribs for 3 to 4 minutes on each side, applying barbecue sauce with a basting brush as you turn them, until the sauce is nicely caramelized and the ribs are lightly charred in a few places. Remove them from the grill, let them rest for a few minutes, cut into single ribs, and serve with classic barbecue accompaniments—corn on the cob, slaw, beans, etc.

All Praise the Mighty Pig: Pork

REAL BARBECUED RIBS

MAKES 2–4 SERVINGS

To get the taste of authentic barbecued ribs, you need to cook them slowly, the traditional way, in a water smoker or barbecue pit at a low temperature. This is how we do ribs in competition. You can also accomplish something close to this using indirect low heat on your covered charcoal or gas grill.

2 racks pork side ribs, St. Louis cut (with the breast plate attached)

2 Tbsp [25 mL] prepared mustard

1 tsp [5 mL] or so granulated garlic

½ cup [125 mL] Championship Barbecue Rub (see page 50)

apple juice in a spray bottle

Ron's Rich, Deeply Satisfying Dipping Sauce (see page 57) or your favorite Kansas City–style sauce

Prepare your smoker for barbecuing, bringing the temperature up to between 200 and 220°F (95–100°C). Cut along the gristly part of the ribs to separate each rack from the breast plate. Remove the shiny membrane on the inside of the ribs.

Coat the ribs evenly with mustard on both sides. Sprinkle them lightly with garlic, then give them a medium coating of rub, coating the convex (inner) side first and finishing with the convex side facing down (this prevents the rub from getting smudged).

Let the ribs sit for at least 15 minutes, or until the rub starts to draw moisture out of the meat and looks shiny.

Place the ribs on the cooking grate, with the convex side up (⌒), or place them on a rib rack. Cook them for 5 to 7 hours, depending on the size of the ribs, spraying them with apple juice at the 3-hour point and then again about every hour or so afterward.

At the beginning of the last hour of cooking, paint the ribs with a light coating of barbecue sauce.

BARBECUE SECRET

Pork rib membrane is slippery and frustrating to remove unless you use this technique: Separate a corner of the membrane from the rib cage with a sharp knife. Using a dry paper towel as a gripper, grab the loosened membrane and peel it off the ribs with steady pressure, reestablishing your grip as more membrane comes off. Once you have removed it, trim off any excess fat from the ribs, along with any remaining bits of membrane.

All Praise the Mighty Pig: Pork

(continued)

Real Barbecued Ribs *(continued)*

Half an hour before the end of the cooking time, test the ribs for doneness. If they pass the pull test (see Barbecue Secret on page 181) give them one more coat of sauce, wrap them in foil, and return them to the cooker for another half hour or so.

Remove the wrapped ribs from the cooker and let them rest for 20 to 45 minutes. Unwrap them, cut them into single ribs, and serve them with your favorite accompaniments.

RAVENSWOOD RIBS

MAKES 4–6 SERVINGS

Zinfandel is one of the best wines you can drink with grilled or barbecued food, and California winemaker Ravenswood makes some of the tastiest, most popular Zins around. Ravenswood's Executive Chef, Eric Lee, was kind enough to share this rib recipe. This versatile rub/mop combination also works well with other cuts of pork, as well as beef and lamb.

NOTE: I've used my Real Barbecued Ribs technique for this recipe, but you can also do them Cheater Ribs–style (see page 181).

RIBS
2 racks of back ribs, trimmed by your butcher
a couple of chunks of applewood

RUB
1 Tbsp [15 mL] kosher salt
2½ tsp [12 mL] garlic powder
1½ tsp [7 mL] dried oregano
1½ tsp [7 mL] dried thyme
1½ tsp [7 mL] onion powder
1½ tsp [7 mL] paprika
¾ tsp [3 mL] fennel seed, toasted and ground
¾ tsp [3 mL] chili powder
½ tsp [2 mL] cumin seeds, toasted and ground
½ tsp [2 mL] mustard seeds, toasted and ground

½ tsp [2 mL] freshly ground black pepper
¼ tsp [1 mL] cayenne
¼ tsp [1 mL] sugar
⅛ tsp [0.5 mL] ground ginger

"MOP"
½ bottle [1½ cups/375 mL] Ravenswood Zinfandel wine
1 cup [250 mL] sparkling apple cider
2 Tbsp [25 mL] extra virgin olive oil
2 Tbsp [25 mL] dark Karo syrup
1 Tbsp [15 mL] molasses
1½ Tbsp [22 mL] kosher salt
1½ tsp [7 mL] garlic powder
¼ tsp [1 mL] ground nutmeg
¼ tsp [1 mL] ground cloves
⅛ tsp [0.5 mL] ground cinnamon
1 bay leaf

(continued)

All Praise the Mighty Pig: Pork

Remove the membrane from the ribs if your butcher hasn't already done it for you (see Barbecue Secret on page 183).

Prepare your smoker for barbecuing, bringing the temperature up to between 200 and 220°F (95–100°C).

Combine all the rub ingredients in a medium bowl and mix them together thoroughly. Set the rub aside.

Combine all the mop ingredients in a medium saucepan. Simmer for 15 minutes on medium-low heat, uncovered.

Generously coat the ribs on both sides with the rub. Let the ribs sit for at least 15 minutes, or until the rub starts to draw moisture out of the meat and looks shiny.

Place the ribs on the cooking grate, with the convex side up (⌒), or place them on a rib rack. Place a chunk of applewood on the coals. Cook the ribs for 5 or 6 hours, depending on their size, mopping them about every half hour and adding another chunk of applewood about an hour before the ribs are done.

Half an hour before the end of the cooking time, test the ribs for doneness. If they pass the pull test (see Barbecue Secret on page 181) give them one more coat of sauce, wrap them in foil, and return them to the cooker for another half hour or so.

Remove them from the cooker and let the wrapped ribs rest for 20 to 45 minutes. Unwrap them, cut them into single ribs, and serve them with your favorite accompaniments, including, of course, some Ravenswood Zinfandel!

TASTY PLANKED
TENDERLOIN TREATMENTS

When I set out to research my second book, *Planking Secrets*, I knew that planking worked great for fish and for summer fruits like peaches and pears, but I had no idea what a perfect match this cooking style was for pork tenderloin. These little cylinders of tender, juicy pork are a staple of Chinese cooking and are wonderful on the grill, but they're also ideally suited to planking. Their size allows two or three to fit nicely on a plank, and they have just the right amount of surface area to cook quickly without losing moisture. They go with all flavors of smoke, from cedar to mesquite. And they take to marinades and rubs extremely well. Here are some basic techniques and a little collection of ideas for how to flavor pork tenderloin, but use your imagination and experiment with your favorite rubs, marinades, and basting sauces.

TECHNIQUE

1. Marinate and/or rub the tenderloin and have it ready to go before you start the grill. (Three tenderloins are usually enough for 4 servings.)

2. Preheat the grill on medium-high for 5–10 minutes, or until the chamber temperature rises above 500°F (260°C). Rinse the soaked plank and place it on the cooking grate. Cover the grill and heat the plank for about 4–5 minutes, or until it starts to throw off a bit of smoke and crackles lightly.

3. Reduce the heat to medium and place the tenderloin on the plank. Cook it for 10 minutes, turn it, and cook it for another 5–10 minutes, basting if you like, until the pork is springy to the touch or reaches an internal temperature of 140°F (60°C). (This will give you juicy pork cooked to a medium doneness. The internal temperature will come up slightly when you let the meat rest.)

4. If you like, just before it's ready, you can move the tenderloin from the plank onto the cooking grate and char the outside, or caramelize it if it's coated with barbecue sauce.

5. Take the tenderloin out of the grill, tent it in foil, and let it rest for a few minutes before serving it. Carve the tenderloin into ½- to 1-inch (1 to 2.5 cm) medallions and apply whatever sauce or garnish is called for.

(continued)

Tasty Planked Tenderloin Treatments *(continued)*

Classic Barbecue   Coat the pork with ballpark mustard, then sprinkle it with Championship Barbecue Rub (page 50). Cook it on a hickory plank till it's nearly done and finish it with a light glaze of Ron's Rich, Deeply Satisfying Dipping Sauce (page 57). Serve more sauce on the side.

Easy Asian   Marinate the pork with Easiest, Tastiest Steak marinade (page 231) and finish it with a coating of Asian Barbecue Sauce (page 61).

Spice-Crusted   Season the pork with salt and pepper, drizzle it with oil, and coat it with minced garlic, toasted fennel and cumin seeds, and a little cinnamon. Serve it with chopped cilantro and your favorite chutney.

Balsamic   Coat the pork with balsamic reduction (see sidebar, page 242). Marinate it overnight. Before cooking, sprinkle on some chopped fresh rosemary and granulated garlic. Serve the pork with a further drizzle of the balsamic reduction and some chopped fresh mint.

Harvest Time   Season the pork with salt and pepper and coat it with a rub made with light brown sugar, powdered ginger, a sprinkle of freshly grated nutmeg, a pinch of clove, and a little cayenne. Baste it with melted apple jelly.

Southwestern   Flavor the pork using Rockin' Ronnie's Grilling Rub (page 51) and serve it with some salsa and cornbread.

NOTE: I love to plank pork tenderloins, but of course they're great cooked for 8 to 10 minutes on the grill. They also cook up nicely in a smoker, where the average pork tenderloin takes about an hour to an hour and a half to come up to medium rare.

Pictured: Spice-Crusted Tenderloin

PLANKED PORK LOIN ROAST
WITH WHISKEY-APRICOT GLAZE

MAKES 4–6 SERVINGS

In this recipe, the aromatic, spicy, mildly astringent flavor of the cedar smoke nicely complements the pork's sweetness and richness. The trick to plank-cooking a roast this big is to get the plank smoldering on high or medium-high heat and then turn it down to medium as soon as you get the meat on. Serve slices of the pork with roasted vegetables on the side and, if you like, some Maple Butternut Squash Purée (page 139).

1 cedar plank, soaked overnight or at least 1 hour
one 3 lb [1.5 kg] pork loin roast with a ⅛-inch [3 mm] fat cap
kosher salt and freshly ground black pepper

GLAZE/SAUCE
one 14 oz [398 mL] can apricot halves in light syrup

¼ cup [50 mL] Jack Daniel's Tennessee Whiskey
¼ cup [50 mL] Dijon mustard
¼ cup [50 mL] brown sugar
¼ cup [50 mL] apricot jam
pinch cayenne

sprigs of fresh parsley and thyme, for garnish

Drain the syrup from the can of apricots into a medium-sized saucepan, reserving the fruit. Add the Jack Daniel's, mustard, brown sugar, apricot jam, and cayenne to the syrup. Bring the mixture to a low boil over medium heat, stirring to melt the sugar and the jam. When it looks like a smooth, fairly thick sauce (which takes about 5 minutes), take it off the heat and set the pan in a bowl of ice cubes to cool.

Lightly score the fat cap of the pork loin in a diamond pattern with a sharp knife. Season it with salt and pepper, and set the meat on a sheet of heavy-duty aluminum foil. Spoon half of the mustard-whiskey mixture over the loin and pat it all over to coat it. Wrap the foil around the meat, sealing it as best you can. Place the wrapped loin in the meat drawer of your fridge. Let it sit for a couple of hours at least, and overnight if possible.

Combine the remaining half of the sauce with the reserved apricot halves, cover the mixture, and refrigerate it.

(continued)

Planked Pork Loin Roast with Whiskey-Apricot Glaze *(continued)*

Preheat the grill on medium-high for 5 to 10 minutes, or until the chamber temperature rises above 500°F (260°C). Rinse the plank and place it on the cooking grate. Cover the grill and heat the plank for 4 to 5 minutes, or until it starts to throw off a bit of smoke and crackles lightly. Reduce the heat to medium-low.

Place the marinated pork loin on the plank, fat side up. Cover the grill and cook the meat for 1 hour, checking periodically for flare-ups.

At the 1-hour mark, take the reserved apricots out of the sauce and place them on the plank next to the roast. Baste the roast with some of the sauce and cook it for another 10 to 20 minutes, until the internal temperature of the pork reaches 140°F (60°C). Take the roast off the heat and lightly tent it in foil.

Transfer the apricot halves to a cutting board and coarsely chop them. Warm the remaining sauce on the stovetop or in the microwave and add the chopped apricots. Let the roast rest for at least 15 minutes (while it's resting, roast some vegetables on the grill). Carve the roast into ½-inch (1 cm) slices and serve them on warmed plates with a spoonful of the apricots and sauce. Garnish the pork with sprigs of parsley and thyme.

CLASSIC NORTH CAROLINA
BARBECUED PULLED PORK SANDWICHES

MAKES 18–24 SERVINGS

The concept here is to cook a pork shoulder butt roast (sometimes called a Boston butt) for many hours in a smoky chamber until it is literally falling apart. One test competitors use for doneness is that if the blade bone can easily be pulled out of the roast, the pork is ready to shred and serve. This is real barbecue the way we prepare it for competition, and the way it is eaten in the southeastern states. You can substitute any good rub you have on hand if you don't have time to make some from scratch, but fellow Butt Shredder Kathy Richardier's Butt Rub is the best! This recipe calls for two butts because if you're going to tend the smoker for such a long time, you might as well fill it up. Pork butt freezes very well, so if you're not feeding a huge crowd, just serve one of the butts, wrap the other in an extra layer of foil, and freeze it for later use.

KATHY'S BUTT RUB

¼ cup [50 mL] paprika

2 Tbsp [25 mL] granulated sugar

2 Tbsp [25 mL] brown sugar

2 Tbsp [25 mL] freshly ground black pepper

2 Tbsp [25 mL] ground cumin

2 Tbsp [25 mL] chili powder (like Chimayo blend, New Mexico, or ancho)

1 Tbsp [15 mL] kosher salt

up to 1 Tbsp [15 mL] cayenne

SANDWICHES

2 pork shoulder butt roasts, about 6–9 lb [2.7–4 kg] each, bone in

1 cup [250 mL] prepared mustard

1 Tbsp [15 mL] granulated garlic

apple juice/maple syrup/Jack Daniel's blend in a spray bottle (see Barbecue Secret on page 28)

2 cups [500 mL] or more of Ron's Rich, Deeply Satisfying Dipping Sauce (see page 57)

1 cup [250 mL] North Carolina–Style Vinegar Sauce (see page 58)

24 fresh, fluffy white buns

Tidewater Coleslaw (see page 112)

Combine the rub ingredients in a bowl and set the rub aside.

Slather the butts with the mustard, sprinkle them with the granulated garlic, and then coat them liberally with the rub. Let the rubbed butts sit for half an hour, until the meat's juices make the rub look wet and shiny.

All Praise the Mighty Pig: Pork

(continued)

❧ VARIATION ❧

Covered grill method You can barbecue pork butts on your covered charcoal or gas grill. Follow this recipe exactly, but use indirect low heat (this is easier on a gas grill because to maintain low heat on a charcoal grill means you have to add coals every hour or two for a whole day). Use soaked wood chips or chunks wrapped in foil and poked with a fork to create a bit of smoke. It won't be as smoky as barbecue made in the traditional style, but it'll still be good! The one advantage of this technique is you can probably get by with a couple of hours less cooking time.

Prepare your smoker for barbecuing, bringing the temperature up to between 200 and 220°F (95–100°C). Line the drip pan of your smoker with a double or triple layer of foil and fill it with apple juice. (If you want a more crispy crust on the butts, just line the drip pan and leave it dry.) Cook the butts for 1½ to 2 hours per pound (500 g) (about 10 to 14 hours, or to an internal temperature of 185°F/85°C), adding coals and chunks of hardwood as required. We use a blend of fruitwood, hickory, and mesquite in competition.

About halfway through the cooking time, turn the butts and spray them with the apple juice mixture. Turn them over and spray them again at the three-quarter mark. Two hours before the butts are due to be ready, turn them over again and, with a basting brush, generously glaze them with barbecue sauce. At the same point, throw a couple of chunks of hardwood on the coals. An hour before the butts are due to be finished, turn and glaze them one more time and wrap them in a double coating of foil. Leave them for one more hour in the smoker, then take them out. Let them rest for at least half an hour (in competition we'll let our butts rest, wrapped in foil, then wrapped in a blanket and placed in an insulated cooler, for as long as 4 hours).

Take the butts out of the foil and place them in a large roasting pan or heavy-duty roasting tray. Pull apart the pork, using 2 forks, "bear claws," or your hands sheathed in rubber gloves, mixing the exterior crusty bits together with the tender, juicy white meat. Drizzle the shredded meat with the vinegar sauce and some barbecue sauce and mix it in.

To serve, pile the shredded pork on the buns, drizzle it with some more of your favorite barbecue sauce, and top it with some coleslaw for a big, juicy, crunchy, messy barbecue sandwich. Take one bite and you will know what real barbecue tastes like!

RON EADE'S FAVORITE
SMOKED PULLED PORK

SERVES 8 OR MORE WITH LEFTOVERS

Ron Eade is the *Ottawa Citizen's* food editor and a die-hard barbecue junkie. He generously shared this easy, simple recipe for pulled pork that eliminates most of the fussing associated with cooking barbecue at home.

I love Ron's minimalist approach to the rub: "My homemade rub involves going to the dollar store and buying a selection of salt-free seasonings, which I mix and then store in the freezer. I choose garlic powder, onion powder, sweet paprika, black pepper, chili powder, ground cumin, a handful of brown sugar, a small handful of salt, dried thyme, oregano, maybe basil, a tablespoon of cayenne—whatever strikes your fancy. It makes lots and you can store the excess in a yogurt tub in the freezer."

one 5–7 lb [2.2–3 kg] Boston butt (shoulder) pork roast, skin intact and bone in (you may have to special order this roast because most pork butts come without skin)

½ cup [125 mL] your favorite dry barbecue rub seasoning mix

about 4 chunks of applewood, for the smoker, soaked 24 hours in water

1½ cups [375 mL] pineapple juice

1½ cups [375 mL] apple cider

1½ cups [375 mL] your favorite barbecue sauce

12 soft-crust white buns

The morning before your dinner event, rub the pork roast well with your favorite dry rub seasoning, especially the exposed meat area where there is no skin. Place it in a food-safe plastic grocery bag and refrigerate it for about 12 hours.

At about 10 p.m. on the night before the dinner, fire up the smoker to maintain a steady interior chamber temperature of 200 to 220°F (95–100°C). Meanwhile, as the smoker is heating, prepare an injection brine by mixing together the pineapple juice and apple cider. Before the pork goes into the smoker, place the roast skin side down on a V-shaped roasting rack that holds the pork at least 1 inch (2.5 cm) above a tray to collect the drippings. Using a barbecue injection syringe, inject the roast completely through the exposed meat side with the pineapple-cider mixture, being careful not to pierce the skin, which acts as a bowl to contain the injected brine. ("It is amazing how much brine the roast will hold," says Ron.)

Place the roast in the smoker. Pour boiling water into the drippings pan to a depth of about 1 inch (2.5 cm). Close the lid, put an applewood chunk on the coals, and go to bed only when you are satisfied the smoker temperature is stable at about 200 to 220°F (95–100°C). Set the alarm clock to 5 a.m. Get up to check the smoker, restocking it with charcoal to maintain optimum cooking temperature and adding an applewood chunk.

By about 10 a.m., having been in the smoker for 12 hours, the pork should have an internal temperature of at least 185°F (85°C).

"The nice thing about this recipe," says Ron, "is that, after smoking the pork butt overnight on my Big Green Egg, I take it off at about 10 a.m. the next day and slather it generously with my barbecue sauce of choice. Then I double- or triple-wrap it in heavy foil, and place it on a baking tray to "hold" in the oven at 200°F (95°C) all afternoon without fear of drying out the meat, or mistiming my dinner. This leaves me free for as many hours as I need to make the side dishes—baked beans and slaw. This way, my guests and I can eat whenever we choose, with no stress."

One hour before serving, remove the roast from the oven and place it inside an empty Styrofoam cooler to rest.

To serve, easily remove the center bone, then pull the pork apart with 2 large carving forks. Serve it on buns with as much additional barbecue sauce as you prefer, but resist the temptation to overpower the meat with sauce. Ideal side dishes are slaw and baked beans.

ALL I REALLY NEED TO KNOW I LEARNED FROM BARBECUE

⋟With Apologies to Robert Fulghum⋞

Most of what I really need to know about how to live, and what to do, and how to be, I learned from cooking barbecue. Wisdom is not at the top of the culinary school mountain, but there on the grill and in the barbecue pit. These are the things I learned.

Put mustard and rub on everything. Don't use MSG. Don't start your coals with chemicals. Barbecue downwind from your neighbors. Oil your grill before you put your meat on. Don't take credit for recipes that aren't yours. Say you are sorry when you undercook the ribs. Wash your hands before you carve the brisket. Drink heavily. Coleslaw and beans are good for you. Strike a balance between work, family, and barbecue. Cook some and eat some and drink some and laugh and sing and dance and play and use your grill or smoker every day.

⋟ ⋞

Take a nap between spraying and turning your pork butt. When you prepare your meat for the judges, use fresh lettuce, present six portions, and go easy on the sauce. Be aware of the internal temperature. Remember the dipping sauce in the little plastic cup? The meat goes in and gets eaten and nobody really knows how or why. Barbecue is like that.

⋟ ⋞

And then remember that book about Barbecue Secrets and the first meat you ever barbecued, and the most flavorful hardwood of all: HICKORY! Everything you need to know about barbecue is there somewhere. Slow and low and smoke and sweet, salty, sour, bitter, and hot, fat and protein and the beauty of perfectly cooked meat.

⋟ ⋞

Think of what a better world it would be if we all, the whole world, had barbecue and peach daiquiris at about three o'clock every afternoon and then laid down for a nap with a bag of charcoal for a pillow. Or if we had a basic policy in our nation (and other nations) to always cook great barbecue and scrape the grill when we're done.

⋟ ⋞

And it is still true, no matter how old you are, that when you go to a barbecue contest it is best not to eat beforehand.

For Cluck's Sake: Poultry

Chicken is so ubiquitous in modern North American cuisine that it has almost become invisible, part of a kind of culinary background noise that takes up space on fast-food menus and makes for totally forgettable home cooking. We make it worse by insisting that chicken be cooked to extreme temperatures, creating dry, stringy, rubbery stuff that only barely qualifies as food.

In championship barbecue, chicken is one of the hardest dishes to get just right. Its skin can go rubbery in the chamber of the cooker, or it can be overcooked to the point where it becomes grainy and tastes too smoky.

But when cooked properly on a grill, or barbecued to perfection, chicken can transcend its boring modern life to transport us to a place where comfort food and dining adventure meet.

One more thing. It's worth the money to buy free-range organic chickens, which are much more flavorful than the regular kind. I like the corn-fed ones that have yellower skin and orange-toned flesh.

MEDITERRANEAN ROAST CHICKEN

MAKES 4 SERVINGS

This is a great way to roast chicken. Don't use too much hardwood smoke or it will overpower the flavor of the herbed rub. Serve the chicken with your favorite roasted vegetables and Dilled Smashed Potatoes (page 133).

➤ **BARBECUE SECRET** ≈

For extra flavor when grilling, place some hardwood chips on the coals. In a gas grill, place a chunk of hardwood below the cooking grate.

one 5 lb [2.2 kg] chicken
kosher salt to taste
1 Tbsp [15 mL] Dijon mustard
2 Tbsp [25 mL] Mediterranean
   Dried Herb Rub (see page 52)
1 Tbsp [15 mL] coarsely chopped
   fresh rosemary
1 tsp [5 mL] freshly ground
   black pepper

1 tsp [5 mL] granulated garlic
1 tsp [5 mL] granulated onion
½ tsp [2 mL] cayenne
½ cup [125 mL] extra virgin
   olive oil
1 tsp [5 mL] fresh lemon juice

Prepare your grill for indirect medium heat, with a drip pan underneath the unheated portion of the grill to catch the drippings. Rinse the chicken in cold water and pat it dry with paper towels. Generously season it with salt and coat it with mustard. Combine the rub, rosemary, pepper, garlic, onion, and cayenne in a small bowl. Coat the chicken with the mixture, patting it on with your hands to ensure it sticks. Drizzle the rubbed chicken with 1 Tbsp (15 mL) of the olive oil. Place the chicken, breast side up, on the unheated side of the cooking grate.

In a small bowl, combine the rest of the oil with the lemon juice.

Cook the chicken, using a small amount of fruitwood like apple or cherry as a flavoring agent, for about 1 hour, basting it every 20 minutes or so with the oil/lemon juice mixture, until the internal temperature at the thickest part of the thigh reaches 160°F (71°C). Remove the chicken from the grill, tent it with foil, and let it rest for 10 to 15 minutes. Carve it and serve it immediately.

For Cluck's Sake: Poultry

201

REALLY EASY CHICKEN

MAKES 6–8 SERVINGS

One of the biggest challenges of championship barbecue is finding a way to cook chicken so the skin doesn't turn out rubbery. This simple recipe is based on a technique some barbecue competitors use to get chicken skin that melts in the judges' mouths. The secret is the acid in the dressing, which softens the skin while the chicken is marinating.

2 chickens, cut into pieces, or 12 chicken thighs kosher salt and freshly ground black pepper	one 16 oz [475 mL] bottle store-bought zesty Italian salad dressing

Reserve ½ cup (125 mL) of the Italian dressing. Season the chicken pieces with salt and pepper and place them in an extra-large freezer bag. Add the rest of the dressing, making sure all the pieces are coated, and marinate the chicken in the refrigerator overnight.

Prepare your grill for indirect medium cooking. For propane grills, this means preheating the grill on high, turning off the burner underneath where you're going to place your meat, and then turning the other burner or burners to medium.

Place the chicken pieces on the cooking grate, skin side up, leaving at least a little space between them to ensure good air circulation. Cook the chicken, turning and basting it periodically with the reserved salad dressing, for 25 to 35 minutes, or until the internal temperature at the thickest part of the breast reads 160°F (71°C). Transfer the chicken from the grill to a serving platter and tent it with foil to rest for about 5 to 10 minutes. Serve it with your favorite accompaniments.

ALTERNATIVE METHOD: This recipe also works really well cooked on a hardwood plank, like maple or hickory. You just need to be careful to watch for flare-ups.

IF YOU DECIDE TO PLANK CHICKEN

Everyone has had to deal with chicken fat flare-ups and outright fires in the grill. Plank-cooking reduces the risk of chicken-related fires in your grill, but doesn't eliminate it. Remember that the lower the cooking temperature, the less risk of fatty flames.

Planks give a great smoky flavor, but they don't produce grill marks. If you like, take your chicken off the plank a few minutes before it's ready, remove the plank, and toss the chicken around on the cooking grate to crisp up the skin and create some flavorful caramelization.

The thing to know about planking poultry is that it seems to work best with hardwoods rather than cedar. For some reason, the astringent flavor of cedar just doesn't go quite as well with the delicate taste of chicken. But planking chicken on hickory or fruitwood gives it a classic smoky barbecue flavor, and the gentle heat of planking makes for juicy, succulent meat.

For Cluck's Sake: Poultry

CHAMPIONSHIP BARBECUE CHICKEN

This recipe was first developed by my old friend and fellow Butt Shredder, Ann Marie "Amo" Jackson, and it has won us some trophies over the years. The sauces are based on recipes by Paul Kirk, the one and only Baron of Barbecue. The key with this recipe is to cook at a low heat and baste often to keep the skin moist and tender. You'll have lots of barbecue sauce left over. It keeps indefinitely in the refrigerator.

two 4–5 lb [1.8–2.2 kg] chickens,
    quartered and backbones removed
1 recipe Asian Poultry Brine (see
    page 56)

BARBECUE SAUCE
2 cups [500 mL] ketchup
1 cup [250 mL] white vinegar
1 cup [250 mL] tightly packed dark
    brown sugar
½ cup [125 mL] pineapple juice
2 Tbsp [25 mL] soy sauce
1 tsp [5 mL] kosher salt
1 tsp [5 mL] cayenne or chipotle
    chili powder

CHICKEN BASTE
¾ cup [175 mL] pineapple juice
¼ cup [50 mL] butter, melted
2 Tbsp [25 mL] fresh lime juice
2 Tbsp [25 mL] soy sauce
2 Tbsp [25 mL] clover honey
1 Tbsp [15 mL] finely chopped fresh
    parsley
1 clove garlic, smashed or pushed
    through a garlic press
½ tsp [2 mL] kosher salt

Marinate the chicken with the brine in a nonreactive pot in the refrigerator for 2 to 4 hours.

Make the barbecue sauce by mixing all the ingredients in a saucepan. Bring the mixture to a boil and then simmer it for 15 to 20 minutes, stirring it occasionally. Cool completely.

Make the baste by combining all the ingredients in a saucepan. Heat it just enough to melt the butter. Keep it warm. The baste is best freshly made, but it can be kept in a covered nonreactive container for up to a week in the refrigerator.

Barbecue Secrets DELUXE!

Take the chicken pieces out of the brine and pat them dry. At this point, you can sprinkle them with a little barbecue rub, but it's not necessary.

Prepare your smoker for barbecuing, bringing the temperature up to 200 to 220°F (95–100°C). Line the drip pan of your smoker with a double layer of foil and fill it with apple juice.

Place the chicken pieces in the smoker. Cover it and cook the chicken for about 1½ to 2 hours, painting the chicken with the baste every 15 minutes, until the internal temperature at the thigh joint reaches 160°F (71°C). Give the chicken a coat of the barbecue sauce and cook it another 5 minutes. Transfer it to a serving platter, tent it loosely with foil, and let it rest for 5 to 10 minutes. Serve the chicken with some barbecue sauce on the side for dipping.

GRILLED ACHIOTE CHICKEN BREASTS
WITH MIXED GREENS

MAKES 4–6 SERVINGS

Achiote is a rust-colored paste made from annatto seeds, which are a common ingredient in Mexican cooking. You can find it in Latin grocery stores and gourmet specialty food stores. It adds an unusual and distinctive flavor and wonderful color to grilled food, and is fantastic with chicken and shrimp. Serve this with Confetti Rice (page 144).

six 5 oz [150 g] boneless, skinless
    chicken breasts

MARINADE
2 cloves garlic
½ tsp [2 mL] kosher salt
1¾ oz [50 g] achiote paste (half of a
    standard-sized brick of paste)
1 tsp [5 mL] ground cumin
1 tsp [5 mL] dried oregano
½ tsp [2 mL] granulated onion
1 Tbsp [15 mL] honey
½ cup [125 mL] fresh-squeezed
    orange juice
1 Tbsp [15 mL] lime juice
1 Tbsp [15 mL] extra virgin olive oil

SALAD
3 Tbsp [45 mL] orange-infused olive oil
    (available at most supermarkets)
1 Tbsp [15 mL] rice vinegar or
    champagne vinegar
1 tsp [5 mL] Dijon mustard
1 shallot, finely minced
kosher salt and freshly ground black
    pepper
5 oz [150 g] bag mixed salad greens
1 ripe avocado, peeled and cut into
    bite-sized chunks
12 cherry tomatoes, halved
chopped cilantro for garnish

Peel and chop the garlic cloves; place them in a large bowl. Sprinkle the salt on top of the chopped garlic and mash it into a fine paste with the back of a fork. Place the mashed garlic in a bowl and add the achiote paste, cumin, oregano, granulated onion, and honey. Wet the ingredients with a splash of the orange juice and mash everything together, making a smooth paste. Add the rest of the orange juice, the lime juice, and the olive oil and mix thoroughly. Place the chicken breasts in the bowl and toss to coat them with the marinade. Marinate the chicken, covered, in the refrigerator for at least 2 hours or overnight, turning it once or twice to keep it coated.

(continued)

Pictured with Confetti Rice (page 144)

Grilled Achiote Chicken Breasts with Mixed Greens *(continued)*

Make the vinaigrette by combining the oil, vinegar, mustard, and shallot in a salad bowl and whisking the ingredients together. Season the vinaigrette to taste with salt and pepper and set it aside.

Prepare your grill for direct medium heat. Remove the chicken breasts from the marinade and grill them for about 4 to 5 minutes, turning them every couple of minutes, until the breasts reach an internal temperature of 160°F (71°C) at the thickest part of the breast. Transfer the chicken to a cutting board and let it rest, tented in foil, for 5 minutes.

While the chicken is resting, toss the mixed greens, avocado, and tomatoes with the vinaigrette and place a pile of the salad on each serving plate. Slice the chicken into bite-sized chunks and arrange it on top of the greens. Garnish the dish with chopped cilantro and a light sprinkling of salt and pepper.

SOUTHWESTERN GRILLED
CHICKEN CLUB SANDWICH

MAKES 2–4 SERVINGS

You may never go back to Subway after eating this juicy, tender chicken club sandwich, a great postgolf Saturday lunch.

4 large boneless, skinless chicken
   breasts, fillet removed

RUB

1 Tbsp [15 mL] kosher salt

1 Tbsp [15 mL] granulated garlic

1 Tbsp [15 mL] granulated onion

1 Tbsp [15 mL] ground coriander

1 Tbsp [15 mL] ground toasted cumin

1 tsp [5 mL] cayenne

1 tsp [5 mL] freshly ground black
   pepper

SANDWICHES

extra virgin olive oil

4 soft white hoagie buns

softened butter

granulated garlic

1 lemon

kosher salt and freshly ground black
   pepper to taste

1 cup [250 mL] Margie's Chipotle &
   Roasted Garlic Mayo (see page 68)

1 bunch fresh arugula, washed and dried

2 large ripe tomatoes, thinly sliced

1 red onion, peeled and thinly sliced

Combine all the rub ingredients in a medium bowl and set aside. Prepare your grill for direct medium heat.

Place the chicken breasts in a large resealable plastic bag and pound them with a mallet to an even ½-inch (1 cm) thickness. Place the breasts on a platter, sprinkle them generously with the rub on both sides, and drizzle them with olive oil to moisten the rub.

Slice the buns in half, butter them, and sprinkle them with the granulated garlic. When the grill is hot, place the breasts oiled side down on the cooking grate, close the grill, and cook them for no more than 1 to 2 minutes per side. After you have turned the breasts, put the buns on the grill, buttered side down. When the breasts are just barely done and the buns are toasted, transfer them to 2 separate plates. Drizzle the breasts with olive oil and a squeeze of lemon and season them with salt and pepper.

Generously slather the toasted buns with the mayo and make a bed of arugula on the bottom half of each bun. Top with the chicken breasts and tomato and onion slices, seasoning the works with salt and pepper. Close the sandwiches, slice them in half, and serve.

For Cluck's Sake: Poultry

209

TUSCAN GRILLED GAME HENS

MAKES 2 MAIN COURSE SERVINGS OR 4 SERVINGS AS PART OF A MULTICOURSE MEAL

This is a delicious way to enjoy Cornish game hens. I've adapted this recipe from one given to me by my Italophile brother, Allan. Serve these with grilled vegetables and your favorite risotto, polenta, or pasta.

2 Cornish game hens
¼ medium onion
2 large cloves garlic
¼ cup [50 mL] tightly packed fresh
   basil leaves
1 tsp [5 mL] Mediterranean Dried Herb
   Rub (page 52)
1 Tbsp [15 mL] chopped fresh rosemary
4 slices pancetta, chopped (about 2 oz/
   60 g)

5 Tbsp [75 mL] good-quality
   balsamic vinegar
1 Tbsp [15 mL] extra virgin olive oil
kosher salt and freshly ground black
   pepper to taste
½–1 cup [125–250 mL] dry white wine
½ cup [125 mL] extra virgin olive oil
sprigs of fresh rosemary, parsley, or
   thyme for garnish

Wash the hens and pat them dry with paper towels. Mince the onion, garlic, fresh and dried herbs, and pancetta by hand or in a food processor. Blend 2 tsp (10 mL) of the vinegar with the 1 Tbsp (15 mL) of oil and add it to the mixture. Season it with salt and pepper.

Cut through the hens' backbones and open them out flat, skin side up. Firmly press down on the breast area to flatten them. Stuff most of the herb mixture under the skin of the thighs, legs, and breasts. Rub the rest all over the hens. Refrigerate for 1 or 2 hours.

Prepare your grill for indirect medium heat with a pan under the cooking grate. Combine the wine and the ½ cup (125 mL) of oil. When your grill is hot, place the birds skin side up on the grate. Grill them for 20 minutes, baste them with the wine mixture, and turn them. Cook them for another 20 minutes, basting and turning them every 5 minutes, until the internal temperature at the base of each thigh is 160°F (71°C). If the hens are not golden brown, crisp them, skin side down, over direct heat for a few minutes, watching out for flare-ups.

Let the hens rest for 5 minutes tented with foil. Drizzle them with oil, season them with salt and pepper, and garnish with fresh herbs.

Pictured with Asian Noodle Salad with Sesame Mayonnaise (page 119)

KATE'S TASTY ASIAN CHICKEN THIGHS

MAKES 4–6 SERVINGS

These tangy, flavorful chicken thighs are based on a recipe by Anya Von Bremzen and John Welchman in their *Terrific Pacific Cookbook*. They go well with Asian Noodle Salad with Sesame Mayonnaise (page 119). This recipe calls for grilling, but you can also barbecue the chicken in a smoker for a truly unforgettable dish, and then finish it by crisping the skin on a hot grill. Because this is a relatively complicated recipe to make, Kate likes to do a double batch and freeze half for later enjoyment.

12 chicken thighs, bone in, skin on (about 3½ lb/1.6 kg)
2 tsp [10 mL] ground coriander
1 tsp [5 mL] freshly ground black pepper
1 tsp [5 mL] kosher salt

MARINADE
1½ Tbsp [22 mL] tamarind pulp (Thai is best)
⅓ cup [75 mL] chicken stock, boiling
6 Asian dried red chilies, each 2–3 inches [5–8 cm] long
4 large cloves garlic, chopped

3 Tbsp [45 mL] chopped shallots
2 tsp [10 mL] chopped fresh ginger
1 Tbsp [15 mL] chopped fresh lemongrass or 2 tsp [10 mL] grated lime zest
1½ Tbsp [22 mL] vegetable oil
3 Tbsp [45 mL] dark soy sauce
3 Tbsp [45 mL] packed light brown sugar
1½ Tbsp [22 mL] rice vinegar
1½ Tbsp [22 mL] ketchup
½ cup [125 mL] finely chopped fresh basil

> **BARBECUE SECRET**
>
> Chicken thighs cooked with wood smoke will usually develop a smoke ring—turning the meat close to the outside a characteristic pink color. Inexperienced guests can sometimes mistake this for underdone fowl. Reassure them by making sure you monitor the internal temperature of the meat during cooking and remove the chicken only after it has reached the desired 160°F (71°C) at its thickest part.

Rinse the chicken pieces well in cold water and pat them dry with paper towels. Prick the skin all over with the tines of a fork. In a small bowl, combine the coriander, pepper, and salt, and rub the mixture into the chicken pieces. Set the chicken aside.

(continued)

Kate's Tasty Asian Chicken Thighs *(continued)*

Add the tamarind pulp to the boiling stock, remove it from the heat, and soak it for 15 minutes. Stir the mixture and mash it with a fork to help the tamarind dissolve. Strain it through a fine strainer into a bowl, pressing on the solids with the back of a wooden spoon to extract all the liquid. Discard the tamarind that remains in the strainer and set aside the liquid.

Stem the chilies and shake out and discard the seeds. Using scissors, cut the chilies into ¼-inch (6 mm) pieces. Soak them in enough warm water to cover for 10 minutes. Drain them well. Combine the chilies, tamarind liquid, garlic, shallots, ginger, lemongrass or lime zest, oil, soy sauce, sugar, vinegar, ketchup, and basil in a food processor and process them into a purée. Arrange the chicken in a large, shallow dish and pour the marinade over it. Cover and refrigerate it for at least 2 hours, but preferably overnight.

Remove the chicken pieces from the marinade and pour the marinade into a saucepan. Heat it to a boil and let it simmer for 10 minutes. Taste it and adjust the seasonings. Remove it from the heat and transfer it to a bowl.

Prepare your grill for indirect medium heat, with a pan underneath the unheated side of the grill to catch the drippings. Place the chicken on the grill and cook it for 20 to 25 minutes, or until the internal temperature reaches 160°F (71°C), basting it every 5 minutes with the marinade. At the last minute, move the chicken thighs to the hot side of the grill and toss them about to crisp the skins, taking care not to burn them. Place the chicken on a serving dish, spoon over the remaining basting sauce, and serve it immediately.

BIG DADDY'S
BARBECUED THAI CHICKEN THIGHS

MAKES 4 SERVINGS

Ian "Big Daddy" Baird is a sometime Butt Shredder who has traveled in Asia. He tells me that one of the best pieces of meat he's ever eaten was a whole chicken thigh and drumstick he purchased from a street vendor out the window of a train as he waited to cross the Thai/Malaysian border. He tried numerous times to re-create it himself, but it wasn't until he married this recipe with real barbecue technique that he came close. Serve this chicken with cold beer.

10–12 chicken thighs, bone in, skin on

MARINADE
6 Tbsp [90 mL] fresh lime juice
¼ cup [50 mL] fresh-squeezed
   orange juice
¼ cup [50 mL] Thai fish sauce
¼ cup [50 mL] peanut or canola oil
¼ cup [50 mL] raw sugar or lightly
   packed brown sugar
¼ cup [50 mL] minced fresh basil

¼ cup [50 mL] green onions
¼ cup [50 mL] fresh cilantro
5–10 cloves garlic, finely minced
2 Tbsp [25 mL] finely minced
   fresh ginger
1 Tbsp [15 mL] Asian chili sauce

BASTING MIXTURE
½ cup [125 mL] peanut oil
1 Tbsp [15 mL] fresh lime juice

Trim the chicken thighs of excess fat. Mix all the marinade ingredients together and put them in a resealable plastic bag. Place the chicken in the bag, remove the air, and seal it. Marinate the chicken for at least 2 hours, and up to a maximum of 8 hours, in the fridge.

Prepare your smoker for barbecuing, bringing the temperature up to 200 to 220°F (95–100°C). Make the basting mixture by combining the peanut oil and lime juice in a bowl.

Discard the marinade and place the chicken in the smoker for 2½ hours, turning and basting it every hour. If you wish, give the skin side a quick sear on a hot grill to really crisp the skin before you take it off the heat. Let it rest, tented with foil, for 5 minutes before serving.

For Cluck's Sake: Poultry

THE WINGS VARIATIONS

Chicken wings are so easy to grill or barbecue. To trim them, just cut the wing tips off and discard them. I like to leave the wing/drumettes together, but you can separate them if you like. Flavor the wings with your favorite rub or marinade.

On the grill, cook the wings for 8 to 12 minutes using direct medium-to-high heat, turning them regularly, until they're almost charred, basting them with your favorite barbecue sauce for the last few minutes of cooking.

To barbecue wings, prepare your smoker for barbecuing, bringing the temperature up to 200 to 220°F (95–100°C). Cook the wings for about an hour with hickory, mesquite, or fruitwood as a flavoring agent, and then crisp them up on a grill if you like. They're great just with a mustard slather and Championship Barbecue Rub (page 50), but try these variations.

Fiery Southwestern Wings Make a simple rub with 1 part chipotle chili powder, 1 part ancho chili powder, and 1 part garlic salt. Grill the wings till they're crispy and finish them with a drizzling of olive oil, a pinch of kosher salt, and a squeeze of lemon.

Teriyaki Wings Marinate the wings in teriyaki sauce for 2 hours. Grill them till they're crispy, basting them with more sauce. Finish them with extra sauce and a sprinkle of toasted sesame seeds.

Buffalo-Style Grilled Wings Melt ¼ cup (50 mL) of butter and add ½ cup (125 mL) of Louisiana-style hot sauce (Frank's RedHot, Tabasco, etc.). Salt and pepper the wings and grill them till they're crispy. Take the wings off the grill and immediately toss them in the butter/hot sauce mixture. Serve them with blue cheese dressing and celery and carrot sticks.

Lemon Dijon Rosemary Wings Season the wings with salt and pepper and coat them with Dijon mustard. Sprinkle them with dried rosemary and a very light dusting of cayenne. Grill them until they're crispy, season them with a little more salt and pepper, and squeeze a lemon over them just before serving.

Cumin Seed Wings Season the wings, slather them with mustard, and coat them lightly with cumin seeds. Then sprinkle them with Rockin' Ronnie's Grilling Rub (page 51). Grill them till they're crispy, drizzle them with olive oil, and season them with salt and pepper.

Pictured: Fiery Southwestern and
Lemon Dijon Rosemary Wings

JAMAICAN JERK CHICKEN

SERVES 4–6

I had the pleasure of visiting the north coast of Jamaica in 2007 and got to taste some fantastic cooking in Montego Bay and Ocho Rios, including the spicy, smoky jerk chicken that's as close to the taste of the original *barbacòa* as you can get. Jerk Centres—local restaurants—are everywhere, and each one has its own distinctive style. The common flavors are extreme chili heat and intense smoke—the heat derived from the infamously fiery habanero or Scotch bonnet chili and the smoke coming from pimento wood, which has a sharp, mesquite-like aroma. The pimento tree berry is known outside of Jamaica as allspice, which is another of the key flavors of any jerk seasoning.

I often use skinless chicken thighs for this recipe because the slow-cooking technique tends to make chicken skin rubbery. If you leave the skin on, finish the dish by crisping the skin side of the chicken pieces over direct medium heat.

NOTE: The habaneros make this quite hot. If you want a milder jerk, use less or substitute jalapeños or serranos. In any case, wear vinyl gloves when you're handling them and watch not to get any chili in your eyes!

4 lb [1.8 kg] skinless chicken thighs
   (or 1 whole chicken cut into parts)

MARINADE

2 medium onions, coarsely chopped

1½ cups [375 mL] green onions,
   trimmed and coarsely chopped

1 cup [250 mL] water

1 or 2 habanero chilies, chopped

1½ Tbsp [22 mL] fresh thyme (or
   1 tsp/5 mL dried thyme)

2 tsp [10 mL] whole Jamaican allspice,
   lightly toasted in a dry sauté pan and
   then finely ground (or use ground
   allspice if you don't want to fuss)

2 tsp [10 mL] sugar

1 tsp [5 mL] freshly ground black pepper

1 tsp [5 mL] freshly grated nutmeg

1 tsp [5 mL] kosher salt

½ tsp [2 mL] ground cinnamon

3 Tbsp [45 mL] neutral-flavored cooking
   oil like canola or corn oil

2 Tbsp [25 mL] cider vinegar

1 tsp [5 mL] browning (liquid caramel—if
   you don't have any, use 1 Tbsp/15 mL
   dark soy sauce or liquid gravy seasoning like Kitchen Bouquet or Bovril)

splash of Appleton Estate dark rum

Combine all the marinade ingredients in a blender or food processor and blend them thoroughly. Reserve about one-third of the mixture and set it aside.

Put the chicken in a lasagna pan or large baking dish and pour 1 cup (250 mL) of the marinade over it. Move the chicken pieces around so they are covered completely. Cover the chicken with plastic wrap and refrigerate it for at least 3 or 4 hours or overnight, turning it once or twice to make sure the pieces are coated evenly.

Prepare your smoker for barbecuing, bringing the temperature to 200 to 220°F (95–100°C). Just before you're ready to put the chicken on, toss 1 chunk of mesquite (or pimento wood if you can get it) on the coals. Place the chicken pieces on the cooking grate and smoke for 1½ to 2 hours, basting the chicken regularly with the remaining marinade, until the temperature at the thickest part of the biggest piece reads 160°F (71°C). (At this point, if you're using chicken with skin on, you can crisp it up on a medium grill.)

Remove the chicken from the cooker and let it rest, lightly tented in foil, for 5 minutes. Garnish it with Red Onion, Green Mango, and Jalapeño Pickle (page 312) or Tropical Salsa (page 63) and serve it with Jamaican-Style Rice and Beans (page 143) and Jamaican Coleslaw (page 113).

ALTERNATIVE METHOD: If you want to cook the chicken on a gas or charcoal grill, prepare the grill for indirect medium-low heat (about 250°F/120°C) and cook it as above, using mesquite as a flavoring agent, if you like. At the end of the cooking time, raise the temperature of the grill to medium and crisp up the chicken pieces for a few minutes over direct heat.

DILLED YOGURT CHICKEN KEBABS

MAKES APPETIZERS FOR 12 OR A MAIN COURSE FOR 4–6

Yogurt and dill do something wonderful to chicken. Using chicken thighs instead of breast meat gives these kebabs added richness. Serve these as an appetizer or as a main course with Field Greens with Toasted Walnut Oil and Pumpkin Seeds (page 116) and Dilled Lemony Rice (page 145).

8 metal skewers or 12 presoaked
    bamboo skewers
2 lb [1 kg] boneless, skinless chicken
    thighs, cut into bite-sized chunks

MARINADE

1 cup [250 mL] plain full-fat yogurt
½ cup [125 mL] chopped fresh dill
½ tsp [2 mL] dried dill
1 Tbsp [15 mL] granulated onion
2 cloves garlic, forced through a
    garlic press
1 tsp [5 mL] fresh lemon juice

pinch cayenne
grinding of black pepper

KEBABS

2 medium sweet white onions, quartered
    and separated into bite-sized chunks
    (or use a cut-up fennel bulb, or a
    combination of the two)
kosher salt and freshly ground black
    pepper to taste
extra virgin olive oil for drizzling
1 lemon, cut into wedges

Combine the yogurt, fresh and dried dill, granulated onion, garlic, lemon juice, cayenne, and pepper in a nonreactive container. Add the chicken pieces and refrigerate the chicken for at least 2 hours or as long as overnight.

Thread the chicken pieces onto the skewers, alternating the meat with the onion (or fennel) chunks. Prepare your grill for direct medium heat. Place the kebabs on the grate and cook them for 3 to 5 minutes per side, or until they're just done. Take the kebabs off the grill, season them with salt and pepper, drizzle them with some olive oil, and serve them immediately. Garnish them with lemon wedges.

TIKKA-STYLE CHICKEN KEBABS

MAKES 4 SERVINGS

My friend Jagreet's mom, a great East Indian home cook, shared her chicken marinade recipe with me, and I'm sharing it with you. Serve these kebabs on a bed of steamed basmati rice with some of your favorite chutney.

8 bamboo skewers, soaked in cold
    water for at least half an hour
4 large boneless, skinless chicken
    breasts, cut into bite-sized chunks

MARINADE
1 cup [250 mL] plain yogurt
3 Tbsp [45 mL] neutral-flavored oil,
    like canola or peanut
3 Tbsp [45 mL] minced fresh ginger
3 Tbsp [45 mL] minced garlic
1 tsp [5 mL] kosher salt

2 Tbsp [25 mL] fresh lime juice
1 Tbsp [15 mL] tandoori paste
1 Tbsp [15 mL] garam masala
1 large red onion, peeled and cut
    into chunks
1 lime

KEBABS
extra virgin olive or canola oil
kosher salt to taste
1 lime

Make the marinade by combining the yogurt, oil, ginger, garlic, salt, lime juice, tandoori paste, and garam masala in a large nonreactive bowl and mixing the ingredients together well. Add the onion chunks and the chicken, cover the mixture with plastic wrap, and marinate the chicken overnight in the refrigerator.

Prepare your grill for direct medium heat. Thread the chicken pieces and marinated onion pieces onto the skewers. Grill the kebabs for 4 to 6 minutes, turning them 2 or 3 times. (Don't overcook the chicken or it will have a mealy texture!) Remove the kebabs from the grill, drizzle them with a little oil, season them with salt, squeeze some fresh lime juice over each skewer, and serve them immediately.

For Cluck's Sake: Poultry

AMO'S APPLE-SMOKED TURKEY
WITH FRUIT & SAVORY STUFFING

MAKES 12–14 SERVINGS

Amo Jackson is a fantastic cook and a longtime member of the Butt Shredder team. She likes to cook this turkey overnight, because it needs to cook for about one hour per pound (500 g). Please plan accordingly, and note that you will need about 20 lb (9 kg) of charcoal, plus a bunch of fist-sized chunks of applewood. You'll also need a spray bottle and a turkey rack, available at most cookware stores.

TURKEY

one 15–20 lb [6.75–9 kg] fresh
    turkey (rinsed with cold water and
    patted dry)
1 cup [250 mL] yellow mustard
granulated garlic
6 quarts [6 L] apple cider or apple
    juice for the water pan
8 strips bacon

RUB

1 cup [250 mL] sugar
¼ cup [50 mL] celery salt
¼ cup [50 mL] garlic salt
¼ cup [50 mL] onion salt
¼ cup [50 mL] seasoning salt
¼ cup [50 mL] poultry seasoning
⅓ cup [75 mL] chili powder

⅓ cup [75 mL] freshly ground black
    pepper
⅓ cup [75 mL] smoked paprika

STUFFING

2 apples, cut into eighths
1 onion, cut into eighths
1 orange, cut into eighths
1 lemon, cut into eighths
1 bunch fresh thyme
3 sprigs fresh rosemary
3 sprigs fresh sage
7 whole cloves garlic, peeled

MOP

2 cups [500 mL] apple juice
½ cup [125 mL] maple syrup

Combine all the rub ingredients in a medium bowl.

    Toss together the stuffing ingredients along with ¼ cup (50 mL) of the rub in a large bowl. Loosely pack the stuffing into both cavities of the turkey. Cover the large opening (by the legs) with a doubled piece of cheesecloth. Secure it to the turkey skin with wooden skewers. This holds in the stuffing while allowing the applewood smoke to enter the cavity.

    Combine all the mop ingredients in another medium bowl, then pour the mixture into a spray bottle.

Coat the turkey with the mustard. Sprinkle the granulated garlic, and then the rub, on the breast side of the turkey first. Turn the bird over and repeat the process on the underside. Place the turkey on a turkey rack breast side down. Cover the turkey with the bacon strips. Tent the turkey with foil or plastic wrap, put it in the refrigerator, and let it rest for at least 1 hour, or overnight.

Plan ahead so you'll have time to cook the turkey for 1 hour per pound (500 g) and let it rest afterward. About an hour before you need to put the turkey on, fill the charcoal basket of the smoker with about 15 lb (6.75 kg) of charcoal. Add 5 chunks of applewood to the charcoal and mix it in.

Start a charcoal chimney half full of coals. When the charcoal is white, dump the coals on top of the cold coals in the smoker to create a seed fire. Close the smoker. Line the water pan with foil, put it back in the smoker, and fill it with apple cider or apple juice.

Transfer the turkey rack, with the turkey on it, from the refrigerator directly onto the bottom grill, just above the water pan.

Make sure the smoker temperature is maintaining a stable temperature of 200 to 220°F (95–100°C), adjusting the air vents accordingly.

Go to bed!!!

About 6 to 8 hours later, replenish the charcoal and wood chunks. Refill the water pan with apple cider and start to spray the turkey with the mop. Mop the turkey every hour or two, until it reaches an internal temperature of 160°F (71°C) at the center of the thickest part of the breast, or right at the thigh joint.

Remove the turkey with the rack and place them on a rimmed baking sheet; spray the turkey with the mop one more time and tightly tent it with foil.

Let the turkey rest for at least 1 hour before removing the stuffing to carve it.

AMO'S CRANBERRY BERRY SAUCE

MAKES ABOUT 6 CUPS [1.5 L] SAUCE

Amo always makes this sauce to go with the juicy, smoky turkey.

one 12 oz [375 g] bag cranberries (about 3 cups/750 mL)

2 cups [500 mL] fresh berries (any combination of blackberries, raspberries, and blueberries, or, in the summer months, chopped fresh peaches)

1½ cups [375 mL] orange juice

¾ cup [175 mL] sugar

½ cup [125 mL] maple syrup

Combine all the ingredients in a medium saucepan over medium heat. Bring the mixture to a boil, then turn the heat down to low and simmer the mixture, uncovered, for half an hour. Serve hot or cold.

SMOKED & GRILLED
MEDITERRANEAN-STYLE TURKEY
IN A HURRY

MAKES ENOUGH TO SERVE A FESTIVE GATHERING OF AT LEAST 15 PEOPLE

My friend and fellow foodie Don Genova is a well-known Canadian media personality. He hosts a great blog (http://blog.dongenova.com) and his podcast, "All You Can Eat," is consistently ranked among the most popular food podcasts on iTunes. I asked him to contribute one of his favorite recipes to this book. This great dish is what he came up with. The trick to this recipe is to start the turkey in a hot smoker and finish it on a hot grill so you get a nice crispy skin.

NOTE: This is the one recipe in this book in which I call for you to prepare your smoker for a higher temperature than the normal 200 to 220°F (95–100°C). Don uses an electric Traeger smoker, which uses hardwood pellets and is easy to get to a higher cooking temperature. I've adapted this recipe with the assumption that you're using a standard bullet-style water smoker like a Weber Smokey Mountain Cooker.

one 10–12 lb [4.5–5.5 kg] turkey
1 cup [250 mL] extra virgin olive oil
½ cup [125 mL] fresh oregano and
   rosemary, chopped

4–5 cloves garlic, finely chopped
smoked paprika, sea salt, and freshly
   ground black pepper to taste
4–6 Tbsp [60–90 mL] fresh lemon juice

Mix together the oil, herbs, garlic, spices, and lemon juice in a small bowl.

Cut the wing tips off the turkey and save them for making stock. Then cut off the turkey thighs and legs, keeping the thigh and leg as 1 piece. Cut the backbone out of the turkey and save it for stock, then butterfly the breast by squishing it flat, skin side up.

Smear the oil and herb mixture all over the turkey pieces, working some of it under the skin wherever possible, and marinate it, refrigerated, for at least 1 hour and up to overnight.

Let the turkey sit at room temperature for about 1 hour before you start cooking.

Barbecue Secrets DELUXE!

Remove the turkey pieces from the marinade and reserve the marinade for basting.

Prepare your smoker for barbecuing, bringing the temperature up to 250 to 300°F (120–150°C). To achieve this higher temperature on a water smoker, don't put any liquid in the water pan, start with a full chimney of charcoal, and make sure all vents are wide open.

Put the turkey pieces on the smoker for about 2 hours, skin side up, using hickory or applewood as the flavoring agent. Remove the turkey pieces from the smoker and set them aside. (To avoid wasting charcoal, either use the remaining cooking time to smoke some tomatoes, onions, nuts, etc., as described on page 104, or close off all air vents to shut down the fire.)

Prepare your grill for direct medium heat. Grill the turkey pieces for about half an hour, turning regularly, until the skin crisps, the juices run clear, and a meat thermometer inserted at the thickest part of the thigh reads 160°F (71°C). Remove the turkey pieces from the grill and let them rest, tented in foil, for about half an hour. Carve the turkey pieces into slices and serve them with your favorite accompaniments.

THE OLD MAN & ➤ THE BEEF ➤

by Kate Zimmerman

[Here's a classic piece of humor from my lovely, sarcastic wife, Kate.—R.S.]

It is true that in this world there are men who cook every day, well or poorly, and do not expect acclaim. There are women like this as well. But in the experience of this writer, a man prepares for a dinner party quite differently from a woman.

He does not perceive the need for a marathon of cleaning and tidying. He does not trouble himself with the sordid details of scouring the bathroom, making three courses that complement each other, or setting the table with ironed napkins rather than paper towels.

Instead, he selects the most spectacular cooking job for himself, fusses over every tiny aspect of it, and then reaps the accolades not just for making this dish, but for being a man and being able—and willing!—to make this dish.

It is to this sort of man, and to this man's companion, that the following article is dedicated.

When a man, just any man, but for the purposes of this story, Everyman, enters the kitchen, it must be in the spirit of the matador.

He must strut, he must flap his apron like a cape at the snorting oven, and he must (preferably to the strains of "Toreador" from Bizet's *Carmen*) sharpen his knife in the air, with great drama.

For HE is going to prepare the MAIN COURSE.

It will be no ORDINARY main course. Men's main courses are never ordinary. If they were, men would not cheapen themselves by preparing them. They would rather not participate in the dinner party at all than prepare something ordinary, or worst of all, vegetarian.

This extraordinary main course will require the death of an animal, perhaps the fiercest of animals. If not a bull, then an extremely bitchy cow. An extremely bitchy cow that is now a thick, bloody porterhouse steak.

The matador knows his task, and it is a good, fine task. He will torture this steak and singe this steak and turn this steak into a feast for which the crowds will cheer and the ladies will throw down the flowers they are wearing in their long, flowing hair.

On this day, just any day, but for the purposes of this story, a Saturday, there is silence in the bullring. From a distant room, the brave matador can hear the whine of the vacuum cleaner as the picador prepares for her minute role in his drama.

The matador is cool. He approaches the thickly marbled beast as if to befriend it, muttering softly in Spanish. With his two enormous hands he slowly coats it in rock salt and black pepper, which he has just finished crushing with forceful bashes of an empty champagne bottle. Gently, he

Men's main courses are never ordinary. If they were, men would not cheapen themselves by preparing them.

slides the brute onto a broiling pan. Then he lets it sleep.

The matador must now preserve his stamina. He leaves the kitchen and enters the bedroom, which is suddenly full of the irritating noise of the picador dusting and picking the matador's socks, shoes, and magazines off the floor.

He lies down on his bed in the coolness of the afternoon, and he sleeps.

Hours later, he is awakened by the sound of clinking as the picador attempts, somewhat clumsily, to set a table somewhere in the vast and still-dusty plain of the house.

Cursing to himself at this interruption, the matador rises and feels the need to refresh himself with a shower. He emerges from the billowing steam like a proud, nude flamenco dancer and prances about the house singing "Carmen, You Is My Woman Now." He is confused from his long sleep.

He passes the picador in the hall as he strides purposefully toward the kitchen. The picador glares at him angrily, as if the spirit of the bull has infused her.

But the matador cannot be distracted. He brushes aside evidence of the picador's meddling. In the arena of the kitchen, dirty bowls and pans signifying some unimportant project of hers are cluttering up the ledges.

The matador sighs the long, deep sigh of the martyr. He throws the dirty bowls aside, where the wild dog of the house will soon draw sustenance from the batter encrusting them.

He cannot be drawn away from his purpose. At the edge of the arena, the bullfighter stands quietly, head bowed. Suddenly, he thrusts his chest forward and struts proudly to the center of the ring. With a dazzling smile at the dog, he unfurls his blood-red apron, aims a sharp glance at the clock, and approaches the dormant, pepper-encrusted monster.

The matador, and the beast, must now wait. They eye each other cautiously, but with intensity. The matador circles the bull—a difficult task since it is resting on the counter.

A bell rings. The matador looks up from his prey angrily. The picador answers the door and greets the crowd in a hushed tone, leading the men and women to their places round the ring of the arena.

They stand in silence; they are not allowed ice cubes in their drinks. They do not want to frighten the bull or enrage the matador. The picador also knows better. She knows, as well, that the matador didn't bother to make any ice.

The matador tosses his head. He knows he must melt some butter on top of the stove; he knows he must add some chopped tarragon to the butter. And he must do it now.

The matador tosses his head. He knows he must melt some butter on top of the stove; he knows he must add some chopped tarragon to the butter. And he must do it now.

He clicks his heels together. He snaps his castanets. He turns on the front element and places the small pot on top. The butter begins to sizzle. The people in the crowd gaze at him and then at each other in wonderment. They say nothing. They are not stupid, these people. Even the matador, so proud and so arrogant, will grant them that.

The picador has not done her job. The oven is not yet as hot and red as a Madrid sunset. The matador once again sighs the long, deep sigh of the martyr. With a deft movement, he turns the switch and an angry red light goes on.

It is time. He clicks his castanets thrice, brusquely, in a manner that at once suggests

He strikes a pose, then strikes a match, touching it to the liquor. It bursts into fire.

blood, death, resurrection, and the Clapper. The crowd has stopped breathing. The picador wonders if she should call 9-1-1. She knows the matador will not allow it.

Now he picks up the beast, recumbent in its broiling pan, and approaches the glowering oven. As the matador eases open the door, smoke billows into the kitchen. He smiles the smile of the devil. He slides the pan so close to the upper element it seems the bull must explode. The smell of singed meat and roasting peppercorns fills the arena.

Even so, the crowd knows it must not yet utter even a small "bravo." The tarragon butter is bubbling in its pot. The matador seizes a bottle of caramel-colored Calvados and lifts it to his lips. He takes a draught, then wipes his mouth with his sleeve, sneering. The picador does not register her usual disgust, which is both the disgust of the co-host and the disgust of the long-suffering wife. She waits. Everyone waits.

They watch as the matador pours the Calvados freely into another small pot, turns a switch, and sets the pot on the element.

He steps back. He leans down and squints into the oven. He sees a blackened beast, a proud savage now broken. He turns the slab of meat over and jabs it back under the broiler. The moment of truth is near. Two minutes pass. The beast is pulled out again, this time to be slashed dramatically into helpless bloody strips and thrust back into the fire once more.

Now the matador rolls up his apron and uses it to protect his massive hands as he slides the conquered monster out of the oven. The picador springs into action, prodding the crowd to take its seats. The matador struts to the table bearing the beast. He returns to the arena for a low, dramatic bow and comes back, holding the hot Calvados. He strikes a pose, then strikes a match, touching it to the liquor. It bursts into fire.

Then, as the crowd stares, transfixed, the matador pours the flaming Calvados upon his trophy.

He hears a roar. Has the ferocious bull come back to life? For a moment, and it is the first moment in a very long while, the bullfighter experiences fear. But then he realizes the roar is that of the crowd, which has risen to scream its approval. The ladies are throwing down the roses from their hair. The picador, also, looks faintly impressed, even though her appetizer has been forgotten.

The matador douses the flames with the tarragon butter. He sits down. He bows his head. He rests. He waits for more applause. He knows that on this day, he has made himself a legend.

This article first appeared in City Palate *magazine.*

Steer It Up: Beef

What can one say about beef, the King of Meats? What *can't* one say? This meat offers so many variations, so much flavor, and it's so easy to cook. Salt and pepper and a hot fire are all you really need for a profound beef experience. This section of the book is my humble tribute to what, in the end, is my all-around favorite food.

Most barbecue cooks use meat thermometers to carefully monitor the internal temperature of big cuts of meat, but for most purposes, you can easily tell whether a steak or chicken breast is done simply by applying pressure to it with your forefinger. If the meat does not spring back, it's still pretty raw. If it has a soft springiness, it's medium rare and ready to take off the grill. If you press it and it feels firm and stiff, it's overdone.

Here's a great way to learn these hand readings. Hold your left hand in front of your chest, palm side down. Touch the meaty area between your thumb and forefinger. That's what rare meat feels like. Now, extend your fingers so they are evenly spread out in the universal "stop right there" sign. Press the same place and you'll find out what medium rare meat should feel like. Now make a fist and press again. That's well done, and if your meat feels like this you should make use of the fist you just made and punch yourself in the forehead.

EASIEST, TASTIEST STEAK

MAKES 4 SERVINGS

I've been grilling steaks bathed in this marinade for over 25 years and I have not found a way to improve on it. It's so easy and adds so much flavor that every backyard cook should have it in his or her repertoire. These steaks go well with just about any side. I like them with roasted baby potatoes and grilled asparagus. The marinade is also great with pork chops as well as rich, meaty fish like salmon, halibut, tuna, and swordfish.

4 well-marbled beef rib steaks, about
   1½ inches [4 cm] thick

MARINADE
1 cup [250 mL] dark soy sauce
2 cloves garlic, finely minced
1 Tbsp [15 mL] finely chopped or
   grated fresh ginger

1 Tbsp [15 mL] fresh lemon juice
   or ¼ cup [50 mL] mirin (Japanese
   sweet rice wine)
1 tsp [5 mL] toasted sesame oil
1 Tbsp [15 mL] tapioca starch
   (cornstarch will also do)
freshly ground black pepper

Combine the marinade ingredients in a nonreactive baking dish. Add the meat, turn it to coat it, and marinate it for 10 minutes to half an hour, turning it once or twice. Do not marinate it overnight, as this is a fairly salty marinade.

   Prepare your grill for direct medium heat. Place the steaks on the grill and cook them for about 4 minutes. Turn the steaks, spoon a little more marinade on top, and then cook them for another 4 minutes for medium rare. Let them rest about 4 minutes and serve.

Steer It Up: Beef

COWBOY STEAKS

MAKES 4 SERVINGS

This is pretty close to my favorite steak. The earthiness of the cumin seeds, the sharpness of the cracked pepper, the sweetness of the onion and garlic granules, and the smoky, tart bite of the chipotle creates an explosion of flavor. Serve whole steaks with beans, a slab of cornbread, and some coleslaw. Alternative serving suggestion: slice up the cooked steaks and serve them fajita-style with salsa, guacamole, and shredded Jack cheese alongside some warm flour tortillas.

4 big rib-eye steaks, bone in, about
   1½ inches [4 cm] thick
½ cup [125 mL] black peppercorns
kosher salt (or another fancy coarse salt
   like Maldon or fleur de sel) to taste
1 Tbsp [15 mL] granulated onion

1 Tbsp [15 mL] granulated garlic
1 tsp [5 mL] chipotle chili powder
   (if you can't find chipotle, use the
   same amount of cayenne)
1 Tbsp [15 mL] toasted cumin seeds
extra virgin olive oil

Place the steaks in a dish or on a large cutting board and let them come to room temperature (it'll take about 1 hour). Use a spice mill or a mortar and pestle to give the peppercorns a coarse grinding, or put them in a thick paper or plastic bag and pound them with a hammer or rolling pin until they reach the desired consistency. They shouldn't be powdery, but more like coarse sand. Generously season the steaks with salt and pepper. Combine the granulated onion and garlic, ground chipotles, and cumin seeds in a bowl. Coat the steaks on 1 side with the mixture, patting it on so it sticks nicely. Drizzle the rubbed steaks with a light coating of olive oil, turn them over and repeat the seasoning, rub it in, and drizzle some oil on top.

Prepare your grill for direct medium heat and cook the steaks 4 to 6 minutes per side for medium rare. If using a charcoal grill, toss a couple of chunks of mesquite (or a handful of wood chips) onto the coals just prior to grilling. With a gas grill, use a foil pack of presoaked chips with holes punched into it with a fork.

Be sure not to overcook the steaks! Remember, they will continue to cook after they are taken off the heat. Remove them from the grill and let them rest for 4 to 5 minutes before serving.

Steer It Up: Beef

233

STEAK, ITALIAN STYLE

MAKES 4 SERVINGS

The Ruby Lake Restaurant on the Sunshine Coast of British Columbia serves great Italian food in a rustic resort setting. Legend has it that some days the restaurant owners put a fresh fish on a stump near the restaurant patio and a local bald eagle makes a show of swooping down and grabbing the fish in its talons. I had a juicy T-bone there once that showed me that sometimes the simplest treatments are the best ones when you're grilling a steak.

4 well-marbled T-bone steaks, at least 1 inch [2.5 cm] thick kosher or Maldon salt and coarsely ground black pepper to taste	1 bunch fresh arugula, washed and dried dried Greek oregano best-quality extra virgin olive oil lemon wedges

Bring the steaks to room temperature by leaving them out of the fridge for 1 hour. Season them generously on both sides with salt and pepper. Drizzle them lightly with olive oil. Prepare your grill for direct medium heat. Grill the steaks 4 to 6 minutes per side, or until they're done the way you and your guests like them (I recommend taking the steak off the heat when the meat springs back slightly when poked, which is when it reaches an internal temperature of about 125°F/52°C). Remove the steaks from the grill and let them rest, tented in foil, for 4 to 5 minutes.

Make a little bed of arugula on each plate and put the steaks on top. Crumble a little oregano on each steak, drizzle it with olive oil, and season it with a little more salt and freshly ground pepper. Garnish it with lemon wedges. The juice and oil from the steak and the squeeze of lemon will create a fabulous natural dressing for the slightly bitter arugula.

LEMONY HERBED FLANK STEAK

MAKES 4 SERVINGS

This dish uses a lemony vinaigrette to marinate the steak as well as to dress it. The clean, simple flavors make for a perfect summer meal. Serve it with Grilled Asparagus (page 129) on the side.

1 large flank or skirt steak, about
   1½–2 lb [750 g–1 kg]
kosher salt and freshly ground
   black pepper

MARINADE
½ cup [125 mL] lemon-infused olive oil
1 Tbsp [15 mL] finely grated lemon zest
3 Tbsp [45 mL] white balsamic vinegar
1 Tbsp [15 mL] Dijon mustard

2 cloves garlic, peeled and finely minced
½ cup [125 mL] finely chopped fresh
   herbs (oregano, thyme, and parsley
   work well)
kosher salt and freshly ground black
   pepper to taste

GARNISH
lemon wedges
sprigs of fresh herbs

Place the flank steak in a baking dish and season both sides with salt and pepper. Let it come up to room temperature for about half an hour.

Combine the marinade ingredients in a bowl and thoroughly whisk them together. Divide the mixture in half, and set aside one half for finishing the dish.

Coat the steak with the remaining half of the mixture. Cover the baking dish with plastic wrap and marinate it for 2 hours or overnight.

Prepare your grill for direct high heat. Remove the steak from the marinade and pat it dry. Place the steak on the cooking grate and grill it on high for 30 seconds per side, just long enough to get some nice grill marks on the meat. Reduce the heat to medium and cook it, turning it once or twice, for about 4 to 6 minutes per side, or until the thickest part of the steak has an internal temperature of 125°F (52°C). Transfer the steak to a cutting board and let it rest, loosely tented in foil, for 5 to 10 minutes.

To serve the steak, carve it across the grain into thin slices and arrange the slices on serving plates. Sprinkle it with a little salt and pepper and spoon on some of the reserved dressing. Garnish with lemon wedges and herb sprigs.

FLANK STEAK FAJITAS ADOBO
WITH MANGO STRAWBERRY SALSA

MAKES 4 SERVINGS

This recipe, which once won me a brand new grill in a cooking contest, makes use of the flank steak, one of the tougher and leaner cuts of beef, but also by far the most flavorful. The trick to great flank steak is to make sure you don't overcook it, let it rest before carving it, and cut thin slices across the grain. This recipe contrasts a spicy marinade with a fruit salsa. The fajitas go well with cold Mexican beer or a light red wine like a Beaujolais.

1 large flank or skirt steak, about
   1½–2 lb (750 g–1 kg)

MARINADE
½ tsp [2 mL] kosher salt
¼ cup [50 mL] fresh lime juice
2 tsp [10 mL] vegetable oil
1 Tbsp [15 mL] ground cumin
1 Tbsp [15 mL] ancho or New Mexico
   chili powder
6 cloves garlic, peeled
2 canned chipotle chilies in adobo
   sauce
freshly ground black pepper to taste

MANGO STRAWBERRY SALSA
2 ripe (but not too ripe) mangoes,
   peeled, pitted, and roughly chopped
½ cup [125 mL] ripe but firm
   strawberries, stems removed and
   roughly chopped
1 jalapeño, seeded and finely chopped
2 Tbsp [25 mL] fresh lime juice
½ tsp [2 mL] kosher salt
½ tsp [2 mL] sugar
1 or 2 dashes Louisiana-style hot sauce
freshly ground black pepper to taste

FAJITAS
12 flour tortillas, wrapped in foil and
   warmed in a 250°F [120°C] oven
1 bunch fresh cilantro, roughly chopped

Blend all the marinade ingredients together in a food processor until you have a fairly smooth paste. Place the steak in a nonreactive baking dish and spoon on the marinade, thoroughly coating the steak on both sides. Cover the steak with plastic wrap and refrigerate it for at least 6 hours or overnight, turning it once or twice.

Half an hour before cooking the steak, combine the salsa ingredients and lightly toss them in a bowl. Season the salsa to taste, cover it, and put it in the refrigerator.

Prepare your grill for direct high heat. Place the flank steak on the grill. Flip it after 3 minutes and spoon 1 or 2 Tbsp (15 or 25 mL) of the marinade on top. Cook it for 3 more minutes and flip it again. Grill it for 1 more minute for rare; add 1 or 2 minutes per side for medium rare. Set the steak on a cutting board, tent it with foil, and let it rest for at least 5 minutes.

Thinly slice the flank steak across the grain, creating juicy strips of meat, and place it in a warmed serving dish. Put out the salsa, cilantro, and warmed tortillas. People can now serve themselves by placing a couple of slices of meat, then a dollop of salsa, then a sprinkling of cilantro, on a tortilla, folding it up, and wolfing it down.

GRILL

GRILLED TURKEY HILL PEPPER STEAK

MAKES 4 SERVINGS

Turkey Hill Pepper Steak comes to us from gourmand and log-home builder John Boys, who got it from someone else who lived in a place called Turkey Hill. The original recipe is the one that inspired the story The Old Man and the Beef, which appears on page 226 of this book. I have adapted the recipe, which is usually broiled, for the grill. The classic accompaniments are scalloped potatoes and peas, but Grilled Asparagus (page 129) and Dilled Smashed Potatoes (page 133) would work great.

one 2 lb [1 kg] porterhouse steak,
    about 2–2½ inches [5–6 cm] thick
kosher salt to taste
½ cup [125 mL] whole black
    peppercorns

½ lb [250 g] butter
1 Tbsp [15 mL] chopped fresh tarragon
½ cup [125 mL] Calvados (French
    apple brandy)

Take the steak out of the fridge at least 1 hour before you plan to cook it and pat a fairly generous amount of salt on both sides. Lightly crush the peppercorns in a spice mill or put them in a paper bag and pound them with a flat mallet. Coat the salted steak liberally with the pepper. Let the steak sit until it reaches room temperature, about another half hour.

Gently warm the butter in a small saucepan until it is just melted but not sizzling. Add the tarragon and set it aside, keeping the butter on the stovetop to keep it warm. Preheat your grill for direct high heat and turn your oven to 200°F (95°C) to warm 4 plates and a serving platter.

Gently warm the Calvados in a small saucepan, being careful not to boil it or expose it to a flame. Keep the Calvados and tarragon butter warm and ready.

Grill the steak for about 3 minutes per side, until the peppercorns are throwing off a spicy fragrance. Turn off 1 side of the grill and cook the steaks over indirect heat for another 3 minutes per side, or until the steak is not quite medium rare (it should have an internal temperature of about 120°F/50°C). Transfer the steak from the grill to a warmed plate and tent it with foil.

When the steak has rested for at least 5 minutes, cut the meat off the bone and slice it into ½-inch (1 cm) strips. Place the steak slices on the warmed platter and bring the platter, the Calvados, and the tarragon butter to the table. As your guests watch in awe, pour the warmed Calvados over the steak slices and immediately light the platter of meat with a match. Toss the steak slices around until the flames subside and then pour the tarragon butter over them, tossing the steak again before serving. Be sure you spoon some of the buttery sauce over each serving.

BEEF TENDERLOIN STEAKS
WITH GORGONZOLA BUTTER

MAKES 6 SERVINGS

This is dead simple, and deadly delicious. Just make sure you don't overcook it! Serve the tenderloin with your favorite steak accompaniments.

six 6 oz [175 g] tenderloin (filet
    mignon) steaks, about 2 inches
    [5 cm] thick
kosher salt and coarsely ground
    black pepper

extra virgin olive oil
Gorgonzola Butter (see page 67), at
    room temperature
balsamic reduction (see sidebar
    page 242)

Generously season the steaks with salt and coarsely ground black pepper. Let them sit for 1 hour to bring them to room temperature.

Prepare your grill for direct medium heat. Drizzle the steaks with a little oil and place them on the cooking grate. Cook the steaks for 2 to 4 minutes per side (depending on how rare you like them). Take them off the grill, tent them in foil, and let them rest for a few minutes. Serve them with a pat of Gorgonzola Butter and a few drops of balsamic reduction.

T-BONE STEAK
WITH ROSEMARY & BALSAMIC MARINADE

MAKES 4 SERVINGS

➤ BALSAMIC REDUCTION ≈

This incredible tangy, sweet, rich syrup has a multitude of uses. It supercharges any vinaigrette. It's great in marinades (or as a simple marinade on its own), and you can even drizzle it on ice cream or fruit.

Pour a 10 oz (300 mL) bottle of cheap balsamic vinegar (you could use more or less as your need dictates; this is just a handy amount to prepare) in a small saucepan and bring it to a boil over medium-high heat. Cook it at a gently rolling boil, watching it carefully, until the vinegar has reduced to about one-third of its original volume (10–15 minutes). When it's ready, it should be a thick syrup that coats the back of a spoon. Set it aside to cool. Transfer it to a squeeze bottle and store it in a cool, dry place. It keeps indefinitely.

Man, I love a good T-bone. It's the ultimate steak, in a way, because it combines the strip loin and the fillet in one handy cut (the two live in peaceful harmony on either side of the bone). The key ingredient here is the balsamic reduction, which penetrates the steak and gives it a bright, distinctive flavor.

two 16–20 oz [500–625 g] T-bone steaks, each about 2 inches [5 cm] thick
kosher salt
cayenne
1 Tbsp [15 mL] chopped fresh rosemary
2 cloves garlic, smashed or pushed through a press
⅓ cup [75 mL] balsamic reduction (see sidebar)
kosher salt and freshly ground black pepper
¼ cup [50 mL] finely chopped fresh parsley
extra virgin olive oil

Take the steaks out of the fridge and put them in a nonreactive dish. Season them with salt and a pinch of cayenne on both sides. Evenly spread the rosemary and garlic over the steaks. Set aside half of the balsamic reduction and drizzle the rest over the steaks, turning them to coat both sides. Refrigerate the steaks, uncovered, for at least 2 hours or overnight, turning them once or twice.

Prepare your grill for direct medium heat. Grill the steaks 4 to 6 minutes per side, or until they have an internal temperature of 125°F (52°C).

Remove the steaks from the grill and let them rest, loosely tented in foil, for about 5 minutes. Using a paring knife, carve the steaks from the bone and slice them into ½-inch (1 cm) slices. Divide the slices between 4 plates and drizzle them with the remaining balsamic reduction. Finish them with a sprinkle of salt, a grinding of pepper, some chopped parsley, and a drizzle of olive oil.

KOREAN-STYLE RIB-EYES

MAKES 6 SERVINGS

Koreans like a little sweet and sour in their marinades and so do I. This recipe draws on the flavors of Korean barbecue, but with a distinctly North American cut and portion size. This goes well with Asian Slaw (page 114), Wasabi Mashed Potatoes (page 137), and Grilled Asparagus (page 129).

three 16 oz [500 g] rib-eye steaks, about 2 inches [5 cm] thick, with rib bones attached

MARINADE
1 cup [250 mL] soy sauce
¼ cup [50 mL] rice vinegar
⅓ cup [75 mL] chopped green onions
2 Tbsp [25 mL] liquid honey

2 Tbsp [25 mL] finely minced garlic
2 Tbsp [25 mL] finely minced fresh ginger
1 tsp [5 mL] toasted sesame oil
1 tsp [5 mL] Vietnamese hot sauce

GARNISH
1 green onion, chopped
toasted sesame seeds

Combine the marinade ingredients in a nonreactive bowl or pan. Place the steaks in the marinade and turn them to coat them. Refrigerate them, uncovered, for at least half an hour and up to 2 hours, turning them once or twice. Remove the steaks from the marinade and pat them dry. Transfer the marinade to a small saucepan and cook it over medium-high heat until it comes to a boil. Reduce the heat to medium-low and simmer the marinade for 5 minutes. Set it aside.

Prepare your grill for direct medium heat. Cook the steaks for 4 to 6 minutes per side, or until they have an internal temperature of 125°F (52°C). Remove them from the grill and let them rest, loosely tented in foil, for about 5 minutes.

Remove the steaks from the bone and cut them into ½-inch (1 cm) slices. Divide the slices between 4 plates and drizzle them with a little of the sauce. Garnish the meat with chopped green onion and sesame seeds. Put the remaining sauce in a serving dish so guests can help themselves.

GRILL-ROASTED TRI-TIP

MAKES 6–8 SERVINGS

Tri-tip is the bottom half of a sirloin roast. It looks like a mini brisket, but it's more tender and doesn't need long cooking because it's quite lean and doesn't have as much connective tissue.

one 3 lb [1.5 kg] well-marbled tri-tip (bottom sirloin) roast	½ tsp [2 mL] crushed dried red chili flakes
kosher salt to taste	1 Tbsp [15 mL] fresh rosemary
3 cloves garlic, peeled and coarsely chopped	1 tsp [5 mL] dried oregano
2 large shallots	1 Tbsp [15 mL] coarsely ground black pepper
	¼ cup [50 mL] extra virgin olive oil

Let the roast sit out of the fridge for half an hour to 1 hour to bring it up to room temperature. Prepare the grill for indirect medium cooking.

Place the remaining ingredients in a food processor and whiz them together until they're blended but not completely puréed. Coat the roast in the paste, reserving 2 Tbsp (25 mL) for basting, and let the meat sit until the grill is ready.

Grill the roast for 45 minutes to 1 hour on the unheated side of the grill, using hickory wood as a flavoring agent. Turn the roast once or twice and baste it with the reserved paste. When it's nearly done—it starts to feel springy to the touch, or the temperature at the thickest part reaches about 130°F (55°C) for medium rare—move it to the hot side of the grill, turn up the heat to high, and sear it on both sides for a few minutes to crisp up the crust. Remove the roast from the grill, tent it in foil, and let it rest for at least half an hour.

Slice the roast across the grain as thinly as you can, sprinkle it with a little salt, and serve it with your favorite accompaniments.

HAWAIIAN-STYLE GRILLED TRI-TIP

MAKES 6–8 SERVINGS

I love everything about Hawaii. This tri-tip recipe conjures memories of warm sea breezes and tropical sunsets. This recipe is based on one by famed Hawaiian chef Sam Choy. Serve this with Tropical Salsa (page 63) and Grilled Rice Cakes (page 146).

one 3 lb [1.5 kg] well-marbled tri-tip (bottom sirloin) roast

MARINADE
2 Tbsp [25 mL] Japanese soy sauce (or Hawaiian shoyu, if you can get it)
2 Tbsp [25 mL] brown sugar
1 Tbsp [15 mL] finely minced fresh garlic or 1 tsp [5 mL] granulated garlic

1 Tbsp [15 mL] grated fresh ginger
1 Tbsp [15 mL] sea salt (or the red Hawaiian type if you can get it)
1 Tbsp [15 mL] cracked black peppercorns
1 tsp [5 mL] freshly ground black pepper
1 tsp [5 mL] granulated onion

extra sea salt to finish

Combine all the marinade ingredients in a large nonreactive bowl. Place the tri-tip in the bowl and thoroughly coat it with the mixture. Cover the bowl and place it in the refrigerator for 1 or 2 hours, turning the roast periodically.

Prepare the grill for indirect medium cooking. Grill the roast for 45 minutes to 1 hour on the unheated side of the grill, using fruitwood like apple or cherry as a flavoring agent. Turn the meat once or twice. When the roast is nearly done—it starts to feel springy to the touch, or the temperature at the thickest part reaches about 130°F (55°C) for medium rare—move it to the hot side of the grill, turn up the heat to high, and sear it on both sides for a few minutes to crisp up the crust. Remove the roast from the grill, tent it in foil, and let it rest for at least half an hour.

Slice the roast across the grain as thinly as you can and serve it sprinkled with a little sea salt.

Steer It Up: Beef

CALGARY-STYLE
GINGER BEEF TRI-TIP

MAKES 6–8 SERVINGS

In Calgary, Alberta, most Chinese restaurants serve a special version of ginger beef—strips of beef that are lightly battered, deep-fried, and then candied with a sweet, sticky, tangy sauce that has lots of heat. I was inspired by fond memories of the dish to create this tasty grilled tri-tip.

one 3 lb [1.5 kg] well-marbled tri-tip
   (bottom sirloin) roast

RUB

2 Tbsp [25 mL] sugar
1 Tbsp [15 mL] ground ginger
1 Tbsp [15 mL] granulated garlic
1 Tbsp [15 mL] kosher salt
1 tsp [5 mL] ground cumin
1 tsp [5 mL] paprika
1 tsp [5 mL] freshly ground black pepper
½ tsp [2 mL] Chinese five-spice powder
½ tsp [2 mL] cayenne

FINISHING GLAZE

one 12 oz [355 mL] jar sweet orange
   marmalade
3 Tbsp [45 mL] frozen orange juice
   concentrate
¼ cup [50 mL] soy sauce
½ cup [125 mL] apple cider vinegar
1 clove finely minced garlic
2 tsp [10 mL] grated fresh ginger
1 tsp [5 mL] crushed dried red
   chili flakes

Combine all the rub ingredients in a bowl and set the mixture aside.

Put the glaze ingredients in a saucepan and bring the mixture to a simmer over medium heat, stirring occasionally. Set aside.

Generously sprinkle the tri-tip with the rub (you will have some left over). Let it sit for half an hour or so, until the roast starts to glisten.

Prepare the grill for indirect medium cooking. Grill the roast for 45 minutes to 1 hour on the unheated side of the grill. Turn it once or twice. When the roast is nearly done—it starts to feel springy to the touch, or the temperature at the thickest part reaches about 125°F (52°C) for medium rare—move it to the hot side of the grill, turn up the heat to high, and paint it generously with the glaze, turning and coating it until the glaze is sticky and caramelized (be careful not to burn it).

Remove the roast from the grill, tent it in foil, and let it rest for at least half an hour. Slice it across the grain as thinly as you can and serve it with a drizzle of the remaining glaze.

VINCE'S HERBED VEAL RIBS

MAKES 4 SERVINGS

Vince Gogolek is a fellow Butt Shredder who has perfected this recipe for veal ribs. They're not usually available in supermarkets, but if you can find them at a butcher shop, they make a delicious alternative to pork or beef ribs (which also work well in this recipe). They're also relatively inexpensive (for veal, anyway). This recipe uses a fresh herb rub, which acts like a marinade, getting the herb flavor deep into the meat. Serve the ribs with grilled vegetables and Minty Potato Hobo Pack (page 138).

one 2–3 lb [1–1.5 kg] rack veal ribs

HERB RUB
¼ cup [50 mL] fresh rosemary, finely chopped
¼ cup [50 mL] fresh parsley, finely chopped
2 Tbsp [25 mL] fresh oregano, finely chopped

4 fresh sage leaves, finely chopped
2 fresh basil leaves, finely chopped
2 cloves garlic, finely minced
½ cup [125 mL] extra virgin olive oil
2 Tbsp [25 mL] kosher salt
2 Tbsp [25 mL] coarsely ground black pepper

Remove the shiny membrane from the back of the ribs. Combine all the herb rub ingredients in a medium bowl and apply the rub to the ribs, ensuring it gets into all the crevices so it can permeate the meat like a marinade. Refrigerate the ribs overnight.

Prepare your grill for direct medium heat. Grill the ribs, turning them often, for 45 minutes to 1 hour, using direct medium heat to brown them and get grill marks, then moving them to indirect heat for another half an hour after browning.

ALTERNATIVE METHOD: For extra flavor and instead of grilling, smoke the ribs for 5 hours using fruitwood as the flavoring agent.

BARBECUED BEEF SHORT RIBS
WITH ASIAN DRY RUB

MAKES 6 SERVINGS

I love short ribs because they have so much fat and connective tissue. With slow cooking and a little smoke, they transform into rich, succulent, fork-tender morsels of pure carnivore love. This dish goes well with Grilled Rice Cakes (page 146) and Asian Slaw (page 114).

six 10 oz [300 g] pieces of beef short ribs, at least 2 inches [5 cm] thick, preferably on the bone

DRY RUB
1 Tbsp [15 mL] kosher salt
1 tsp [5 mL] freshly ground black pepper
1 tsp [5 mL] granulated garlic

½ tsp [2 mL] ground ginger
½ tsp [2 mL] Chinese five-spice powder

TO FINISH
prepared mustard
vegetable oil
Asian Barbecue Sauce (see page 61)

Combine all the rub ingredients in a small bowl. Coat the ribs with a thin layer of mustard. Lightly coat them with the rub and drizzle them with a little oil, patting it on gently so the ribs are glistening. Set them aside.

Prepare your smoker for barbecuing, bringing the temperature to 200 to 220°F (95–100°C). Make sure you line your water pan with a double layer of extra-wide foil and fill the pan with apple juice.

Put the ribs in the smoker. Cover and cook them for 4 to 5 hours. Use hickory or applewood chunks as a flavoring agent. The ribs are done when the meat has come away from the bone and has a soft, jellylike feel. Glaze them with the sauce once or twice in the last half hour of cooking. Remove the ribs from the smoker and let them rest, tented in foil, for 10 minutes. Serve them with more sauce on the side for dipping.

PLANK

PLANK-ROASTED PRIME RIB

MAKES 6–8 SERVINGS

☞ PLANKING SECRET ☜

The flavor of cedar smoke goes well with so many foods, from salmon to cheese, and even beef. But most of the time, when I'm planking beef, I want classic hardwood flavor. I choose planks made of oak, hickory, and mesquite, although fruitwoods also work well.

This is a novel way to cook a classic cut of beef because it imparts an unexpected smoky flavor (even more unusual if you use a cedar plank). The key with cuts like this is to be careful not to overcook.

1 plank, any kind you like,
  soaked overnight or at least
  1 hour
one 5 lb [2.2 kg] rib roast,
  bones attached

DRY RUB
1 Tbsp [15 mL] granulated garlic
  or garlic powder
1 Tbsp [15 mL] granulated onion
  or onion powder
1 Tbsp [15 mL] coarsely ground
  black pepper

1 Tbsp [15 mL] dried rosemary
¼–½ tsp [1–2 mL] cayenne

kosher salt
2 Tbsp [25 mL] Dijon mustard
1 Tbsp [15 mL] coarsely chopped
  fresh rosemary
extra virgin olive oil
4 or 5 whole fresh rosemary
  branches, each about 5 inches
  [12 cm] long

Combine all the rub ingredients in a small bowl and set aside.

Take the roast out of the fridge and let it sit for 1 hour to come to room temperature. Season it on all sides with kosher salt. Coat it with the mustard. Sprinkle the rosemary evenly on the roast, then sprinkle it generously with the dry rub (you'll have some left over). Drizzle it with olive oil and pat the rub and rosemary into the roast.

Preheat the grill on medium-high for 5 to 10 minutes, or until the chamber temperature rises above 500°F (260°C). Rinse the soaked plank and place it on the cooking grate. Cover the grill and heat the plank for 4 to 5 minutes, or until it starts to throw off a bit of smoke and crackles lightly. Reduce the heat to medium-low.

(continued)

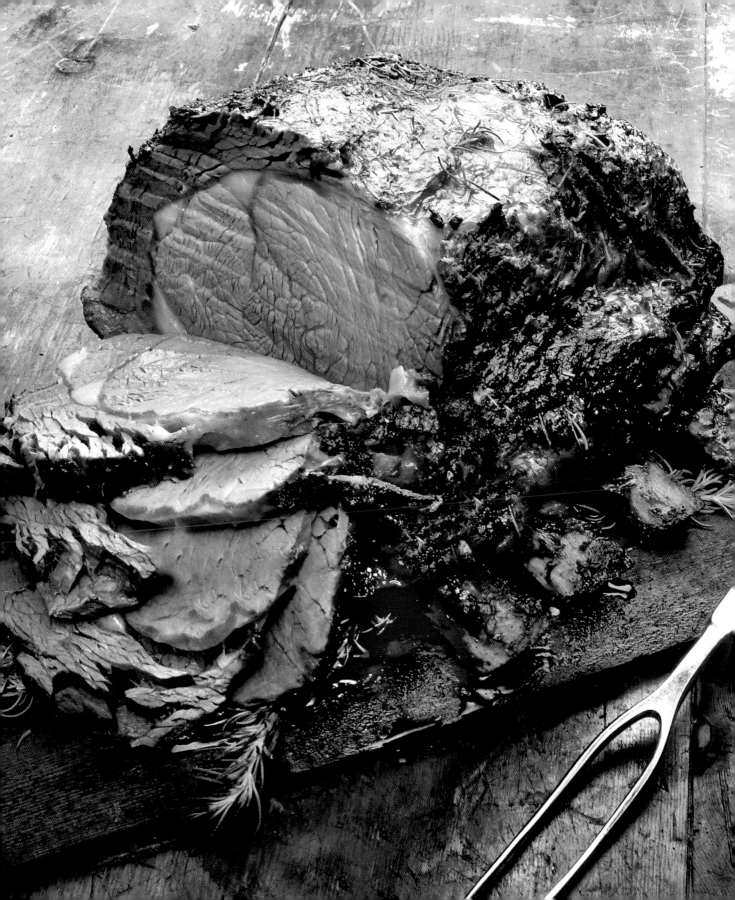

Plank-Roasted Prime Rib *(continued)*

Lay the rosemary twigs across the plank to make a bed for the roast. Place the roast on the rosemary and cover the grill. Cook for 1½ to 2 hours, until the core of the roast reaches an internal temperature of 125°F (52°C) for medium rare. Remove the roast from the grill, tent it loosely in foil, and let it rest for half an hour to 1 hour before serving it with your favorite sides. The long resting time gives you plenty of time to grill some veggies.

ALTERNATIVE METHOD: You can also cook this roast over indirect medium heat on a gas or charcoal grill.

BEAUTIFUL BRONTO BEEF RIBS

MAKES 4–6 SERVINGS

These are the ribs that tipped over Fred Flintstone's car. You can use the rub on anything, but it goes exceptionally well with this dish.

2 racks beef prime ribs, 6–8 bones
    per rack

RUB
1 Tbsp [15 mL] black peppercorns
1 Tbsp [15 mL] dried mushrooms
    (porcini, morels, or chanterelles
    work well)

1 tsp [5 mL] cumin seeds
1 Tbsp [15 mL] ancho chili powder
½ tsp [2 mL] chipotle chili powder or
    cayenne

kosher salt
extra virgin olive oil

Grind the pepper, dried mushrooms, and cumin seeds using a spice mill or electric coffee grinder until they are the consistency of coarse sand. Combine the mixture in a bowl with the ancho and chipotle chili powders. Season the ribs with a generous coating of salt and then give them a light drizzle of oil. Coat them liberally with the rub. Let the ribs sit for up to half an hour, or until the rub starts to glisten.

    Prepare the grill for indirect medium heat with a pan to catch the drippings. Grill the ribs for 1 to 1½ hours, turning them every 15 minutes or so and basting them with olive oil, until the internal temperature in the thickest part of the ribs reaches 140°F (60°C). For the last 10 minutes of the cooking time, put the ribs over direct heat to char and crisp them up. You can finish these with your favorite barbecue sauce but I prefer them just like this. Serve them with classic barbecue accompaniments.

BBQ

ALTERNATIVE METHOD: For a whole 'nuther layer of flavor, smoke these ribs for 4 to 5 hours, using oak or mesquite as a flavoring agent, and finish them on the grill.

CHEF ALLEMEIER'S WILD SAGE-RUBBED
BEEF TENDERLOIN
WITH ALBERTA MUSTARD SAUCE

MAKES ENOUGH FOR 1 AWARD-WINNING PLATTER TO SERVE 6 BARBECUE JUDGES

Michael Allemeier is Executive Chef at Mission Hill Family Estates, one of the world's premier destination wineries. Michael is also a barbecue fanatic and honorary Butt Shredder. He's competed twice in the Jack Daniel's World Championship Invitational Barbecue, and at the last one, he won a coveted JD oak-barrel trophy for this dish, which was his first-place entry in the "Home Cookin' from the Homeland" contest, an opportunity for international teams to chance to compete in an unlimited category. He's pictured here with Queen of Smoke, Sharma Christie.

WARNING: This is an outrageously elaborate recipe that's designed to win an international barbecue contest, so if you're going to do it, study the instructions carefully. For me, it's a great read and an insight into the mind of a world-class chef.

BEEF TENDERLOIN

1 whole beef tenderloin
12 cloves garlic, chopped
20 large fresh sage leaves, sliced into superthin strips (chefs call this a chiffonade)

2 lemons and their grated zest
1 tsp [5 mL] freshly ground black pepper
⅓ cup + 2 Tbsp [100 mL] extra virgin olive oil

To prepare the tenderloin, clean the tenderloin by removing the train and the head. Clean up the head and use it for something else, like tenderloin steaks or kebabs. Square off the remaining loin to create a large chateaubriand. All the remaining trim and train can be ground for something else. Mix the garlic, sage, lemon zest, pepper, and olive oil in a bowl and mix them together well. Lay out a large piece of plastic wrap and place the beef on top. Rub in the herb mixture to fully cover the beef. Wrap up the tenderloin *tightly* in the plastic and chill it overnight. The next day, remove the meat from the fridge and bring it to room temperature. Preheat a charcoal grill to 400°F (200°C). Place the meat on the grill and close the lid. Turn it every 5 minutes to sear it well. Reduce the heat to 325°F (160°C) and cook the tenderloin to an internal temperature of 120°F (50°C). Remove it and let it rest in a warm place for 30 minutes.

Barbecue Secrets DELUXE!

SMOKED ONIONS

4 medium cooking onions

oak chunks

To prepare the smoked onions, prepare your smoker for barbecuing, bringing the temperature up to 200 to 220°F (95–100°C). Smoke the onions in their skins for about 1½ hours, or until they're al dente. Use oak as a flavoring agent and apple juice in the water pan. Let the onions cool. Peel them carefully and cut them in half. Remove the inner cores, leaving only the 2 to 3 outer layers, which will become bowls that will contain the sauce for the tenderloin. Chop up the cores and reserve them for use in the sautéed mushrooms.

GRILLED PORTOBELLO MUSHROOMS

8 portobello mushrooms, stems removed and gills scraped out

½ cup [125 mL] extra virgin olive oil

5 Tbsp [75 mL] canola oil

5 Tbsp [75 mL] balsamic vinegar

3 Tbsp [45 mL] chopped fresh rosemary

kosher salt and freshly ground pepper

To prepare the grilled portobellos, combine the olive oil, canola oil, vinegar, and rosemary together in a bowl. Add the mushrooms and toss them in the marinade. Cover them well and chill them overnight. Prepare the grill for direct medium heat. Grill the mushrooms for about 3 minutes per side, or until they are soft and shiny, and season them well with salt and pepper. Cut each mushroom into a perfectly round shape and add the trim to the mushroom sauté.

SAUTÉED MUSHROOMS

10 slices thick bacon, diced

smoked onion pieces, removed from the center of the smoked onions and chopped

3 cloves garlic, minced

1 lb [500 g] assorted mushrooms, quartered

1 bunch green onions, thinly sliced

kosher salt and freshly ground black pepper

(continued)

Chef Allemeier's Wild Sage–Rubbed Beef Tenderloin with Alberta Mustard
Sauce *(continued)*

To sauté the mushrooms, put the diced bacon into a hot sauté pan and cook it until it's crispy. Remove the bacon and set it aside. Add the chopped smoked onion to the bacon fat and sauté it until it's tender. Add the minced garlic and cook it until it's fragrant. Add the mushrooms and sauté them until they're tender. Add the sliced green onions and reserved bacon at the last minute. Adjust the seasoning with salt and pepper.

MUSTARD SAUCE

7 oz [225 g] butter, melted and all solids removed (clarified)

¾ cup + 2 Tbsp [200 mL] tarragon vinegar

2 large shallots, finely diced

5 sprigs fresh tarragon

½ tsp [2 mL] freshly ground black pepper

1⅓ cup + 2 Tbsp [350 mL] dry white wine

4 egg yolks

3 Tbsp [45 mL] grainy mustard

2 Tbsp [25 mL] whipping cream

Tabasco sauce

Worcestershire sauce

kosher salt

To make the mustard sauce, prepare the clarified butter and set it aside (keeping it warm). Place the tarragon vinegar, shallots, fresh tarragon, and black pepper in a small stainless steel pot. Reduce the vinegar slowly over medium heat until the mixture is almost dry, being careful not to burn it. Add the white wine and reduce the mixture again by half. Remove the sauce from the heat and leave it to steep for 30 minutes. Strain the mixture through a fine sieve. Place the reduction in a stainless steel bowl that will fit over a pot of simmering water. Place the egg yolks in the bowl with the reduction and place it over the simmering water. Cook the sauce, whisking it constantly, until it's thick and ribbonlike. Do not overcook it. Carefully whisk in the butter, drop by drop. Add the mustard and cream and adjust the seasoning with Tabasco, Worcestershire, and salt. Keep the sauce warm until it's needed.

To-do list

The day before:
- Clean and marinate the beef tenderloin.
- Smoke the onions.
- Marinate the portobellos.

The day of the contest:
- Bring the meat to room temperature.
- Prep the onions—peel and clean them.
- Make up the reduction for the mustard sauce.
- Melt the butter and keep it warm until needed.
- Prepare the grill for the beef.
- Cook the beef and make the sauce while the beef is cooking.
- Once the beef comes off and is resting, grill the portobellos and make the cutouts.
- Sauté the mushrooms using the chopped smoked onion cores and the portobello trim.
- Heat a serving platter.
- Place the sautéed mushrooms in a line down 1 side of the platter. Place the rounds of grilled portobellos next to the sautéed mushrooms. Quickly and carefully heat the onions on the grill to warm them, then place them on the portobellos as if they are a bowl on a little saucer. Carve the beef into ½-inch (1 cm) slices and place them on top of the sautéed mushrooms. Season the beef with sea salt and black pepper. Carefully spoon the sauce into the smoked onion halves and top the sauce with the sliced green onions.
- Turn in the platter and wait for the judges to deliver you a taste of barbecue glory!

THE KING OF BARBECUE:
BEEF BRISKET

MAKES 10–16 SERVINGS, DEPENDING ON THE SIZE OF THE BRISKET AND APPETITES

This sinewy, fatty cut of beef may not be something you see often in the supermarket's meat section, but it's one of the most flavorful meats, and it's the classic barbecue choice in Texas. The bigger the brisket, the juicier the end product. Smaller cuts can end up dry. Cooking a brisket requires a long-term commitment. Plan to do this overnight, or on a day when you can stay around the house doing yard work or watching sports on TV. The process I've described here is as close as possible to what we do in competition. The end result is succulent, fork-tender slices of meat that need no accompaniment, but if you insist, serve them with a little dipping sauce, some coleslaw, beans, and pickled onions.

For large cuts like pork butts and briskets, the rule of thumb is to cook them for 1½ hours per pound (500 g). That means a 10 lb (4.5 kg) brisket will take 15 to 20 hours to cook, so you really need to start cooking it the night before you're going to serve it. Your timing doesn't have to be exact, so you shouldn't have to get up at three in the morning to put on the roast (I usually put a big brisket on just before going to bed). Sealed in foil and wrapped in a blanket (or in a 160°F/71°C oven), a cooked brisket can sit for several hours before you serve it.

one 10–14 lb [4.5–6.4 kg] whole beef brisket, with a nice white fat cap

3 quarts [3 L] apple juice

1 cup [250 mL] prepared mustard

1 Tbsp [15 mL] granulated garlic

1½ cups [375 mL] Championship Barbecue Rub (see page 50) or Texas-Style Rub (see page 51)

2 cups [500 mL] apple juice mixed with Jack Daniel's and maple syrup in a spray bottle (see Barbecue Secret on page 28)

2 cups [500 mL] Ron's Rich, Deeply Satisfying Dipping Sauce (see page 57)

⋟ BARBECUE SECRETS ⋞

For some reason, freezing helps to tenderize a brisket. I often freeze mine and then thaw it in the refrigerator for at least 2 days before cooking. Once it's thawed, store it in the refrigerator.

⋟ ⋞

When a brisket is done, it looks like a meteorite—so dark and crusty that you can't see the grain of the meat. Barbecue competitors mark the brisket before cooking it to make carving easy. Before you start preparing the brisket for cooking, cut off a 3 or 4 oz (90 or 125 g) chunk of meat from the flat end of the brisket, perpendicular to the grain of the meat. This marks the roast so you know where to start carving slices.

⋟ ⋞

The charred, fatty crust of the brisket can be cut off and roughly chopped to make "burnt ends," which are superb either in a bun or thrown into some baked beans to give them an extra jolt of smoky, fatty flavor.

(continued)

Steer It Up: Beef

The King of Barbecue: Beef Brisket *(continued)*

Take your thawed brisket out of the refrigerator and let it sit for 1 or 2 hours so it starts to come up to room temperature. Prepare your smoker for barbecuing, bringing the temperature to 200 to 220°F (95–100°C). Make sure you line your water pan with a double layer of extra-wide foil and fill the pan with apple juice. Use as much charcoal or hardwood as your smoker or pit will hold. A good water smoker will hold close to 15 lb (6.75 kg) of charcoal, which will burn for almost 24 hours. (You should know your smoker well before you attempt to cook a brisket.)

There should be a nice fat cap on the brisket. Trim the excess fat off it with a sharp knife so you're left with a layer about ⅛ to ¼ inch (3–6 mm) thick.

Coat the brisket with the mustard. Sprinkle both sides with a light coating of granulated garlic. Coat both sides of the brisket with a heavy sprinkling of barbecue rub so that it is evenly coated.

Let the brisket rest for about half an hour, until the rub starts to get moist and tacky—the salt in the rub pulls some of the juices out of the roast, and this helps to make a nice crust. Put the brisket, fat side up, into your smoker and place some hickory or mesquite chunks on top of the coals. Cook the brisket for 1½ hours per pound (500 g).

The internal temperature of the brisket should rise very gradually throughout the cooking time, reaching a final temperature of about 180°F (82°C). If you're going to use a meat thermometer, keep it in the roast—don't use one that you poke into the meat every time you use it, because it will cause the juices to run out. Halfway through the cooking time (first thing in the morning), turn the brisket, spraying it on both sides with the apple juice/Jack Daniel's mixture. At this point, be sure to add some more hardwood chunks and top up the water pan with hot water. Also, make sure you have plenty of coals left, and replenish them if you're running low.

Three-quarters of the way through the cooking time, turn the brisket and spray it again. About 2 hours before you take it out of the smoker, turn it and give it a good coating of barbecue sauce on both sides. Cook the sauce-coated brisket for about another half hour, just enough so the sauce starts to set. Give the brisket one more coating of glaze, take it off the cooking grate, and wrap it in a double layer of foil (the extra-wide foil works best). Put the wrapped brisket back in to cook for 1 more hour.

Remove the brisket and let it rest for at least 1 hour. In competition, our briskets often rest for as many as 3 or 4 hours wrapped in a blanket and kept in a cooler.

Take the brisket out of the foil and slice it, perpendicular to the grain, into ⅛- to ¼-inch (3–6 mm) slices. Serve it just like that, on a plate, with a little barbecue sauce on the side for dipping.

I. LOVE. STEAK.

A lip-smacking tribute to the king of grilled meat, the glorious beef steak.

As I write this, the giant rib eye that I just finished devouring is pleasantly stretching my overfull belly, which is throbbing happily as it begins processing its glorious, meaty cargo.

The aftereffects of that superdelicious steak are still with me. My lips are greasy, the gaps in my teeth hang on to the remaining shards of flesh, and my taste buds resonate with a familiar peppery afterglow.

Licking my lips nostalgically, I have a steak flashback.

Cut to five minutes ago. There it is, glistening on the plate as it throws off the classic aroma of seared fat, mesquite smoke, and charred spices. Atop the steaming slab sits a slowly liquefying daub of Gorgonzola butter. The dark mass of the steak is framed nicely by slices of ripe red tomato, a few spears of grilled asparagus, and a handful of roasted nugget potatoes, all drizzled with fruity olive oil, spritzed with fresh lemon juice, and dusted with a sparkling skiff of Maldon salt.

That bite. That first bite! Sawn from a corner of the steak with the serrated edge of my knife, the freshly exposed surface shines with juice as I draw the slice to my mouth. Its warm red core is silky on my tongue, and the crusty, chewy outer layers give my teeth the most meaningful assignment of their lives.

I liberate another shiny slice from the beautiful hunk and ceremoniously drag it through the mixture of juice, savory butter, and olive oil that has pooled on the plate. The next forkful includes a tangy chunk of tomato. The next, a creamy bite of potato. Then, a lemony, palate-refreshing bite of asparagus.

Oh, yes, almost forgot the wine. A big, jammy Shiraz, of course. A slug of that, and then back to the motherlode of a steak, which looms on the plate, its edge now jagged like a mine face, waiting to be carved away.

Many satisfying chews and gulps of wine later, I reach my final destination—the rib bone, with its familiar curve. Setting down my implements, I grab the meat-sicle with my bare hands and gnaw away at it, reveling in the fattiest, richest, chewiest bites, my cheeks shining in the candlelight.

I grab the meat-sicle with my bare hands and gnaw away at it, reveling in the fattiest, richest, chewiest bites, my cheeks shining in the candlelight.

Finally, I can wrest no more flesh from the bone. The job is done, and all that's left is to release a meal-crowning burp and loosen my belt. Hallelujah.

So, now you know what I do when my wife's away for the weekend.

A beef steak primer

And now for some advice on how you can have equally satisfying steak experiences at home (with your spouse or not).

Okay. First, and perhaps most important, you have to get a perfect piece of meat, well-aged and nicely marbled. My favorite, as you just found out, is the rib-eye steak with the bone attached. I like it because it has lots of fat, and it also has nice chewy connective tissue that makes for an interesting texture (and makes for a steak that kids often don't like).

Here's a list of the great cuts you may want to consider:

The rib eye, the king of grilling steaks, is one of the most marbled and delicious cuts. It's rich and juicy, and because it's got so much fat, it's hard to overcook. Even better when it's on the bone, which is called a "cowboy rib eye" in some circles.

Flank/skirt/hanger steak, from the diaphragm of the animal, is the most flavorful cut of beef, in my opinion. It's best when treated with an overnight marinade, seared quickly on the grill to a maximum doneness of medium rare, and then sliced thinly across the grain and served fajita-style in warmed tortillas with all the fixings.

Strip loin or New York strip is the classic restaurant steak. With its perfect shape and thin edge of white fat, it's hard to ruin one of these. No need for complex treatment—a quick dry or wet rub or a short bath in a soy sauce–based marinade is all you need. Or maybe just coarse salt and freshly cracked pepper.

The filet mignon or tenderloin steak is among the most expensive cuts. This superlean steak is a favorite with the ladies. Its mild flavor benefits from a wrapper of bacon, a pat of compound butter, or a rich sauce, but, as with all steaks, it's also nice with just salt and pepper. This one is also best served as rare as possible. Overcook it and it gets mealy.

Sirloin is a less expensive cut. Like the flank, this sinewy steak has lots of flavor, but it's relatively lean. This is a great breakfast steak, cut thin, fried fast, and served with a couple of sunny-side-up eggs laid on top.

The porterhouse/T-bone is gloriously complex, with a tasty, chewy piece of loin on one side of the bone and a round of fillet on the other. This is a rich steak. I like to get one custom cut to about a 3-inch (8 cm) thickness, cook it over medium heat, and then carve the meat off the bone and preslice it for my guests.

Round steak is my least favorite cut of beef. It's extremely lean, kind of tough, and doesn't have much flavor. It's acceptable if cooked quite rare, and, like sirloin, it's not bad for breakfast.

Chuck. It's not good for the grill, but this delicious cut is rippled with intramuscular fat and grisly connective tissue. Simmer or bake it for a long time and it takes on magical properties. But in the summer, just never mind.

Steak your reputation

Cooking a steak is easy—almost as easy as ruining one. Heed these words and avoid grill-related emasculation:

Turn it down High heat is important for grilling a great steak because it makes grill marks, which give a nice charred taste to the steak

and make it look appetizing. So preheat your grill on high, get some nice grill marks in the first couple of minutes of cooking, and then turn it down to medium-high or even just plain medium. Your steak will cook more evenly and you'll avoid it being burned on the outside and raw and cold on the inside.

Pay attention   I've said this before and I'll say it again. Don't walk away from the grill. Or, if you do walk away, set a kitchen timer to prompt you to come back. Most steaks take about three or four minutes per side, which means if you want to pay full attention it might take eight minutes out of your day. The alternative: go watch TV and come back to the grill when your steak is ruined.

Don't oversauce   I rarely use barbecue sauce on a steak because I prefer to taste the steak. But if you do use barbecue sauce, use it for the last minute or two as a finishing glaze. Slather it on at the beginning and you'll have a black steak that tastes of burnt sugar.

Let it rest   Here's a rule of thumb: If it's done on the grill, it's overdone on the plate. Take your steak off the grill when it's almost done, then let it rest, tented in foil, for at least four or five minutes before serving. This allows the residual heat to complete the cooking process and lets the juices in the steak redistribute into the meat so they won't spurt out when you carve your first bite.

Thick is better than thin   Most steaks you buy in the supermarket are cut too thin. Get your butcher to cut a 1½- to 2-inch (4 to 5 cm) steak, cook it a little longer and on a little lower heat, and you'll get a juicier, more succulent result.

I could go on. But, really, cooking a great steak is pretty simple. Follow these rules and you will experience excellent steak flashbacks that will keep you licking your lips for days.

This article originally appeared in Calgary's great food publication, City Palate.

Get Your Wild On: Lamb & Game

I love the extra flavor you get with lamb and game. Chicken, beef, and pork are delicious domesticated meats, but we modern carnivores eat so much of them that we almost forget that each kind of meat has a distinctive taste. Not so with lamb and venison, whose slightly wild flavor helps to connect us with our animal selves. When we bite into a perfect lamb kebab or venison chop, a part of us is transported back to the distant past, in which our ancestors worked hard hunting or herding to earn the next good meal.

The beauty of modern lamb and farm-raised venison is that their flavors are distinctive but not so strong as to be unappealing. They certainly hold up to the outdoor cooking techniques of grilling, planking, and barbecue, and their flavor is greatly enhanced by strong herbs and spices.

To enjoy the best cuts of lamb or game properly, they can't be overcooked; the meat is so naturally lean that to retain its succulent quality it needs to be done rare or medium rare.

TANDOORI LAMB KEBABS

MAKES 4 SERVINGS

Tandoori paste is available in the Indian food section of most supermarkets, and it's a great thing to have in your fridge. It adds intense flavor to chicken and lamb, and if you have the foresight to marinate the meat overnight, it also has a tenderizing effect. Serve these lamb kebabs with steamed basmati rice, a vegetable curry, and your favorite chutney.

eight 7-inch [18 cm] bamboo skewers,
   soaked for at least 1 hour
one 3 lb [1.5 kg] boneless leg of lamb,
   cut into bite-sized chunks

MARINADE
½ cup [125 mL] tandoori paste
⅓ cup [75 mL] yogurt
2 Tbsp [25 mL] fresh lemon juice
3 Tbsp [45 mL] chopped fresh cilantro

KEBABS
1 large Spanish onion, cut into bite-
   sized chunks
3 oz [90 g] butter
lemon wedges and fresh cilantro sprigs
   for garnish

Mix together the tandoori paste, yogurt, lemon juice, and cilantro in a medium nonreactive bowl. Add the lamb chunks and coat them with the marinade. Refrigerate the lamb overnight if possible, or at least 1 hour.

Thread the lamb chunks onto the skewers, alternating them with pieces of onion. Heat the butter in a small saucepan just until it's melted. Set it aside and keep it warm.

Prepare your grill for direct medium heat. Place the kebabs on the cooking grate and grill them for 6 to 8 minutes, or until the lamb chunks are springy to the touch. Every couple of minutes, turn and baste the kebabs with butter (be sure to have your spray bottle at the ready; the butter can cause flare-ups). Remove the kebabs from the grill and serve them garnished with lemon wedges and cilantro sprigs.

LAMB MEATBALL KEBABS
WITH MINT JELLY GLAZE

MAKES 4 MAIN COURSE SERVINGS OR 8 APPETIZERS

The combination of toasted pine nuts and fresh and dried herbs gives these kebabs a rich flavor and a tender but nutty texture. Serve as an appetizer or as a main course with Dilled Lemony Rice (page 145), Mimi's Tabouleh (page 120), and some grilled vegetables.

eight 7-inch [18 cm] bamboo skewers,
    soaked for at least 1 hour

½ cup [125 mL] mint jelly
¼ cup [50 mL] water
½ cup [125 mL] pine nuts
1 lb [500 g] ground lamb
½ cup [125 mL] fresh breadcrumbs
1 egg, slightly beaten
¼ cup [50 mL] chopped fresh cilantro
¼ cup [50 mL] chopped fresh flat-leaf
    Italian parsley

¼ cup [50 mL] chopped fresh mint
½ tsp [2 mL] dried mint
1 Tbsp [15 mL] chopped fresh chives
½ tsp [2 mL] dried oregano
¼ tsp [1 mL] freshly grated nutmeg
½ tsp [2 mL] kosher salt
generous grinding black pepper
2 or 3 small zucchini, sliced into
    ¾-inch [2 cm] discs
10 ripe cherry tomatoes
10 smallish button mushrooms, or
    5 larger ones cut in half

Combine the mint jelly and water in a small saucepan and heat the mixture, stirring, until the jelly is melted. Set it aside.

Toast the pine nuts in a dry skillet over medium heat until they turn golden brown. Cool and coarsely chop them. Gently but thoroughly combine the ground lamb, pine nuts, breadcrumbs, egg, cilantro, parsley, fresh and dried mint, chives, oregano, nutmeg, salt, and pepper in a nonreactive bowl.

Wetting your hands to prevent sticking, shape the lamb mixture into about 25 balls, about 1 inch (2.5 cm) each. Thread the meatballs onto the skewers, alternating with the zucchini, cherry tomatoes, and mushrooms. At this point, you can refrigerate the skewers, covered with plastic wrap, for 1 to 2 hours.

Prepare your grill for direct medium heat and oil the grill. Spray the kebabs with cooking spray or brush them with oil and place them on the grill. Cook them for 4 to 5 minutes per side, or until the meatballs are cooked through, brushing them with the mint jelly glaze during grilling.

Pictured with Dilled Lemony Rice (page 145)

GROUND LAMB & BEEF KEBABS
WITH SAFFRON RICE & GRILLED TOMATOES

MAKES 4 SERVINGS

I live in North Vancouver, which has a large Iranian population. This dish, called *Kebab Kubideh*, is an Iranian staple, cooked at home on festive occasions and offered on the menu of most Iranian restaurants. The kebab meat, which is usually a mixture of ground lamb and ground beef, is traditionally squeezed onto special long, flat steel skewers, which are rotated above a gas or charcoal fire. Getting the meat to stay on the skewers is a special skill. Based on my futile efforts, it seems to me that only Iranians can master it. With my own incompetence in mind, I've adapted the recipe to make it easy to cook, without skewers, on a standard covered grill. Special thanks to my barbecue pal Reza Mofakham for sharing this recipe with me.

KEBABS

1 medium onion, finely grated

½ lb [250 g] ground lamb

½ lb [250 g] ground beef

¼ cup [50 mL] fine, dry breadcrumbs

1 egg

1 tsp [5 mL] kosher salt

½ tsp [2 mL] freshly ground black pepper

SAFFRON RICE

1½ cups [375 mL] basmati rice

4 cups [1 L] water

2 Tbsp [25 mL] kosher salt

2 Tbsp [25 mL] melted butter

¼ tsp [1 mL] saffron, dissolved in 2 Tbsp [25 mL] warm water

regular olive oil

8 small ripe tomatoes

1 tsp [5 mL] ground sumac (an earthy, sour spice found in most Middle Eastern grocery stores—if you can't find it the dish is still delicious without it)

4 pats of butter, at room temperature

Put the grated onion in a clean tea towel and squeeze the liquid out of it. With your hands, thoroughly mix all the kebab ingredients in a bowl. Cover and refrigerate the mixture for at least 2 hours.

About 1 hour before you want to eat, rinse the rice several times in warm water. Place the water and salt in a large pot and bring the water to a boil. Add the rice and cook it for 5 to 10 minutes. Drain the rice in a large sieve. Cover the bottom of the pot with about half of the butter. Carefully transfer the drained rice back into the pot, heaping it at the center so as not to touch the sides of the pot. Add the saffron-infused water and the rest of the melted butter. Cover the underside of the pot lid with a tea towel and place the lid tightly on the pot. Cook the rice over moderately low heat until the rice is tender and a golden crust has formed at the bottom, about 30 to 35 minutes.

While the rice is cooking, prepare your grill for direct medium heat. Divide the meat into 4 portions. On a place of aluminum foil or parchment paper, shape each portion into an oblong shape about 1½ inches (4 cm) thick, 3 inches (8 cm) wide, and about 6 to 8 inches (15–20 cm) long, sort of like a long hamburger patty. Drizzle the patties with olive oil. Use the foil or parchment paper to lift the patties and transfer them, oiled side down, on to the cooking grate. Grill them for about 4 minutes per side, taking care to keep them together when you turn them (you may need to use two spatulas). Halfway through the cooking time for the kebab patties, put the tomatoes alongside on the cooking grate and grill them, turning them regularly. Remove the patties and tomatoes from the grill and let them rest for a few minutes.

Spoon the loose rice from the pot onto a platter. Immerse the bottom of the rice pot in cold water. This should help release the golden crust at the bottom. Remove and reserve it.

Slice each kebab patty into bite-sized pieces and slice the tomatoes in half. Serve the kebab and tomato slices on a bed of rice and sprinkle with a little ground sumac. Accompany each portion with a pat of butter and a chunk of the golden crust, which is called *tah-dig.*

PLANKED LEG OF LAMB
WITH RED WINE REDUCTION

MAKES 4–6 SERVINGS

Yes, you can plank a whole leg of lamb. And, surprisingly, cedar works very nicely, although any of the hardwoods, particularly apple or cherry, are also excellent.

1 plank, soaked overnight or for at least
    1 hour
one 6 lb [2.7 kg] leg of lamb, bone in
kosher salt and freshly ground black
    pepper
extra virgin olive oil
16 cloves garlic
1 Tbsp [15 mL] dry mustard
12 sprigs fresh thyme

RED WINE REDUCTION
one 25 oz [750 mL] bottle Cabernet
    Sauvignon or other red wine
1 cup [250 mL] chicken stock
3 large shallots, finely chopped

Season the lamb with salt and pepper and drizzle it with olive oil. Use your hands to evenly coat the leg in the oil. Push 4 of the garlic cloves through a garlic press and spread the garlic evenly over the lamb. Dust the leg with the dry mustard and massage it into the flesh. Lightly crush the rest of the garlic cloves with the flat side of a knife and set them aside.

Preheat the grill on medium-high for 5 to 10 minutes, or until the chamber temperature rises above 500°F (260°C). Rinse the soaked plank and place it on the cooking grate. Cover the grill and heat the plank for 4 to 5 minutes, or until it starts to throw off a bit of smoke and crackles lightly. Reduce the heat to medium-low.

Make a bed of the reserved crushed garlic and half of the thyme sprigs on the plank. Place the lamb leg on top, fat side up, and place the rest of the thyme sprigs on top of the roast, patting them so they stick to the meat. Cook the leg for about 1½ hours, or until the lamb has an internal temperature of 125°F (52°C) at the thickest part of the roast.

While the lamb is roasting, pour the wine and chicken stock into a heavy saucepan and add the shallots. Bring the mixture to a medium boil and reduce it until you have about a cupful of syrupy sauce. Set it aside and keep it warm.

When the lamb is ready, take it off the grill and tent it loosely with foil. Let it rest for 30 to 45 minutes. Carve the lamb at the table and pass the sauce around.

SEXY MINTY LAMB RACKS
FOR TWO

MAKES 2 SERVINGS

My friend Arnold Smith says this recipe is one of the sexiest. His wife, Yvette, calls it an "I want you now" meal, which means when he serves it he usually ends up being dessert.

2 racks of lamb, frenched by your
    butcher (trimmed to bare the ribs
    and remove the silverskin)
½ cup [125 mL] finely chopped
    fresh mint

½ cup [125 mL] dark brown sugar
1 Tbsp [15 mL] white wine vinegar

Combine the mint, sugar, and vinegar, and mix them together until you have a thick, wet paste, adding a splash more of vinegar if it seems too thick. Prepare your grill for direct medium heat. Coat the lamb racks generously with the paste and grill them for 8 to 12 minutes, or until the internal temperature reaches 130°F (55°C) for medium rare. Turn the lamb every couple of minutes to allow the brown sugar on both sides of the rack to gently caramelize and the flavor of the mint to intensify. Be sure to let the racks rest for at least 5 minutes before serving with your favorite accompaniments.

PLANKED ASIAN-FLAVORED LAMB RACKS

MAKES 4 MAIN COURSE SERVINGS OR 8 APPETIZER SERVINGS

Too often we just reach for the mint or rosemary when it comes to lamb, when it also happens to be delicious with Asian flavors. Planking is a great way to cook lamb racks because the complex flavors are preserved by the gentle heat. The inspiration for this recipe comes from food stylist Nathan Fong.

1 cedar or fruitwood plank, soaked overnight or at least 1 hour

4 racks of lamb, frenched by your butcher (trimmed to bare the ribs and remove the silverskin)

kosher salt

MARINADE/SAUCE

½ cup [125 mL] hoisin sauce

2 Tbsp [25 mL] smooth peanut butter

2 Tbsp [25 mL] soy sauce

2 Tbsp [25 mL] dry sherry

2 Tbsp [25 mL] fresh-squeezed orange juice

1 tsp [5 mL] finely chopped or grated orange zest

1 tsp [5 mL] finely chopped or grated fresh ginger

½ tsp [2 mL] toasted sesame oil

2 cloves garlic, smashed or pushed through a garlic press

½ tsp [2 mL] crushed dried red chili flakes

TO FINISH

½ cup [125 mL] coarsely chopped dry-roasted peanuts

¼ cup [50 mL] chopped green onions

Whisk together the marinade/sauce ingredients in a medium bowl. Divide it into 2 equal portions and set one half aside in the fridge. Lightly season the lamb racks with salt. Coat the lamb racks with 1 portion of the marinade. Cover the lamb and refrigerate it for at least 2 hours or overnight.

Preheat the grill on medium-high for 5 to 10 minutes, or until the chamber temperature rises above 500°F (260°C). Rinse the soaked plank and place it on the cooking grate. Cover the grill and heat the plank for 4 to 5 minutes, or until it starts to throw off a bit of smoke and crackles lightly. Reduce the heat to medium-low.

Place the lamb racks on the plank in pairs, facing one another, so the ribs interlock like fingers. Cook them for 15 to 20 minutes, or until the lamb has an internal temperature of 125°F (52°C). Remove the meat from the grill and tent it loosely in foil for 5 to 10 minutes. Slice it into chops and serve it garnished with the chopped peanuts and green onions.

RACK OF LAMB
WITH BALSAMIC REDUCTION

MAKES 4 MAIN COURSE SERVINGS OR 8 APPETIZER SERVINGS

This is a delicious way to grill lamb racks. The balsamic reduction has an incredible sweet tanginess that offsets the earthiness of the dried herbs and brings out the flavor of the meat. Serve the racks cut into chops as an appetizer, or as a main course with Pauline's Wild Rice Salad (page 117).

4 racks of lamb, frenched by your
   butcher (trimmed to bare the ribs
   and remove the silverskin)
kosher salt to taste

MARINADE
2 Tbsp [25 mL] fresh lemon juice
½ cup [125 mL] extra virgin olive oil
2 Tbsp [25 mL] Dijon mustard
1 Tbsp [15 mL] chopped fresh rosemary
½ tsp [2 mL] freshly ground black
   pepper
2 cloves garlic, smashed or pushed
   through a garlic press

BALSAMIC REDUCTION
1 cup [250 mL] balsamic vinegar

FOR GRILLING
2 Tbsp [25 mL] Dijon mustard
1 Tbsp [15 mL] granulated garlic
1 Tbsp [15 mL] granulated onion
½ tsp [2 mL] cayenne
½ cup [125 mL] Mediterranean Dried
   Herb Rub (see page 52)
1 Tbsp [15 mL] olive oil
sprigs of fresh mint for garnish

One to two hours before you are going to cook the lamb racks, lightly season the lamb with salt. Combine all the marinade ingredients in a nonreactive baking dish or resealable plastic bag. Add the racks, turning them once or twice to ensure they are evenly exposed to the marinade.

While the lamb is marinating, pour the balsamic vinegar in a small saucepan and bring it to a boil over medium-high heat. Cook it, watching it carefully, until the vinegar has reduced to about half of its original volume (10–15 minutes). It should be a thick syrup that coats the back of a spoon. Set it aside to cool.

(continued)

Rack of Lamb with Balsamic Reduction *(continued)*

Prepare your grill for direct medium heat. Take the lamb out of the marinade, pat the racks dry with paper towels, and brush them with the remaining 2 Tbsp (25 mL) mustard. Combine the granulated garlic, onion, and cayenne in a small bowl and sprinkle the mixture lightly over the lamb racks. Coat the racks generously with the herb rub, patting it on with your hands so it sticks to the meat. Drizzle the olive oil over the rubbed racks and pat it into the rub.

Using cherry wood as a flavoring agent, grill the racks for 4 to 5 minutes per side, or until the internal temperature at the thickest point is 135 to 140°F (57–60°C). To serve, cut the racks into individual chops, arrange them on plates, and drizzle them with the balsamic reduction. Garnish the lamb with sprigs of fresh mint.

GRILLED VENISON TENDERLOIN
WITH CUMBERLAND SAUCE

MAKES 4 SERVINGS

I love the gamey taste and silky texture of venison tenderloin, which needs
to be cooked rare to medium rare. This recipe treats the venison very simply,
but dresses it up with a lovely, complex, old-school British sauce that I found
in *The Joy of Cooking*. Serve this dish as a course on its own or on a little pile
of Maple Butternut Squash Purée (page 139).

one 1 lb venison tenderloin
kosher salt and coarsely ground
   black pepper
extra virgin olive oil

CUMBERLAND SAUCE
½ cup [125 mL] slivered almonds
1 tsp [5 mL] dry mustard
1 Tbsp [15 mL] brown sugar
¼ tsp [1 mL] ground ginger
pinch cayenne
¼ tsp [1 mL] kosher salt

¼ tsp [1 mL] ground cloves
1½ cups [375 mL] port wine
½ cup [125 mL] seedless golden raisins
2 tsp [10 mL] cornstarch
2 Tbsp [25 mL] cold water
¼ cup [50 mL] red currant jelly
1½ tsp [7 mL] finely grated orange zest
1½ tsp [7 mL] finely grated lemon zest
¼ cup [50 mL] orange juice
2 Tbsp [25 mL] fresh lemon juice
2 Tbsp [25 mL] Grand Marnier liqueur

To make the sauce, gently toast the almonds in a sauté pan over medium
heat, taking care not to burn them. Set the almonds aside.

Combine the mustard, sugar, ginger, cayenne, salt, cloves, port, raisins,
and toasted almonds in a saucepan and bring the mixture to a boil over
medium heat. Reduce the heat to low and simmer the mixture for 8 to
10 minutes.

Thoroughly combine the cornstarch and cold water and stir the mixture
into the sauce. Let it simmer for about 2 minutes. Stir in the red currant
jelly, orange and lemon zest, and orange and lemon juice until you have a
smooth, glossy mixture. Set the sauce aside (it can be served warm or cold).

(continued)

Get Your Wild On: Lamb & Game

279

Grilled Venison Tenderloin with Cumberland Sauce *(continued)*

Prepare your grill for direct high heat. Season the venison tenderloin with salt and pepper and wet it with a little oil. Grill it, turning it often, for just a few minutes, until the exterior is nicely charred and the tenderloin reaches a core temperature of no more than 120°F (50°C). Remove the meat from the grill and set it aside to rest, loosely tented with foil, for 5 minutes.

While the tenderloin is resting, heat up the sauce and stir in the Grand Marnier just before serving.

Slice the tenderloin into ¾-inch (2 cm) medallions and arrange the slices on plates. Spoon the sauce over the meat and serve.

Pictured with Maple Butternut Squash Purée (page139)

A JOURNEY TO THE ANCESTRAL HOME OF ⮞PLANK-COOKING⮜

In the summer of 1986 my wife, Kate, and I came to the west coast of British Columbia on a vacation with her parents, who were looking to retire as far away from the dreaded winters of Ottawa as they could get. We all fell in love with a little town called Sechelt up the Sunshine Coast, a short ferry ride north of Vancouver. During that trip, my father-in-law, Bill, and I rented a 10-foot aluminum boat and went salmon fishing. With simple angling gear and a bucket of live herring for bait, we motored out to a group of small islands and put our hooks in the water.

Before long we had caught a couple of beautiful wild coho salmon, which put up an incredible fight as we reeled them in, flashing in the sun as they jumped out of the water. It was the most exciting fishing experience I've ever had. But even more memorable was the taste of that freshly caught salmon, which we ate within hours. Wrapped in foil and baked with just a little salt, pepper, and lemon juice, it was succulent and delicious—like nothing we had ever tasted before.

We would all eventually move to the coast, the in-laws to Sechelt, and Kate and I to Vancouver. As a German sport fisherman once told me, explaining why he immigrated to British Columbia, "I came to catch the salmon. But the salmon caught me."

The salmon caught me, too—and not only as a food. I became interested in the role salmon has played in the rich history of the First Nations peoples. Before European settlers arrived, thousands of Aboriginal people from many different tribes lived along the coast, harvesting the incredible bounty of seafood and plant life along the fiords and river inlets at the western edge of the coastal rainforest. Ancient stories tell of rivers that were so thick with spawning salmon that a man could walk across on their backs.

With so much food, and such a moderate climate, there was time to build beautiful lodges, boats, and totems, and craft exquisite boxes, bowls, and utensils—as well as to develop extremely sophisticated fishing and cooking techniques.

The First Nations people made fishing hooks with bent wood and bone, fashioned fishing line from woven cedar bark, designed special rakes to sweep schools of herring into canoes, and built elaborate and ingenious traps at the mouths of streams to capture the salmon.

Salmon was, and still is today, at the heart of West Coast Aboriginal culture. Salmon sustained the people through the winter, and the first salmon to return to the rivers to spawn marked the start of another prosperous year. Salmon were preserved and cooked in all kinds of ways, including wind-drying, smoking, boiling, and pit-roasting. The first salmon of the season, filleted and fastened to a cedar post and roasted on an alder fire on the beach, was the direct ancestor of the salmon that you plank on your backyard grill today.

I came to catch the salmon, but the salmon caught me.

As I researched the history of plank-cooking for my second book, *Planking Secrets*, I realized that to become a true planking expert I had to experience this ancient Aboriginal barbecue technique firsthand. So I visited a place where the traditional practice is kept alive and well by the modern descendants of the Quw'utsun' people of Vancouver Island.

Historians estimate that the Quw'utsun' have lived in southern British Columbia and the Upper Puget Sound for more than 4,500 years. When the first European settlers arrived in the 1800s, there were close to 6,000 Quw'utsun' living in 13 villages. Today about 3,500 Quw'utsun' people live in the Cowichan Valley on Vancouver Island. Since 1990 they have showcased their culture to the world through the Quw'utsun' Cultural Centre, a campus-style facility near Duncan, British Columbia. The center offers guests interpretive tours, exhibits of traditional artwork, and the opportunity for non-Aboriginal people to sample traditional food. Its flagship culinary event is the salmon barbecue.

❧ ❧

On a rainy day in the fall of 2005 I make a pilgrimage to the Cowichan Valley for a visit to the center's Riverwalk Café, where executive chef Bev Antoine greets me. She's in the middle of preparations for a big salmon barbecue for an incoming group of Japanese tourists. Chef Antoine has been cooking at the center since 1991 and has built a great team in her kitchen. Sous-chef Raymond Johnston is assigned to show me the salmon barbecue technique.

I arrive about two hours before the meal will be served, and Raymond is getting the salmon ready. He's got some beautiful fresh coho, about five or six pounds each. I watch him prepare one of the fish. He cuts the head off, then removes the backbone, keeping the whole fish intact in a kind of giant butterflied fillet. He carefully removes the remaining bones with a pair of needle-nose pliers.

Now it's time to light the fire. I join him in a trip out to the storage shed behind the restaurant, where we take turns splitting a bunch of alder and hauling it over to the nearby fire pit. The wood is a little green, and we have

to work hard to get it burning, but soon we have a nice crackling fire. Nature is cooperating and it has stopped raining.

Back to the kitchen, where Raymond mounts the fish fillets on piquin sticks—giant wooden tongs made out of cedar posts that have been cut down the middle like old-fashioned clothespins. Raymond makes finger-sized incisions along the outside edge of each salmon fillet, and places the fillets between the tongs. To keep the fish straight and flat, he deftly inserts four cedar sticks through the incisions, across the width of the fillets. The last step is to close the tongs with some wire, firmly clamping the sticks against the salmon.

By the time Raymond is finished mounting all the coho on their sticks, the fire has died down to

Ancient stories tell of rivers that were so thick with spawning salmon that a man could walk across on their backs.

a perfect bed of hot alder coals. It smells incredible—the sweet smoke seems to transport us back thousands of years as we place the sticks in the sockets that line the pit. We tend the salmon, turning it every 15 minutes or so, as our lunch guests begin to gather around the fire, taking pictures and chatting. Within an hour the red flesh of the coho has turned orangey pink and is glistening with hot juices.

It's time for the lunch service. Raymond and I take the piquin sticks out of their sockets and carry the salmon back to the kitchen. He cuts the fillets in half and places them on long cedar planks along with bowls of roasted potatoes and steamed vegetables, and a salad of local greens drizzled with blackberry vinaigrette. I join in with the kitchen staff as we work in pairs to carry the planks into the dining hall and dramatically present them to the assembled lunch guests. The Japanese, who aren't used to seeing salmon like this, are in awe.

> **I close my eyes as I chew, thinking about how it must have felt to eat salmon like this after a long winter of surviving on preserved food.**

Back in the kitchen, I grab a fork and pull a chunk of belly meat off one of the fillets. The flavor of the salmon has been touched lightly by the alder smoke. The flesh is juicy and perfectly succulent, with lots of flavor even though the fish has not even been salted. I close my eyes as I chew, thinking about how it must have felt to eat salmon like this after a long winter of surviving on preserved food.

That feast would have been much more than a meal—it was a celebration of the renewal of nature and recognition of the recurring gift of the salmon to the coastal people. In a book called *Indian Fishing: Early Methods on the Northwest Coast*, author Hilary Stewart quotes a prayer that would have been recited at the first sight of the salmon:

> *Welcome, friend Swimmer,*
> *we have met again in good health.*
> *Welcome, Supernatural One,*
> *you, Long-Life-Maker,*
> *For you come to set me right again*
> *as is always done by you.*

When you cook using the recipes from this book, and taste the food that has been enhanced with the smoke of the plank, think about your family, your friends, your health, your work, and the nourishing, delicious meal you're enjoying and take a moment to be thankful for it all.

Salmon
& Other
Spectacular
Seafood

SALMON

Like burgers, salmon deserves a special section of its own in this book, in recognition of the noble fish's growing stature as one of the best things you can cook outdoors—especially when you use a wooden plank, which explains why most of the following recipes are variations of planked salmon.

What's so great about salmon? For one thing, it's extremely good for you, with its heart-friendly fatty acids and nourishing protein. For another, its coral color and fine-grained flesh make it absolutely beautiful on the plate. But mainly, salmon is just plain delicious—rich without being cloying, boldly flavored without a hint of fishiness. And, when done right—which means rare to medium rare—the texture is silky on the tongue, unleashing the primal sensation of what it must have been like to be an ancient hunter devouring his freshly caught bounty.

Salmon is also wonderful because it's so versatile. It's great grilled with salt, pepper, and a squeeze of lemon, but it can be easily enhanced by many different treatments—from the piney tang of rosemary and balsamic vinegar, to the aromatic richness of Indian spices, to the sweet simplicity of Jack Daniel's and maple syrup.

I just love salmon, especially wild salmon. This is a good place for me to proclaim my longstanding support for British Columbia wild salmon, which in my humble opinion is the best-quality salmon available in North America. To find out more, visit www.bcsalmon.ca.

THE FIRE CHEF'S BBQ SALMON
ON A PLANK

MAKES 4–6 SERVINGS

The late David Veljacic was the father of barbecue in Canada, founding the Canadian National Barbecue Championships. David was a firefighter, hence his nickname, "The Fire Chef." He was diagnosed with cancer several years before he succumbed to it in 2001, and while on medical leave he wrote cookbooks and taught a generation of backyard cooks. This is his most famous recipe, adapted for the plank.

> ⤳ **PLANKING SECRET** ⤳

For planking geeks only: Drill eight or ten ½-inch (1 cm) holes through your plank before you soak it to create more air flow, and therefore more smoke. If you do this, take extra care to watch for flare-ups.

1 alder or hickory plank, soaked overnight or at least 1 hour

one 2½ lb [1.2 kg] salmon fillet, deboned, skin on

MARINADE

⅓ cup [75 mL] finely chopped fresh parsley

3 Tbsp [45 mL] oil-packed sun-dried tomatoes, finely chopped

1 Tbsp [15 mL] oil from the sun-dried tomatoes

⅓ cup [75 mL] extra virgin olive oil

1 tsp [5 mL] kosher salt

1 head roasted garlic (see page 68), cloves squeezed out of their skins

Combine the marinade ingredients in a small bowl. Place the salmon fillet in a nonreactive dish and pour the marinade over the fillet. Cover and refrigerate it overnight.

Score the salmon with 2 long slits along the length of the fillet. Don't cut all the way through the fish. Mash the salt together with the roasted garlic and spread the mixture over the fillet and into the slits. Re-coat the fillet with the marinade.

Preheat the grill on medium-high for 5 to 10 minutes, until the chamber temperature rises above 500°F (260°C). Rinse the soaked plank, place it on the cooking grate, cover the grill, and heat the plank for 4 to 5 minutes, until it starts to throw off a bit of smoke and crackles lightly. Place the salmon on the plank and reduce the heat to medium-low. Cook it for 15 to 20 minutes, until it has an internal temperature of 135°F (57°C). Remove the plank and salmon from the grill and serve.

Salmon & Other Spectacular Seafood

CEDAR-PLANKED SALMON
WITH WHISKEY-MAPLE GLAZE

MAKES 6–8 SERVINGS

(continued)

⤜ TYPES OF SALMON ⤜

For North American consumers, there are basically five kinds of salmon available on the market.

Chinook Also known as spring or king salmon, this is my favorite fish, with firm flesh, good fat content, and exceptional flavor. The most exotic and delicious of all salmon is the white spring or white king, which has a light pink, almost ivory-colored flesh. I think it's best for plank-cooking because it's the largest of the salmon species, which means you can often get 4 or 5 lb (1.8–2.2 kg) fillets, or even larger. At its freshest, spring salmon has flesh so firm and flavorful it reminds me of lobster meat.

Sockeye Sockeye has a bright red-orange color and rich, tasty flesh. It's a smaller breed, with fillets in the 2 to 3 lb (1–1.5 kg) range. It's tasty but easy to overcook on the plank because of its small size.

Coho This is the feistiest of the West Coast game fish, renowned for its habit of leaping out of the water while being reeled in. If you can get wild coho, buy it and try it. It's really succulent, and sometimes you can get fairly big fillets.

(continued)

This has become one of my signature recipes. I've cooked it scores of times over the past few years, I've won awards with it, and I often get the comment, "This is the best salmon I've ever eaten." The sweet, woody flavor of the Jack Daniel's and maple syrup complements the richness of the salmon and the aroma of the cedar in this West Coast dish. I like to present it on the plank and then serve it on a bed of field greens tossed with some French walnut oil, kosher salt, and toasted pumpkin seeds.

1 cedar plank, soaked overnight or at least 1 hour
one 3 lb [1.5 kg] whole wild Pacific salmon fillet, deboned, skin on

WHISKEY-MAPLE GLAZE
½ cup [125 mL] Jack Daniel's Tennessee Whiskey
1 cup [250 mL] maple syrup
1 tsp [5 mL] crushed dried red chili flakes

1 Tbsp [15 mL] butter, at room temperature

kosher salt and freshly ground black pepper
1 tsp [5 mL] granulated onion or onion powder
2 lemons, halved
sprigs of fresh parsley for garnish
1 Tbsp [15 mL] finely chopped fresh flat-leaf Italian parsley

Make the glaze by combining the whiskey and maple syrup in a small saucepan. Bring the mixture to a low boil and reduce it by about half, until you have a thick syrup that coats the back of a spoon. Add the chilies and butter and stir the sauce until it's just combined. Set it aside and keep it warm on the stovetop.

Season the skinless side of the salmon with salt, pepper, and granulated onion. Let the salmon sit for 10 to 15 minutes at room temperature, until the rub is moistened.

(continued)

Types of Salmon (*continued*)

Chum Leaner and lighter in color than its cousins, the chum is delicious but milder in flavor than the bigger species.

Pink I love fresh pink salmon, although it's not as good for plank-cooking as some other kinds because it's the smallest and leanest of the salmon species. But it has a delicate flavor and light-colored flesh that make it excellent for pan-frying or quick-roasting.

Cedar-Planked Salmon with Whiskey-Maple Glaze (*continued*)

While the salmon is sitting, preheat the grill on medium-high for 5 to 10 minutes, or until the chamber temperature rises above 500°F (260°C). Rinse the soaked plank and place it on the cooking grate. Cover the grill and heat the plank for 4 to 5 minutes, or until it starts to throw off a bit of smoke and crackles lightly. Reduce the heat to medium-low. Season the plank with kosher salt and place the salmon, skin side down, on the plank.

Cover the grill and cook the salmon for 15 to 20 minutes, or until the fish has an internal temperature of 135°F (57°C). Check it periodically to make sure the plank doesn't catch fire, and spray the burning edges with water if it does, making sure to close the lid afterward.

When the salmon is done, squeeze half a lemon along its length and carefully transfer it, plank and all, to a platter. Garnish it with parsley sprigs and the remaining lemon, cut into slices. Drizzle a spoonful of the sauce over each portion as you serve it, and sprinkle it with a little chopped parsley.

THE K.C. BARON'S
HICKORY-PLANKED SALMON
WITH BROWN-SUGAR CURE

MAKES 8–10 SERVINGS

What can I say about Paul Kirk? He's the one and only Kansas City Baron of Barbecue, a seven-time world champion, and a true barbecue pioneer. He has been generous enough to adapt one of his favorite salmon recipes for the plank especially for this book. If you're ever in New York City or Las Vegas, don't forget to visit his RUB (Righteous Urban Barbeque) restaurants.

1 large hickory plank, soaked in
    water or apple juice overnight
    or at least 1 hour
one 5 lb [2.2 kg] fillet of salmon,
    pin bones removed

RUB
1 cup [250 mL] dark brown sugar
1 Tbsp [15 mL] Morton Tender
    Quick (a cure mixture available
    in the spice or salt section of
    grocery stores)

1 Tbsp [15 mL] Old Bay season-
    ing or Seafood Seasoning
    (recipe below)
2 tsp [10 mL] coarsely ground
    black pepper
2 tsp [10 mL] kosher salt
1 tsp [5 mL] granulated garlic

½ cup [125 mL] Dijon mustard
1 cup [250 mL] dark brown sugar

> **PLANKING SECRET** ≈

Plank-cooking works well in both gas and charcoal grills. As long as it's a covered grill, you'll get the desired smoky flavor from the smoldering plank. If you do use a charcoal grill to do your planking, add a few minutes to the cooking time. Covered charcoal grills generally produce a more moderate heat compared to natural gas and propane grills.

Make the rub by combining all the ingredients in a medium bowl and blending them together well.

Place the salmon on a large piece of plastic wrap. Sprinkle the skin side of the fillet with the rub, turn it over, and cover the fillet with the rest of the rub. Wrap the fillet up in the plastic wrap, place it in the refrigerator, and let it marinate or cure for 2 hours.

When you're ready to cook the salmon, remove it from the refrigerator. Using a pastry brush, paint the top side of the salmon fillet with the mustard and coat it with the brown sugar.

(continued)

Salmon & Other Spectacular Seafood

291

The K.C. Baron's Hickory-Planked Salmon with Brown-Sugar Cure *(continued)*

Preheat the grill on medium-high for 5 to 10 minutes, or until the chamber temperature rises above 500°F (260°C). Rinse the soaked plank and place it on the cooking grate. Cover the grill and heat the plank for 4 to 5 minutes, or until it starts to throw off a bit of smoke and crackles lightly. Reduce the heat to medium-low.

Place the salmon on the plank and cook it for 20 to 25 minutes, or until the fish has an internal temperature of 135°F (57°C).

NOTE: The standard instructions in this book are for planking with a gas grill. Paul is a dyed-in-the-wool charcoal-and-hardwood guy, and his recipe calls for this dish to be cooked in a covered charcoal grill. He recommends a 35- to 40-minute cooking time, with some hickory chips thrown onto the coals for good measure.

SEAFOOD SEASONING
MAKES ¼ CUP (50 ML)

You can use this seafood seasoning as a substitute for Old Bay or other seafood seasonings. It's good on chicken, as well.

1 Tbsp [15 mL] ground bay leaves	¾ tsp [3 mL] ground nutmeg
2½ tsp [12 mL] celery salt	½ tsp [2 mL] ground cloves
1½ tsp [7 mL] dry mustard	½ tsp [2 mL] ground ginger
1½ tsp [7 mL] freshly ground black pepper	½ tsp [2 mL] paprika
	½ tsp [2 mL] cayenne

Combine all the ingredients well in a medium bowl. Store the seasoning in an airtight container. (It's best if made at least a few days before you use it.)

STEVEN RAICHLEN'S PLANKED SALMON
WITH MUSTARD & DILL GLAZE

MAKES 4 SERVINGS

Steven Raichlen is Zeus in the pantheon of barbecue cooking gods, and I'm honored to include this recipe from his book *BBQ USA*. His technique is a little different from mine, but it works just as well.

1 cedar plank, soaked overnight
    or at least 1 hour

SALMON

one 1½ lb [750 g] salmon fillet,
    deboned, with or without skin,
    and ideally cut from the end
    closest to the head
extra virgin olive oil for brushing
coarse salt (kosher salt or sea
    salt) and freshly ground
    black pepper

GLAZE

½ cup [125 mL] mayonnaise
    (preferably Hellmann's)
⅓ cup [75 mL] grainy French
    mustard
2 Tbsp [25 mL] chopped
    fresh dill
½ tsp [2 mL] finely grated
    lemon zest
kosher salt and freshly ground
    black pepper

> **PLANKING SECRET** ≈

Removing the skin from a salmon fillet is pretty easy if you have a sharp, flexible fillet knife. Just start an incision near the tail of the fillet. As you cut, hold the end of the skin down and keep downward pressure on the knife. The skin is tough enough so you won't cut through. If this is too daunting a task, ask your fishmonger to do it for you.

If you're using salmon with skin, generously brush the skin with olive oil. If you're using skinless salmon, brush 1 side of the fish with olive oil. Season both sides with salt and pepper. Place the salmon on the plank, skin side down (or oiled side down for skinless salmon).

Place all the glaze ingredients in a nonreactive bowl and whisk them together. Season the glaze with salt and pepper to taste.

Set up the grill for indirect grilling and preheat it to medium-high. When you're ready to cook, spread the glaze mixture evenly over the top and sides of the salmon. Place the salmon on its plank in the center of the grate, away from the heat, and cover the grill. Cook the salmon until it's cooked through and the glaze is a deep golden brown, 20 to 30 minutes.

(continued)

Make a bed on your plank for extra flavor. Place a bundle of fresh herbs, some chopped scallions, or a handful of crushed garlic cloves on the plank before you put your meat or fish on to cook.

Steven Raichlen's Planked Salmon with Mustard & Dill Glaze
(continued)

To test for doneness, insert an instant-read meat thermometer through the side of the salmon. The internal temperature should be about 135°F (57°C). Another test is to insert a slender metal skewer in the side of the fillet for 20 seconds. It should come out very hot to the touch. Transfer the plank and the fish to a heatproof platter and slice the fish crosswise into serving portions. Serve the salmon right off the plank.

NOTE: You can use fish fillets with or without skin—your choice. (Though Steven loves the skin, he says his wife finds it makes the salmon taste fishy. He recommends this recipe for other rich, oily fish fillets, including bluefish and pompano.)

CHEF HOWIE'S PLANKED SALMON

MAKES 4 SERVINGS

John Howie could be considered a planking pioneer. As executive chef of Seastar Restaurant & Raw Bar in Bellevue, Washington, and a purveyor of fine seafood, cooking planks, and seasonings (www.plankcooking.com), he's been planking for close to 20 years and has demonstrated his techniques on *Martha Stewart Living Television*, the CBS *Early Morning Show* and Food Network's *Best of*, to name a few. John has generously shared his signature planked salmon recipe with me. You can buy the delicious dry rub in this recipe through his website. You'll have some left over; it's a great grilling rub for fish, chicken, or veggies.

1 cedar plank, soaked overnight or at
    least 1 hour
four 6 oz [175 g] fresh salmon fillets,
    about 2 inches [5 cm] thick, skin
    removed

DRY RUB
1 Tbsp [15 mL] kosher salt

1 Tbsp [15 mL] paprika
2 tsp [10 mL] light brown sugar
2 tsp [10 mL] lemon pepper
1 tsp [5 mL] granulated garlic
1 tsp [5 mL] dried tarragon
1 tsp [5 mL] dried basil

2 lemons, cut into 8 wedges

Combine all the rub ingredients well in a bowl.

Place the fillets on wax paper. Sprinkle both sides of the fish evenly with 2 Tbsp (25 mL) of the rub, pressing the seasoning into the fish. Refrigerate the salmon, uncovered, for at least 2 hours and up to 12 hours.

Preheat the grill on medium-high for 5 to 10 minutes, or until the chamber temperature rises above 500°F (260°C). Rinse the soaked plank and place it on the cooking grate. Cover the grill and heat the plank for 4 to 5 minutes, or until it starts to throw off a bit of smoke and crackles lightly. Reduce the heat to medium.

Place the salmon on the plank and cook it for 8 to 10 minutes, or until the fish has an internal temperature of 135°F (57°C). (This temperature is my standard doneness measure for fish. Chef Howie prefers his salmon rarer and removes it from the heat at 120°F/50°C). Transfer the salmon pieces to plates and serve them garnished with lemon wedges.

Salmon & Other Spectacular Seafood

FRED'S PLANKED CITRUS SALMON

MAKES 6–8 SERVINGS

Brian Misko is an enthusiastic barbecuer who took the plunge, along with his friend Glen Erho, and started up a barbecue team called House of Q. Brian passed on this recipe, which he has cooked time and again for his family. "It was originally crafted after salmon fishing in Tofino with my in-laws," he says. "I had never been fishing on the open ocean before, nor had Fred Kraus, my father-in-law. Nonetheless, a nice side of salmon was decorated for the grill with whatever we had in the cabin." And they've cooked it that way ever since.

1 alder cooking plank, soaked overnight
   or at least 1 hour
one 3 lb [1.5 kg] whole wild Pacific
   salmon fillet, deboned, skin on

MARINADE
juices of 1 orange, 1 lime and 1 lemon
   (reserve some slices for garnish)

1 tsp [5 mL] grated zest from the
   3 citrus fruits (optional)
2 cloves garlic, finely minced or pushed
   through a press
¼ cup [50 mL] extra virgin olive oil
kosher salt and freshly ground black pepper

Place the salmon in a nonreactive dish like a lasagna pan.

Whisk together all the marinade ingredients in a medium bowl and pour the marinade over the salmon. Marinate the fish for a minimum of 1 hour at room temperature.

Preheat the grill on medium-high for 5 to 10 minutes or until the chamber temperature rises above 500°F (260°C). Rinse the soaked plank and place it on the cooking grate. Cover the grill and heat the plank for 4 to 5 minutes, or until it starts to throw off a bit of smoke and crackles lightly. Reduce the heat to medium-low.

Remove the salmon from the marinade and season it with salt and pepper. Place it on the plank and cook it for 15 to 20 minutes, or until the fish has an internal temperature of 135°F (57°C). Halfway through the cooking time, spoon some of the marinade on top of the fish. When the salmon is done, serve it on the plank, garnished with the extra citrus slices.

Salmon & Other Spectacular Seafood

297

PLANKED SALMON
WITH PESTO

MAKES 6 SERVINGS

This is another classic way to plank salmon. Serve it with a tossed green salad and Florida-Style Grilled Zucchini (page 131).

1 alder cooking plank, soaked overnight
   or at least 1 hour

SALMON
one 2½ lb [1.2 kg] deboned salmon
   fillet, skin on
kosher salt and freshly ground
   black pepper
2 lemons, 1 for juice, 1 for garnish
½ cup [125 mL] extra virgin olive oil

PESTO
1 cup [250 mL] fresh basil leaves,
   washed and dried
6 cloves garlic, peeled
⅓ cup [75 mL] pine nuts
1 cup [250 mL] grated Parmesan cheese
¾ cup [175 mL] extra virgin olive oil
kosher salt and freshly ground black
   pepper

Cut the salmon fillet into 6 even portions. Season them on all sides with salt and pepper. Combine the juice of 1 lemon with the olive oil and pour it over the salmon. Let it marinate at room temperature for about 1 hour.

In a food processor, purée the basil, garlic, pine nuts, and Parmesan cheese with 2 to 3 Tbsp (25 to 45 mL) of the olive oil. With the processor running, slowly add the rest of the oil. Season the pesto with salt and pepper.

Coat the salmon pieces generously with the pesto (you'll have enough pesto left over to toss with some pasta another day; it freezes well, too).

Preheat the grill on medium-high for 5 to 10 minutes, or until the chamber temperature rises above 500°F (260°C). Rinse the soaked plank and place it on the cooking grate. Cover the grill and heat the plank for 4 to 5 minutes, or until it starts to throw off a bit of smoke and crackles lightly. Reduce the heat to medium-low. Place the salmon portions on the plank, leaving room around each for heat to circulate. Cook the fish for 8 to 12 minutes, or to an internal temperature of 135°F (57°C). Serve the salmon garnished with lemon wedges.

PLANKED SALMON
WITH ROSEMARY & BALSAMIC VINAIGRETTE

MAKES 6 SERVINGS

Rosemary and salmon are a classic combination. In this recipe, the honeyed balsamic vinaigrette and brown sugar intensify the flavor of this dish. This is excellent with grilled vegetables and Tomatoes in Paradise (page 115).

1 plank (cedar is nice but any kind will do), soaked overnight or at least 1 hour
one 2½ lb [1.2 kg] salmon fillet, deboned, skin on

VINAIGRETTE
kosher salt and freshly ground black pepper
1 tsp [5 mL] granulated garlic
1 Tbsp [15 mL] balsamic vinegar
3 Tbsp [45 mL] extra virgin olive oil

1 Tbsp [15 mL] liquid honey
1 shallot, peeled and finely chopped
1 tsp [5 mL] grainy mustard
½ tsp [2 mL] dried rosemary

3 or 4 sprigs fresh rosemary
extra virgin olive oil for drizzling
1 lemon, cut into wedges
1 green onion, finely chopped, for garnish
balsamic reduction (optional, see sidebar page 242)

Combine all the vinaigrette ingredients in a bowl and mix them together thoroughly. Coat the salmon fillet with the vinaigrette and set it aside.

Preheat the grill on medium-high for 5 to 10 minutes, or until the chamber temperature rises above 500°F (260°C). Rinse the soaked plank and place it on the cooking grate. Cover the grill and heat the plank for 4 to 5 minutes, or until it starts to throw off a bit of smoke and crackles lightly. Reduce the heat to medium-low.

Place the rosemary sprigs on the plank and lay the salmon fillet on top of the herbs, skin side down. Cook it for about 15 minutes, or until its internal temperature is 135°F (57°C). During cooking, watch for flare-ups and put them out with a spray bottle of water.

Take the plank off the grill and transfer it to a heatproof serving platter, tenting the salmon loosely with foil. To finish it, season it lightly with a little more salt and pepper, drizzle it with olive oil, and serve each portion with a wedge of lemon and a sprinkling of chopped green onion. For an extra-fancy touch, dot the plate with balsamic reduction.

Salmon & Other Spectacular Seafood

299

PLANK

PLANKED SALMON WITH CRAB SAUCE

MAKES 4 SERVINGS

Christine Hunt, who lives on beautiful Salt Spring Island, is a member of the Kwakiutl First Nation and the third generation of her family to fish the Pacific waters off the coast of British Columbia. She's also a great cook. Christine's recipe, which I've adapted for planking, is a rich, creamy combination, fit for a special occasion.

1 alder or hickory plank, soaked
    overnight
one 1½ lb [750 g] salmon fillet, skin
    on, cut into 4 pieces
1 tsp [5 mL] lemon pepper

CRAB SAUCE
2 Tbsp [25 mL] butter
2 Tbsp [25 mL] all-purpose flour

2 cups [500 mL] whole milk
1 tsp [5 mL] lemon pepper
4 oz [125 g] light cream cheese, cubed
2 Tbsp [25 mL] fresh lemon juice
finely chopped or grated zest of 1 lemon
1 green onion, thinly sliced
4 oz [125 g] fresh crabmeat (or a 4½ oz/
    128 mL can, with juice)

Season the salmon pieces with the 1 tsp (5 mL) of lemon pepper and set them aside.

Preheat your grill to medium-high heat.

While the grill is heating, melt the butter in a saucepan over medium-low heat. Stir in the flour and cook the mixture for about 1 minute. Gradually whisk in the milk and the lemon pepper. Cook, stirring the sauce often, until it has thickened, about 12 minutes. Whisk in the cream cheese until it melts into the sauce. Stir it occasionally to maintain its smoothness.

While the sauce is cooking, rinse the soaked plank and place it on the cooking grate. Cover the grill and heat the plank for 4 to 5 minutes, or until it starts to throw off a bit of smoke and crackles lightly. Reduce the heat to medium-low. Place the salmon pieces on the plank. They'll be done in 8 to 10 minutes, or when they're springy to the touch.

When the salmon is nearly done, transfer it to a plate and cover it loosely with foil. (While the fish is resting you might want to quickly grill some veggies.)

Finish the sauce by adding the lemon juice and zest, green onion, and crab (include the juice if you're using canned). Plate the salmon pieces, spoon on the crab sauce, and serve.

SOY MAPLE-PLANKED SALMON

MAKES 6 SERVINGS

East meets North in this classic planking recipe based on one shared by email pen pal Kim Peterson, which contrasts the classic sweetness of maple syrup with Asian flavors of ginger and soy sauce.

1 cedar, alder, or maple plank, soaked overnight or at least 1 hour
one 2½ lb [1 kg] salmon fillet, skin on
greens from 1 bunch green onions, chopped

SOY MAPLE SAUCE
1 cup [250 mL] maple syrup

2 Tbsp [25 mL] grated fresh ginger
¼ cup [50 mL] fresh lemon juice
3 Tbsp [45 mL] soy sauce
2 cloves garlic, finely minced
kosher salt and freshly ground black pepper

Make the glaze by combining the maple syrup, ginger, all but 1 Tbsp (15 mL) of the lemon juice, the soy sauce, garlic, and salt and pepper to taste in a small pot. Cook the mixture at a simmer until it's reduced to 1 cup (250 mL), about 30 minutes. Let it cool. Season the salmon with salt and pepper and coat it with about half of the sauce using a basting brush.

Preheat the grill on medium-high for 5 to 10 minutes, or until the chamber temperature rises above 500°F (260°C). Rinse the soaked plank and place it on the cooking grate. Cover the grill and heat the plank for 4 to 5 minutes, or until it starts to throw off a bit of smoke and crackles lightly. Reduce the heat to medium-low.

Quickly place the chopped onion greens on the plank, reserving about 1 Tbsp (15 mL). Place the salmon on the greens. Cook it for about 15 minutes, or until the internal temperature is 135°F (57°C). During cooking, watch for flare-ups and put them out with a spray bottle of water.

Take the plank off the grill and transfer it to a heatproof serving platter, tenting it loosely with foil. Finish the remaining sauce by adding the reserved lemon juice and warming it up a bit. Drizzle the salmon with the sauce and serve it immediately, garnishing it with the reserved chopped onion greens.

PLANK

TOJO-STYLE
MISO-MARINATED PLANKED SALMON

MAKES 6 SERVINGS

Hidekazu Tojo is the owner and chef of Tojo's, one of the world's most famous Japanese eateries. Ever eaten a California roll? Tojo invented it. His flavor and texture combinations are brilliant. Here, I've simplified and adapted one of Tojo's fish recipes for the plank. He uses sablefish fillets rather than salmon, but any rich, dense-fleshed fish would work well. You can find the ingredients in the Asian section of most supermarkets or in Japanese specialty stores.

1 cedar plank, soaked overnight or at
    least 1 hour

SALMON
six 6 oz [175 g] salmon fillets
kosher salt

MARINADE
½ cup [125 mL] miso paste
¼ cup [50 mL] mirin (Japanese sweet
    rice wine)

¼ cup [50 mL] sake
1 tsp [5 mL] sugar
¼ tsp [1 mL] togarashi chili pepper or
    cayenne
1 tsp [5 mL] finely minced fresh ginger

GARNISH
1 Tbsp [15 mL] finely chopped chives
½ cup [125 mL] shredded daikon (Japa-
    nese radish), tossed with a few drops
    each of rice vinegar, tamari, and mirin

Salt the fish pieces on both sides and place them in a nonreactive pan.

Combine the miso, mirin, sake, sugar, chili pepper, and ginger in a medium bowl; the mixture will make a fairly thick liquid. Pour the marinade over the fish and turn the pieces to coat them. Cover the fish and refrigerate it for at least 2 hours or overnight.

Preheat the grill on medium-high for 5 to 10 minutes, or until the chamber temperature rises above 500°F (260°C). Rinse the soaked plank and place it on the cooking grate. Cover the grill and heat the plank for 4 to 5 minutes, or until it starts to throw off a bit of smoke and crackles lightly. Reduce the heat to medium-low.

Place the fish pieces on the plank and cook them for 10 to 15 minutes, or until the fish has an internal temperature of 135°F (57°C). When the salmon is ready, transfer it to a platter and tent it with foil for 3 to 4 minutes. Garnish with chives and serve it with the shredded daikon.

Also pictured: Skewered Prawns Pistou (page 337) and Planked Scallops (page 338)

PLANKED TANDOORI SALMON
WITH PEACH CHUTNEY & MINTED YOGURT

MAKES 6 SERVINGS

I've tried to track down the originator of this recipe, and I'm pretty sure it comes from New York-based Scandinavian chef Christer Larsson. It's one of the greatest combinations of flavors I can imagine. I've adapted it for the plank, which adds another dimension to an already superb dish. Serve this dish with steamed basmati rice and some grilled papadums.

1 alder or cedar plank, soaked overnight
    or at least 1 hour
one 2½ lb [1.2 kg] salmon fillet,
    deboned, skin on

RUB
⅔ cup [160 mL] extra virgin olive oil
1 clove garlic, finely chopped
1 Tbsp [15 mL] tandoori powder or
    garam masala
salt (preferably fleur de sel or other
    coarse sea salt)

PEACH CHUTNEY
1 Tbsp [15 mL] sugar

¼ cup [50 mL] rice vinegar
4 medium peaches, peeled and cut into
    ½-inch [1 cm] dice
2 Tbsp [25 mL] finely grated fresh ginger

MINTED YOGURT
1½ tsp [7 mL] honey
1½ tsp [7 mL] finely chopped fresh mint
pinch ground cumin
pinch turmeric
1 cup [250 mL] plain low-fat yogurt
kosher salt and freshly ground black
    pepper

Combine the olive oil and garlic in a bowl. Rub the mixture all over the salmon. Sprinkle the salmon with the tandoori powder or garam masala and season it lightly with salt. Cover the salmon and refrigerate it for up to 2 hours.

    Dissolve the sugar in the vinegar in a nonreactive saucepan over moderately high heat. Bring the mixture to a boil and cook it for 1 minute. Stir in the peaches and ginger and return the chutney to a boil. Reduce the heat and simmer the chutney, stirring it frequently, until the fruit is softened, about 5 minutes. Transfer it to a bowl.

(continued)

One of the best ways to prepare papadums—the delicious Indian cracker—is to grill it. All it takes is 10 or 20 seconds per side on a hot grill to crisp up the papadums and bring out their flavor.

Planked Tandoori Salmon with Peach Chutney & Minted Yogurt *(continued)*

Combine the honey, mint, cumin, and turmeric in a medium bowl. Whisk in the yogurt until it's blended and season the mixture with salt and pepper. Cover the bowl and refrigerate the sauce.

Preheat the grill on medium-high for 5 to 10 minutes, or until the chamber temperature rises above 500°F (260°C). Rinse the soaked plank and place it on the grate. Cover the grill and heat the plank for 4 to 5 minutes, or until it starts to throw off a bit of smoke and crackles lightly. Reduce the heat to medium.

Place the salmon fillet on the plank. Cook for 10 to 15 minutes, or until the fish has an internal temperature of 135°F (57°C). Serve the salmon with the chutney and the yogurt sauce.

PLANKED SALMON PIZZA

MAKES 4 SERVINGS

My pal Reza Mofakham helps manage a hardware store and caught the barbecue bug a couple of years ago. He's learned to master the Cadillac of charcoal cookers, the Big Green Egg, which is kind of a cross between a covered grill and a tandoor oven—which means you can plank salmon and cook pizza in it. This dish scored well in the open category at the Canadian National Barbecue Championships in 2005, and I think it'll score well with you, too. It's a tasty way to deal with leftover planked salmon. If you don't feel like making your own pizza dough, you can buy it frozen at most supermarkets.

PESTO SAUCE

2 cups [500 mL] fresh basil

¼ cup [50 mL] freshly grated
   Parmesan cheese

¼ cup [50 mL] toasted pine nuts

2 cloves garlic

1 tsp [5 mL] kosher salt

½ tsp [2 mL] freshly ground
   black pepper

¼ cup [50 mL] extra virgin olive oil

PIZZA DOUGH

1 Tbsp [15 mL] sugar

1½ cups [375 mL] lukewarm water
   or beer

2 tsp [10 mL] instant yeast

4¼ cups [1 L + 50 mL] all-purpose flour

1 tsp [5 mL] kosher salt

2 Tbsp [25 mL] oil

TOPPINGS

½ lb [250 g] leftover planked salmon,
   broken into bite-sized pieces

1 Tbsp [15 mL] capers

4 oz [125 g] goat cheese

2 Tbsp [25 mL] sun-dried tomatoes,
   coarsely chopped

For the pesto, place the basil, Parmesan, pine nuts, garlic, salt, and pepper in a blender. Blend them together until they're smooth, slowly adding the oil in a stream, until you have a smooth, light-green sauce. Set the pesto aside.

    For the pizza dough, dissolve the sugar in ½ cup (125 mL) of the water or beer, sprinkle the yeast overtop, and let it sit for about 5 minutes. Place the flour and salt in a food processor. Add the yeast mixture and the oil,

(continued)

Planked Salmon Pizza *(continued)*

and turn on the machine. Pour the rest of the water or beer through the feed tube of the food processor while it's running. Blend the mixture just until the dough forms a ball on the side of the bowl. (If you're using a bread machine, prepare the ingredients according to the manufacturer's instructions).

Remove the dough and knead it on a lightly floured surface for a few minutes. Transfer the dough to a bowl and lightly oil the top. Cover the bowl with plastic wrap and leave it in a warm, draft-free area for about 40 minutes, until it has doubled in size.

Preheat the grill or oven to 375 to 400°F (190–200°C). Press the dough evenly onto a lightly oiled pizza stone or pizza pan. Spread the pesto evenly on the dough and add the salmon, capers, goat cheese, and sun-dried tomatoes. Bake the pizza for 15 to 20 minutes, or until the crust is golden brown and the cheese is melted.

HOT SMOKED SALMON

MAKES 6–8 SERVINGS

When good-quality salmon is barbecued over low heat using hickory, alder, or mesquite smoke as a flavoring agent, the end result is outrageously good. This is my favorite way to barbecue salmon.

one 1½–2 lb [750 g–1 kg]
    whole wild salmon fillet
    (also called a side)
kosher salt and freshly ground
    black pepper to taste
1 Tbsp [15 mL] toasted
    sesame oil

1 tsp [5 mL] crushed dried red
    chili flakes
¼ cup [50 mL] brown sugar
1 lemon, halved
chopped fresh parsley for garnish

⮞ BARBECUE SECRET ⮜

A simple way to barbecue salmon is good ol' mustard and rub. Just slather a fillet with prepared mustard, sprinkle it with Championship Barbecue Rub (page 50), and barbecue it at 200 to 220°F (95–100°C) for 1½ to 2½ hours, depending on the size and thickness of the fillet and how you prefer it done.

Prepare your smoker for barbecuing, bringing the temperature to 200 to 220°F (95–100°C). Put the salmon, skin side down, on a baking sheet or cutting board. With a pair of needle-nose pliers, pluck the pin bones out of the fillet. Season it with salt and pepper and coat it with sesame oil. Sprinkle the chili flakes evenly over the fillet and then sprinkle the brown sugar over the top. Squeeze the juice of half the lemon over the sugared salmon.

Let the fish sit for 15 minutes or so, until the sugar is wet and glistening.

Place the fillet on the cooking grate, put a chunk or two of hardwood on the coals, close the smoker, and barbecue the salmon for 1½ to 2½ hours, or until the internal temperature at its thickest part reaches about 140°F (60°C). Use 2 wide spatulas to remove the salmon from the smoker. Transfer it to a warmed platter. Garnish the salmon with chopped parsley and the remaining lemon half, cut into wedges.

Salmon & Other Spectacular Seafood

WILD BC SALMON
WITH HOMEMADE TARTAR SAUCE &
TOMATO SALAD

MAKES 4 SERVINGS

Rob Clark, Executive Chef of C Restaurant, Nu Restaurant, and Raincity Grill, is the best seafood chef in Vancouver, and that's saying something. This is his recipe, which I've adapted for the grill. It's a sophisticated version of a salmon-grilling technique I learned many years ago that's as easy as pie and as delicious as it gets. The concept is to slather a side of salmon with mayo, put it on a hot grill, skin side down, and cook it until the salmon is done and the mayo has sort of set, like a savory pudding, on the fish. Pair this salmon with some BC Pinot Blanc or Sauvignon Blanc.

TARTAR SAUCE

1 cup [250 mL] mayonnaise

2 tsp [10 mL] dried dill

3 Tbsp [45 mL] finely chopped cornichons (gherkins)

1 Tbsp [15 mL] finely chopped stuffed green olives

1 Tbsp [15 mL] finely chopped shallots

1 Tbsp [15 mL] finely chopped capers

1 Tbsp [15 mL] finely chopped fresh parsley

2 Tbsp [25 mL] fresh lemon juice

1 Tbsp [15 mL] Dijon mustard

TOMATO SALAD

2 Tbsp [25 mL] extra virgin olive oil

2 tsp [10 mL] rice wine vinegar

1 tsp [5 mL] Dijon mustard

1 Tbsp [15 mL] finely minced shallot

⅛ tsp [0.5 mL] cayenne

kosher salt and freshly ground black pepper

4 medium fresh heirloom tomatoes (yellow ones work nicely)

SALMON

four 6 oz [175 g] boneless, skinless wild BC salmon fillets (Rob prefers pink salmon but coho or sockeye also work well)

sea salt

Combine all of the tartar sauce ingredients in a small bowl and stir until well blended. Set the mixture aside.

Prepare the tomato salad by whisking together all the ingredients except the tomatoes. Slice the tomatoes into ¼-inch (6 mm) rounds. Gently toss the tomato slices in the vinaigrette and divide the salad among 4 serving plates.

Season the salmon fillets with salt and let them sit for 10 minutes.

Prepare your grill for direct medium heat. Place the salmon fillets, skin side down, on the cooking grate and slather each of them with 1 Tbsp (15 mL) of the tartar sauce. Cover the grill and cook the salmon for 5 to 7 minutes, until the fillets reach an internal temperature of 135°F (57°C). When they're done they should easily come off the grill, leaving the skin behind.

To serve the salmon, place the fillets on the plates beside the tomato salad and finish the dish with a dollop of the remaining tartar sauce.

GRILLED SALMON TACOS

MAKES 16 TACOS, ENOUGH FOR 4–6 AS A MAIN COURSE, OR 16 APPETIZER SERVINGS

One of the highlights of visiting Maui was the fantastic fish tacos sold by beachside vendors. This is my attempt to replicate this dish, which works extremely well using salmon for the fish. I like to crisp the salmon skin on the grill and offer it as a condiment with the tacos (it's crunchy and rich— the bacon of the sea), but feel free to omit it if that's not to your taste. Serve this dish with cold American beer or a crisp, fruity white wine.

RED ONION, GREEN MANGO, & JALAPEÑO PICKLE

2 cups [500 mL] seasoned rice vinegar

3 Tbsp [45 mL] fresh lime juice

1 Tbsp [15 mL] kosher salt

1 medium red onion, halved lengthwise and cut crosswise into thin strips

2 large jalapeños, stemmed, seeded, and cut into thin strips

1 green (unripe) mango, peeled, cored, and cut into thin strips

SAUCE

½ cup [125 mL] Margie's Chipotle & Roasted Garlic Mayo (see page 68)

¼ cup [50 mL] sour cream or yogurt

1 Tbsp [15 mL] fresh lime juice

SALMON

2 lb [1 kg] side of wild sockeye or coho salmon, skin on

about 1 tsp [5 mL] Rockin' Ronnie's Grilling Rub (see page 51)

TACOS & THE REST OF THE FIXIN'S

16 white corn tortillas

1 batch Chunky Smoked Tomato Guacamole (see page 65)

half a head of iceberg lettuce, chopped

½ cup [125 mL] chopped fresh cilantro

Louisiana-style hot sauce

For the pickle, combine the rice vinegar, lime juice, and salt in a saucepan and cook the mixture over medium-high heat, stirring it until the salt dissolves and the mixture comes barely to a boil. Place the onion, jalapeño, and mango slices in a bowl and pour the hot vinegar mixture over them. Let the pickle stand at room temperature for at least 1 hour and up to 8 hours. Transfer it to a storage container and refrigerate it.

For the sauce, combine all the ingredients and refrigerate until needed.

Prepare your grill for direct medium heat. Sprinkle the salmon with a light coating of the grilling rub. Let the rubbed salmon sit for a few minutes, until it starts to glisten. Place the salmon, skin side down, on the cooking grate and grill it for 8 to 12 minutes, until the salmon springs back to your touch or comes to an internal temperature of about 130 to 140°F (55–60°C).

While the salmon is cooking, heat a sauté pan to medium-high and lightly toast both sides of each of the corn tortillas in the hot, dry pan. Keep the heated pile of tortillas warm by covering them with a clean, damp dishcloth.

Take the side of salmon off the grill with a long spatula (or a couple of short ones). It should come right off the skin. Transfer the salmon to a cutting board and let it rest, tented in foil, for 5 minutes.

While the salmon is resting, return to the grill and try to pull the salmon skin off with a set of tongs. If it comes off easily, flip it over and lightly grill the other side for no more than 30 seconds (if it doesn't come off easily, I usually tear what I can off the grill and eat it right then and there). Transfer the skin to a plate and set it aside. As it cooks, it will become very crisp, like bacon.

Slice the salmon into ½-inch (1 cm) strips (the fish may break apart when you slice it, but that's okay) and place the slices in a serving dish. Coarsely chop the salmon skin and place it in a small serving bowl.

To serve the tacos, lay out the tortillas, salmon, salmon skin, sauce, pickles, guacamole, chopped lettuce, chopped cilantro, and hot sauce on a table and let your guests assemble their own.

OTHER SPECTACULAR SEAFOOD

It's too easy to go for the pork chops or chicken breasts when you're shopping for your next grilled meal. These days there's so much great fresh seafood available that if you don't cook it at least once a week you're missing out on one of life's great pleasures.

Some backyard cooks are intimidated by fish because it often sticks to the grill. If that's a big problem for you, get into hobo-pack cooking—wrapping fish with foil, which is a foolproof way to go. Others worry about picky kids who turn their noses up at anything other than a hot dog or burger. I hate to say it, but give the kids what they want and go through the extra trouble to cook yourself and your spouse some delicious fish. And still others are concerned about freshness and food safety. The solution: find a good fishmonger, make friends with her, and get her to teach you how to distinguish the freshest fish from the yucky stuff. Over time you'll come to know what's best, which is often the fish that is local and in season.

The recipes in this section are designed to give you a nice range of choices so you can experiment with different kinds of seafood and different cooking techniques. Dive in and I think you'll agree that life is better when you make some room for the ocean's bounty on your grill!

HALIBUT & MOREL HOBO PACKS

MAKES 4 INDIVIDUAL PORTIONS

These really pack a punch when it comes to flavor, and the aroma when you open up the packs is out of this world. Serve these with a simple green salad and some nice French bread to sop up all the rich juice.

four 8 oz [250 g] halibut fillets	¼ lb [125 g] butter
kosher salt and freshly ground black pepper	½ cup [125 mL] chopped fresh flat-leaf Italian parsley
4 slices double-smoked bacon	½ cup [125 mL] dry Riesling
1 large white onion	1 cup [250 mL] whipping cream
4 medium Yukon Gold potatoes	truffle oil
½ lb [250 g] fresh morel mushrooms, trimmed, washed well, and patted dry	¼ cup [50 mL] chopped fresh chives
	4 lemon wedges

Season the halibut fillets with salt and pepper. Cut the bacon slices in half and set them aside. Thinly slice the onion and the potatoes and set them aside. Slice the morels into ⅛-inch (3 mm) rounds and set them aside.

Prepare 4 squares of doubled wide aluminum foil, about 18 inches (45 cm) square. Lightly coat each square with butter, leaving a 4-inch (10 cm) margin all the way around. Place 2 half-slices of the bacon in the middle of each sheet. Lay down a layer of onion slices, season with salt and pepper, then add a layer of potato slices and season again. Place the halibut fillets on top. Divide the morels into 4 equal portions and place them on top of the halibut. Sprinkle each with chopped parsley.

Gather the corners of the foil and shape them around each fillet so that when you pour the cream and wine in it won't spill out. Pour a splash of the Riesling and ¼ cup (50 mL) of the cream into each pack. Drizzle a few drops of truffle oil and a daub of butter on each. Seal each pack tightly.

Prepare your grill for direct medium heat. Place the hobo packs on the cooking grate and grill for 12 to 14 minutes. Remove 1 pack, open it, and test the potatoes for doneness. If they're not quite tender, reseal the pack and put it back in the grill for 3 or 4 minutes. Remove the packs from the grill and let them rest for 5 minutes. Let your guests open them up and sprinkle the contents with chopped chives. Garnish with lemon wedges.

Salmon & Other Spectacular Seafood

GRILL

DILLED & GRILLED HALIBUT

MAKES 4 SERVINGS

⮞ BARBECUE SECRETS ⮜

One of the problems with grilling fish is the delicate flesh sticks to the cooking grate and the fish seems to fall apart before you can get it off the grill. But today's covered gas or charcoal grills cook so evenly you don't have to turn your fish, even when you're cooking it over direct heat. For fillets, just cook the fish skin side down. The skin sticks to the grill, allowing the fish to come off cleanly and easily. If you're cooking fish steaks that have no skin, be sure you oil the grill and spray the fish with cooking spray just before putting it on the grate.

Bonus tip: Don't let that skin go to waste. Salmon skin in particular is excellent when crisped up on the grill. After you've taken your salmon fillet off, pry the skin off the grate and grill it for another few minutes. Remove it, and sprinkle it with salt. It's a crispy and delicious cook's treat!

Halibut is such a delicately flavored fish that you don't want to do much to it. The key here is to use the very freshest ingredients. This dish is excellent with your favorite green salad.

four 6 oz [175 g] fresh halibut
   fillets, skin on
kosher salt and freshly ground
   black pepper
¼ cup [50 mL] chopped fresh
   dill (stems removed)

2 Tbsp [25 mL] fresh lemon juice
extra virgin olive oil
lemon wedges for garnish

Place the fish fillets in a nonreactive dish or baking pan. Season both sides of each fillet with salt and pepper and coat them evenly with the dill. Squeeze the lemon over the fish and then drizzle it generously with the olive oil, turning it to coat it. Let it sit for 15 minutes. Meanwhile, prepare the grill for direct medium heat.

Place the halibut pieces on the grill, skin side down. Cook the halibut for about 6 minutes, until it's just cooked through, to an internal temperature of about 140 to 150°F (60–66°C). Remove it from the grill (the skin will stick to the grill but should easily separate from the fish) and let it rest for a couple of minutes. To serve the halibut, season it with a little more salt and pepper, drizzle it with olive oil, and accompany it with lemon wedges.

PLANKED SAFFRON HALIBUT
WITH AVOCADO & TROPICAL FRUIT SALSA

MAKES 4–6 SERVINGS

I get a lot of my fish at Westlynn Meats and Seafood in beautiful Lynn Valley in the heart of British Columbia's rainforest. Mike works there and he knows his fish. His unusual recipe, which I've adapted for the plank, pairs the intense flavor of spiced halibut with a cool tropical salsa. Substitute snapper for halibut for an even stronger flavor. Confetti Rice (page 144) goes very well with this.

1 plank (cedar or fruitwood), soaked overnight or at least 1 hour

1 batch Tropical Salsa (see page 63)
four 6 oz [175 g] halibut fillets
kosher salt and freshly ground black pepper

1 tsp [5 mL] ground cumin
½ tsp [2 mL] turmeric
pinch saffron threads, crumbled
pinch cayenne
1 lime, cut in half
extra virgin olive oil
fresh cilantro sprigs for garnish

Prepare the salsa and set it aside.

Season both sides of the fillets with salt and pepper. Combine the cumin, turmeric, saffron, and cayenne in a bowl and sprinkle the mixture lightly over the fillets. Squeeze the lime halves over the fillets and drizzle them with a little olive oil. Marinate the fish for 15 minutes.

Preheat the grill on medium-high for 5 to 10 minutes, or until the chamber temperature rises above 500°F (260°C). Rinse the soaked plank and place it on the cooking grate. Cover the grill and heat the plank for 4 to 5 minutes, or until it starts to throw off a bit of smoke and crackles lightly. Reduce the heat to medium-low.

Place the fillets on the plank and cook the fish for 15 to 20 minutes, or until the fish has an internal temperature of 135°F (57°C). Remove it from the grill and tent it lightly in foil. Let it rest for 2 or 3 minutes.

Serve the fillets topped with a dollop of salsa and a sprig of cilantro.

GRILLED SABLEFISH
WITH WARM TOMATO & RED ONION SALAD

MAKES 4 SERVINGS

HOW TO CHOOSE & ❧ STORE FISH ❧

When shopping for fresh fish, look for a place that goes through a lot of fish! The faster the fish is selling, the more likely it is to be fresh.

And don't be afraid to buy frozen fish. Which would you rather eat—a fish that was caught in the open ocean and immediately frozen at sea, or one that was freshly caught and has been sitting on a boat, and then in a warehouse, and then in a store?

Thaw fish using cold water. Fresh-frozen fish can be thawed easily by placing it, still in its packaging, in a sink full of cold water. Half an hour in a water bath and the fish is thawed and ready to cook.

Look for firm, shiny flesh that smells as fresh as it looks. Touch the fish. It should be firm to the touch, with a nice sheen, and should smell fresh and not fishy.

Store your fish packed with ice. To keep fish at optimum freshness in your refrigerator, keep it in its sealed packaging and surround it with ice.

My friend Steve Crescenzo from Chicago is a great cook, and I've adapted this from one of his favorite seafood recipes. I love the rich, silky texture of sablefish, also known as black cod. You can substitute halibut or any other white, firm-fleshed fish. Please note: To execute this recipe, you're going to be switching from indirect medium heat to direct medium-high heat, which is easy on a gas grill but a little more challenging with a charcoal-fired grill.

SALAD

2 heads roasted garlic
(see page 68)
¼ cup [50 mL] extra virgin
olive oil
1 small red onion, sliced thinly
1 bay leaf
2 or 3 sprigs fresh thyme
¼ cup [50 mL] high-quality
balsamic vinegar (aged 12
years or more)
2 cups [500 mL] cherry
tomatoes

FISH

four 5–8 oz [150–250 g]
sablefish fillets, skin on
vegetable or canola oil for
brushing
kosher salt and freshly ground
black pepper
pinch cayenne
1 bunch fresh chives
lemon wedges

Prepare the grill for indirect medium heat.

Squeeze the garlic paste out of the heads of roasted garlic into an ovenproof pan. Pour the olive oil over the garlic, add the onion slices, bay leaf, and thyme, and stir everything around. Place the pan in the grill and cook for about 15 minutes, stirring occasionally, until the oil is hot and the onion and garlic are starting to sizzle.

Add the balsamic vinegar and tomatoes to the pan. Mix everything together well. Cover the grill and roast the mixture in the uncovered pan, turning the contents gently every couple of minutes, just until the tomatoes begin to split. (Note: If you can get your hands on yellow or orange cherry tomatoes, you can mix and match; the result is very pretty.)

Put on some oven mitts. Remove the hot pan from the grill and set it aside. Adjust the grill to achieve direct medium-high heat. Rub the fish fillets with the oil, sprinkle them with salt, pepper, and cayenne, and place them on the cooking grate skin side down. Grill them for 8 to 10 minutes, or until the core temperature at the thickest part of the fillets is 135°F (57°C). Do not overcook the sablefish!

Spoon a nice portion of the tomato salad onto the center of a warmed plate. Remove the fish fillets from the grill (the skin should stick to the grill, allowing you to easily separate the cooked fillets from the skin) and place them on top of the salad. Spoon a little more of the tomato salad over that. Garnish the dish with chopped fresh chives and lemon wedges and drizzle it with some olive oil. Have good bread on hand to sop up the juices.

LINGCOD IN FOIL
WITH FENNEL & APPLE SALSA

MAKES 4–6 SERVINGS

My family once went on a guided fishing trip in the waters near Pender Harbor, British Columbia. Once we got past Kate's violent seasickness and our disappointment at not catching any salmon, our son, Jake, got the thrill of the day when he caught a 9 lb (4 kg) lingcod. The lingcod is a long, greenish-blue bottom fish with a big, ugly face and a giant mouth that can take an octopus in one bite. It also has incredibly succulent, delicate, bluish-white flesh that's so tender it falls apart if you try to grill it, but it's just great cooked in foil.

SALSA

1 fennel bulb, stalk and fronds attached
1 navel orange
3 Tbsp [45 mL] orange-infused extra virgin olive oil (or regular if you can't find the orange-infused kind)
1 Tbsp [15 mL] white balsamic vinegar
½ tsp [2 mL] Dijon mustard
kosher salt and freshly ground black pepper
2 Granny Smith apples

FOIL PACKS

1 medium yellow onion
2 oz [60 g] butter
granulated garlic
1½ lb [750 g] boneless lingcod fillet (halibut would also work)
1 tsp [5 mL] finely grated orange zest
2 Tbsp [25 mL] Pernod liqueur
extra virgin olive oil for drizzling

Trim the fronds from the fennel, discarding the woody stems. Finely chop the fennel fronds and set them aside.

Halve the orange and set one half aside. Combine the olive oil, vinegar, and mustard in a bowl along with the juice of half the orange and 1 tsp (5 mL) of the chopped fennel fronds. Whisk the ingredients together and add salt and pepper to taste. Set this vinaigrette aside.

Cut the fennel bulb in half from top to bottom. Cut one half of the fennel bulb into very thin slices using a mandoline or a very sharp chef's knife. Set the sliced fennel aside.

Chop the other half of the fennel bulb into a ¼-inch (6 mm) dice and place it in the mixing bowl containing the vinaigrette.

Peel and core the apples and chop them into a ¼-inch (6 mm) dice. Transfer them to the bowl with the vinaigrette and diced fennel and toss them together. Set the salsa aside.

Trim and peel the onion and then cut it into the same kind of thin slices as the fennel using the mandoline. Set the sliced onion aside.

Fold a 4-foot (1.2 m) strip of wide, heavy-duty aluminum foil in half and lay it down on your counter. Coat the foil with a thin layer of the butter, leaving a 4-inch (10 cm) margin around the rectangle of foil. Lay down the sliced onion on the foil and sprinkle the onion slices with a little salt. Season both sides of the lingcod fillet with a very light sprinkle of salt, pepper, and granulated garlic. Lay it on top of the onions, and then lay the shaved fennel slices on top of the fish. Top with the orange zest. Drizzle the fish with the Pernod and some olive oil. Sprinkle a teaspoon of the chopped fennel fronds and a pinch of salt over the shaved fennel. Tightly seal the foil around the ingredients.

Prepare the grill for direct medium heat. Place the foil packet, onion layer facing down, on the grill and cook for 12 to 15 minutes, or until the onions are soft and the fish is cooked through. Transfer the packet to a heatproof serving platter and let it rest for about 5 minutes. To serve, open up the packet at the table and divide its contents among you and your guests with a large serving spoon, making sure everyone gets some of the liquid. Top each serving with a dollop of the salsa and a wedge of the remaining half of the orange.

NOTE: Because fennel bulbs and onions come in different sizes, it's hard to estimate exactly how much of these ingredients you'll have when you come to assembling the foil packet. Use your best judgment—if it looks like you have too much fennel or onion for everything to fit comfortably, feel free to change the amounts to suit the situation.

CARAWAY-CRUSTED PLANKED MONKFISH
WITH TOMATO & GREEN ONION SAUCE

MAKES 4 SERVINGS

Monkfish is often referred to as the poor man's lobster because it has very firm, rich, flavorful white flesh. The fillet looks kind of like a pork tenderloin, and it cooks up very nicely on a plank.

1 cedar plank, soaked overnight or at
    least 1 hour

MONKFISH
1½ Tbsp [22 mL] caraway seeds
one 1 lb [500 g] skinless monkfish fillet
kosher salt and freshly ground
    black pepper
2 Tbsp [25 mL] extra virgin olive oil
1 large clove garlic, finely minced
finely grated zest of ½ lemon
pinch cayenne

SAUCE
¼ cup [50 mL] mayonnaise
1 ripe tomato, chopped into a ¼-inch
    [6 mm] dice
3 green onions, finely chopped, 1 Tbsp
    [15 mL] reserved for garnish
1 Tbsp [15 mL] finely chopped fresh
    parsley
1 small clove garlic, finely minced
pinch cayenne
1 Tbsp [15 mL] fresh lemon juice
kosher salt

Lightly toast the caraway seeds in a dry sauté pan, transfer the caraway to a plate to cool, and set it aside.

Season the monkfish fillet with salt and pepper. Combine the olive oil, garlic, lemon zest, cayenne, and granulated onion in a small bowl and coat the fillet with the mixture. Sprinkle all but 1½ tsp (7 mL) of the caraway seeds evenly over the fillet. Let it sit for 15 minutes.

To make the sauce, combine all the ingredients in a medium bowl and mix them together thoroughly. Set the sauce aside.

Preheat the grill on medium-high for 5 to 10 minutes, or until the chamber temperature rises above 500°F (260°C). Rinse the soaked plank and place it on the cooking grate. Cover the grill and heat the plank for 4 to 5 minutes, or until it starts to throw off a bit of smoke and crackles lightly. Reduce the heat to medium.

Place the fish on the plank and cook it for 15 to 20 minutes, turning it halfway through the cooking time, until the fish is springy to the touch or has an internal temperature of 135°F (57°C).

Cut the fish into medallions and serve it with a dollop of the sauce, a sprinkling of salt and pepper, and a tiny drizzle of olive oil. Garnish it with the reserved caraway seeds and green onions.

BLACKENED SNAPPER ON THE GRILL

MAKES 4 SERVINGS

If you've ever tried to cook this spectacular dish indoors, you'll know it's a bit of a nightmare—it generates a huge amount of white smoke. Cooking this dish outdoors takes a special technique that uses a gas grill to preheat cast iron pans to create the same effect as chef Paul Prudhomme's restaurant kitchen. Don't cook this dish if you're worried about smoking out your neighbors! You'll need two 9-inch (23 cm) heavy cast iron skillets to pull off this recipe.

WARNING: It's extremely easy to severely burn your hand if you absent-mindedly grab the handle of the insanely hot pan when you take the fish off the grill. Please be careful!

four 8–10 oz [250–300 g] snapper fillets	¾ lb [375 g] butter 1 batch Cajun Rub (see page 53)

Warm 4 serving plates and 4 small ramekins in an oven on low heat.

Prepare your gas grill (sorry, charcoal grills just don't generate enough heat for this recipe) for direct high heat. Place 2 cast iron skillets on the cooking grate with their handles pointed away from you. Let the pans heat up in the grill for at least 15 minutes, until they are extremely hot.

While the pans are heating, melt the butter in a sauté pan until it is just melted. Turn off the heat but leave the pan on the stovetop to keep it warm.

Dip the snapper fillets in the melted butter and sprinkle them generously on both sides with the rub mixture. Drizzle a little of the remaining butter over the rubbed fillets.

Open the grill and quickly place the fillets in the pans. This will cause a lot of white smoke and the butter may flame up, so be careful. Cover the grill and cook the fish for just a couple of minutes. Carefully and quickly turn the fillets over with a spatula and cook them for another 1 to 2 minutes, until the outside of the fish is nicely blackened.

Put on some oven mitts, just in case you grab a pan handle by mistake. With your spatula, remove the fillets from the pans and place them on the serving dishes. Transfer the remaining butter into the warmed ramekins. Serve the snapper immediately, with the ramekins of butter for dipping.

PLANKED CUMIN CURRY BASA
WITH BANANA YOGURT SALSA

MAKES 4 SERVINGS

Basa is the tofu of the sea—it easily takes on flavors while retaining its succulent texture. Any white-fleshed fish will also work here. This dish goes nicely with plain basmati rice and your favorite grilled vegetable.

1 cedar plank, soaked overnight or at least 1 hour
two 12 oz [375 g] basa fillets
kosher salt

RUB
1 Tbsp [15 mL] curry powder
1 tsp [5 mL] light brown sugar
pinch cayenne
1 Tbsp [15 mL] toasted cumin seeds
1 lime, cut in half

BANANA YOGURT SALSA
1 medium-ripe banana
½ cup [125 mL] plain yogurt
1 Tbsp [15 mL] chopped fresh cilantro

fresh cilantro sprigs for garnish
your favorite chutney

Cut the basa fillets in half to make 4 equal pieces. Season them with salt and put them in a nonreactive dish or bowl. Mix together the curry powder, sugar, cayenne, and cumin seeds in a bowl and lightly coat the fillets on both sides with the rub. Squeeze half the lime over the rubbed fish pieces. Refrigerate the fish for at least 15 minutes but not longer than 1 hour.

Meanwhile, chop the banana into ½-inch (1 cm) chunks and combine them in a bowl with the yogurt and chopped cilantro. Cover and refrigerate the yogurt salsa until you're ready to use it. This should be made shortly before you serve it.

Preheat the grill on medium-high for 5 to 10 minutes, or until the chamber temperature rises above 500°F (260°C). Rinse the soaked plank and place it on the cooking grate. Cover the grill and heat the plank for 4 to 5 minutes, or until it starts to throw off a bit of smoke and crackles lightly. Reduce the heat to medium-low.

Put the fish pieces on the plank and cook them for 10 to 15 minutes, or until the fish has an internal temperature of 135°F (57°C). Remove from the grill, garnish with cilantro sprigs, and serve immediately with the banana yogurt salsa and some chutney.

PEPPER-GRILLED TUNA
WITH WASABI LIME MAYO

MAKES 4 SERVINGS

Grilled tuna is one of the most succulent dishes I know. The key here, as with almost all things grilled, is to avoid overcooking it. Some like tuna done this way blue-rare, so just the outside of the tuna is seared. I prefer it a little more done, like a medium-rare steak, still translucent in the middle. Serve it with Grilled Rice Cakes (page 146).

WASABI LIME MAYO
½ cup [125 mL] mayonnaise or aïoli
1 Tbsp [15 mL] fresh lime juice
1 tsp [5 mL] prepared wasabi paste or
    wasabi powder
kosher salt and freshly ground black
    pepper to taste

TUNA
2 Tbsp [25 mL] kosher salt

1 cup [250 mL] freshly cracked black
    peppercorns
four 8 oz [250 g] tuna steaks, as fresh
    as you can get them
olive oil for drizzling

lemon wedges and fresh cilantro sprigs
    for garnish

To make the wasabi lime mayo, combine the mayonnaise or aïoli, lime juice, and wasabi in a bowl and season the mixture with salt and pepper. Make the mayonnaise ahead of time—preferably the night before, but at least 1 hour before serving—to allow time for the flavors to combine nicely.

Prepare your grill for direct high heat. In a bowl, combine the salt and cracked pepper. Press the tuna steaks into the seasoning mixture until they are well coated on all sides. Drizzle the steaks with olive oil and grill them for 30 seconds to 3 minutes per side, depending on how thick the steaks are and how rare you want them. For tuna, which is extremely firm and lean and doesn't really leak any juice, the easiest test for doneness is to cut into the steak with a sharp knife.

Remove the tuna from the grill, and slice it thinly. Place it on individual plates, and serve it surrounded by a drizzle of the wasabi lime mayo and garnished with 1 or 2 sprigs of cilantro and a lemon wedge.

Pictured with Grilled Rice Cakes (page 146)

PROSCIUTTO-WRAPPED
CEDAR-PLANKED TUNA

MAKES 4 SERVINGS

~ TOM'S ~
BARBECUE SECRET

My friend Tom Riglar calls this the inverted aluminum pan secret, and it's an interesting way to focus and fine-tune the heat of your grill.

Here's how it works:

1. Prepare your grill for indirect high heat.
2. Put the food you want to cook on the hot side of the grill to brown it.
3. Move the food off the hot side toward the cool side.
4. Place an inverted aluminum roasting pan over the food.
5. The more of the pan you have over the heat source, the more heat it will draw to what you're cooking. The movement of this pan is now your heat regulator for a mini convection oven! "The size of this oven is governed by the size of your aluminum pan," says Tom. "The number of applications is governed only by your imagination."

This unusual dish was developed by my friend Tom Riglar, who is what I would call a true grilling geek. It's an unconventional but delicious way to cook tuna steaks, using Mediterranean flavors and contrasting textures. Serve with Confetti Rice (page 144) or grilled nugget potatoes and a flavorful Gewürztraminer or Riesling.

1 cedar plank, soaked for at least 2 hours or overnight
four 6 oz [175 g] tuna steaks, about 3–4 inches [8–10 cm] in diameter
8 thin slices Italian prosciutto

RELISH
2 Tbsp [25 mL] olive oil

1 medium sweet onion, diced
2 large cloves garlic, minced
1 red pepper, seeded and diced
¼ cup [50 mL] pitted kalamata olives, coarsely chopped
¼ cup [50 mL] finely chopped fresh basil
2 Tbsp [25 mL] capers, drained
1 Tbsp [15 mL] white wine vinegar

Heat the olive oil in a sauté pan and cook the onion, garlic, and red pepper over medium heat, stirring them regularly, until they're soft. Remove the mixture from the heat. Add the olives, basil, capers, and vinegar and set the mixture aside.

Rinse the plank. Form cone shapes around each piece of tuna with the prosciutto, using toothpicks to hold it in place, if necessary. Place these on the plank, leaving room around each one. Fill the top cavities with the relish.

Preheat the grill on medium-high for 5 to 10 minutes, or until the chamber temperature rises above 500°F (260°C). Place the plank with the tuna rounds on the cooking grate and cover the grill. Cook the tuna for 4 to 5 minutes, or until the plank starts to crackle and throws off some smoke. Reduce the heat to medium and cook the tuna to an internal temperature of 135°F (57°C). Remove the plank and tuna from the grill and serve immediately with the remaining relish.

GRILLED OCTOPUS SALAD

MAKES 4 SERVINGS

When I was a teenager traveling in Europe, my friend Rich and I rented Vespas in Rome and motorcycled to Lido, the beach community just west of the city. We stopped at a restaurant and the garrulous proprietor talked us into ordering a seafood salad that featured marinated octopus. I'll never forget the chewy, tangy chunks of octopus in that salad. It was one of the most satisfying meals I had on that trip.

one 2 lb [1 kg] octopus arm

2 Tbsp [25 mL] extra virgin olive oil

1 tsp [5 mL] crushed dried Greek
    oregano

1 tsp [5 mL] crushed dried red chili
    flakes

1 Tbsp [15 mL] fresh lemon juice

splash red wine vinegar

kosher salt and freshly ground black
    pepper

1 Tbsp [15 mL] chopped fresh flat-leaf
    Italian parsley

lemon wedges

Put a wine cork in a pot of cold water. (Adding a cork to the water while boiling octopus is thought to make it more tender.) Place the octopus arm in the water and bring it to a boil over high heat. Turn the heat down to low and simmer the octopus for about 1 hour, or until it is tender when you poke it with a knife. Rinse it, dry it, and set it aside.

Prepare your grill for direct high heat. Brush the octopus arm with a little of the olive oil and grill it just until it has some nice char marks on both sides. Slice it diagonally into bite-sized pieces and put it in a salad bowl. Add the rest of the ingredients except the parsley and lemon wedges and toss the salad. Cover the bowl and place it in the refrigerator overnight. Toss and serve the salad the next day, garnished with the chopped parsley and wedges of lemon.

GRILLED TROUT IN FOIL

MAKES 2 SERVINGS

The following simple technique gives the fish a more subtle and delicate flavor and texture than grilling over direct heat, and the orange adds a lovely flavor and aroma. Get the freshest possible fish—preferably one you caught in a mountain lake, hours earlier, on a fly rod!

3 Tbsp [45 mL] butter, at room
    temperature
one 2 lb [1 kg] cleaned whole
    rainbow trout
kosher salt and freshly ground black
    pepper to taste

2 Tbsp [25 mL] chopped fresh parsley
½ medium white onion, peeled
2 oranges
sprigs of fresh parsley for garnish

Prepare your grill for direct medium heat. Tear off a strip of heavy-duty foil 2½ times as long as the fish and double it. Spread 1 Tbsp (15 mL) of the butter evenly over the top surface of the foil. Place the fish on the buttered foil. Lightly season the fish inside and out with salt and pepper, and sprinkle it with the chopped parsley. Slice the onion and one of the oranges into thin rounds and place half of the onion and orange slices inside the body cavity and the other half on top of the fish. Daub the remaining 2 Tbsp (25 mL) of butter inside the fish and on top of the onion and orange slices. Squeeze half the remaining orange over everything and wrap the foil around the fish, sealing it tightly.

    Place the foil package on the cooking grate, cover the grill, and cook the trout for 8 to 12 minutes, until the fish is just done, or it has an internal temperature of 140 to 150°F (60–66°C). You can poke a meat thermometer through the foil in the last few minutes of cooking to check for doneness. To serve, open up the foil, carefully transfer the fish to a warmed platter, and pour the juices left in the foil over the fish. Garnish the trout with orange wedges and parsley sprigs.

PROSCIUTTO-WRAPPED
PRAWN & LYCHEE KEBABS

MAKES 4 MAIN COURSE SERVINGS OR 12 APPETIZER SERVINGS

This combo might sound strange, but the sweetness of the lychees and the prawns and the saltiness of the prosciutto complement one another very nicely, and the lychee liqueur gives the kebabs a superb aroma. This is ideal as a cocktail-party appetizer, but also goes well with rice and a green salad as a main course. (Note: Wrapping prawns with thin slices of prosciutto is pretty fussy. If you're in a hurry, this dish tastes great even without this embellishment.)

twelve 7-inch [18 cm] bamboo skewers, soaked for at least 1 hour

one 20 oz [565 g] can lychees in syrup
¼ cup [50 mL] Soho lychee liqueur (mainly used in fancy lychee martinis)
1 tsp [5 mL] crushed dried red chili flakes
1 shallot, minced
1 Tbsp [15 mL] finely minced fresh ginger
¾ cup [175 mL] unsweetened coconut milk

¼ cup [50 mL] sunflower oil or other neutral-flavored oil
24 large fresh prawns (about 13–15 to the pound), peeled and deveined, with the tails still on
12 thin slices Italian prosciutto, halved lengthwise
1 Tbsp [15 mL] cornstarch
½ cup [50 mL] cold water
2 Tbsp [25 mL] finely chopped fresh mint
limes for squeezing

Drain the canned lychees, reserving ¾ cup (175 mL) of syrup. In a bowl, combine 12 lychees, the reserved lychee syrup, the liqueur, chili flakes, shallot, ginger, coconut milk, and oil. Gently toss the prawns in the mixture in a medium bowl and marinate them for 1 hour at room temperature or 3 hours in the refrigerator.

Remove the prawns and the fruit from the marinade, reserving the liquid. Wrap each prawn with half a slice of the prosciutto, as if you are putting a little belt around the middle of the prawn, taking care that about half of the prawn is still visible. Thread the prosciutto-wrapped prawns onto the

(continued)

Prosciutto-Wrapped Prawn & Lychee Kebabs *(continued)*
presoaked bamboo skewers, placing a lychee after every second prawn. (For cocktail-party canapés, thread 1 lychee and 2 prawns on each skewer.)

Prepare the grill for direct medium heat. While the grill is heating, pour the reserved marinade into a medium saucepan and bring it to a slow simmer over medium heat. Mix the cornstarch with the water and pour it into the liquid. Bring it to a boil and simmer it for about 5 minutes, or until the sauce is shiny and thick. Set it aside.

Oil the cooking grate, place the skewers on the grill, cover them, and cook them for no more than 1 or 2 minutes per side, or until the prawns are barely cooked through. Serve the kebabs drizzled with the sauce and garnished with chopped mint and a squeeze of lime.

SKEWERED PRAWNS PISTOU

MAKES 4 MAIN COURSE SERVINGS OR 12 APPETIZER SERVINGS

Pistou is the French equivalent of the Italian pesto sauce. In this version I've added toasted nuts, anchovies, and lemon zest for an extra kick. This sauce also works well as a coating for roast lamb.

twelve 6-inch [15 cm] bamboo
skewers, soaked for at least
1 hour

PISTOU

¼ cup [50 mL] lightly toasted
pecans (almonds or pine nuts
are also excellent)

2 cups [500 mL] loosely packed
fresh basil leaves

1 cup [250 mL] loosely packed
fresh flat-leaf Italian parsley

12 anchovy fillets, rinsed

2 cloves garlic, peeled

⅓ cup [75 mL] extra virgin olive oil

zest of 1 lemon, finely grated or
chopped

PRAWNS

12 jumbo prawns, in their shells

kosher salt and freshly ground
black pepper

12 cherry or grape tomatoes

lemon wedges for garnish

To make the pistou, combine the pecans, basil, parsley, anchovies, and garlic in a food processor and process them until they're smooth. Add the oil slowly in a thin stream while the processor is running. Transfer the pistou to a bowl, add the zest, and stir the pistou thoroughly. Transfer about ½ cup (125 mL) of the pistou to a serving bowl and reserve it for dipping.

Season the prawns with salt and pepper. Toss them with the remaining pistou and refrigerate them for 20 minutes or up to 1 hour. When you're ready to cook them, thread 1 prawn onto each skewer, with a cherry tomato threaded between the tail and the head.

Prepare the grill for direct medium heat. Place the skewers on the cooking grate, cover the grill, and cook for 1 or 2 minutes per side, or until just cooked through. Serve them with the extra pistou for dipping and garnish them with lemon wedges.

> **⮞ BARBECUE SECRET ⮜**

Don't marinate fish too long in strongly acidic marinades. Acid breaks down the proteins in fish in the same way as heat. So if you keep fish in very acidic marinades for much longer than 15 minutes, it will literally start to cook. That's fine if you want to make ceviche, a dish that uses a citrus marinade to essentially cook raw fish, but not good if you're planking or grilling the fish.

SUPEREASY GRILLED
⮞ JUMBO PRAWNS ⮜
WITH CURRY PASTE

My pal Kosta the fishmonger shared this great, simple way to grill jumbo prawns. Butterfly them (split them in half lengthwise, which makes it easy to remove the vein) and coat them with a mixture of your favorite curry paste cut with a little neutral-flavored oil (about 3 Tbsp/45 mL curry paste mixed with 1 Tbsp/15 mL oil will coat a dozen prawns). Grill the prawns over high heat for about a minute or two per side, and finish them by tossing them in a pan with some melted butter. Serve them with lemon wedges for an outstanding appetizer.

Salmon & Other Spectacular Seafood

PLANKED SCALLOPS

MAKES 4 SERVINGS

The sweet flavor and meaty texture of scallops is excellent with a little wood smoke. Food stylist Nathan Fong, who helped make my recipes look gorgeous for my *Planking Secrets* book, came up with this delicious dish when I asked him how we should present the scallops for one of the photos.

1 plank (cedar is great, but any kind will do), soaked overnight or at least 1 hour
12 large or 16 medium-sized scallops
kosher salt

MARINADE/SAUCE
1 Tbsp [15 mL] fresh lemon juice
1 tsp [5 mL] finely grated lemon zest
1 Tbsp [15 mL] sherry vinegar

2 Tbsp [25 mL] butter
1 tsp [5 mL] chopped fresh dill
½ tsp [2 mL] crushed dried red chili flakes
1 Tbsp [15 mL] liquid honey

TO FINISH
butter lettuce leaves
lemon wedges and sprigs of fresh dill for garnish
Garden Salsa (see page 62)

Place the scallops in a nonreactive bowl. Season them with a little salt and set them aside.

Combine the lemon juice and zest, vinegar, butter, chopped dill, chili flakes, and honey in a saucepan over low heat. Cook the sauce, stirring it constantly, just until the butter is incorporated. Remove it from the heat and pour half the sauce over the scallops, tossing them to coat them.

Preheat the grill on medium-high for 5 to 10 minutes, or until the chamber temperature rises above 500°F (260°C). Rinse the soaked plank and place it on the cooking grate. Cover the grill and heat the plank for 4 to 5 minutes, or until it starts to throw off a bit of smoke and crackles lightly. Keep the heat on medium-high.

Place the scallops on the plank, cover the grill, and cook them for 2 to 3 minutes. Turn and baste the scallops and cook them for another minute, or until they're almost done. If you like a little charring, you can move the scallops onto the cooking grate for the last 1 or 2 minutes of cooking.

Remove the scallops from the grill and toss them with the rest of the basting sauce. Serve them on a leaf of butter lettuce garnished with a lemon wedge, a sprig of dill, and a spoonful of Garden Salsa.

SMOKED OYSTERS

MAKES 4–8 APPETIZER SERVINGS

The canned smoked oysters you can buy at the supermarket taste like oily cardboard compared to these plump, delicious beauties. This is a great thing to do when you've got your smoker up and running for something else. When you've finished your main project, take advantage of the hot smoker and barbecue a few tubs of oysters for later consumption. You can keep them in the refrigerator for a few days, or freeze them for a month or two, but I'll bet they won't be around that long!

one 1-pint [500 mL] container shucked large fresh oysters (8–12 oysters)	2 Tbsp [25 mL] butter
extra virgin olive oil	kosher salt and freshly ground black pepper
¼ cup [50 mL] Championship Barbecue Rub (see page 50)	1 lemon
	barbecue sauce (optional)

Prepare your smoker for barbecuing, bringing the temperature to 200 to 220°F (95–100°C). Drain the oysters and pat them dry with a paper towel. Coat them lightly with oil and sprinkle both sides with the rub. Let them sit for a few minutes, until the rub starts to glisten. Spray your cooking grate with vegetable cooking spray and place the oysters on the grate. Smoke them for 1 hour, using hickory as the flavoring agent, until the oysters are springy to the touch and have taken on a smoky golden hue. Remove them from the smoker.

At this point, you can just put them on a serving tray and pass them around. They're best fresh out of the smoker, dipped in barbecue sauce. I also like to let them cool and then quickly pan-fry them in the butter, finishing them with a sprinkling of salt and pepper and a squeeze of fresh lemon.

Salmon & Other Spectacular Seafood

FEAR & LOATHING ON ~THE BARBECUE TRAIL~

The Further Adventures of Rockin' Ronnie

The Butt Shredders' glorious victory at the 2001 Oregon State Open was the beginning of an excellent adventure that would bring the team to new competitive heights—and bring me, its chief cook, to a few new lows. Here are a few snippets and stories to bring you up to date.

As I sliced into the hot, glistening pork butt, I saw it was perfectly juicy and tender. The smell of pork fat and hardwood smoke jacked my nostrils. Ten minutes to go till turn-in. The sun beat down on the carving board and I could feel my barbecue mojo working at peak capacity. I had never been so intent on winning in my life.

It was judging day at the 2004 Canadian National Barbecue Championships in Whistler, BC. The sports hypnotherapy session I had gone through the day before was working like a charm. Thanks to that, our traditional round of martinis at dawn, and a steady stream of cold German beer, I was able to reach deep into the recesses of my smoky subconscious to find a calm, confident place that sharpened my focus and steadied my hands.

We Butt Shredders needed all the focus we could muster if we were going to win the contest that day. The competitive field was the best in the history of the Nationals, including seven-time world barbecue champion Paul Kirk and Memphis in May winner Myron Mixon.

The sun beat down on the carving board and I could feel my barbecue mojo working at peak capacity.

With minutes to go to the turn-in deadline, my teammates gathered around me and I passed them slices from different parts of the three steaming, juicy roasts resting in front of me on the carving board. We quickly traded notes on which had the best flavor and tenderness, and agreed on the butt that would produce the six slices for turn-in.

Three hours later, we had repeated the process to enter the three other categories—chicken, ribs, and brisket—and our fate was in the hands of the judges.

There was victory in the smoky air around the Butt Shredders as we waited for the results to be announced. One by one, the winners of each category were revealed. We came first in pork shoulder. Second in brisket. Fifth in ribs. We didn't place in chicken, but those three places were enough to make the Butt Shredders the first Canadian team to take the Grand Champion trophy in the 15-year history of the Canadian National Barbecue Championships. Until that day, US teams had almost always triumphed at every Canadian contest because, after all, barbecue is an American sport. But with our win at Whistler it felt like we had finally brought barbecue home to Canada for good.

The winning streak had started with our historic victory at the 2001 Oregon State Open (see page 70), and continued with two back-to-back Grand Champion titles at Barbecue on the Bow in Calgary. Those victories earned us entry into a whole new level of competition, with invitations to the American Royal in Kansas City and the most prestigious and coveted contest on earth, the Jack Daniel's World Championship Invitational Barbecue. For a while there, the Butt Shredders were living the barbecue dream.

> ≈

If a normal barbecue contest is like a charming little hobo village, the American Royal is a smoky megalopolis populated by huge, Shrek-like meat eaters in ball caps and barbecue sauce–stained t-shirts. On the Saturday night of the contest, something like 60,000 locals crowd into the competition grounds to watch 400 teams. The Budweiser flows like water, and funnel cakes are the closest thing you'll find to a vegetable.

My biggest highlight from the Royal—meeting one of barbecue's true rock stars, David Klose, who was helping out with one of the teams. David is the barbecue equivalent of Orange County Choppers. In the same way that the California outfit makes themed motorcycles, David makes themed pits. He's done everything conceivable in that arena, from converting a NASCAR car body into a barbecue to constructing a pit in the shape of a giant Jack Daniel's bottle.

Not only is David a famous pit maker, he's also a colorful storyteller. I stood listening to him while he recounted a barbecue pit building project for the owner of the Dallas Cowboys. As part of that assignment he got a chance to meet the famous cheerleaders. As David told it, "If I could

The Budweiser flows like water, and funnel cakes are the closest thing you'll find to a vegetable.

ever get a couple of them to help me at a barbecue contest, I think I'd just drizzle some honey on 'em and turn 'em in to the judges! That would really be somethin', wouldn't it?"

> ≈

I'll never forget the Butt Shredders' first visit to The Jack. There we were in Lynchberg, Tennessee, home of the famed distillery, competing against the very best barbecue teams in the world—50 state and regional US champions, along with about a dozen other international teams. The competition grounds are just a short walk from the distillery, in a little valley called The Holler, alongside a beautiful stream.

As we drove on to the site for the first time, we realized we had never seen so much high-end barbecue hardware gathered in one place. There were rolling barbecue pits in every style imaginable, and all the competitors had smiles pasted on their faces that said, "We made it to The Jack!" We all had a chance at the ultimate prize in barbecue—global bragging rights.

Strangely, my favorite memory of The Jack has little to do with barbecue. We'd been up half the night tending our cookers and we were just starting to prep our chickens. It was about eight in the morning and this guy who looked like a character straight out of King of the Hill, in sunglasses and a ball cap, came driving through the competition grounds in a golf cart. He'd stop every few dozen yards and let out a yell, in a thick Southern accent: "FRIED PIES! FRIED PIES! GIT YER HOMEMADE FRIED PIES! I GOT PEACH PIES, APPLE PIES! FRIED PIES!"

One of my teammates gave him a good-morning glare and yelled back in her wonderfully crusty style: "Are those pies any good?"

The man smiled, looked Kathy in the eye, and said, "Darlin', these pies are so good, if you put one on top of yer head, yer tongue would slap you to death just tryin' to get at it!"

❧ ❧

It was easy for me to get hooked on competitive barbecue. It's the ultimate combination of adrenaline-soaked team sport, grease-soaked eating and unlimited drinking. What's not to love?

Back then, I figured you couldn't really get too much of it. Then all those competition victories went to my head, and eventually the whole thing kind of spiraled out of control.

> **"Darlin', these pies are so good, if you put one on top of yer head, yer tongue would slap you to death just tryin' to get at it!"**

I happily left my well-paying but crappy corporate job so I would have time to write and promote my cookbooks. I spent countless hours organizing and delivering cooking demonstrations and workshops. I published a newsletter called *Barbecue Times* and produced *The Barbecue Secrets Podcast*, a homemade Internet audio show. I founded something called Barbecue Academy, a corporate teambuilding workshop based on championship barbecue. And I even acted as a motivational speaker, delivering a special workshop at an international conference based on the theme, "Everything I Know about Communication, I Learned from My Barbecue." Sheesh.

I truly was relentless in my pursuit of barbecue glory. But eventually my barbecue dream would become a treadmill. In the summer of 2005, I delivered close to 20 workshops and cooking demonstrations and pushed the team to compete in seven barbecue contests.

I got to the point where I was so tired and distracted that one night I came home from doing a cooking class too weary to unpack the car and left a portable charcoal grill in the back seat. Early the next morning, my neighbor rang the doorbell. When I came to the door he said, "Hate to bother you, but I think your car is on fire."

A piece of smoldering charcoal had fallen out of the cooker and onto the back seat, and, overnight, a slow fire had spread. By morning, smoke was billowing out of the half-open window and the seat had melted into a disgusting, toxic mess. The back seat had to be replaced and it took two years for the smell of burning plastic to disappear from that car.

❧ ❧

The lowest point in my barbecue career came in the spring of 2006, when I took a look at my 2005 personal income tax return and my bank account. I finally came to the realization that, during the three years I was pursuing my barbecue dream with no full-time job, I had literally been going broke.

A few months later I had a new corporate job in a downtown office and was finally making a decent living again.

❧ ❧

As I write this, it's a year and a half later. My self-imposed barbecue sabbatical was a refreshing break, although every time I smelled mesquite I got a pang in my brisket.

Lately, the phone has been ringing. It's barbecue calling, with opportunities to apply everything I've learned to some fresh and exciting projects. As I consider my options, I realize I may have stepped away from barbecue, but all that blue smoke has penetrated deep into my soul.

My adventures in outdoor cooking have made me a wiser, humbler man. I can't help but trust that the world of barbecue will now take me to new places and introduce me to people who will enrich my life further still.

Deeee-licious Desserts

You'd think that once you've stuffed yourself with barbecue you couldn't even consider dessert, but the opposite is true. A rich meal of barbecued or grilled food simply begs for a sweet, satisfying ending. I am lucky enough to be married to the best dessert cook on earth. My wife, Kate, does not make a huge variety of desserts, but when she discovers a great recipe she perfects it. And you, dear reader, are lucky enough to now own the distillation of more than 20 years of home dessert cooking in the Shewchuk household. Although the inspiration for these recipes comes from different sources, most of them have been perfected by Kate. Read on, bake on, and enjoy.

ZOË'S PARFAIT

MAKES 6–8 SERVINGS

Here's a simple dessert invented by my daughter, Zoë (who always got an A in home economics).

2 flavors of ice cream, gelato, or sorbet
(try mango and raspberry, or banana
and coconut)
1 cup [250 mL] blueberries

½ cup [125 mL] strawberries
shredded unsweetened coconut
1 Tbsp [15 mL] lemon zest, grated or
finely minced

Place 3 scoops of ice cream, gelato, or sorbet for each person being served in individual serving dishes. Zoë recommends that you put them together in a wine or champagne glass for a semiformal appearance. Top with blueberries and strawberries. Sprinkle with coconut and lemon zest. Voilà!

DISAPPEARING GINGERSNAPS

MAKES ABOUT 30 COOKIES

These are crispy cookies for spice lovers. Cook a batch of these and watch them disappear.

1 cup [250 mL] sugar, plus extra for rolling

¾ cup [175 mL] vegetable shortening (Crisco works well)

½ cup [125 mL] molasses

1 egg, beaten with a fork

2 cups [500 mL] all-purpose flour

1 tsp [5 mL] ground ginger (or to taste)

1 tsp [5 mL] ground cinnamon

½ tsp [2 mL] baking soda

pinch kosher salt

Cream the sugar with the shortening, molasses, and egg in a large bowl. Sift together the flour, ginger, cinnamon, baking soda, and salt and add them to the mixture. Cover and chill the batter for several hours.

Preheat the oven to 325°F (160°C).

Take a heaping tablespoon of the mixture and roll it into a ball in your hands. Pour about ¼ cup (50 mL) of sugar into a small bowl. Roll each ball in the sugar, then place it on a baking sheet, with about 3 inches (8 cm) between them. Take a tumbler with a flat, round bottom, dip it first into the sugar, then squash each ball into a flat disc. You may need to re-dip the tumbler frequently.

Bake the cookies for 8 to 10 minutes. Let them cool, snap your fingers, and they'll be gone.

LEMON CURD SQUARES

MAKES ABOUT 16 SQUARES

This is one of the best desserts of all time, a classic from *The Joy of Cooking*, which I'm including here simply because it's one of the best ways to end a summer meal. Keep an eye on how these are doing, both when the crust is baking and when it is baking with the topping. You may well need a little less time at each stage. Serve these on a platter with The Ultimate Triple Chocolate Brownies (page 351).

CRUST
1 cup [250 mL] sifted all-purpose flour
¼ cup [50 mL] icing sugar
½ cup [125 mL] melted butter

FILLING
1 cup [250 mL] sugar
½ tsp [2 mL] double-acting
 baking powder

2 slightly beaten eggs
2 Tbsp [25 mL] fresh lemon juice
2 tsp [10 mL] grated lemon zest
½ cup [125 mL] flaked unsweetened
 coconut (optional)
½ cup [125 mL] icing sugar for
 sprinkling overtop

Preheat the oven to 350°F (180°C).

To make the crust, sift the flour and the icing sugar into a medium mixing bowl. Stir in the melted butter. Press the mixture into an 8-inch (2 L) square greased baking pan and bake the crust for 20 minutes.

While the crust is baking, make the filling by combining the sugar, baking powder, eggs, lemon juice, lemon zest, and flaked coconut (if desired) in a medium bowl.

When the crust has baked about 15 minutes (keep an eye on it), take it out of the oven. Pour the filling mixture over the warm crust and put it back into the oven for an additional 25 minutes (or less; watch to make sure it doesn't burn). Chill the dessert.

Before serving, sprinkle the dessert with icing sugar and cut it into 2-inch (5 cm) squares.

THE ULTIMATE
TRIPLE CHOCOLATE BROWNIES

MAKES ABOUT 12 BROWNIES

This recipe, plus an icing, won a brownie contest about 20 years ago. When these brownies were first served to me and Kate by my fellow barbecue team member Kathy Richardier without the icing that was called for in the original recipe, we all agreed that frosting these babies would be overkill—even to us, which is really saying something.

Triple Chocolate Brownies have been served at least 100 times in my house, and they never fail to provoke ecstatic approval. They freeze superbly, too, although the fact that they are frozen doesn't always keep eager fingers away. Note: Use the big, good-quality European-style chocolate bars. You can probably mess around with the chocolate combination, using chocolate bars with nuts or fruit, but this basic recipe is so outrageously good you ought to try it as is at least once.

½ cup [125 mL] butter

3 oz [90 g] unsweetened chocolate, chopped

2 eggs, at room temperature

pinch kosher salt

1 cup [250 mL] sugar

2 tsp [10 mL] vanilla extract

one 3 oz [90 g] bar white chocolate

one 3 oz [90 g] bar milk chocolate

one 3 oz [90 g] bar bittersweet or dark chocolate

½ cup [125 mL] all-purpose flour

vanilla ice cream, whipped cream, or fruit (optional)

Preheat the oven to 325°F (160°C).

Line an 8-inch (2 L or 1.2 L) square or round cake pan with foil; grease the inside of the foil generously. Melt the butter in a saucepan over low heat. Remove the saucepan from the heat and add the unsweetened chocolate. Allow the chocolate to melt completely.

Beat the eggs and salt together at high speed for 30 seconds in a large bowl. Gradually add the sugar and keep beating until the batter is very thick and pale. Mix in the butter-chocolate mixture and the vanilla. Chop the chocolate bars into pieces and toss them in the flour. Add them to the mixture in the bowl and mix well by hand.

Pour the batter into the pan. Bake it for 30 to 35 minutes, or until the brownies are firm to the touch. Serve them warm with vanilla ice cream, whipped cream, fruit, or nuthin' at all.

Deeee-licious Desserts

MOM'S CHOCOLATE CAKE
WITH CHOCOLATE ICING

MAKES 8–10 SERVINGS

Everybody needs a great chocolate cake recipe; this, from an old *Food &.
Wine* magazine, is the one our family and friends love the most. Kate has
messed around with the recipe occasionally, and has found that using milk
chocolate instead of dark in both the cake and the icing results in a much
sweeter cake that younger kids like. This is a version geared more to grown-
ups. Nevertheless, a big glass of milk is the ideal accompaniment. This is
best baked the day before you serve it.

CAKE

2 cups [500 mL] all-purpose flour
2 tsp [10 mL] baking powder
2 tsp [10 mL] baking soda
1 tsp [5 mL] kosher salt
2 cups [500 mL] sugar
2 cups [500 mL] water
4 oz [125 g] unsweetened chocolate
6 Tbsp [90 mL] unsalted butter
1 tsp [5 mL] vanilla extract
2 eggs, lightly beaten

CHOCOLATE ICING

1⅓ cups [325 mL] whipping cream
1½ cups [375 mL] sugar
6 oz [175 g] unsweetened chocolate
½ cup plus 2 Tbsp [150 mL] unsalted
   butter
1½ tsp [7 mL] vanilla extract
pinch kosher salt

Preheat the oven to 350°F (180°C).

Butter and flour two 8-inch (1.2 L) round cake pans. Line the bottoms
of the pans with wax paper or parchment (don't skip this step or you'll never
get this moist cake out of the pan).

Sift together the flour, baking powder, baking soda, and salt in a medium
bowl; set it aside. Combine the sugar and water in a medium saucepan. Bring
the mixture to a boil over high heat and stir it until the sugar dissolves, then
pour it into a large bowl. Add the chocolate and butter and let the mixture sit,
stirring occasionally, until the chocolate is melted and the mixture has cooled
slightly. Stir in the vanilla.

Beat the eggs into the chocolate mixture at medium speed until they're
combined. Add the dry ingredients all at once and beat the batter at medium

speed until it's smooth. Divide the batter evenly between the prepared pans and bake it for about 25 minutes, or until the top springs back when pressed lightly and a cake tester comes out clean. Cool the cakes in their pans for about 25 minutes, then invert them onto a rack to cool completely.

To make the icing, bring the cream and sugar to a boil in a medium saucepan over moderately high heat. Reduce the heat to low and simmer the mixture, stirring it occasionally, until the liquid reduces slightly, about 6 minutes. Pour the mixture into a medium bowl and add the chocolate, butter, vanilla, and salt. Let it stand, stirring occasionally, until the chocolate and butter have melted.

Set the bowl inside a larger bowl of ice water. Using a hand-held electric mixer, beat the icing on medium speed, scraping the sides occasionally with a rubber spatula, until it's thick and glossy, about 5 minutes.

When the icing is ready, set 1 cake on a serving platter. Using a metal spatula, spread one-third of the chocolate icing over the cake. Top with the second cake and ice the top and sides with the rest of the icing.

LEMON CHIFFON CAKE

MAKES 8–10 SERVINGS

My old friend Jennifer Wah loves to bake, and she's darn good at it. I begged her to share the recipe for this fragrant, moist, tangy, fluffy cake and she was happy to oblige. Just writing this, I can taste it! It's great as a follow-up to barbecue, with "a perfect light, fresh finish that still keeps your mouth alive," says Jen. She likes to serve it with fresh raspberries and blueberries jumbled around the edges.

CAKE

7 eggs
½ tsp [2 mL] cream of tartar
2 cups [500 mL] all-purpose flour
1¼ cups [300 mL] sugar
1 Tbsp [15 mL] baking powder
1 tsp [5 mL] sea salt
½ cup [125 mL] safflower oil
¾ cup [175 mL] fresh lemon juice
   (or ½ cup/125 mL lemon juice and
   ¼ cup/50 mL orange juice if you
   like a slightly sweeter cake)
2 Tbsp [25 mL] grated lemon zest
1 tsp [5 mL] vanilla extract

LEMON GLAZE

2 Tbsp [25 mL] butter, at room
   temperature
pinch kosher salt
3 cups [750 mL] icing sugar, sifted
grated zest of 1 lemon (make sure
   the zest is very fine for the glaze)
¼ cup [50 mL] fresh lemon juice

raspberries and blueberries for
   garnish (optional)
lemon and orange crescents for
   garnish (optional)

Preheat the oven to 325°F (160°C).

Separate the eggs. Reserve the whites in a large metal bowl. Put the yolks, unbeaten, into another bowl and set them aside. Beat the whites until soft peaks form, then add the cream of tartar and continue beating until very stiff peaks form. Set the mixture aside.

Measure the flour, sugar, baking powder, and salt into another large bowl. Make a well in the centre.

Add the oil, juice(s), lemon zest, and vanilla to the unbeaten egg yolks. Add the egg yolk mixture to the well in the flour mixture and beat them together until the batter is smooth.

Using a spatula, very gently fold the beaten egg whites into the flour-sugar mixture, just until they are incorporated.

Pour the batter into an ungreased 10-inch (4 L) nonstick tube cake pan and bake the cake for 1 to 1¼ hours, until a skewer or knife comes out clean.

While the cake is baking, make the lemon glaze. Put the butter, salt, icing sugar, and zest in a bowl and mix them together with an electric mixer until the ingredients are combined. Gradually add the lemon juice until the glaze is the consistency of a thick syrup, adding more icing sugar or lemon juice if needed to get it just right. Set the glaze aside.

When the cake is done, allow it to cool on a cooling rack for half an hour or so before running a knife around the inside of the pan and inverting it onto a serving plate. While the cake is still warm, drizzle the glaze over the cake and let it run down the sides, or use a knife to help spread it evenly and glaze the whole cake, if you prefer.

Garnish the cake with lemon and orange crescents and serve it with fresh berries.

PAVLOVA

This classic is one of my family's favorite party desserts. It contains no flour, which is great for your gluten-intolerant friends, and can be tarted up with almost any combination of fresh fruit. Mangoes and strawberries and grapes, for instance, with pomegranate seeds sprinkled overtop. It's best to make pavlova when the weather is dry, so the meringue doesn't lose its delicious crunch.

scant ¾ cup [175 mL] egg whites (from 5 large eggs), completely yolk-free, at room temperature
¼ tsp [1 mL] cream of tartar
pinch kosher salt
2 Tbsp [25 mL] cornstarch, plus more for the baking sheet
1⅔ cups [410 mL] sugar

2 tsp [10 mL] white vinegar
1 tsp [5 mL] vanilla extract
2 cups [500 mL] whipping cream, chilled
1 Tbsp [15 mL] honey (optional)
3 cups [750 mL] (or so) cut-up fresh fruit or berries
sprigs of fresh mint for garnish (optional)

Position the oven rack a little below the middle of the oven. If your oven is electric, put a shallow pan of water on the bottom rack of the oven. Preheat the oven to 275°F (140°C).

Line a baking sheet with cooking parchment (foil also works) and dust the sheet with cornstarch to make sure the meringue doesn't stick to it.

Warm a large stainless steel bowl under hot water, then dry it thoroughly. Add the egg whites, cream of tartar, and salt. Surround the bowl with a warm, damp dishtowel to make sure the egg whites stay warm.

Combine the cornstarch with 2 Tbsp (25 mL) of the sugar and set it aside. Whip the egg white mixture at medium-high speed until it's stiff and starts to pull away from the sides of the bowl. Immediately begin adding the remaining sugar by sprinkling it into the egg whites slowly, 1 tablespoon at a time. Then add the cornstarch and sugar mixture. Scrape down the sides of the bowl and keep whipping, slowly adding the white vinegar and vanilla. Continue whipping for 1 minute more. At this point, the mixture should be glossy.

For individual pavlovas, use an ice cream scoop and stack 2 scoops together, then use the back of the scoop to sculpt each meringue into a volcano with a depression in the center. For a large pavlova, use a spatula or spoon to spread the meringue into a 7-inch (18 cm) round, about 3 inches (8 cm) high, making a shallow depression in the middle. Feel free to give the edges some swirls.

Put the meringue in the heated oven and immediately reduce the heat to 250°F (120°C). It's important that you don't open the door of the oven for at least 45 minutes (less for the smaller meringues). The meringue should be crisp and dry looking. Bake the large meringues for 1½ hours; bake the smaller ones for 1 to 1¼ hours. Leave the meringues in the oven, with the heat turned off and the oven door cracked open, for another 30 minutes after baking. Then remove them from the oven and set the baking sheet on a rack to cool.

You can assemble the pavlova up to 1 hour before serving. Any longer and it will start to get soggy. Whip the chilled cream until it holds soft peaks. Add the honey, if you're using it, and whip it another few seconds to blend it in. The cream should be holding slightly firmer peaks. Fill the center of the pavlova with the cream and gently top it with the fruit. Keep it cool. Serve it garnished with mint sprigs, if desired.

NOTE: For added luxury you can dress the pavlova with dollops of lemon curd. (You can halve the filling subrecipe for Lemon Curd Squares on page 349.)

BLACK & BLUE BERRIES
WITH LIME ZEST CONFIT

MAKES 6–8 SERVINGS

This one's inspired by a dessert from celebrity chef Anthony Bourdain, who has "Blueberries with Lime Sugar" on the menu at Les Halles restaurant in New York. It's great with just blueberries, but Kate decided it would benefit from the addition of blackberries. The combination works beautifully and kids love it, too. Don't forget to drink the juice!

LIME ZEST CONFIT

2 limes
1 cup [250 mL] water
½ cup [125 mL] sugar

BERRIES

3 Tbsp [45 mL] sugar
2 Tbsp [25 mL] fresh lime juice

¾ pint [375 g] fresh blueberries
¾ pint [375 g] fresh blackberries
¼ cup [50 mL] fresh mint, finely chopped
sprigs of fresh mint for garnish
½ cup [125 mL] crème fraîche or sour cream, or enough vanilla ice cream for 6–8 (optional)

To make the confit, remove the peel from the limes with a paring knife, being sure not to include the white pith. Slice the peel into thin pieces. (It's much easier to zest the limes if you use a zester, which is a wonderful tool for all kinds of reasons.)

Combine the water and sugar in a small saucepan and bring the mixture to a boil. Add the zest and reduce the heat so the mixture simmers. Loosely cover the pot and let the liquid cook until it has reduced by half. Remove it from the heat, cool it completely, and strain it (or not, if you aren't averse to shreds of lime). You can store the confit in an airtight container and refrigerate it until you need it.

To finish the dish, combine the sugar with the lime juice in a large, presentable bowl and stir to dissolve the sugar. Add the berries and toss them well, coating all the berries with the mixture. Add the fresh mint and the lime zest confit and toss the berries well again. The mixture is even better after the flavors have had time to marry, so refrigerate the berries for 1 hour or more. Garnish them with more fresh mint and serve them with crème fraîche, sour cream, or vanilla ice cream, if you like.

BLACKBERRY NECTARINE COBBLER

MAKES 6 SERVINGS

You can use peaches instead of nectarines in this cobbler—or any fruit combination you like. It's nice to have a mix of the tart and the sweet, though, as you do when you mix blackberries with peaches or nectarines. Rhubarb is another great fruit to use in a cobbler.

1 cup [250 mL] sugar

1 Tbsp [15 mL] cornstarch

3 large nectarines, cut into ½-inch
   [1 cm] pieces (about 3 cups/
   750 mL)

3 cups [750 mL] blackberries

1½ cups [375 mL] all-purpose flour

1½ tsp [7 mL] baking powder

¾ tsp [3 mL] kosher salt

7½ Tbsp [110 mL] cold, unsalted butter,
   cut into bits (the large-holed section
   of a grater also works well for this)

¾ cup [175 mL] milk

6 Tbsp [90 mL] sliced almonds

whipped cream or vanilla ice cream,
   if desired

Preheat the oven to 400°F (200°C). Butter a 9- × 13-inch (3.5 L) baking dish.

Stir together the sugar and cornstarch in a bowl. Add the fruit and gently but thoroughly toss it to distribute the sugar and cornstarch evenly. Spread the fruit mixture in the baking dish.

Whisk together the flour, baking powder, and salt in another bowl. Add the cold butter (if it's not cold, it won't blend properly). Cut the mixture together with a pastry blender or 2 knives until it resembles coarse meal. Add the milk and stir the dough until it's just combined.

Drop the dough onto the fruit in mounds, 1 or 2 per person. Sprinkle the almonds over the cobbler and bake it in the middle of the oven for 20 minutes, or until the top is golden. Serve the cobbler hot or warm with whipped cream or ice cream.

KATHY'S KEY LIME PIE

MAKES 8 SERVINGS

Unfortunately for my waistline, Kate is not the only person I know who makes great desserts. This recipe, from fellow Butt Shredder Kathy Richardier, is a loose adaptation of a Martha Stewart recipe. Kathy says you can also use the one on the back of the key lime juice bottle when you can find key lime juice.

1¾ cups [425 mL] graham cracker
   crumbs
3 Tbsp [45 mL] sugar
6 Tbsp [90 mL] butter, melted
pinch kosher salt
one 14 oz [398 mL] can sweetened
   condensed milk

5 large egg yolks
¾ cup [175 mL] key lime juice, or the
   juice of about 25 key limes (the fresh
   juice is wonderfully fresher than
   bottled, if you can find the limes and
   want to bother juicing them)
whipped cream

Preheat the oven to 375°F (190°C). Mix together the graham cracker crumbs, sugar, butter, and salt and press the mixture into a 9-inch (23 cm) pie plate. Bake it for about 12 minutes, until the crust is slightly browned. Cool it completely. Reduce the oven temperature to 325°F (160°C).

    Whisk the condensed milk, egg yolks, and lime juice together. Pour the filling into the cooled crust and return the pie to the oven. Bake it until the center is just set, about 15 minutes. Cool it completely. The pie should be chilled for several hours in the refrigerator before serving it. Top it with whipped cream.

MEXICAN HOT FUDGE SUNDAES
WITH CARAMELIZED PINEAPPLE

MAKES 8 SERVINGS

This recipe, from my friend and fellow foodie Angie Quaale, is a delicious variation on the grilled pineapple theme.

1 whole fresh pineapple

3 Tbsp [45 mL] brown sugar

¾ cup [175 mL] whipping cream

½ cup [125 mL] (or more) freshly brewed strong coffee

1 lb [500 g] semisweet chocolate chunks

1 tsp [5 mL] ground cinnamon

½ tsp [2 mL] vanilla extract

1 Tbsp [15 mL] ancho chili powder

vanilla ice cream

2 Tbsp [25 mL] toasted pine nuts

Remove the top and bottom from the pineapple. Carefully remove the outer skin and discard it. Cut the pineapple in half vertically and then again in half vertically so you have 4 separate long pieces. With a sharp knife, remove the core from each piece and then cut each quarter into about 8 chunks. Transfer the pineapple chunks to a baking dish or baking sheet, sprinkle them with the brown sugar, and let them sit for 10 minutes.

While the pineapple is resting, prepare the grill for direct medium-high heat. Make the hot fudge sauce by bringing the cream and coffee to a boil in a medium saucepan. Remove it from the heat and add the chocolate, cinnamon, vanilla, and ancho chili powder. Stir the mixture until the chocolate is melted and the sauce is smooth. Set it aside.

Place the pineapple chunks on the cooking grate, taking care they don't fall through. Cook them until they're soft and well caramelized. Remove them from the grill and set them aside.

To serve the pineapple, place scoops of vanilla ice cream in serving bowls. Add 2 or 3 pieces of the caramelized pineapple, top them liberally with the hot fudge sauce, and sprinkle the toasted pine nuts overtop. Serve the sundaes immediately.

Deeee-licious Desserts

GRILLED PINEAPPLE
WITH CARAMEL SAUCE

MAKES 6 SERVINGS

⤳ BARBECUE SECRET ⤴

You can also use grilled pineapple slices to top an Asian Chicken Burger (page 165). Cut the pineapple into rounds instead of spears.

This easy and delicious summer recipe is the perfect end to a grilled dinner.

1 fresh pineapple
coarsely ground black pepper
caramel ice cream topping or
  Mexican cajeta sauce (available at most Latin specialty stores or gourmet food shops)

¼ cup [50 mL] whipping cream (only if you're using the cajeta sauce)

Prepare your grill for direct medium heat. Peel and core the pineapple. Cut it into spears about 1 inch (2.5 cm) thick and sprinkle them with a little coarsely ground black pepper. Grill the pineapple spears for about 4 minutes per side, until they're slightly charred.

Warm the sauce in a microwave or double boiler. If you're using cajeta sauce, you'll need to whisk in a little cream to loosen it up. Drizzle the pineapple slices with the warmed sauce and serve.

WHISKEY & HONEY PLANKED PEACHES

MAKES 8 SERVINGS

This delicious recipe is based on the technique of planking god Ted Reader. You can easily substitute ripe pears or nectarines for the peach halves. The key is to use perfectly ripe freestone peaches so it's easy to halve and peel them.

1 cedar plank, soaked for 6 hours or overnight
¾ cup [175 mL] Jack Daniel's Tennessee Whiskey
½ cup [125 mL] honey
freshly ground black pepper to taste
freshly grated nutmeg to taste

8 ripe but firm freestone peaches, peeled and halved
1 Tbsp [15 mL] fresh lemon juice
1 cup [250 mL] whipped cream, sweetened with a dash of Amaretto, or premium vanilla ice cream
8 sprigs fresh mint

Combine the whiskey and honey in a small saucepan over medium-high heat. Season the mixture with the pepper and nutmeg. Bring it to a boil, reduce the heat, and simmer it until the liquid is reduced by half. Remove it from the heat and cool it.

Arrange the peaches cut side up in a dish just large enough to hold them in 1 layer, and brush them with the lemon juice. Spoon 1 Tbsp (15 mL) of the bourbon-honey mixture over each peach and let them marinate for 1 hour.

Preheat the grill to high. Place the soaked plank on the grill, close the lid, and bake it for 3 to 5 minutes, or until it begins to crackle and smoke. Carefully lift the lid, place the peaches on the plank, cut side up, and close the lid. Cook them for 3 to 5 minutes, or until the peaches are hot and tender and starting to char on the edges. Remove them from the plank and transfer them to dessert plates. Garnish each peach with a dollop of whipped cream or ice cream, drizzle it with the remaining bourbon-honey mixture, add a sprig of mint, and serve the peaches immediately.

Deeee-licious Desserts

PLANKED GRAPEFRUIT
WITH GRAND MARNIER & HONEY

MAKES 8 SERVINGS

Trust me. This is delicious. I got the idea from one of the pioneers of plank-cooking, Malcolm York. Malcolm wrote the excellent book *Introduction to Plank Barbecuing*, which includes a planked grapefruit recipe featuring sweet vermouth and cherries. I took this concept and ran with it.

1 cedar plank, soaked overnight or at least 1 hour	Grand Marnier liqueur
4 pink grapefruits, cut in half	½ cup [125 mL] liquid honey
	vanilla ice cream

Prepare the grapefruits as if you were going to have them for breakfast, making cuts to loosen the segments in the skin. Drizzle each grapefruit with about 1 tsp (5 mL) of the liqueur.

Preheat the grill on medium-high for 5 to 10 minutes, or until the chamber temperature rises above 500°F (260°C). Rinse the soaked plank and place it on the cooking grate. Cover the grill and heat the plank for 4 to 5 minutes, or until it starts to throw off a bit of smoke and crackles lightly.

Place the grapefruit halves, cut side up, on the plank. Close the grill and reduce the heat to medium. Cook the grapefruit for about 10 minutes. Remove the halves from the plank, place them on dessert plates, and drizzle them with a little more Grand Marnier and some honey. Place a small scoop of ice cream on top of each half and serve.

PLANKED PEARS
WITH WALNUTS & BLUE CHEESE

MAKES 8 SERVINGS

This is a classic flavor combination, adapted for the plank. Serve these with a scoop of vanilla ice cream and/or a glass of the fortified wine you used to top off the pears.

1 cedar plank, soaked overnight or at
    least 1 hour
½ cup [125 mL] walnuts
4 large ripe pears, peeled and halved,
    with the cores scooped out

¼ cup [50 mL] dark brown sugar
½ cup [125 mL] crumbled blue cheese
port or sherry
vanilla ice cream (optional)

Preheat the oven to 400°F (200°C). Toast the walnuts on a baking sheet for about 10 minutes, or until they start to darken and produce a nice aroma. Remove them from the oven and cool them slightly. Coarsely chop them and set them aside.

Place the pears, cut side up, on a baking sheet (if they don't balance well, slice a bit from the bottom to make them sit evenly). Sprinkle them with the brown sugar and put about 1 Tbsp (15 mL) of cheese in the depression of each pear. Top each off with just a touch of port or sherry.

Preheat the grill on medium-high for 5 to 10 minutes, or until the chamber temperature rises above 500°F (260°C). Rinse the soaked plank and place it on the cooking grate. Cover the grill and heat the plank for 4 to 5 minutes, or until it starts to throw off a bit of smoke and crackles lightly. Reduce the heat to medium-low.

Place the pears on the plank, taking care not to tip them, and cook them for 10 minutes, or until the cheese is melted and the pears are golden and tender. Remove them from the plank, sprinkle some chopped walnuts over each pear, place a scoop of ice cream beside each pear, if you like, and serve them immediately.

Deeee-licious Desserts

PLANKED PEAR CRISP

MAKES 6–8 SERVINGS

The late, great essayist Laurie Colwin wrote about food in a way that was funny, homey, and totally inviting. My wife Kate has made this pear crisp of Colwin's many times, but one of the most memorable was on an early fall evening at Vancouver's Spanish Banks beach. We reheated it in its pan on our portable grill. The sound of the surf, the lights starting to twinkle on the opposite shore, and the warm, pear crisp—bliss. Plank-cooking the crisp sends it over the top, but it works well in a good old convection oven, too.

1 fruitwood plank (apple or cherry would work well, but cedar also works fine), soaked overnight or at least 1 hour	zest of 1 lemon
	1 sprig fresh rosemary (optional)
4 lb [1.8 kg] ripe pears, cut in chunks	¾ cup [175 mL] brown sugar
¼ cup [50 mL] granulated sugar, or less	1 cup [250 mL] all-purpose flour
¼ cup [50 mL] fresh lemon juice	½ cup [125 mL] cold butter
	vanilla ice cream (optional)

Toss the pear chunks with the granulated sugar, lemon juice, and zest in a large bowl. Grease an 8-inch (2 L) square baking pan. Place a sprig of rosemary in the bottom of the pan; if children are going to run away screaming, omit this step. Gently pour in the pears.

Rub together the brown sugar, flour, and butter in a medium bowl. (An easy way to achieve the desired texture is to freeze the butter beforehand, then grate it using a large-holed grater.) The topping should be crumbly. Sprinkle it over the pears.

Preheat the grill on medium-high for 5 to 10 minutes, or until the chamber temperature rises above 500°F (260°C). Rinse the soaked plank and place it on the cooking grate. Cover the grill and heat the plank for 4 to 5 minutes, or until it starts to throw off a bit of smoke and crackles lightly.

Reduce the heat to low (you want the chamber temperature to stabilize at 350–400°F/180–200°C), and place the baking dish on top of the plank (if the plank is warping from the heat, turn it upside down and wait a few minutes until it flattens). Bake the crisp until the pears are tender and the topping is golden brown and crunchy, about 1 hour. Cool the crisp for 20 minutes before serving it with vanilla ice cream.

High-End Belly Wash: Cocktails & Beverages

What does one drink with barbecued, planked, or grilled food? During competition, cold beer goes down great—and, if you pace yourself, you won't get too hammered by judging time. We also have a tradition of martinis at dawn . . . or was that shots of tequila at dawn? For some reason the memory is fuzzy. Generally I like to serve beer and wine to accompany grilled or barbecued food. Dry, hoppy beers go nicely with richer barbecue, as do fruity, spicy white wines like Gewürztraminer and crisp, citrusy Sauvignon Blancs. And, of course, there's nothing like a big chewy red to go with steak or lamb. The key is to maximize your eating and drinking pleasure, and one way to turn up the fun volume is to start off the party with a nice cocktail. Here are a few of my favorites.

ACK-ACK-A-DAQ!

This, my friends, is the ultimate summer blender drink. It should only be made when local peaches are at the peak of their ripeness, the sky is deep blue, and the ambient temperature is over 90 degrees. This is the kind of drink that should be hand-delivered to your beautiful wife as she reads a trashy novel in a chaise longue wearing a cheap straw hat. One of these and she will love you forever. Two of them and she will love you as soon as she's finished the drink.

1 Tbsp [15 mL] sugar
ice cubes
3 or 4 ripe peaches, peeled, pitted,
   and cut into chunks
5 oz [150 mL] white rum

1½ oz [45 mL] peach schnapps
chilled soda water
sugar to taste
fresh lime juice to taste

Rim 4 wide-mouthed glasses with the sugar and set them aside. Fill a blender about half full with ice cubes. Place the peach chunks on top of the ice. Pour the rum and schnapps into the blender, then top them up with soda water to cover the ice and peaches. Whiz the mixture in the blender until it's smooth and frothy. Jack up the flavor with a little sugar and some fresh lime juice (that's especially important if the peaches aren't quite ripe). Pour the daiquiris into the glasses and serve them immediately.

BUDAPEST MARTINI

MAKES 1 DRINK

Wendy Vallaster, manager of TC Lions Pub in Vancouver, was kind enough to share the recipe for this fabulous cocktail, which she developed to pair with a tapa.

1 oz [30 mL] chilled vodka
½ oz [15 mL] golden pear liqueur
½ oz [15 mL] sour apple liqueur

club soda
1 ripe pear

Shake the first 3 ingredients well in a martini shaker and strain the drink into a chilled martini glass. Top it with 1 to 2 oz (30 to 60 mL) of club soda. Cut a thin, round slice of fresh pear and drop it in.

CAMPARI COCKTAIL

MAKES 1 DRINK

Pretentious? *Mais oui.* But delicious? *Bien sûr.*

1 measure Campari
2 oz [60 mL] fresh-squeezed
    orange juice

Perrier or soda water
1 lemon or lime slice

Fill a short, wide (old fashioned) glass with ice cubes and add the Campari, juice, and Perrier or soda water. Stir the drink and garnish it with a slice of lemon or lime.

CRAZY TEXAS PUNCH

This festive, kitschy punch from my friend Amy may sound crazy, but it's a crowd-pleaser!

1 small box Jell-O (Amy prefers straw-
    berry or cherry, but any flavor will do)
2 cups [500 mL] hot water
2 cups [500 mL] sugar

2 cups [500 mL] cold water
one 2-quart [2 L] can pineapple juice
two 2-quart [2 L] bottles ginger ale
13 oz [385 mL] vodka or white rum

Combine the Jell-O, hot water, and sugar and stir the mixture until the granules have completely dissolved. Add the cold water and pineapple juice. Pour the punch into a 1-gallon (4 L) milk carton that has been well rinsed and freeze it overnight.

Let the Jell-O mixture thaw for 2 to 4 hours (Amy says it only takes 1 hour in Texas). Remove the milk carton and put the semifrozen brick in a large punch bowl. Add one of the bottles of ginger ale and the vodka or rum before serving. People like this punch so much, you will need the extra bottle of ginger ale to pour in at the end.

CUBA LIBRE

Have one of these and it's summer . . . even if it's 20 degrees below zero.

1½ oz [45 mL] best-quality white rum (I like Appleton best) juice of ¼ lime	cold Coca-Cola 1 lime slice

Fill a highball glass with ice cubes, pour in the rum, squeeze in the lime juice, and top the glass up with Coke. Garnish the drink with the slice of lime.

DIRTY BANANA

MAKES 1 DRINK

This rum-based drink, from my friend Chris Brown, makes any time, or day, or location, a tropical celebration.

1½ oz [45 mL] Appleton Estate V/X ½ oz [15 mL] Sangster's Jamaica Rum Cream 2 oz [60 mL] pineapple juice	2 oz [60 mL] orange juice quarter of a banana (half if you really like banana) fresh fruit for garnish

Blend the ingredients until they're smooth. Serve the drink in a hurricane glass. Garnish it with fresh fruit.

D.J. SMOOTHIE

My son Jake is the pickiest eater on the planet—not easy for parents who want him to eat something other than chicken nuggets and plain cheese pizza. But his sensitive palate is going to serve him well one day as a chef or sommelier. It's already starting to pay dividends. Watching me experiment with planking recipes, he decided he was going to develop some blender drinks. So far his favorite is a S'More Smoothie, consisting of chocolate sauce, ice cream, and graham crackers—a bit sweet for some tastes. The following tangy treat, however, has wide appeal, and with a little rum might even make it on the cocktail circuit. (The D.J. Smoothie is named after Jake and his friend David, who co-developed the recipe and helped mess up the kitchen in the process.)

2 ice cubes	pinch sugar (optional)
juice of 2 lemons, 2 limes, and	3 chunks watermelon, seeds removed
2 oranges	3 chunks cantaloupe
1 banana	small handful blueberries

Whiz the ingredients together in a blender and serve the drink. Then run around, turning the house into a junk heap, or go play some video games.

KIR

MAKES 1 DRINK

Hand one of these to your guests as they arrive and suddenly it's a special occasion.

| ½ oz [15 mL] crème de cassis | 4 oz [125 mL] crisp dry white wine (white Burgundy Aligoté is the classic) |

Pour the crème de cassis into a white wine glass. Gently pour the wine overtop, taking care not to mix them too much. The drink should look like a clear version of a Tequila Sunrise, with the heavier cassis lurking at the bottom. (For an extra-special Kir Royale, substitute chilled champagne for the white wine.)

PIMM'S NO. 1 CUP & GINGER

MAKES 1 DRINK

These sneaky little cocktails are innocuous enough, until you've had a couple and your face starts to feel as if it's made of rubber.

| 1½ oz [45 mL] Pimm's No. 1 Cup liqueur | cold ginger ale 1 orange slice |

Fill a highball glass with ice, pour in the liqueur, top it with ginger ale, and garnish the drink with an orange slice.

ROCKY MOUNTAIN MARGARITAS

MAKES 2 BLENDERS OF MARGARITAS, ENOUGH FOR 8–12 DRINKS

I call these Rocky Mountain Margaritas because the blue Curaçao combined with the green limeade concentrate gives the drinks an emerald glow like a glacier-fed river or a high mountain lake.

kosher salt

2 limes, cut into wedges

one 12 oz [355 mL] can limeade
   concentrate, thawed

1 cup [250 mL] water

one 8½ oz [235 mL] bottle unsweetened
   lime juice from concentrate

10 oz [300 mL] tequila

6 oz [175 mL] blue Curaçao
   (or triple sec)

Pour 2 Tbsp (25 mL) of coarse salt onto a small plate. Wet the rims of 4 large margarita glasses (or however many you're serving) with a wedge of lime and dip the rims into the salt. Set the glasses aside. Combine the thawed limeade concentrate, water, lime juice, tequila, and blue Curaçao in a jug or a large measuring cup. Fill a blender with ice cubes. Pour in the mixture to cover the ice cubes and whiz it until it has the consistency of a Slurpee. Fill the glasses and go for it!

SANGRIA

MAKES 1 LARGE PITCHER

Make this great Spanish-style cooler a day ahead to give all the flavors time to meld into the ultimate summer drink. Thanks to Sean "The Judge" Dunnigan for passing this one on to me.

2 bottles red wine (Cabernet Sauvignon, Merlot, Rioja, Zinfandel, or Shiraz)
2 tsp [10 mL] Cointreau
2 oz [60 mL] brandy
2 oz [60 mL] Curaçao
¼ cup [50 mL] sugar
2 navel oranges, cut into ½-inch [1 cm] slices

2 ripe peaches, peeled, cored, and cut into ½-inch [1 cm] slices
2 ripe pears, peeled, cored, and cut into ½-inch [1 cm] slices
half a ripe pineapple, peeled, cored, and cut into ½-inch [1 cm] slices
2 cups [500 mL] club soda

Combine all the ingredients except the club soda in a pitcher. Mix them together, cover the sangria, and refrigerate it, overnight if possible but for at least a couple of hours before serving. Just before serving, stir in the club soda. Serve the sangria in tall glasses.

SHAKEN JAMAICAN

MAKES 1 DRINK

Jamaican distilling giant Appleton sponsors the Canadian National Barbecue Championships in Whistler, British Columbia. Appleton has been a great supporter of championship barbecue, and I am a great supporter of Appleton. Whether it's winter or summer, you can bring on some Jamaican sunshine with this delicious drink.

1½ oz [45 mL] Appleton Estate V/X
1 oz [30 mL] cherry brandy

3 oz [90 mL] pineapple juice
3 oz [90 mL] orange juice

Shake the ingredients together with ice and strain the drink into a martini glass.

Extra Stuff

MUSIC TO BARBECUE BY

Remember, barbecue is not just a food, it's a lifestyle, and a lifestyle needs a soundtrack. There have been many songs written about barbecue and there have even been some CD compilations of barbecue music. But I think the place to start is by asking yourself the question, "What music do I most associate with the good life—great food, best friends, summer fun?" Whatever the answer is, that's what you should throw onto your music player when you're cooking and serving up barbecue. Of course, classic blues and country music go naturally with outdoor cooking, but so do jazz, rock 'n' roll, and world music.

Top 20 Albums

After many years of intensive, liver-damaging research, here are my top 20 albums to barbecue by. Some go back to my university days and are part of my genetic makeup. Others are more recent discoveries. All are full of great songs that will shake your body and heal your soul, much like a perfect grilled or barbecued meal.

1. *American IV: The Man Comes Around* Johnny Cash
2. *Avalon Sunset* Van Morrison
3. *Blood on the Tracks* Bob Dylan
4. *Blue Horse* The Be Good Tanyas
5. *Car Wheels on a Gravel Road* Lucinda Williams
6. *Clandestino* Manu Chao
7. *Classic Bluegrass* Larry Sparks
8. *A Collection of Hits* Kathy Mattea
9. *The Essential Waylon Jennings* Waylon Jennings
10. *In Spite of Ourselves* John Prine
11. *Legend* Bob Marley and the Wailers
12. *Live at Blues Alley* Eva Cassidy
13. *Loaded* The Velvet Underground
14. *The Mountain* Steve Earle and the Del McCoury Band
15. *Nashville* Solomon Burke
16. *O Brother Where Art Thou* soundtrack Various artists
17. *People Gonna Talk* James Hunter
18. *The Return of the Grievous Angel/ A Tribute to Gram Parsons* Various artists
19. *Trampoline* The Mavericks
20. *Uprooted* Various artists

Best Playlist

With the help of a computer and a CD burner, you can make your own custom barbecue CD—and with online music services like Apple's iTunes, you can grab songs for a buck or so apiece. Here's my ultimate barbecue mix—a bit of a hodgepodge, but I guarantee that if you listen to this playlist you will be a step closer to barbecue nirvana.

1. "Seminole Wind" John Anderson
2. "Sweet Is the Melody" Iris DeMent
3. "You're a Big Girl Now" Bob Dylan
4. "Walking in Memphis" Marc Cohn
5. "Uncle John's Band" Grateful Dead
6. "A Song for You" Gram Parsons
7. "I'd Rather Go Blind" Etta James
8. "Hound Dog" Big Mama Thornton
9. "Burning Love" Elvis Presley
10. "Sweet Home Alabama" Lynyrd Skynyrd
11. "La Grange" ZZ Top
12. "Pride and Joy" Stevie Ray Vaughn and Double Trouble
13. "Takin' Care of Business" Bachman-Turner Overdrive
14. "Superfly" Curtis Mayfield
15. "Jamming" Bob Marley and the Wailers
16. "Take Me to the River" Al Green
17. "Dream in Blue" Los Lobos
18. "Rocket" Kathy Mattea
19. "It's a Great Day to Be Alive" Travis Tritt
20. "Windfall" Son Volt
21. "Hallelujah" Rufus Wainwright

My Kind of Country

I like all kinds of music, but I have a soft spot for country. I think it exemplifies the spirit of barbecue. Here is the playlist on my iPod that I turn to most.

1. "Save a Horse (Ride a Cowboy)" Big & Rich
2. "Devil's Right Hand" Johnny Cash
3. "Big River" Rosie Flores
4. "Wichita Lineman" Glen Campbell
5. "Always Late (With Your Kisses)" Lefty Frizell
6. "Bubbles in My Beer" Bob Wills & His Texas Playboys
7. "Amarillo by Morning" George Strait
8. "Look at Miss Ohio" Gillian Welch
9. "Good Time Charlie's Got the Blues" Danny O'Keefe
10. "Lodi" Jeffrey Foucault
11. "The Road Goes On Forever" Robert Earl Keen
12. "Lovesick Blues" Hank Williams
13. "Hello Darlin'" Conway Twitty
14. "Kiss an Angel Good Morning" Charley Pride
15. "I Fall to Pieces" Patsy Cline
16. "Make the World Go Away" Eddy Arnold
17. "I Will Always Love You" Dolly Parton
18. "You've Still Got a Place in My Heart" George Jones
19. "Feel Like Going Home (demo)" Charlie Rich

A SELECTION OF MENUS

Championship Barbecue Feast

There's a reason some of these recipes have the word "classic" in them. Serve your favorite summer beverages, like cold beer and Jack Daniel's and Coke.

Classic North Carolina Barbecued Pulled Pork
Sandwiches (page 193)
North Carolina–Style Vinegar Sauce (page 58)
Ron's Rich, Deeply Satisfying Dipping Sauce
(page 57)

Tidewater Coleslaw (page 112)
Classic Baked Beans for a Crowd (page 142)
Blackberry Nectarine Cobbler (page 359)

Asian-Themed Barbecue Supper

A hot summer night, some good friends, and delicious Asian flavors. What could be better? Serve cold Asian beer like Kirin, Tsingtao, or Kingfisher, and a nice, crisp, fruity Riesling or Sauvignon Blanc.

Prosciutto-Wrapped Prawn & Lychee Kebabs
(page 334)
Kate's Tasty Asian Chicken Thighs (page 213)
Asian Noodle Salad with Sesame Mayonnaise
(page 119)

Grilled Asparagus (page 129)
Zoë's Parfait (page 347)

Southwestern Heat

I would recommend starting out this evening with a round or two of Rocky Mountain Margaritas (page 379) and then moving to Mexican beer and/or a big chewy red wine like a Shiraz.

Funky Quesadillas (page 97)
Fiery Southwestern Wings (page 216)
Chunky Smoked Tomato Guacamole (page 65)
Margie's Chipotle & Roasted Garlic Mayo
(page 68)

Flank Steak Fajitas Adobo with Mango
Strawberry Salsa (page 236)
Confetti Rice (page 144)
Grilled Pineapple with Caramel Sauce
(page 362)

A Supereasy Family Dinner

It's Friday night, the kids are home, and everyone needs an end-of-week lift. This easy but very satisfying menu will start the weekend off on the right foot.

Supercharged Grilled Corn on the Cob (with plain
or savory butter) (page 130)
Easiest, Tastiest Steak (page 231)
Field Greens with Toasted Walnut Oil & Pumpkin
Seeds (page 116)

The Ultimate Triple Chocolate Brownies
(page 351) with vanilla ice cream

RESOURCES

Your higher-end cookbooks seem to always have a section at the end that goes into all kinds of detail on where you can get the best mail-order ingredients, so I figured I should do something. But I rarely get food other than from my local suppliers, so I hope this list will at least make some new connections for you.

Rockin' Ronnie Connections

Website: www.ronshewchuk.com

Facebook group: Barbecue Secrets

Barbecue Secrets blog/podcast home page:
   http://barbecuesecrets.libsyn.com

Twitter feed: rockinronnie

Email: rockinronnie@ronshewchuk.com

Telephone: 604-929-6451

Skype handle: Ron Shewchuk

Other Places You Should Visit on the Web

The Smoke Ring: The center of the online barbecue universe. www.thesmokering.com

Kansas City Barbecue Society: The leading governing body of barbecue. www.kcbs.us

National Barbecue News: You should subscribe to this print publication. www.barbecuenews.com

The BBQ Forum: A running conversation about barbecue that you shouldn't miss. www.rbjb.com/rbjb/rbjbboard/

Barbecue'n on the Internet: A great resource. www.barbecuen.com

The Virtual Weber Bullet: A great online community for users of the most popular backyard barbecue pit. www.virtualweberbullet.com

Pacific Northwest Barbecue Association: The online home of the PNWBA. www.pnwba.com

Barbecue on the Bow: Calgary's long-running Alberta Championship barbecue contest. www.bbqonthebow.com

Johnstone's Barbecues and Parts: The place to go in Canada for the widest selection and best service. www.johnstones.com (Order online from across Canada at www.bbqparts.ca)

Cobb Canada: The best portable charcoal grill EVER. www.cobbcanada.ca

Planking Resources

These days you can find cooking planks at most gourmet food stores, barbecue specialty stores, home improvement centers, hardware stores, and big super-markets. If you can't find planks in your neighborhood, visit these websites to find good-quality mail-order planks. (For hard-to-find mesquite planks, order by phone from Rancho Lobos in Mexico at 520-225-0415 (www.rancholobos.com).)

www.westcoastlifestyles.com

www.plankcooking.com

www.barbecuewood.com

The Best Sauces

For award-winning "Natural Champions" barbecue sauces, check out Ronnie and Denzel's at www.denzelshotsauce.com.

ACKNOWLEDGMENTS

Where do I begin? With my beautiful wife, Kate Zimmerman, of course. Kate has put up with my "barbecue lifestyle" for our 26 years of marriage, including my irritating habits: filling our carport and backyard with barbecue gear and related detritus; spending countless weekends writing books, delivering workshops, and traveling to competitions; drinking barrel after barrel of various alcoholic beverages consumed in the name of "field research"; and making many empty promises of "Yes, honey, that's the last grill I'll buy." In addition to exhibiting godlike patience, Kate also made a huge contribution to this book, with some great recipes and a couple of hilarious articles. Thank you, darling, for getting used to the taste of my smoky kisses . . . and tolerating the smell of my smoky farts on Sunday mornings.

Thank you, Robert Mackwood, for being my agent and friend, and for getting me into this mess!

Next in line for a giant thank you is my old friend and mentor, Bob Lyon, the Granddaddy of Barbecue in the Pacific Northwest. It was Bob's superb all-day workshop on championship barbecue nearly 20 years ago that gave me my first mind-blowing exposure to real Southern-style barbecue and inspired me to join a team and enter my first competition. Through the years Bob has always been generous with his sage advice and support—for me, and for countless others whom he helped catch the barbecue bug. It's impossible to mention Bob without tipping my hat to the late, great David "The Fire Chef" Valjacic and his wife, Pat, the dynamic couple who helped Canada get its start in competitive barbecue. They are missed and won't be forgotten, and David's famous salmon recipe lives on in this book.

Southern-style barbecue has a rich history and deep traditions, which I've tried to document in this book. I owe a lot of my knowledge to some of the icons of American barbecue, including Paul "The KC Baron of Barbecue" Kirk, Rocky Danner, and Myron Mixon, who have shared a lot of great stories (and some of their secrets) with me. And speaking of history, I was honored to have the opportunity to learn about West Coast Aboriginal cooking techniques from those who are still carrying on these traditions. Special thanks to Chef Bev Antoine, sous-chef Raymond Johnston, Kathy Parkinson, and the rest of the team at the Quw'utsun' Cultural Centre on Vancouver Island for educating me and allowing me to participate in preparing salmon according to tradition.

And where would I be without my beloved competition teammates? From the day Kathy Richardier, Amo Jackson, Rocco Ciancio, and I formed the original Rockin' Ronnie's Butt Shredders, our lives would never be the same. Over the years the team grew, including barbecue stalwart Ian "Big Daddy" Baird and West Coast Shredder originals, Stephen Robertson, Heather Rooke, Kenny Stef, Tom Masterson, and Vince Gogolek. Other stellar additions to the team have included Dave Thurgar, Margie Gibb, Carol and Sandy Dougall, Sharma Christie, Bryan O'Connor, and real-life chefs Michael Allemeier, Bob Haselbach, and Neil Wyles. Championship barbecue is truly a team sport and I can honestly say I would not have a barbecue career without the Butt Shredders. An extra thank you goes out to Kathy, Amo, Margie, Ian, Vince, and Michael for contributing some great recipes.

Speaking of contributions, the core of this book is its collection of recipes, cooking techniques, and even snapshots, many of which were provided by family, friends, and barbecue fans who answered my call and shared their favorite dishes. They are my brother Allan Shewchuk, my daughter Zoë and son Jake, Michelle Allaire, Carolyn Rowan, Brian Misko, Glen Erho, Fred Kraus, Jenny Neidhart, Amo Jackson, Mike Dos Santos, Christine Hunt, Chris Brown, Pauline Bahnsen, Wendy Vallaster, Kim Peterson, Rob Clark, Diane Reid, Gail Norton, Jennifer Wah, Terry and Cathy Kelly, Lawrence Davis, Nathan Fong, Tom Riglar, Arnold Smith, Reza Mofakham, Sean Dunnigan, Wendy Vallaster, Michael Allemeier, Kosta Zogaris, Angie Quaale, Don Genova, Amy Walker, Steve Crescenzo, Mike Dos Santos, Dee Hobsbawn-Smith, Eric Giesbrecht, Eric Lee, and Jane Mundy. I was also lucky enough to have some of the icons of outdoor cooking contribute recipes: Ted Reader, Stephen Raichlen, Paul Kirk, and John Howie. Thanks for lending me your support!

I talk a lot about how important gear is to the barbecue lifestyle. Let me take a moment to thank my old friend Gary Johnstone, his wife, Janice, and the whole team at Johnstone's Barbecues and Parts in North Vancouver for always being there when I need them. Gary's showroom is truly a candy store for barbecue aficionados and I'm lucky to know him and his superb team. And, speaking of gear, a guy who does a lot of planking needs a lot of planks. My crazy friends at Westcoast Lifestyles—Alex and Chris Robertson, and Geordie Monro—have always been there to supply me with the best-quality planks on the market, and they've sold a lot of books on my behalf. You guys deserve a good planking and I thank you for your generous support.

And finally, a huge and heartfelt thank you to everyone who helped produce this book, starting with my friends at Whitecap Books. Michael Burch, Robert McCullough, Taryn Boyd, Michelle Mayne, Amanda LeNeve, Setareh Ashrafologhalai, Paula Ayer, and Grace Yaginuma put in a huge amount of time and effort into the project, from the initial conception all the way to making sure it's properly distributed and promoted. I am also grateful to everyone who helped make the food photos look fantastic, including food stylists Joanne Facchin and Nathan Fong and photographers John Sinal and the late Greg Athans, along with Jacqui Thomas, Roberta Batchelor, Bryan O'Connor (who took a lot of the photos scattered throughout the book), Thom Koplar, Elaine Schick, and Zsuzsi Palotai.